THE MADONNA

CULTURAL STUDIES

Series Editors
Janice Radway, Duke University
Richard Johnson, University of Birmingham

The Madonna Connection: Representational Politics, Subcultural Identities, and Cultural Theory edited by Cathy Schwichtenberg

Dreaming Identities: Class, Gender, and Generation in 1980s Hollywood Movies Elizabeth G. Traube

Enlightened Racism: The Cosby Show, *Audiences, and the Myth of the American Dream* Sut Jhally and Justin Lewis

FORTHCOMING

Reconceptualizing Audiences edited by Jon Cruz and Justin Lewis

Frameworks of Culture and Power: Complexity and Politics in Cultural Studies Richard Johnson

An Introduction to Media Studies edited by Stuart Ewen, Elizabeth Ewen, Serafina Bathrick, and Andrew Mattson

Art and the Committed Eye: Culture, Society, and the Functions of Imagery Richard Leppert

photo by Alberto Tolot, *courtesy of Warner Brothers*

The Madonna Connection

REPRESENTATIONAL POLITICS, SUBCULTURAL IDENTITIES, AND CULTURAL THEORY

edited by
CATHY SCHWICHTENBERG

Routledge
Taylor & Francis Group

NEW YORK AND LONDON

First published in paperback 2024

First published 1993 by Westview Press

Published 2019 by Routledge
605 Third Avenue, New York, NY 10158
4 Park Square, Milton Park, Abingdon, Oxon OX14 4RN

Routledge is an imprint of the Taylor & Francis Group, an informa business

Library of Congress Cataloging-in-Publication Data
The Madonna connection : representational politics, subcultural
  identities, and cultural theory / edited by Cathy Schwichtenberg.
      p.   cm. — (Cultural studies)
  Includes bibliographical references (p.   ) and index.
  ISBN 0-8133-1396-1—ISBN 0-8133-1397-X (pbk.)
  1. United States—Popular culture.   2. Madonna, 1959–
Influence.   I. Schwichtenberg, Cathy.   II. Series.
E169.12.M275   1993
306'.0973—dc20   92-24760
                                                                       CIP

Publisher's Note
The publisher has gone to great lengths to ensure the quality of this reprint but points out that some imperfections in the original copies may be apparent.

ISBN 13: 978-0-367-29365-9 (hbk)
ISBN 13: 978-0-367-30911-4 (pbk)
ISBN 13: 978-0-429-31240-3 (ebk)

DOI: 10.4324/9780429312403

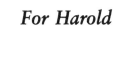
For Harold

Contents

One Out of Bounds: Reading Race and Madonna's Audiences

Two The Sapphic Insurgent: Madonna and Gay Culture

Three   Gender Trouble: Madonna Poses the Feminist Question

Four   The Political Economy of Postmodernism: Madonna as Star-Commodity

Acknowledgments

The Madonna Connection has been, above all, a collaborative effort. My greatest acknowledgment goes to the volume's contributors, who "kept the conversation going" with me and among themselves. The book's scope and vitality attest to their enthusiasm, hard work, and cooperation (not to mention a sustained interest in Madonna). In addition, I am grateful to those interdisciplinary allies who helped me locate such a fine array of scholars who regularly cross disciplinary boundaries. I also thank my former colleagues in the Department of Communication at the University of Massachusetts at Amherst, whose intellectual challenges provided some of the impetus for this book's premise: that Madonna *is,* indeed, a multifaceted phenomenon. Thanks are also due Suzanne LeGrande, my research assistant at the University of Massachusetts during the early stages of this project.

At present, I am grateful for the friendship and support of my new colleagues in the Department of Speech Communication at the University of Georgia, particularly Celeste Condit, Jerry Hale, Cindy Jenefsky, and Ed Panetta. Others further away are responsible for bridging distances and providing intellectual support, among them James Lull, Janice Rushing, Tom Frentz, Michael McGee, Maurice Charland, and Belle Edson.

No project comes to fruition without the foresight and skill of a good editor, and I had the very best: Gordon Lester-Massman at Westview Press and his editorial assistant, Jim Fieser. I am profoundly grateful to have worked with them both. I also thank series editors Janice Radway and Richard Johnson for their helpful comments and suggestions during the book's formative stages. Thanks also to Liz Rosenberg for her interest and cooperation.

I thank Tom Nakayama for intellectual and emotional sustenance during my hours of need (and for supplying all those Madonna tapes and postmodernism articles). Most of all, I owe a debt of gratitude to Harold Schlechtweg, whose encouragement, love, humor, and critical insights made *The Madonna Connection* a reality. Last but not least, I thank Madonna for stirring up trouble and forcing us to think seriously about the politics of popular culture.

Cathy Schwichtenberg

CATHY SCHWICHTENBERG

Introduction:
Connections/Intersections

*D*AVID TETZLAFF notes in this volume that "when tabloid journalists start presenting the activities of academics to their sensation-seeking audiences, it is obvious that some very large cultural power is at hand." This cultural power refers, of course, to Madonna, who needs little introduction given her cultural ubiquity. For almost a decade, Madonna has insinuated herself into public consciousness through media spectacles that have raised public admiration and condemnation to new levels of intensity (see Schulze, Barton White, and Brown, this volume).

Academics are typically the last to know about popular phenomena (or they willfully ignore them), but their reaction to Madonna has proved to be an exception to the rule: Academic commentary on the early phase of her career was soon forthcoming (Brown and Fiske 1987; Fiske 1987; Kaplan 1987; Lewis 1987). However, the full extent of her significance as a cultural power to be reckoned with was emphasized most forcefully for me in 1990 when I began presenting papers at conferences on the later, more political Madonna that were reported on with chagrin by the popular press—an unaccustomed (though at first welcomed) attention that culminated in a particularly nasty exposé about "Madonna scholars" on the television program "Inside Edition."

Yet, the story of academic encroachment into the media's colonized domain did not stop there. If I had been chastised by practitioners of a slanted journalism, jealously guarding their monopoly on public discourse, this did not prevent others from responding. From 1990 to 1991, I was inundated with requests for material on Madonna from young women in Virginia, Oregon, New York, and elsewhere who were writing papers about her. My appearance on "Inside Edition" prompted a generous letter from a college professor I had not heard from in thirteen years (as well as an inquiry from a woman in Minnesota who thought I might be a distant relative). Writing *about* Madonna and her cultural significance had, in effect, produced con-

1

crete examples of that very phenomenon. Unlike my previous forays into popular culture, writing about Madonna had produced connections with others outside academe that dissolved the boundaries between public and private, academic and popular, theory and practice.

Though such boundaries may function in name only, the fact that Madonna broaches divisions underscores the extent of her cultural power—certainly large enough to link total strangers in dialogue and highlight the ephemerality of boundaries. This is what *The Madonna Connection* is, in part, all about: the connections between everyday life and cultural analysis as significant to the ways in which we understand, interpret, communicate, and use the resources of popular culture, as well as the ways in which popular culture can enable or constrain us.

Over the past ten years or so, cultural studies as an interdisciplinary area of inquiry has shifted its focus from text-based to audience-based analyses. This shift, however, has produced polarized views on popular culture. Although some cultural theorists admonish all forms of textual analysis, opting for what they see as the "empirical truth" of audience studies, others continue to embrace the text and its sociocultural manifestations that can be "read" through the analysis of popular discourses. Moreover, there is much debate within cultural studies as to whether certain media representations ideologically manipulate audiences or provide them with the resources to resist such manipulation.

Again, we are confronted with binary oppositions constituted through boundaries between text and audience, between enablement and constraint. Using Madonna and her work as a paradigm case that documents cultural struggle, the contributors to *The Madonna Connection* reject the either/or dichotomies now commonplace within cultural studies debates. In the effort to push scholars to reflect further on the distinctions of cultural studies, this volume engages in dialogue over the political effectivity of Madonna's multifaceted representations. Indeed, the analyses are as provocative as the cultural phenomenon herself. Thus, if *connection* is a key term in the book's title and its foremost activity, then *representational politics* is what is at issue in all discussions of Madonna's impact on the culture at large and within subcultural domains.

By now, it is no secret that many of Madonna's bold representations address subcultural groups. Yet, as Ronald Scott points out in his chapter, unlike black divas who have crossed over into the white mainstream, Madonna's popularity among black audiences has worked in the opposite direction. By integrating symbolic aspects into her performances that reference subcultural groups, Madonna has become a mainstream artist who addresses African Americans, Hispanics, gay men, lesbians, bisexuals, feminists, and others who represent minority or subordinate positions in relation to the dominant cultural and political powers that be. The extent to which

Madonna poaches from the repertoires of subcultural groups or celebrates those "others" in whose name she speaks is the subject of thoughtful and nuanced discussion throughout this anthology in ways that indicate new directions for cultural studies.

A key term in the book's subtitle, *subcultural identities,* is, then, a reflexive marker, indicative of the workings of subjectivity and identification that inform the constitution of subjects. These operations are especially important for subcultural groups that must "pass" in the mainstream as well as construct and celebrate their own unique differences. Whether subcultural identities are constructed through sites of memory (Patton, this volume), the history of the black church (Scott, this volume), or rearticulation (Henderson, this volume), all must negotiate the treacherous terrain of white, heterosexual, cultural privilege that threatens to efface all traces of "otherness." Subcultural identities are, therefore, always forged in struggle over and against the dominant. Madonna's subculturally evocative texts may very well present the conditions for the coalescence and mobilization of identities yet to be pacified by commodity culture: a perspective that warrants some disagreement within the larger purview of late capitalism, as some contributors argue (Tetzlaff; Bordo; and Mandziuk).

As the last key term in the subtitle, *cultural theory* indicates the overarching cultural framework within which Madonna's multiple texts operate. No text, popular or otherwise, functions in a vacuum. Much like Karl Marx's "social hieroglyph," Madonna can be read as a barometer of culture that directs our attention to cultural shifts, struggles, and changes. From concrete instances that ignite public debate and controversy, one can develop and theorize the complex workings of a culture to gauge future directions. Thus, Madonna and her work in film, video, music, and performance incite us to reflect on the larger cultural issues at stake. The "Madonna paradigm" serves as a touchstone for theoretical discussions on issues of morality, sexuality, gender relations, gay politics, multiculturalism, feminism, race, racism, pornography, and capitalism (to name a few). This volume demonstrates Madonna's usefulness as a paradigm case to advance further developments in cultural theory, whether influenced by ideology critique, postmodernism, poststructuralism, or other theoretical frameworks that systematize the workings of culture.

It is perhaps fitting to return this general introduction to the issue with which I began: the issue of banality as constructed by tabloid journalism. In the final chapter of this book, Greg Seigworth, taking to heart the criticism advanced by Meaghan Morris (1988) and Simon Frith (1991), addresses the problem as follows: "With Madonna, the stakes are even higher: A cultural studies analysis that already runs the risk of lapsing into banality is suddenly confronted by a subject considered by many to be the utmost in banality herself." But though Madonna's own self-conscious construction may appear to be a transparently obvious come-on for facile forms of academic analysis, academic pundits and trash journalists alike are missing the point. The goal of critical analysis has never been, to my knowledge, to shed light on obscure cultural forms lacking all relevance to individuals' daily lives. In fact, with the possible exception of Elvis, Madonna is without peer in having inscribed herself with such intensity on the public consciousness in multiple and contradictory ways.

If, as Edward Said (1983, 220) points out, the cultural critic is positioned at the intersection between "the power of the dominant culture, and the impersonal system of disciplines and methods (savoir)," then it is the critic's job to dialectically engage in the negotiation of cultural business at that busy intersection. Although Morris (1988, 17) argues that banality arises whenever the subject of theoretical discourse becomes an "emblem of the critic's own activity," her own argument is, in fact, self-involved—a self-consciousness three times removed from popular culture that traps Morris in a purely academic introspection. Rather, we should follow Said's directive to that intersection of politics and popular culture where, as cultural critics and theorists, we make connections between culture as it is lived and culture as it is theorized. Using Madonna as a multifaceted site of contestation, this volume attempts to do just that.

The four parts of *The Madonna Connection* each highlight different theoretical and cultural dimensions of Madonna's repertoire and its effects according to the following issues: race and audiences, reception and interpretation within the gay community, foundationalist or antifoundationalist conceptions of feminist theory and praxis, and the ideological force of commodity culture. The reader will find interesting overlap between these parts as well as within them, and though the individual chapters express different views, the book as a whole is structured much like an in-depth dialogue, with the Madonna paradigm as its unifying core. Many contributors explore the political tensions within the current postmodern debate (Nakayama and Peñaloza; Schwichtenberg; Kaplan; Mandziuk; Pribram; Bordo; and Seigworth); others look to Foucaultian poststructuralism (Patton; Henderson; and Morton); and still others consider different theoretical frameworks (Scott; Tetzlaff; and Schulze, Barton White, and Brown). Although postmodernism figures prominently in most of the selections, there is no universal agreement that the Madonna paradigm is necessarily postmodern. In light of this, each contributor uses the methodology best suited to the facet of representation she or he wishes to explore, thereby demonstrating the range of critical and interpretive approaches that can be brought to bear on an evolving (and lively) cultural phenomenon.

Part One of the anthology, "Out of Bounds: Reading Race and Madonna's Audiences," presents theoretically informed audience studies of Madonna's work, with special attention to race and audience perceptions of the Madonna phenomenon. Many of Madonna's music videos address aspects of race, whether related to musical form or visual representation. Although some of her videos depict a multiracial entourage (as in *Borderline*), others more explicitly foreground the issue of race within the narrative (as in *Like a Prayer* or *La Isla Bonita*). Because Madonna "pushes boundaries" in the areas of race and sexuality, negative as well as positive audience responses are telling, whether they originate in the mainstream or among subcultural groups.

For this reason, Laurie Schulze, Anne Barton White, and Jane Brown examine the discursive construction of Madonna haters in a wide-ranging audience study and in the popular press. Although they do not explicitly deal with the issue of race, their findings reveal a complex construction of Madonna as "low-Other," which redefines the terms for what constitutes a resistive reading. Schulze, Barton White, and Brown find that those respondents who dislike Madonna locate themselves in opposition to what they perceive as her universal acceptance. The authors also caution against disqualifying readings such as those of Madonna haters because this "too easily permits overly romanticized notions that audiences of popular culture always valiantly resist dominant ideology in progressive ways." Such findings fit well within the current political climate, where conservatives typically construct themselves as an embattled minority, which is most clearly exemplified in their attacks on multiculturalism.

Against this backdrop, Thomas Nakayama and Lisa Peñaloza's study of multiracial readings of Madonna's music videos underscores the difficulties for people of color who must navigate the dangerous terrain of white privilege in their struggle for visibility. Using the prism metaphor to highlight race as multiply inflected, Nakayama and Peñaloza disparage the binary notion of race (i.e., black or white) and contend that one's racial self-identification does not guarantee a particular type of reading. In their audience study, they discover variable interpretations of Madonna's videos that fall within four categories: (1) Asian/Asian American, (2) Hispanic/Latino(a)/Mexican American, (3) black/African American, and (4) white/Caucasian/European American. Nakayama and Peñaloza find that, although dominant reading patterns emerge, respondents generally resort to survival tactics such as game-playing, indicating the power of the "white center." So, too, they caution against the uncritical celebration of resistive readings and note that "the dominance of the white center creates a tension between inherent whiteness and potential multicultural identification."

Ronald Scott's analysis of *Like a Prayer* and Madonna's reception in the black community concludes Part One. Although he does not employ the methodologies of audience research, he contextualizes *Like a Prayer* in reference to the black church, historically rooted in African-American culture, politics, and religion. Charging the media with complicity in perpetuating racism, Scott challenges Madonna's detractors who perceive her video as sacrilegious and likewise castigates those who impose sexual interpretations on the interracial relationship between Madonna and the black male character in the video. This, he argues, serves to reinforce (white) stereotypes about black religion, black men, and white women. Scott unflinchingly explores the tensions between religion, sexuality, and race, and in the end, he champions *Like a Prayer* as Madonna's tribute to black culture. Although he acknowledges that every member of the black community may not agree with every aspect of the video, he believes that, in its totality, *Like a Prayer* is about making moral choices, and in his opinion, Madonna reflexively incites viewers to "do the right thing."

Part Two, "The Sapphic Insurgent: Madonna and Gay Culture," explores Madonna's reception and interpretation within the gay community. Much of Madonna's later work (i.e., *Express Yourself, Vogue, Justify My Love,* the Blond Ambition tour, and *Truth or Dare*) deals explicitly with representations of sexuality that have particular resonance for gay and lesbian audiences but are typically misread or ignored by the mainstream. Indeed, if Madonna has poached elements from gay culture for mass distribution, then the chapters in this section recontextualize those elements within gay history, fantasy, and political struggle. The Madonna paradigm provides the impetus to shift the margins to the center, and thus it highlights the complexities of gay and lesbian politics and pleasures as they are lived, constructed, and contested.

For Cindy Patton, Madonna's *Vogue* video serves as a touchstone from which she develops a poststructuralist theory that explains the formation of subaltern memory in relation to gay politics, identity, and representation. Here, Patton explores the tensions between Madonna's libertarian body politic in *Vogue* and the lived experience of voguing as a kind of "folk" dance that originated among black and Hispanic queens (a particular gay, subaltern formation). Although Patton's analysis does not diminish Madonna's significance to gay culture, her theoretical exploration confronts the problems of gender, race, and sexuality mainstreamed for mass consumption. Patton notes with concern that "*Vogue* alludes to a popular memory of repression that it then anxiously undercuts by atomizing and 'dequeening' the performance of the dance." Through her chapter, Patton weaves a provocative and nuanced account of the political stakes invested in popular embodiments of subaltern memory. More than simply presenting a "pose," she suggests, *Vogue* opens up cultural theory to previously hidden (gay) sites that must be reckoned with.

Similarly, Lisa Henderson explores the Madonna phenomenon from a gay cultural perspective in order to map out and assess Madonna's contributions to the "politics of queer sex." Using the censorship controversy around *Justify My Love* as a centerpiece, Henderson traces the multiple discourses

that situate Madonna within the context of the sex and pornography debates—a highly charged nexus that invokes 2 Live Crew, the National Endowment for the Arts (NEA), Jesse Helms, acquired immune deficiency syn-
drome (AIDS), Robert Mapplethorpe, Christian fundamentalists, sado-
masochistic (S/M) lesbians, Women Against Pornography, and, of course,
Madonna's own sex-radicalism as reported in the mainstream and gay
presses. Henderson deftly draws together these interlocking networks of discourse to place Madonna's sexual politics in stark relief against the backdrop of gay culture, which has been increasingly under siege by the right
wing.

Arguing from an *anti*-antiporn position, Henderson affirms the pleasures
of Madonna's gay-directed rearticulations and visibility; however, she con-
cedes that, unlike Madonna, gay and lesbian people represent an oppressed
minority for whom self-identification entails tremendous risk. Thus, Madonna's poaching and flaunting may only provide a provisional challenge,
yet it is not one to be overlooked. Henderson provokes a rethinking of the
very terms of the politics of sexual representation by focusing on gay and
lesbian struggle, where a sexualized visibility and identity are paramount to
survival.

My own analysis of Madonna's sex-radical tactics provides a bridge between the gay and lesbian discussions in Part Two and the issue of feminism,
developed more fully in Part Three. Arguing from a postmodern feminist
perspective, I situate Madonna's later music videos (i.e., *Express Yourself*
and *Justify My Love*) within the context of the ongoing feminist/postmod-
ernist debate to illustrate how Madonna's postmodern representational
strategies challenge the foundational "truths" of sex and gender. The gender
deconstruction and sexual multiplicity at work in Madonna's texts may not
be amenable to a feminism based on an identity politics, but such strategies
address those marginalized groups (such as gay men and lesbians) that can
provide feminism with a model for an intricate, coalitional politics not
based on immanent notions of identity. Thus, Madonna's postmodern interventions pry open "a space in the mainstream to provide sexual minorities
with visibility and confirmation, while provoking feminism to rethink its
own lines, limits, and boundaries."

Part Three, "Gender Trouble: Madonna Poses the Feminist Question,"
foregrounds and situates Madonna's repertoire within the current context of
feminist theory—a fluid field that provides multiple avenues of approach to
the problem of female representation. The selections included here contribute to furthering dialogue between realist and postmodernist positions as
advanced within feminist theory. Although such positions are not mutually
exclusive, Madonna's constant reinventions bring to the foreground the
complexities of representational politics as authentic or inauthentic, constructed or lived, theorized or practiced. In the effort to break down these

boundaries and explore the nuances that typify feminist differences as well as connections, contributors highlight the various dimensions of the Madonna paradigm as an equivocal challenge to feminism as it is both lived and theorized within patriarchal culture.

E. Ann Kaplan, in a wide-ranging analysis of the various cultural discourses constructing Madonna, explores two theories of the mask in relation to strategies of subversion. This entails an examination of Madonna's use of masks in resisting the "patriarchal feminine," as well as her ability to disrupt the bourgeois illusion of the "real" individual. Kaplan analyzes the investments of numerous constituencies—the Parents' Music Resource Center, teenage consumer culture, the U.S. media, neo-Marxist critics, women and feminist scholars, and Madonna herself—in a series of discourses that conflictually construct "Madonna." Kaplan unwraps the layers that constitute the Madonna phenomenon, shedding new light on how middle America defines itself in terms of sexual mores, inhibitions, constraints, and fantasies. She cautions against interpretations of Madonna's work that celebrate girl culture as necessarily resistive to patriarchy, but she also advances a compelling argument for the subversive potential of Madonna's masks that eschew any inherent notion of an identity. The Madonna phenomenon engenders complex debates that, as Kaplan amply illustrates, "have great implications for cultural studies methods in general."

Roseann Mandziuk, in an alternate approach to Kaplan's discursive constructions, offers a critical reassessment of postmodern theory and its viability for a feminist theory and politics based on praxis. Arguing from a feminist realist position, Mandziuk examines a series of Madonna's texts (i.e., her "Nightline" interview, the "Rock the Vote" spot, and *Vogue*) to illustrate the political dangers inherent in mistaking individual play for social intervention. Mandziuk presents a thoroughgoing critique of postmodernism's contributions to feminism, which she believes are based on ephemeral promises of liberation that seduce women into silence once more and deny them a position from which to speak. Although Mandziuk acknowledges the shortcomings of feminist identity politics, she advocates a more critical and reflexive construction of such politics and warns against postmodern seductions of the type exemplified by Madonna. To relinquish political ground, from which women as real social subjects can speak, is, for her, tantamount to "sleeping with the enemy."

E. Deidre Pribram, on the other hand, suggests that postmodernism is not necessarily antithetical to feminism. In an in-depth discussion and analysis of Madonna's performance-documentary *Truth or Dare*, Pribram deconstructs the simple binary terms of truth and illusion that have characterized commentary on the film in the popular press. As a filmmaker herself, Pribram demonstrates the visual acuity that can be brought to bear on a film that defies easy categorization. Likewise, she explores the subject/object dichotomy that has led feminist critics and others to position Madonna not only as inauthentic but as object. Drawing from postmodern theorist Jean Baudrillard's concepts of "simulation" and "seduction," Pribram counters the reality-based criticism leveled at Madonna and argues that Madonna's simulated, seductive techniques display a large measure of control over her own images—a model that "may be a point of departure in the articulation of postmodern feminism."

This point of departure is taken up by Melanie Morton, who situates Madonna's multimedia interventions within various contexts of domination, inscribed by turn as modernity, bourgeois ideology, and the historical avant-garde. Drawing from poststructuralist theory, Morton demonstrates how Madonna outdistances the avant-garde through a detailed comparative analysis of the visual codes governing Fritz Lang's *Metropolis* and those codes that Madonna simulates and subverts in her music video *Express Yourself.* This further extends to Madonna's refusal of closure in the musical score of *Express Yourself,* illustrated through a musicological analysis of the keys and tonalities that govern a musical semiotics. Morton takes us on a playful, yet thoughtful, excursion into *Express Yourself* and its strategic points of intersection. By emphasizing a postmodern feminist reinscription, Morton shows the multiple ways that Madonna refuses the subjugation of both visual and musical conventions, indicating her politically subversive sexuality.

The final part of this book, "The Political Economy of Postmodernism: Madonna as Star-Commodity," situates the Madonna paradigm within the mainstream of consumer culture, where star packaging and targeted audiences are critical for profitability. Advancing various forms of cultural and ideological criticism, this part highlights the symbiotic relationship between postmodernism and political economy. Here, Madonna's high measure of success as a postmodern phenomenon signals the media, beauty, and music industries' ability to flexibly respond to inauthenticity and reinvention as marketing strategies. In light of late capitalism's postmodern approach, the three chapters in Part Four examine how Madonna's novelty, beauty, power, and autobiography are used in the packaging of her star personae. Contributors underscore the complexities informing representational politics on a larger scale, where mainstream concerns and a savvy ideology efface local struggles.

David Tetzlaff offers a relentless ideology critique of Madonna's postmodern penchant for constant transformation. In an incisive analysis that questions her mass audience appeal and takes to task those critics who celebrate her, Tetzlaff discusses Madonna's lack of authenticity, which figures in her ability to market herself and thus adapt to the late capitalist marketplace. Tetzlaff focuses on Madonna's metatextual narratives that document her rise from rags to riches to explore how power, as a material issue, is linked to her success. In the process, he illuminates the ways in which capitalism accommodates the feminism that is personified by Madonna as successful career woman. For Tetzlaff, her popularity indicates the extent to which late capitalist values have been absorbed by popular culture. Given the precepts of 1980s Reaganism on which Madonna hitched her star, it would seem that advanced capitalism and postmodernism make fine bedfellows. As Tetzlaff notes, "Madonna's power is tied to her ability to have her image reproduced and distributed . . . 'America's Funniest Home Videos' notwithstanding, the masses cannot follow Madonna's path to empowerment."

In a similarly provocative essay, Susan Bordo surveys and critiques current discourses that promote plastic surgery, bodybuilding, liposuction, exercise regimens, and other bodily enhancements that contribute to "plasticity" as a postmodern paradigm. Within the context of bodily transformation, Bordo situates the physical reconstruction of Madonna, who has come to represent the perfect postmodern body in both theoretical and popular discourse. Bordo advances a feminist critique of Madonna's bodily transformations as emblematic of postmodernism's tendency to efface women's physical differences in accordance with a "plastic" standard of beauty. Sharing some of Mandziuk's concerns, Bordo highlights Madonna's physical iconography to emphasize the political dangers postmodernism poses for feminism, particularly when this postmodernism is aligned with capitalism. Within this larger purview, Bordo illustrates how commercial imperatives inform a "plastic aesthetics of the body."

Greg Seigworth, taking up some of the points raised by Tetzlaff and others in the volume, concludes Part Four with the question of autobiography in the age of postmodern hypercommercialism. Focusing on the new system of stardom within the contemporary music industry, Seigworth explores issues of character, persona, and personality in relation to Madonna's largely autobiographical albums. For Seigworth, Madonna, particularly when compared with Elvis, signals important shifts in the way we perceive musical performers both aurally and visually. Drawing from Fredric Jameson's theory of "cognitive mapping," Seigworth uses his expertise as a music critic to provide a theoretical account of postmodern musical stardom that engages the notions of "star," "system," and "meaning." This chapter, which appropriately concludes the book with autobiography, compels us to reflect on our own activities as writers and cultural critics without lapsing into solipsism or (even worse) banality.

Together, the chapters in this volume present a multifaceted approach to a cultural phenomenon that has the longevity and dimension to ignite public controversy. All of the contributors agree that Madonna has insinuated herself into individuals' daily lives, offering connections between their lived experiences and the various discourses in circulation; what is at issue is the interpretation of such cultural ubiquity. In an age in which popular culture and mass culture enjoy a symbiotic relationship, it is more difficult than ever to discern the "progressive" or "ideological" character of representational politics, particularly as it affects subcultural groups.

As the chapters that follow indicate, the Madonna phenomenon, when multiply inflected, can generate nuanced accounts that challenge the cultural studies dichotomies of text/audience and enablement/constraint. Given this, cultural critics and theorists should worry less about methodological turf or lapsing into banality and concentrate more on making those connections that dissolve boundaries. This volume does just that by offering a series of in-depth analyses that, taken as a whole, replicate a thoughtful and inquiring conversation. Although no discussion is without disagreement, the chapters included here go beyond mere differences of opinion to complement and add to the growing body of work on popular culture. If Madonna has served as a vehicle for such discussion, then that is all to the better.

REFERENCES

Brown, M. E., and Fiske, J. (1987). "Romancing the Rock." *One, Two, Three, Four: A Journal of Very, Very Popular Music* 5:61–73.

Fiske, J. (1987). "British Cultural Studies and Television." In R. C. Allen (ed.), *Channels of Discourse: Television and Contemporary Criticism.* Chapel Hill: University of North Carolina Press, pp. 254–289.

Frith, S. (1991). "TV Guides." *Village Voice,* January 15, p. 72.

Kaplan, E. A. (1987). *Rocking Around the Clock: Music Television, Postmodernism, and Consumer Culture.* New York: Methuen.

Lewis, L. A. (1987). "Form and Female Authorship in Music Video." *Communication* 9:355–377.

Morris, M. (1988). "Banality in Cultural Studies." *Discourse* 10:3–29.

Said, E. W. (1983). *The World, the Text, and the Critic.* Cambridge, Mass.: Harvard University Press.

Part One

Out of Bounds: Reading Race and Madonna's Audiences

photo by Neal Preston, *courtesy of Warner Brothers*

LAURIE SCHULZE
ANNE BARTON WHITE
JANE D. BROWN

1

"A Sacred Monster in Her Prime": Audience Construction of Madonna as Low-Other

*T*HROUGHOUT her career, Madonna has polarized critics and audiences. As John Fiske (1987, 275) has said, Madonna is "much loved or much hated." One critic called her "a sacred monster in her prime," which perfectly captures the extremities of her audiences. Her fans idolize her; she is worshipped, a postmodern deity. Her detractors loathe her; she is shunned and despised, a contemporary monster (Hoberman 1991, 51). For every fan who tells a reporter: "I love her. Madonna, she's so cool. She's like a great gifted personality. She's not just sexy... she's what she wants to be," there is a letter to the editor that snarls, "Why appall your readers with the mug shot of America's favorite social disease, Madonna?" (Kastor and Spolar 1985, C6; *Rolling Stone* 1985, 9).

Madonna is incredibly popular. She has had sixteen consecutive top-five hits (only Elvis had more) and the most successful record of any music star in the 1980s (Ayers 1990, 20; Gilmore 1987, 36). As one critic wrote, "Let's get it clear from the start that we're talking about the most successful female solo pop performer ever" (Garratt 1986, 12). *Rolling Stone* flatly calls her "the world's most famous woman" (Zehme 1989, 51).

But Madonna's success may be due less to her artistic talent and more to her ability to tap into and disturb established hierarchies of gender and sexuality. Since the beginning, Madonna has been the subject of vehement criticism and hostility. Feminists, fundamentalist groups, Planned Parenthood, and the Veterans of Foreign Wars, among others, have publicly denounced Madonna's songs, music videos, public service announcements, or television commercials.[1] She has been accused of being anti-Christian and antifamily (Wildmon 1985) and has been called a bimbo, a tart, and a man-eater.

The rather substantial body of critical scholarship on Madonna certainly acknowledges that she is not universally admired. But most academic work has focused on how Madonna's texts make meanings and pleasures available to her fans instead of her critics and how they have positioned Madonna as a positive role model for young adolescent girls (Fiske 1987; Lewis 1987). In this chapter, we look more closely at those who hate, rather than love, Madonna, to try to explain why such a popular woman engenders such hostility as well as praise.

We find that Madonna can be seen as a striking contemporary instance of what Peter Stallybrass and Allon White (1986) call the "low-Other." The low-Other is a symbolic and cultural construct, involving the production of a hierarchical order. Something is designated as base, gross, freakish, marginal, abject—pushed down into a "low" place and pushed away as "Other." The result is the normalizing and the elevation of whatever "it" is *not*. Powerful social conflicts are taken up in such representational practices, and often constructions of the low-Other are mobilized around gender, race, ethnicity, class, sexual orientation, and so on. Paradoxically, then, as Stallybrass and White point out, what is "socially peripheral" often assumes a "symbolically central" position. Low-Others of various sorts are heavily represented in popular culture and constructed by popular audiences. Interpretations of Madonna and her texts that are produced by Madonna haters evidence this practice at work.

Madonna is criticized from a variety of perspectives, but each assumes a higher social, moral, or aesthetic ground from which she can be seen as unworthy of emulation. To some critics, Madonna is the lowest form of popular culture and promotes debased and unsophisticated taste, thus undermining high cultural standards. Others worry more about Madonna as a model of unsavory morals for our children. For some, this concern is linked to an apparently even more dangerous possibility—that Madonna corrupts the meaning of *womanhood*. A sort of female grotesque, Madonna is reviled for the carnivalesque transgressions of traditional gender roles and sexuality that characterize her various personas and performances.[2]

Our analysis also shows the paradoxical position from which Madonna's critics speak. Even as they critique Madonna, they give her symbolic power, probably among the young, in particular, who adore her precisely because she does transgress high cultural norms. The vociferousness of the haters' anger and revulsion also suggests the allure they fight against. As Stallybrass and White (1986, 4–5) explain, elite or high culture, try as it might to repulse and expel the low, is inextricably bound to it: "The result is a mobile, conflictual fusion of power, fear and desire in the construction of subjectivity: a psychological dependence upon precisely those others which are being rigorously opposed and excluded at the social level."

This paradox is clear, too, when we try to apply traditional definitions of the resistive reader to this audience. *Resistive Reader* is a term that cultural studies usually reserves for an audience that goes against the grain of dominant ideological meanings. Yet, some readers use a patriarchal discourse of

the feminine to understand Madonna and identify themselves as resistive audiences: "I'm so glad to hear that not all professionals think Madonna is
great," one woman who refers to Madonna as "Miss Whore" wrote. Our
analyses suggest that we may need to rethink what is meant by resistance to
the dominant culture in a way that can include an audience like the one we
describe here.

Our study of Madonna haters drew on three sources of information.
First, an extensive amount of popular discourse on Madonna, generated
from 1984 through 1991, was analyzed. Second, we examined the responses
to a letter-writing contest sponsored by *Rocky Mountain News* columnist
Justin Mitchell in Denver, Colorado.[3] In the contest, readers were asked to
complete one of two statements about Madonna in twenty-five words or
less: (1) "I think Madonna is a supremely gifted and talented artist who deserves more media attention as well as the Nobel Prize for body chemistry
because . . . " or (2) "I think Madonna should be forced to work third shift
for below the minimum wage in a fish-processing plant for the rest of her life
because. . . . " The newspaper received some 130 entries, about evenly split
between fans and haters. Only the haters were included in this analysis. Finally, the open-ended responses of 332 college students to Madonna's videos *Papa Don't Preach* and *Open Your Heart* were analyzed. Discriminant
function analysis was also run on these 332 cases to determine differences
between those who hated Madonna and those who loved her or were
"somewhat" fans of hers.[4]

The survey of Madonna's bad press, the letters from the newspaper contest, and the responses by the college students revealed four recurrent and
overlapping critical perspectives: (1) Madonna as emblematic of the lowest
form of aesthetic culture—utterly commercial, formulaic, trivial, and shallow pop music (as opposed to authentic, original, and substantial rock); (2)
Madonna as the lowest form of socially irresponsible culture—the infec-
tious source of a media effect that corrupts innocent children; (3) Madonna
as the female grotesque—the lowest and/or most dangerous form of the feminine—the whore, the sacrilegious anti-Madonna, the narcissistic woman
who deliberately makes a spectacle of herself, the voracious man-eating
vamp(ire); (4) Madonna as the antithesis of feminism and feminist identity
politics. We examine each of these critical perspectives in turn.

MADONNA AS THE LOWEST FORM
OF AESTHETIC CULTURE

One critic so nicely summed up the various alliances operating within a high
popular culture/low popular culture antagonism that his words are worth
quoting at length:

Carole King, Joni Mitchell and Carly Simon, the rock singer-songwriters who were at the peak of their popularity in the mid-70's, wrote probing confessional songs that tried to expand the vocabulary of adult pop music into an art form. But Madonna's music . . . revels in . . . cartoon fantasies of self-gratification. Carole King, in particular, stood for an unglamorous socially concerned humanism. Madonna, by contrast, offers only impetuous romantic fantasy to those who can afford it, the world outside her own juvenile dreams barely exists . . . [T]he antiintellectual, artifice-flaunting female pop tradition that Madonna represents . . . rejected artistic goals for deadpan ironic attitudinizing, [and the pop-stars representing this tradition] traded in their complicated real selves to become preening music-video products with self-christened brand names (Holden 1985, 22).

"Rock," therefore, according to this and other critics, is adult, innovative, authentic, serious, and committed actively and unselfishly to social issues. "Rock" is art. Madonna, in contrast, is "pop"—juvenile, formulaic, artificial, shallow, self-centered, escapist fantasy, committed to making a profit. Madonna is a commodity produced by industry. Clearly, pushing Madonna to the bottom rungs of the pop cultural ladder makes a space at the top for pop music "art."

Furthermore, despite the fact that Madonna is located in opposition to female singer-songwriters, it is Madonna and pop that are feminized. As Patrice Petro (1986), Tania Modleski (1986), and Andreas Huyssen (1986) have pointed out, when the high culture versus mass culture distinction is invoked, a "gendering" strategy that attributes "active" masculine values to high culture (art) and "passive" feminine characteristics to mass culture (entertainment) often is at work. A number of music critics link Madonna, pop, and "feminine" qualities (using adjectives like fluffy, coy, bubbly, etc.) to construct a transcoded version of the art versus mass culture distinction within the domain of popular music.

Described as "shallow, kitschy pop entertainment," "pure, commercial hokum," "gleaming and superficial," and "manipulative," Madonna signifies the low-Other of popular art, the media package that demonstrates the power of the culture industry to successfully commodify a performer with no talent. Even reviews that discuss Madonna's vision have been framed by this construction of her. For example, a recent article asserted that "by reinventing herself clip by clip [in videos], Madonna has exploited the potential of the MTV revolution more astutely than any contemporary star" and went on to say that she "infuses each clip with her vision." The headline on the magazine cover, however, read, "How Video Created Madonna" (Ayers 1990).

These themes also are evident in the haters' responses to the videos *Papa Don't Preach* and *Open Your Heart*. One male viewer of the second video responded that it did not appear to have one specific theme: "To me, it was just a vehicle to sell more records." Another male viewer of *Open*, when asked to identify the dancing woman in the video, responded: "The woman is Madonna and she is dancing because that's what society wants to see. If she just sat in the chair and sang her song not too many people would like her video and it wouldn't make any MONEY!!"

As respondents to the newspaper contest put it, Madonna is "the epitomy of style over substance," and "her popularity relies on marketing and packaging rather than the artistic product." Thus, Madonna is seen as all artifice and no art. One male viewer of *Open Your Heart* commented that the "video was interesting but the song sucked." Certainly, as Madonna continued to demonstrate she was no flash in the pan, turning out hit after hit and making increasingly elaborate tours, more critical voices began to say (sometimes grudgingly) that Madonna was a talented popular artist. But the "Madonna as anti-art" discourse persists. As a recent article put it:

> Nowhere...is the dissonance between musical value and spectacular stardom more jarring than with Madonna. On the one hand, she has managed to remain hugely famous for as long as the Beatles lasted after they hit it big. On the other hand, she has not advanced musically much beyond the level of Milli Vanilli.... Madonna has managed to maintain consumer interest by constantly repositioning herself in new media, by constantly repackaging" (Reid 1990, 24).[5]

Notice, too, that Madonna's fans are characterized as consumers. The gendering strategies that assign allegedly masculine qualities to art and feminine qualities to low and mass culture frequently are deployed with respect to audiences as well. Audiences for high culture are active and productive; audiences for mass culture are passive consumers and hence are particularly at risk of being affected and infected by low entertainment.

In sum, Madonna often is positioned as the low-Other in the domain of aesthetic culture. She is not perceived as a musical artist, nor, perhaps, can she "rise" from the low to become one. Writing on women and art, Roszika Parker and Griselda Pollock (1981, 8) state: "Women and all their activities are characterized as the antithesis of cultural creativity, making the notion of a woman artist a contradiction in terms." They quote Octave Uzanne, a nineteenth-century writer, who sums it up perfectly: "So long as a woman refrains from *unsexing* herself by acquiring genius let her dabble in anything. The woman of genius does not exist but when she does she is a man." Clearly, Madonna has not "unsexed" herself—on the contrary, her gender and sexuality are the centerpiece of her work. Madonna's embrace of this feminine position makes her a part of low art; she is *not* part of a high art tradition of selfless, inspired vessels (read genderless) who see, understand, and create art that illuminates the complexities of our culture. Madonna's perceived inspiration, unlike that of the selfless artist, is base; she openly desires fame and wealth. Madonna's art also is suspicious because, unlike the works of Vincent van Gogh or Henri Matisse, it is readily available for purchase at any record or video store. As John Berger has suggested in his analysis of cultural status, such availability may contribute to reducing the perceived value of Madonna's work.

MADONNA AS THE LOWEST FORM OF
IRRESPONSIBLE CULTURE: A SOCIAL DISEASE

Madonna's most visible fans in the first two or three years of her career were the "wanna-bes," adolescent girls who reinterpreted Madonna's look to become a cultural phenomenon in their own right. Little wonder that they often were positioned as a passive audience or that there was a moral panic about the effects that Madonna was having on them. As Terry Lovell (1983, 62) has noted, "Every successive penetration of capital into cultural production has produced an outbreak of 'moral panic' in its wake," from novel reading in the eighteenth century to film in the 1930s to television in the 1950s. Inevitably, the audiences thought to be at risk were and are described as "weak-minded women" and/or "weak-minded children and adolescents." Much of the initial concern over the effects of Madonna coincided with concern over the effects of MTV, yet another benchmark of capital's "penetration into cultural production."[6] As a consequence, the discourse constructing Madonna as a social disease infecting vulnerable adolescent girls has a particular vehemence.

Popular music criticism is much less likely to be the vehicle for configuring Madonna as the deviant source of social or moral contagion than other forms of popular discourse. On the contrary, popular music critics have tended to launch counterdiscourses against groups such as the National Coalition on Television Violence and the Parents' Music Resource Center, strongly contesting their arguments that sexually explicit and violent imagery or lyrics in music videos, heavy metal, rap, and so on have deleterious effects on youth (R. Johnson 1985; Goldberg 1990). Nevertheless, even pop music critics have implied that Madonna's audiences are different in a way that renders them more susceptible to her so-called messages. For example, in one review of a Madonna concert, the writer pointed out that the crowd, "primed by the records and the videos, shrieked . . . before [Madonna] had sung a note" and complained that the audience's "Pavlovian responses suggest[ed] the results of an experiment set up by behavioral psychologists in order to prove that Skinner was right after all" (Palmer 1985, C4).

Another critic, worrying about the effects of what she termed "bimbo rock" on the gains women have made within the music industry, interviewed a clinical social worker who said:

> My work involves counseling pregnant and parenting teen-age girls, and I know how impressionable they are. Rock stars like Madonna . . . are important to them. They buy their records, sing their songs, and dress like them. They get the message of what it means to have sex, and it puts a lot of pressure on them to live up to that image. They . . . get the notion that it's great to have sex. Why worry about the consequences? In fact, they never even hear about the consequences (C. Johnson, 1985, 54–55).

The popular press has reported that even Madonna fans themselves are concerned, quoting female fans in their early twenties who say, "We think it's bad for all these little kids to admire her. Did you see her movie [*Desperately Seeking Susan*]? She was a slut, she smoked" (Kastor and Spolar 1985, C6).

Most of the discursive work contributing to the Madonna-as-social-disease configuration has circulated in the arena of social commentary rather than music criticism. Concern that the wanna-bes might go beyond style imitation escalated with the release of Madonna's "Papa Don't Preach" in the summer of 1986. Alfred Moran (1986), the executive director of Planned Parenthood, wrote a widely circulated memo to the entertainment media stating that Madonna's single "sends a potent message to teenagers about the glamour of sex, pregnancy and childbearing" that will "encourage more teens to engage in sex prematurely." Popular social commentators like Ellen Goodman (1986, 5) called Madonna's *Papa Don't Preach* video a "commercial for teen-age pregnancy" and asked Madonna to "call off the propaganda." Goodman pointed out that Madonna, twenty-seven years old, married, and rich, was irresponsibly sending a message that would lead her gullible adolescent female fans not into the romantic fantasy of the *Papa* video but into the harsh reality of poverty and single parenthood.

"Papa Don't Preach" has been a remarkably persistent focal point for criticism of Madonna as a corrupter of youth. One critic writing five years after the song's release flatly stated that Madonna "has contributed to the immorality of minors (millions of them)" and, citing "Papa" as an example, called her "a shallow millionairess encouraging her followers toward the royal road to poverty" (Charen 1991, 50).

As further illustration of this theme, one of the female Madonna haters, when asked to whom she might give the *Papa* video, wrote: "I'd give it to a early pre-teen girl. She'd probably think it was really romantic and sweet and nine months later she'd be thinking how stupid she was to think it was ever meaningful or realistic."

Almost 20 percent of the Madonna haters who responded to the newspaper contest said that they hated her because of what they perceived to be her effects on fans. "In my opinion," one woman wrote, "Madonna is one of the poorest yet most influential role models for our young people. Many young girls imitate and even worship her. She promotes sexual promiscuity, incest, and rebellion in society. I am a teacher in middle school and I see the product of her influence."

Another woman wrote that "she irresponsibly and without consideration for her adoring and imitative fans is a role model for teenage parenthood, disrespect for others' religious beliefs, and materialism." A man claimed that Madonna is "an inconsiderate tramp who has no social values and abuses her popularity by trashing the minds of our youth today."

A number of the haters read the *Open Your Heart* video as a portrayal of Madonna as a child abuser. One female wrote that the video disgusted her because it had "overtones of sexual molestation of children." Another female hater wrote that she was bothered by the video, particularly the "thought of some little boy being subjected to this kind of smut." When asked why Madonna kissed the little boy at the end of *Open,* one female wrote, "Maybe Madonna wants to be in every little boy's fantasies." One male responded that Madonna kissed the boy because "she's a child molester." When asked what happens to the boy and Madonna after the video ends, one female hater wrote, "Madonna probably wanted us to believe the little boy is taking her away from this horrible world but if he goes with her he'll end up molested!"

This theme of impropriety on the part of Madonna is continued in the haters' responses to the question of to whom they would give the *Open* video. One female wrote, "A perverted young man because it seems too extreme for average people." Another woman wrote that she would give the video to "some slease ball in New York who has an hour to live and likes Madonna and little boys. Maybe it would cheer someone like *that* up." The video's display of Madonna's "inappropriate" behavior with the little boy is read by these haters as befitting the interests of the most perverted segments of our society.

Two letters spoke from an overtly religious standpoint, inscribing the discourse of what Todd Gitlin (1983, 250) has referred to as "the far righteous." A man wrote that "Madonna is leading our children to hell and deserves far worse than the fish-processing plant treatment. Jesus Christ says those who corrupt the children should have 'a millstone hanged about their necks, and drowned in the depths of the sea.' Matthew 18:6." A woman, writing as the Antichrist (who, she claimed, is a Madonna fan), imagined that the Antichrist would say that he loves Madonna because "she is obediant to my will and does a good job in luring the impure, unchaste, and unstraight to my cause; like pride, greed, drugs, crime, sodomy, she tempts the weak and rebellious, adding to my army."

The *Papa* video was not the only controversial piece that stimulated religious discourses to position Madonna as a source of moral contagion. The Reverend Donald Wildmon, of the American Family Association, wrote an article in 1985 claiming that the publication of nude photographs of Madonna in *Playboy* and *Penthouse* would encourage child pornography. Judith Reisman, an investigator of the Department of Juvenile Justice and Delinquency Prevention, concluded, according to Wildmon, that "many children would be more easily victimized by child pornographers since they would only be doing what Madonna (their idol) did" (Wildmon 1985, 2).

In the same article, Wildmon called Madonna "anti-Christian" and "anti-family" for wearing crucifixes as jewelry. In 1989, he and the American Family Association threatened to boycott Pepsi-Cola if the company used Madonna's *Like a Prayer* in a commercial because the music video was blasphemous and anti-Christian and because Madonna was a horrible "role model for America's youth ("Pepsi Refuses" 1989). Pepsi-Cola shelved the commercial.

Madonna-as-social-disease is a site where disparate discourses converge: discursive strands of liberal and socially concerned humanism, the conservative religious Right, and feminism form a strange alliance against the low-Other, Madonna. This powerful opposition to Madonna's work parallels the response to burlesque during the mid-nineteenth century. Robert C. Allen (1991, 128) states that burlesque "had become a disease, a contagious infection; the burlesque performer had become both the diseased body and the carrier of the disease within the civic body." It is no surprise, then, that rumors of Madonna testing HIV-positive have been incredibly persistent (Browne, DiMartino, Jordan, and Kilday 1991); certain segments of our culture, no doubt, find comfort in identifying her as a carrier of the AIDS virus—a disease perceived by some as a punishment for immoral behavior. Making Madonna HIV-positive establishes her moral guilt and provides for her ultimate containment by death.

MADONNA AS THE LOWEST FORM
OF THE FEMININE

Fiske (1987, 273) claims that the real threat Madonna poses to patriarchy is not "the traditional and easily contained one of woman as whore" but rather "the more radical [threat] of woman as independent of masculinity." Madonna's most flagrant trespasses involve crossing the established boundaries of appropriate gender roles and sexuality drawn by patriarchy and heterosexism. But few critics take on the more radical threat and instead resort to reducing Madonna to a figure they consider the lowest form of womanhood—the prostitute—perhaps in an effort to discourage other women from emulating her, a warning to women who might follow her lead.

"Madonna's bare-bellied, fondle-my-bra image is strictly bimbo-city, and of course it sells [but] take away the ravaged-tart trappings and there's nothing else to talk about" (Loder 1984/1985, 107). The word *tart* often is used to describe Madonna, especially in her early "boy toy" phase, when she appeared with masses of blond hair with dark roots, wore underwear as outerwear, dressed in what one critic called "mix-and-mismatch and flea sale fashions," and piled on excessive makeup and junk jewelry. One of the most salient details of her look in this boy toy phase was the deliberately exposed stomach and navel, displaying a body that was out of step with fashion—lush and Rubenesque, rather than slim. Madonna celebrated the body, an excessive body, and deliberately emphasized the lower strata of the body. She enacted parodic and exaggerated performances of femininity and heterogeneously combined the virgin and the whore, little-girl-playing-dress-up and seasoned gold digger. (This last pairing threatens all the social repressions around the sexuality of children and may be one of the most unsettling aspects of Madonna's performances for some audiences.) Madonna's carnivalesque transgressions of gender and sexuality, the source of much pleasure for her fans, are extremely disturbing to her haters, and often this hate is focused on the body and expressed in a discourse about the body.[7]

Consider these excerpts from popular criticism: "Madonna [in concert] was a sweaty pinup girl come to life. She wiggled her tummy and shook her ass. She smiled lasciviously and stuck out her tongue." "You've seen Madonna wiggling on MTV—right, she's the pop-tart singer with the trashy outfits and the hi-there belly button." "In her videos and on stage, [Madonna] is more the vamp, wriggling and writhing in her revealing outfits, puckering her lips, looking sultry and so on." "Madonna has an action-packed body, always prominently on display, and doleful, knowing eyes that seem to encourage every male fantasy of lust with no limits. In truth, she is an indifferent singer, but her voice has the whispered assurance of one of those phone-for-sex girls" (Cocks 1985, 74; Goldberg 1985, 20; Skow 1985, 74; Palmer 1985, C4).

Most critics stop short of calling Madonna a whore, opting for euphemistic phrases like "tarted-up floozy" instead. An article in *New Republic*, however, pulls no punches and refers to Christopher Lasch's *Culture of Narcissism* to explain why Madonna is hot. The writer says that when Lasch argued that the Happy Hooker, rather than Horatio Alger, is now the "prototype of American success," he "was talking about the prostitute as a social type, but he could just as well have been describing Madonna." The article quotes Lasch's description of the prostitute extensively and adds that it is "too true" of Madonna (J. T. 1985, 42). Joni Mitchell, when asked about Madonna in a recent interview, said, "What's the difference between her and a hard hooker, you know?" (Wild 1991, 64).

Even discourses that evidence more fascination and desire than repulsion often have an uneasy undertone when attempting to make sense of Madonna's body and her sexuality. "She's tart but delicious, she's campy but coy . . . that bad girl of boy dreams and bawdy snatcher of hearts [who]

writhes, wiggles, shimmies her semi-liquid assets and gleefully misbehaves."
Besides imaging a body that threatens to overspill its boundaries, the description is also interesting in the way it puns on *bawdy*, evoking the ghoul-
ish and alien *body snatcher*. The writer goes on to say that Madonna has
"plowed through boyfriends like party snacks" (McBride 1985, 41, 43).
"The bawdy snatcher of [boy's] hearts" is really "the snatch that eats boys,"
a voracious, overappetited feminine monster, the vagina dentata.[8] The "tabloid" Madonna is often constructed in these terms, as in a recent *Globe*
cover story: "Man-eater Madonna Used Sex to Climb to the Top!"
(Nelander 1990, 17).[9]

Another mythical feminine monster summoned up to make sense of Madonna is the succubus. "Madonna," says *Boston Phoenix* editor Milo Miles,
"is the kind of woman who comes into your room at three A.M. and sucks
your life out" (Marsh 1985, 161). A succubus, according to legend, is a female demon, a (hetero)sexual predator. While men lie sleeping, the succubus
descends on them and essentially rapes them, forcing them to have sexual intercourse with her. The proximate root of the word is the late Latin *succuba*,
which means *prostitute*. The woman-as-whore threat may be traditional,
but it may not be as easily containable as Fiske suggests it is. Or, perhaps, in
Madonna's case, as a strategy of containment, it leaks.

What we do find is ample confirmation of Fiske's point that Madonna's
"enjoyment of her own sexuality" is the most serious transgression. Descriptions of her sexuality as whorish are often linked with charges that Madonna is selfish and self-interested, which rephrases a woman's pleasure in
her own sexuality as vanity, narcissism, and selfishness (Holden 1985, 21–
22). One critic wrote, "She is a slutty, self-obsessed, sometimes cruel, always
manipulative woman" (Charen 1991, 50). A review of *Truth or Dare* called
Madonna a "vain icon" and the film "a one-woman show ad nauseum,"
adding "you've never seen such a series of publicity stunts. Madonna's only
art lies in self-promotion, in the sheer depth of her narcissism" (Gallo 1991,
36).

Madonna is a woman who deliberately "makes a spectacle out of herself"
and obviously takes great pleasure in it.[10] Letters from the newspaper contest were rife with a hatred that centers on Madonna's autoerotic aesthetic.
One woman wrote that "anyone with that much of an obsession with her
own body needs a bit of serious therapy"; another commented, "Talent,
overclouded by too much body . . . can wear on the mind. You were sexy,
Madonna, but now you're shabby, tacky and gauche!!!" Two other letters,
also from women, made similar points: "Her flaunting herself is bad," and
"'Proverbs 11:22—A beautiful woman lacking discretion and modesty is
like a fine gold ring in a pig's snout.' I NEED SAY NO MORE."

A striking number of letters in the newspaper's contest were from women
who constructed the meaning of Madonna as whore. A thirty-one-year-old

mother wrote, "Madonna is a sleez, she's a tramp, she's a slut. She's a disgrace to the woman's race." Another wrote: "I think Madonna should work at what she portrays in her music because she portrays a young woman longing for sex to be her door to love and yet wants to be in control of her male victims. . . . Sorry its not in 25 words or less but to put a limit on words to discribe a whore is unrealistic." Still another woman wrote: "Any slut can strip and sing professionally. She's a repulsive ho. Since she first started being overly slutty (since she's always been a ho) I turned the station before even her second note. Over time I've grown to loathe her and her metal tits." One woman found the slippage between virgin and whore disturbing: "Madonna went from acting like Miss Innocent Virgin to Miss Whore of the '90s."

In responding to the *Papa* video, one woman wrote she disliked the part when Madonna "is singing (dressed in black) and dancing around. It adds a somewhat whore-ish aspect to this video." One male viewer of *Open* wrote that his most memorable image from the video was of "an untalented Bimbo dancing." Similarly, another male viewer wrote that his most memorable image was "the incessant gyrations of a sex-crazed nymph dressed in black."

In the terms of this discourse, the lowest form of the feminine is the whore. Madonna's critics are quick to cast her in this role. We might see this as a strategy to contain Madonna herself as the boy toy and to resist the implications of a reversed interpretation—that for Madonna, *boys* are the toys, that in Madonna's world boys exist solely to satisfy *her* desires. Sometimes, Madonna seems to go even further, posing an autoeroticism that suggests that when she tires of her playthings, she may not really need men at all. Perhaps, as Fiske suggests, that is the threat that drives individuals coming from patriarchal frameworks to reduce Madonna to the lowest of the low.

MADONNA AS THE ANTITHESIS OF FEMINISM

Although feminism is hardly a univocal discourse and although some feminists have been Madonna fans from the beginning (Garratt 1986, 12–13; Williamson 1985, 46–47; Simmonds 1985, 60), there is and was, especially early in Madonna's career, a certain tendency in the popular press to construct a unified position for feminism against Madonna. For example, one article reported that "some feminists clearly feel that Madonna's self-parody as an eye-batting gold digger. . . is a joke too damaging to laugh at," but the writer neglected to mention what other feminists might feel (Skow 1985, 74). Another asserted that "Madonna's whole image, in fact, is like a finger-flip to feminists" (Cocks 1985, 74). Kurt Loder (1984/1985, 107) remarked in *Rolling Stone* that "Madonna's whole act . . . seems custom-designed to gag feminists of both sexes."

Indeed, articles written by male feminist rock critics dominated the discursive construction of Madonna as an antifeminist, at least in the first phases of her career. For example, Jim Miller (1985, 48–57) wrote: "As one of the most influential strong-holds of knee-jerk misogyny, the rock scene has long cried out for women with power, ideas and an independent sense of style. . . . The current upsurge, however, has many different and even contradictory facets. Striking new figures like Cyndi Lauper . . . flourish beside much more traditional starlets like Madonna." To Miller, Cyndi Lauper signified the creative artist and progressive feminist and Madonna signified the "fluffy" pop entertainer and "old-fashioned" sexist female stereotype.[11] Another male critic called Madonna "a pretty dinosaur," noting that though women in pop used to have to "play the bimbo" to succeed, feminism "has changed all that, allowing women to be whatever they want." Madonna, he argued, is an "old-fashioned throw-back" (Watrous 1985, 111).

Not all spokespeople for the early Madonna-as-antifeminist movement in music criticism were male feminists, however. For example, Connie Johnson (1985, 54) asked, rhetorically, "Don't you think Madonna's sex-bomb, 'boy-toy' posture is a step backward for everyone who wanted to topple the notion that women's only purpose and pleasure in life is to serve men?" She gave this answer: "Unfortunately, Bimbo Rock only reinforces that notion. Rather than challenge the long-standing stereotype, these eager pop stars willingly mold their images around it."

With Madonna's very successful *True Blue* album, her Who's That Girl? tour, and her new look (a slimmer body, sophisticated close-cropped platinum hair, high-fashion clothes [Gross 1986]), something of a counterdiscourse began to emerge in the popular press that gave Madonna a profeminist inflection. The Madonna-as-antifeminist critique persists, of course, but its hegemony has weakened. Reviewing the Who's That Girl? tour, a critic for *Rolling Stone* (the previous site of savage criticism denouncing Madonna as "bad mass culture" and antifeminist) said that the performance of "Papa" "takes sharp aim at some of the current batch of male authority figures (including the pope and the president) who would presume to have the power to make key decisions regarding a woman's control of her own body" (Gilmore 1987, 87). The article nominated Madonna as a "genuine hero" to "little girls across the world" and called the tour the most "forceful showcase for the feminine sensibility in pop" to date.

When Madonna appeared on ABC's "Nightline" in December 1990 to defend the video *Justify My Love,* banned by MTV, her answers to Forrest Sawyer's questions about feminist criticism of her videos kicked off a series of competing bids for the meanings of Madonna vis-à-vis feminism. Caryn James (1990, H38, 44) claimed that Madonna "is redefining feminism itself" and that to "judge Madonna by traditional [feminist] standards is to miss the point." According to James, Madonna is "the woman who most astutely embodies how feminism has shifted in the last decade" because for Madonna, "feminism means the freedom to be sexy as well as sexual, to be in control of one's image as well as one's life." Camille Paglia (1990, 39), also writing in response to the "Nightline" appearance, argued that "Madonna is the true feminist. She exposes the puritanism and suffocating ideology of American feminism . . . Madonna has taught young women to be fully female and sexual while still exercising total control over their lives." Madonna, Paglia contended, is a postmodern feminist who, in contrast to an outmoded feminism that proclaimed "no more masks," reveals that "we are nothing but masks." Reveling in "the eternal values of beauty and pleasure," Madonna is "the future of feminism."

On the other hand, Madonna is still anathema for some feminists. Barbara Grizzuti Harrison's (1991, 80, 82) reply to Paglia and James was: "Is Madonna a feminist? Gimme a break. Do pigs fly?" Harrison objected to the postmodern position that valorizes "this inventing/reinventing business" over "constancy" and argued that the "we are nothing but masks" claim is antithetical to feminist identity politics. "In the '50's, when women wore the same push-up bras and high, high heels that Madonna postures in today, rebels against conformity spoke one word: authenticity. They knew that to wear a mask is an act of extreme defensiveness or aggression. What it is not is an act of existential courage. As long as Madonna wears masks—and confuses the person with the image—there is no real person there (and no real risk)."

Harrison also referred to the "putrid images" in the video *Express Yourself,* including the sequences where Madonna is chained to a bed and crawls on her hands and knees across the floor. On "Nightline," Madonna defended *Express Yourself* against what the interviewer called "feminist criticism" by saying, "Okay, I have chained myself, though, okay? . . . I'm in charge, okay? Degradation is when somebody else is making you do something against your wishes, okay?" In response to this, Harrison wrote, "It really is not okay, okay? It makes me inexpressibly weary to have to say the obvious—that the very worst degradation is that which we inflict upon ourselves" (Harrison 1991, 80, 82).

A similar division is evident in academic criticism. Susan Bordo (1990 and this volume) believes that postmodern interpretations that depict Madonna as deconstructing essentialist notions of gender and sexuality (Schwichtenberg 1990 and this volume; McClary 1990) separate Madonna's videos and performances from their historical and social circumstances, wherein the "containment, sexualization, and objectification of the female body" continues. Madonna's videos do put her body on display; the parodic or destabilizing elements claimed for them by a postmodern reading are simply tacked on to what is "really just cheesecake—or perhaps, pornography." Furthermore, Bordo (1990, 674–676) claims, the so-called liberation of multiple, shifting nonessential identities that Madonna offers in fact inscribes a new "mind/body dualism"—"what the body does is immaterial, so long as the imagination is free." But it is a false freedom, one that ignores "the material praxis of people's lives, the normalizing power of cultural images, and the sadly continuing social realities of dominance and subordination."

Despite the fact that the newspaper contest ran just a few days after Madonna's appearance on "Nightline" and that a good deal of subsequent commentary put the "Madonna: feminist or antifeminist?" issue into heavy cultural circulation, none of the Madonna haters who responded to the contest wrote letters explicitly inscribed as feminist discourse. However, one woman did write that she disliked Madonna because "she sends out the message to impressionable fans that a girl's self-worth exists only thru her body how it is used. She promotes immature defiance at the expense of 'self.'" Although this writer does not identify herself as a feminist nor define her critique as a feminist one, her response is very much in line with a feminist position against the patriarchal notion that "woman is body" and the patriarchal objectification of women's bodies.

The systematic backlash against American feminism in the 1980s, so forcefully documented by Susan Faludi (1991), may have something to do with the absence of the word *feminism* from what appears to be a feminist critique of Madonna. That backlash has been remarkably effective, and one of its consequences is that *feminism* has been made to signify radical, bitter, man hating, separatist, and lesbian. Eleanor Smeal, former president of the National Organization for Women, has suggested that despite disavowing the label *feminist,* many women *are* feminists; they hold feminist beliefs and even support feminism's political and social efforts but will not take the name *feminist* for themselves because efforts to redefine feminism in conservative and patriarchal terms have been so effective (Bolotin 1982, 30).

Thus, we are very reluctant to say that the "Madonna: feminist or antifeminist?" debate is not a part of the cultural capital of popular audiences, despite the absence of the term *feminism* in the newspaper contest letters. It may not always be named as such, but, for instance, when a "concerned" thirty-one-year-old mother writes that Madonna is "a disgrase to the womans race," we cannot presume that this is *not* a feminist reading of Madonna merely because the woman has not first identified herself as a feminist. [12]

Though haters were the group in the college sample most likely to identify themselves as feminists, few of their open-ended responses to the *Papa* and *Open* videos clearly mentioned feminism. One white female student from the Northeast wrote that she disliked *Open* because of "the way Madonna chose to represent herself. As a sexual object. . . . It sets back feminist ideals—things women have worked hard to establish." But later in the survey, this same person explained that she worked in the rock-and-roll industry and recognized "it's admittedly sexist . . . [a] woman just don't stand a chance unless there can be some sort of 'sexual connotations' attached to her." Two other white female students from the Northeast commented that Madonna's dancing style in *Open* was sexist and that the video reminded them of "sex exploitation of women." In his critique of *Papa*, one white male from the Southeast wrote that he did not agree with the video's message, which he thought was that abortion is wrong; he wrote, "I think a woman should have the right to make the decision on her own."

Three haters offered positive feminist commentary on the meaning or statement made by the video *Open*. Two white females wrote similarly about Madonna's control of her sexuality. "The video is about the ability of a woman to use her sexuality to influence others, gain power and get what she wants," one woman offered. The other woman wrote that *Open* was about "a woman controlling her body and sexuality—even if in a bizarre way."

These haters' feminist critiques of Madonna's work were rare, however, and almost equally split between positive and negative evaluations. They centered on Madonna's representations of female sexuality. If seen as self-conscious and controlled by Madonna, the representations were judged positively; if understood as embodiments of social stereotypes, they were evaluated negatively.

How can we explain this puzzling absence of feminist critiques and the ambiguities in those critiques that do appear? We thought we might find some explanation by looking at the three groups (Madonna fans, middle-of-the-roaders, and haters) in the college student sample. We found that haters were the group most likely to agree with the statement "feminism has benefited society" and to identify themselves as feminists. Then, to explore the meaning of the haters' self-proclaimed feminism, we used a discriminant function analysis, a statistical technique that predicts group membership to see how the opinions about women's sexual autonomy and freedom expressed in the college sample were related to the respondents' feelings about Madonna. [13] The statistical analysis showed that the students' attitudes toward women's sexual freedom were significant in predicting attitudes about Madonna. The haters, although more likely to consider themselves feminists, did not include sexual freedom in their definition of the term *feminism*. Of the three groups (haters, fans, and middle-of-the-roaders), haters were the least likely to agree with premarital childbearing and were more likely than fans to agree that women should not initiate sex.

Thus, we see that the definition of feminism is contested across audiences. Madonna is interpreted under different definitions of feminism in different social and discursive formations, and the result is a case study in the ways that popular culture may be articulated to competing social and political practices. There is no way to settle, once and for all, the argument about whether Madonna's texts are feminist. That issue depends on the uses to which these texts are put and on the contexts in which they are interpreted and inscribed.

CONCLUDING THOUGHTS

Clearly, Madonna is not universally loved. She is, in fact, strongly disliked by many who share a vision of her as the low-Other—the symbolic center of much that is wrong with the culture aesthetically, socially, and/or morally. As we have seen, Madonna engenders strong criticism from at least four perspectives: For some, she is the worst of popular culture; others fear that she will corrupt our youth; and still others see her as dangerously antifeminine or, ironically, antifeminist. To all of her critics, she is something to be reviled rather than revered.

Madonna may not intend that she be read as a modern Medusa, but it is clear that some audiences are quite actively producing meanings that place her in the pantheon of female grotesques and feminine monsters. When Madonna haters say that she is "disgusting" and "nauseating" or that "she makes me retch," one can almost feel the maelstrom of repulsion and desire that threatens to pull them down but nevertheless also fascinates them. When the hater is a woman, one might speculate that the rejection is manifestation of a barely displaced "abjection of self," a self-loathing resulting from the interiorization of the patriarchal feminine. As one female Madonna fan replied to Mitchell, in trying to explain Madonna haters, "I think some men hate Madonna because she has 'balls.' Some women also hate women who are powerful. Many women hate themselves and worship men."

From a media studies point of view, one of the most interesting questions this analysis raises is how such a seemingly contradictory set of readings can be understood in terms of the evolution of culture and the position of the audience in it. Some of the audiences we investigated identified themselves as resistive readers. One woman in the newspaper contest, for example, who called Madonna a "repulsive ho" added, "I began to wonder if I was the only one left with standards, since all I heard was praise [for Madonna]. By reading your article, I see that at least there's two decent people left." Apparently, this woman saw the dominant reading of Madonna as one that endorses Madonna's refusal to maintain the virgin/whore dichotomy and that valorizes her obvious pleasure in her own sexuality. However, from what she perceives to be an embattled and marginalized position, this woman used

Madonna to redraw the borders between virgin and whore ever more emphatically.

This is quite the reverse of how scholars in cultural studies typically think of dominant and resistive readings. In his seminal discussion of Madonna's fans and detractors, Fiske, for example, credits only a certain kind of fan with the power of resistance. To Fiske (1987, 271), resistive readers are those who resist the interpretation of Madonna as an "agent of patriarchal hegemony," a "sex/lust object," and who are able to find independent "meanings of their own feminine sexuality that suit them." Fiske would not consider Madonna fans who see her as "the compleat Boy Toy" to be resistive readers because they use a dominant patriarchal discourse of gender to control the meanings of Madonna, which reduces her to "whore" and "sex object."

As we have seen, however, at least some of those who hate Madonna consider themselves resistive readers, and we believe we should give them serious consideration. The danger in disqualifying readings such as theirs as dominant readings is that it too easily permits overly romanticized notions that audiences of popular culture always valiantly resist dominant ideology in progressive ways. To disabuse one of such a notion, there is nothing like reading through a stack of letters from actual audiences (young and old, African-American and white, male and female, working-class and bourgeois) who loathe Madonna in multiple and contradictory ways.

Allen (1991, 32) points out that just as it is a gross oversimplification to suppose that there is a unified "dominant culture," it is equally problematic to imagine that there is "solidarity among the discourses of subordination." Allen argues that what we find instead is "the coalescence and dissipation of multiple sets of interests all along the scale of power, in shifting and frequently contradictory patterns of alliance and contestation." Allen finds that resistant practices are just as likely to be "constructing yet another object of subordination" as they are to be struggling upward against a power bloc. This is precisely the sort of resistance we have found in the cultural practices of some Madonna haters. A woman who probably is a working-class African American constructed the meaning of Madonna as "slut" and "ho." But just because the trajectory of this resistive force points down, does that make it any less resistive?

Allen suggests that we might think more productively of cultural power relations in terms of ordination and insubordination rather than domination or submission: "Power is expressed through ordination, that is, by attempting to regulate through the arrangement of things in ranks and orders—what is high, what is low; what is us, what is them" (Allen 1991, 34). Resistance, then, may be expressed through insubordinate discourse that attempts to invert or transgress existing orders. Some of these Madonna haters are doing just that, challenging what they perceive as the ordinating authority of a discourse that praises Madonna, that validates her popularity and commercial success. They are insubordinate readers, despite the fact that many cultural critics would be hard pressed to identify them as progressive, resistive ones.

NOTES

1. For a list of "Madonna controversies," see Holden (1991).

2. There is a useful discussion of the "female grotesque" in Russo (1986).

3. We thank Justin Mitchell for allowing us to use the letters generated by the contest. We have not edited quotes from the letters and survey responses for grammatical or syntactical errors—they appear as they were written.

4. The data set contains observations of two Madonna videos, *Papa Don't Preach* and *Open Your Heart,* made by students in undergraduate communication classes at three state universities. *Papa* was seen by 186 students (68 blacks and 118 whites); 290 students (69 blacks and 221 whites) watched *Open.* Because only 24 of the students were Hispanic or Asian, they were excluded from the analysis of the data. For more details, see Brown and Schulze (1990).

The survey contained both closed and open-ended questions. Most of the open-ended questions were designed to determine each viewer's response to and reading of the video, such as "What do you think happened in this video?" and "How did this video make you feel?"

Several of the open-ended questions addressed the specific narrative events in the video and how the reader had interpreted them. For example, in regard to *Open Your Heart,* the respondents were asked, "Who are the people watching the dancer and why are they there?" For both videos, the respondent was asked to predict what would happen to the characters after the conclusion of the video: "What would you say happens to the little boy and the woman [in *Open*]?" Other questions tapped into the readers' interaction with the text, such as to whom they would give the video and why.

Each viewer had been asked, "How much do you like Madonna?" (possible responses were: "a whole lot, she's one of my favorites," "some," or "not at all"). Viewers who responded "a whole lot" after seeing either video were categorized as "fans." Viewers who responded "not at all" after seeing either video were designated as "haters." Those who answered that they liked Madonna "some" on both of their video responses were categorized as "neutrals." The largest number of respondents, 207, were neutrals (62 percent). There were 35 fans (almost 11 percent of the sample), and the haters numbered 90 (a little more than 27 percent of the sample).

5. For some scathing reviews that position Madonna as the "anti-artist," see also Palmer (1985), Goldberg (1985), Lambert (1985), Pareles (1986), and Sante (1990).

6. See, for instance, Gelman (1985) about the possible effects on youth of music videos in general. Most prominently featured, however, are two photographs of Madonna wanna-bes, captioned "Madonna's mirror images." And the article includes an account of one mother's "encounter with the power of video" that describes her "shock" when her fourteen-year-old daughter began dressing like Madonna.

7. As Stallybrass and White say, "The 'carnivalesque' mediates between a classical/ classificatory body and its negations, its Others, what it excludes to create its identity as such. In this process, discourses about the body have a privileged role, for transcodings between different levels and sectors of social and psychic reality are effected through the intensifying grid of the body. It is no accident, then, that transgressions and the attempt to control them obsessively return to somatic symbols, for these are the ultimate elements of social classification itself" (Stallybrass and White [1986, 26]).

8. In this regard, see Creed (1987) for a useful discussion of feminine monsters, from classical mythology to the contemporary horror film. Creed bases much of her analysis on Kristeva's (1982) theorization of abjection. We would argue that abjection is a central aspect of the phenomenon of Madonna hatred and would direct attention toward Kristeva's theory of the maternal in patriarchal cultures, rooted as it is in her notion of the abject. The very name *Madonna* may well act as a lightning rod for unconscious processes that replay the abjection of the mother by the child in the key stages of subject formation. Similarly, abjection figures in constructing the feminine and maternal as monstrous in the symbolic order.

9. The tabloids are not alone, though. One of the nastiest pieces ever written about Madonna is by Christopher Connelly (1984), who frames Madonna's career as a series of seductions, describing how she used and then discarded men on her way to pop stardom.

10. See Russo (1986) for an insightful analysis of how "making a spectacle," though it has its dangers, can be a useful strategy in feminist praxis.

11. Employing the Cyndi Lauper/Madonna dichotomy was a very popular strategy in rock music criticism from at least 1984 through 1986, invariably functioning to position Madonna as revisionist, antifeminist, and formulaic, as an unoriginal "poptart." See, for example, Cocks (1985) and Pareles (1986).

12. As Faludi (1991) notes in the introduction of her book, the postmodern disavowal of feminism apparently is more an upper-class phenomenon than a working-class one. In a 1986 Gallup poll, 41 percent of upper-class women said they were not feminists, yet only 26 percent of the women who occupied the low-income bracket said the same.

13. This statistical technique is discriminant function analysis. The responses to the following statements constituted the significant construct: "Women should not initiate sex"; "men can tell from a woman's dress if she wants to have sex"; and "women can have children before marriage." These constitute a measure of women's sexual freedom and autonomy.

REFERENCES

Allen, R. C. (1991). *Horrible Prettiness: Burlesque and American Culture*. Chapel Hill: University of North Carolina Press.
Ayers, A. (1990). "TV's In-Vogue Video Vamp." *TV Guide,* May 19–25, pp. 20, 21, 22, cover.
Berger, J. (1977). *Ways of Seeing*. New York: Penguin Books.

Bolotin, S. (1982). "Voices from the Post-feminist Generation." *New York Times Magazine,* October 17, p. 30.

Bordo, S. (1990). "'Material Girl': The Effacements of Postmodern Culture." *Michigan Quarterly Review* 29, no. 4 (Fall): 653–677.

Brown, J. D., and Schulze, L. (1990). "The Effects of Race, Gender, and Fandom on Audience Interpretations of Madonna's Music Videos." *Journal of Communication* 40, no. 2 (Spring): 88–102.

Browne, D., DiMartino, D., Jordan, T., and Kilday, G. (1991). "Truth or Scare." *Entertainment Weekly,* December 20, pp. 28–29.

Charen, M. (1991). "Madonna: The Girl Needs Some New Material." *Rocky Mountain News,* June 20, p. 50.

Cocks, J. (1985). "Big Girls Don't Cry." *Time,* March 4, p. 74.

Connelly, C. (1984). "Madonna Goes All the Way. " *Rolling Stone,* November 22, pp. 14–20, 81.

Creed, B. (1987). "Horror and the Monstrous-Feminine: An Imaginary Abjection." *Screen* 27, no. 1 (January/February): 44–70.

Faludi, S. (1991). *Backlash: The Undeclared War Against American Women.* New York: Crown Publishers.

Fiske, J. (1987). "British Cultural Studies." In R. C. Allen (ed.), *Channels of Discourse.* Chapel Hill: University of North Carolina Press, pp. 254–289.

Gallo, B. (1991). "Grand Delusions." *Westword,* May 22–28, p. 36.

Garratt, S. (1986). "How I Learned to Stop Worrying and Love Madonna." *Women's Review Number Five,* March, pp. 12, 13.

Gelman, E. (1985). "MTV's Message." *Newsweek,* December 30, pp. 54–56.

Gilmore, M. (1987). "The Madonna Mystique." *Rolling Stone,* September 10, pp. 36, 87.

Gitlin, T. (1983). *Inside Prime Time.* New York: Pantheon.

Goldberg, M. (1985). "Madonna Seduces Seattle." *Rolling Stone,* May 23, p. 20.

———. (1990). "At a Loss for Words." *Rolling Stone,* May 31, pp. 19–22.

Goodman, E. (1986). "No Sermon, Madonna, If You Cut the Propaganda." *Los Angeles Times,* September, 23, p. 5.

Gross, M. (1986). "Classic Madonna." *Vanity Fair,* December, pp. 102–107, 155–156.

Harrison, B. G. (1991). "Can Madonna Justify Madonna?" *Mademoiselle,* June, pp. 80, 82.

Hoberman, J. (1991). "Blond on Blond." *The Village Voice,* May 14, pp. 51, 56.

Holden, S. (1985). "Madonna's Siren Song." *New York Times,* January 6, sec. 2, pp. 21–22.

———. (1991). "Madonna's Love Affair with the Lens." *New York Times,* May 5, p. H20.

Huyssen, A. (1986). "Mass Culture as Woman: Modernism's Other." In T. Modleski (ed.), *Studies in Entertainment.* Bloomington: Indiana University Press, pp. 188–207.

James, C. (1990). "Beneath All That Black Lace Beats the Heart of a Bimbo . . . and a Feminist," *New York Times,* December 16, pp. H38, 44.

Johnson, C. (1985). "What Wrong's with Bimbo Rock?" *Los Angeles Times,* March 10, pp. 54–55.

Johnson, R. (1985). "Shock the Monkey, Punch the Clown." *Rock Video,* June, pp. 46–49.

J. T. (1985). "Washington Diarist: Like a Virgin." *New Republic,* August 12–19, p. 42. of Horror: An Essay on Abjection. New York: Columbia University Press.

Kaplan, E. A. (1987). *Rocking Around the Clock.* New York: Methuen.

Kastor, E., and Spolar, C. (1985). "Loading Up on Lace in Tribute to Their Idol's Material Whirl." *Washington Post,* June 3, p. C6.

Kristeva, J. (1982). *Powers*

Lambert, P. (1985). "Everything Old Is New Again." *Wall Street Journal,* January 23, p. 31.

Lewis, L. (1987). "Consumer Girl Culture: How Music Video Appeals to Women." *OneTwoThreeFour* 5 (Spring): 5–15.

Loder, K. (1984/1985). "1984 Record Guide." *Rolling Stone Yearbook 1984,* December 20, 1984–January 3, 1985, p. 107.

Lovell, T. (1983). *Pictures of Reality.* London: BFI Publishing.

McBride, J. (1985). "That Man-Smasher Madonna on Tour." *People,* May 13, pp. 41, 43.

McClary, S. (1990). "Living to Tell: Madonna's Resurrection of the Fleshly." *Genders* 7 (Spring): 1–21.

Marsh, D. (1985). "Girls Can't Do What the Guys Do: Madonna's Physical Attraction." In D. Marsh (ed.), *The First Rock & Roll Confidential Report.* New York: Pantheon, p. 161.

Miller, J. (1985). "Rock's New Women." *Newsweek,* March 4, pp. 48–57.

Modleski, T. (1986). "Femininity as Mas(s) querade: A Feminist Approach to Mass Culture." In C. MacCabe (ed.), *High Theory/Low Culture.* New York: St. Martin's Press, pp. 37–52.

Moran, A. F. (1986). *Memorandum RE: The Need for Balanced Messages in the Media.* New York: Planned Parenthood of New York City.

Nelander, J. (1990). "Man-eater Madonna Used Sex to Climb to the Top." *Globe,* September 18, p. 17.

Paglia, C. (1990). "Madonna—Finally, A Real Feminist." *New York Times,* December 14, p. A39.

Palmer, R. (1985). "Madonna Sings at Radio City. " *New York Times,* June 7, p. C4.

Pareles, J. (1986). "Madonna Vs. Lauper: Who's Better?" *Mademoiselle,* December, pp. 102, 232.

Parker, R., and Pollock, G. (1981). *Old Mistresses: Women, Art and Ideology.* New York: Pantheon.

"Pepsi Refuses to Drop Madonna as Role Model for Youth Despite Offensive Video." (1989). *AFA Journal,* April, pp. 1, 23.

Petro, P. (1986). "Mass Culture and the Feminine: The 'Place' of Television in Film Studies." *Cinema Journal* 25, no. 3 (Spring): 5–21.

Reid, J. (1990). "Posing, the Question." *In These Times,* December 5–11, p. 24.

Rolling Stone. (1985). "Letters" column, January 17, p. 9.

Russo, Mary. (1986). "Female Grotesques: Carnival and Theory." In T. de Laurentis (ed.), *Feminist Studies/Critical Studies*. Bloomington: Indiana University Press, pp. 213–229.

Sante, L. (1990). "Unlike a Virgin." *New Republic*, August 20/27, pp. 25–29.

Schwichtenberg, C. (1990). "Postmodern Feminism and Madonna: Toward an Erotic Politics of the Female Body." Paper presented at the National Conference on Re-writing the (Post)Modern, March 30–31, Salt Lake City, Utah.

Simmonds, D. (1985). "Close-Up on Madonna." *Marxism Today*, October, p. 60.

Skow, J. (1985). "Madonna Rocks the Land." *Time*, May 27, p. 74.

Stallybrass, P., and White, A. (1986). *The Politics and Poetics of Transgression*. Ithaca, N.Y.: Cornell University Press.

Watrous, P. (1985). "Madonna: Retro Sex?" *Vogue*, March, p. 111.

Wild, D. (1991). "A Conversation with Joni Mitchell." *Rolling Stone*, May 30, p. 64.

Wildmon, D. (1985). "The Problem of Describing Pornography." *National Federation for Decency Journal*, September, p. 2.

Williamson, J. (1985). "The Making of a Material Girl." *New Socialist* 31 (October): 46–47.

Zehme, B. (1989). "Madonna: The *Rolling Stone* Interview. *Rolling Stone,* March 23, p. 51.

THOMAS K. NAKAYAMA
LISA N. PEÑALOZA

Madonna T/Races: Music Videos Through the Prism of Color

*M*UCH HAS BEEN WRITTEN, in both academic publications (Curry 1990; Hayward 1991; Kaplan 1987; Lewis 1987; McClary 1990; Schwichtenberg 1992 and this volume) and the popular press (Deevoy 1991; Drucker 1991; Fisher 1991; Goodman and Lavoignat 1991; Rabinowitz 1991; Svetkey 1990), about Madonna and issues of sexuality. Her success at constantly shifting her media images "makes her the ultimate postmodern video star" (Rubey 1991, 902). Her continual probing into questions of sexuality and her reinvented images have been thrust on us relentlessly, giving rise to critical reflection on both the sexual politics of media representations and the construction of gender.

Feminist critics have offered insights into some of the gender politics of Madonna's music videos and the complex relationships that women have with these videos. Such critiques have expanded the fields of communication and cultural studies by contributing to our understanding of how gender is played out on the field of cultural struggle.

Although gender has attained the status of being one of "the most important concepts . . . encounter[ed] in communication studies" (O'Sullivan et al. 1983, XIII), the racial dimension of communication is strangely absent in most analyses. For example, *race* is not included in *Key Concepts in Communication* (O'Sullivan et al. 1983), nor does this book list related terms (*ethnicity, minorities, black*) as key concepts.

In the politically charged terrain of cultural studies, race has fared little better. In his introductory text to cultural studies, for example, Graeme Turner (1990) offers no discussion of the work of Paul Gilroy or the Race and Politics Group at the Birmingham Centre, nor is there much discussion of racial issues, although Turner does recognize in Stuart Hall's work "the issue of race as one of concern to cultural studies" (1990, 76). Regarding their overview of the treatment of color in feminist cultural studies, Sarah Franklin, Celia Lury, and Jackie Stacey conclude that "the *influence* of debates about, and struggles against, racism in cultural studies continues to be rather uneven" (1991, 177). These writers, while nodding in the direction of race, do little to advance it from the margins and make it a critical element of social and political relations.

One important aspect of Madonna's music videos that has been noticeably ignored involves issues of racial politics. This is particularly surprising given the inclusion of a number of people of color in her music videos, beginning in her earlier ones (e.g., *Borderline* and *Material Girl*) and including her more recent works (e.g., *Like a Prayer, Justify My Love,* and *Vogue*). Although some studies (Brown and Campbell 1986; Brown and Schulze 1990) have examined racial readings of music videos, such studies have taken a binary approach to understanding racial difference. In these studies, the two juxtaposed audiences were black and white students. Studies of this type are important in opening up music videos and other texts to the issue of racial readings and racial representations, but they risk continuing to perpetuate a binary understanding of race. And ultimately, the use of binary frameworks to conceptualize race can lead to distortions and misunderstandings of racial difference (Altman and Nakayama 1991).

In this chapter, we explore Madonna's music videos within the context of multiple racial and ethnic categories. In what follows, we examine readings given to several of Madonna's videos in order to understand how racial and ethnic differences play an important role in the videos' reception and interpretation. Of particular interest here is the play of individual identity within the U.S. social structure.

THE PROBLEMATIC OF THE RACIAL PRISM

We use the trope of the prism to examine the racial politics of interpretation, to explore the way in which colors are played out in the texts of Madonna. The refraction of light through the prism is not binary; it always displays a multiplicity of colors. And it is this multiple character that guides our inquiry. The prism allows us to make two significant moves in this chapter: First, we foreground race as the critical ground from which readings are negotiated by the audience, and thus we move away from simply celebrating different readings as potential sites of resistance; second, we examine Madonna's use of race within her cultural products (videos/text) in an effort to understand the resistive potential of these readings.

Identity, as a stable subject position for reading, has been problematized by a number of contemporary theorists, chiefly along gender lines (Butler 1990; Devor 1989), though our interest here focuses on racial lines. As such, we locate the multiplicity of colors both within our readers and within the text. However, to acknowledge multiplicity does not necessarily address issues of location among the various racial groups within these two domains, nor the critical juncture that is formed between them. In the context of such recent work, on the one hand, it would be naive for us to assume that racial identity forms a coherent, stable foundation from which subjects create reading formations independent of existing social relations. On the other hand, we do not wish to assume that racial identity is chosen freely, although some individuals may claim this luxury (e.g., Roosens 1990). For others, physical characteristics denote membership in a given group. San Juan (1991, 216) warns of the critical dangers of collapsing race into ethnicity because "it erases the crucial difference between the incorporation of the colonized minorities by force and violence—not only the intensity of their repression but its systematic nature—and that of the European immigrant groups." This erasure of history makes it difficult to discuss racisms and racial politics. Between these two camps, there is considerable room for maneuvering identity as the individual shifts between possible perspectives and interpretations.

Of course, it is also important to keep in mind that identity is a social construction, and as such, racial and ethnic identity may not be the sole explanation for differences in the readings given cultural products. However, the continuing significance of race and ethnicity as a part of social relations suggests that the traces of this identity remain in the readings. The seeming absence of racial and ethnic differences, for example, could be manifest in the form of de-ethnicized, deracialized universals—readings that appear to transcend membership in specific racial and ethnic categories. Finally, it is also possible that identity functions as the fluid, contingent process in which an individual expresses a number of reading positions as identificational practices. In either case, the residual remains of racial and ethnic identity can be traced against the backdrop of social formations.

The celebration of differential reading practices has reflected a concern with the political potential of these differences as sites of resistance. This positive character of cultural studies is clearly articulated in the work of John Fiske (1989), although it is equally characteristic of much work in U.S. cultural studies (e.g., Lewis 1987). Recently, this approach to cultural studies has been critiqued (Budd, Entman, and Steinman 1990). However, to bring the study of race into this framework without recognizing the differential position of specific racial and ethnic groups in society is to miss phenomena. As Paul Gilroy (1987, 11) notes, "Racism does not, of course, move tidily and unchanged through time and history. It assumes new forms and articulates new antagonisms in different situations." The dynamic nature of racism (Fougeyrollas 1985; Taguieff 1987) makes us hesitant to join the party celebrating multiple readings. Somehow the fete loses its affirmative character if we are no longer certain whether we are toasting politically progressive sites of resistance or simply getting drunk and becoming unable to recognize politically regressive sites of racism. Our argument here is quite clear: As critical scholars, it is imperative that we understand both the positive and negative sides of different reading configurations. This approach will help us begin to see how race is negotiated so that we can begin to understand how racist readings can be reaffirmed and repressed. Armed with this knowledge, critical communication scholars can identify and challenge such readings.

METHODOLOGY

Our objective in this study is to investigate the ways in which members of a particular ethnic or racial group read specific cultural products. We selected several of Madonna's music videos (*Borderline, Cherish, Express Yourself, La Isla Bonita, Like a Prayer*) for a number of reasons: her use of actors of various racial and ethnic backgrounds, the somewhat controversial material, the timely nature of the music videos, and their profitability as popular cultural products.

These videos were shown to students at a midsized West Coast university who then answered an open-ended set of questions (Appendix A). Once the students had responded to all of the videos, they were asked to fill out a sheet asking for demographic information (Appendix B). Although this group represents a convenient sample, we felt it was appropriate to the exploratory nature of this study. By incorporating students from both day and night classes, we were able to gather 257 responses from respondents ranging in age from eighteen to fifty; 50 percent were male and 50 percent were female. Appendix C depicts specific age ranges and sex compositions for each of the racial and ethnic groups.

Our open-ended questionnaire consisted of six questions that asked about (1) the meaning of each video, (2) the importance of gender, (3) the significance of ethnicity or race, (4) aspects of the video that were appealing and/or disturbing, (5) general reactions, and (6) anything else the respondents wanted to say about the particular video. (All responses have been reproduced as they were written; no attempt has been made to correct grammatical errors or change the wording of students' responses.)

Several videos were screened in a given class, followed by a period of silence so that the students would have the opportunity to respond to the open-ended questions. After the videos were screened, the students discussed their reactions.

Once the data were collected, a coding scheme was developed. Initially, we avoided focusing on the representations of the racial and ethnic characters in the videos, concentrating instead on patterns of responses. Though the responses varied within each of the racial and ethnic groups, dominant patterns did emerge that reflected some difference in reading formations.

DISCUSSION

In *The Practice of Everyday Life,* Michel de Certeau (1984, 18) writes: "People have to make do with what they have. In these combatants' stratagems, there is a certain art of placing one's blows, a pleasure in getting around the rules of a constraining space. We see the tactical and joyful dexterity of the mastery of a technique." De Certeau's overarching metaphor of an ongoing battle offers us a useful entry into discussing the complexity of the readings given Madonna's videos. The "meaning" (as if there were only one) of the videos does not reside simply in the text but also in issues of representation that guide and constrain the possible readings.

It is necessary to recognize that all of our respondents were students at a predominately white (European-American) institution. Thus, we are sensitive to the dynamics of the context in which we gathered our readings. That is, the tactics and techniques utilized by students of color for survival in a white-dominated institution have to be seen as influencing the responses we received. However, we do not think that the experiences of people of color in the United States can be understood outside the context of a white-dominated society.

Despite the experiential basis for this claim, it is not easy to pinpoint the ways that white domination functions in relation to marginalized groups. In part, this is recognized by Richard Dyer (1988) in his argument that much of the representational power of "whiteness" stems from its ability to remain invisible. We have observed this phenomenon in the classroom as well when our European-American students resist self-identification along racial categories. Their insistence that they are "just people" or that self-identification "isn't important" belies the significance of masking whiteness and its representational power exerted on those in the margins:

> When we say marginal, we must always ask, marginal to what? But this question is difficult to answer. The place from which power is exercised is often a hidden place. When we try to pin it down, the center always seems to be somewhere else. Yet we know that this phantom center, elusive as it is, exerts a real, undeniable power over the whole social framework of our culture, and over the ways that we think about it (Ferguson 1990, 19).

Our initial foray into interpreting the readings of Madonna's videos is done in hopes of making whiteness a little less invisible and, therefore, a less insidious form of power. One way to do this is to conceptualize white as a racial category. Race studies should not be conducted in the margins alone.

In our analysis of the responses, we have identified five dominant reading patterns, all of which must be understood within the context of both social relations and individual identity. Although Madonna's music videos are widely seen as "open" texts, there does appear to be an organization to the readings that were given to them. We see the following reading patterns:

1. *Cultural affirmation:* Simply defined, identity is the articulation of a person's location relative to a social group (such as family, ethnic group, or race). As a member of a group, a reader might be expected to privilege that group in his or her interpretation, in a reading pattern we will refer to as *cultural affirmation.* The focus here is on the group of which the person is a member. It is a positive reading of that group, and it may lead to an idealization of the group because it focuses exclusively on that group's positive characteristics.

2. *Cultural negation:* A second pattern of reading is more indirect, as if by default, in that identity is expressed in terms of negative characterizations of "other" social groups. A person's membership within a group is implicit and acted out by focusing on the "other." This is typically articulated in terms of negative treatments or attributions given to that "other."

3. *Racial rejection/whitewash:* Given existing discrepancies between "minority" and "majority" populations, it is perhaps not surprising that individuals would read videos as favoring whites because this group is the dominant majority. (Currently, whites represent 84 percent of the U.S. population [U.S. Bureau of the Census 1989, 15].) This type of reading has been, at various times, described as "whitewash," *Tio Taco,* or *los vendidos* (sellouts), and it occurs when an individual does not claim membership in a stigmatized group but rather focuses on the possibility of being included in the mainstream.

4. *Pollyanna:* This reading pattern emerges when a person de-emphasizes membership in social categories and instead chooses to identify with some deracialized, de-ethnicized transcendent social group. In this pattern, racial and ethnic differences are viewed as irrelevant or unimportant.

5. *Destabilized Identity Dynamic:* This reading pattern features a chaotic identity dynamic in which a person shifts between and among various cultural spheres, claiming allegiance to no single identity. This is a "cafeteria" approach to identity.

It is important to note here that there is no monolithic reading practice based on racial identity; that is, there is no "black reading," "Hispanic reading," or "Asian reading." Within each group, a multiplicity of readings emerged. However, this observation is nothing new; our contribution involves moving our understanding to the next step: How might we conceptualize the nexus between race and readings?

Much of the contemporary literature on the resistive potential of readings rests on the assumption that individuals buy into a particular form of identity. But can people give readings that are seemingly different from their locations? Based on the readings we collected, we believe this regressive reading practice occurs, and we therefore seek to understand how this constrains and perhaps enables possibilities for resistance. To observe that it is possible for progressive readings to be given neither ensures that this practice happens nor helps us understand why it does not.

What we wish to suggest at this point is that readings tend to fit within a postmodern mainstream. That is, the readings fall within a range of readings, but no one reading is either the dominant or the "correct" one. These readings contain both potential points of resistance and means for reaffirmation of the status quo.

In his study of the complex relationship between postmodernism and popular culture, Jim Collins (1989) turns to the trope of the *musée imaginaire* to articulate the complex process by which subjects arrange the "semiotic glut" with which popular culture bombards them. The significance of Collins's musée imaginaire resides in its clear rejection of a "free market" system of interpretation:

> The situation, then, is not a "democratic" plurality, where aesthetic and ideological alternatives are carefully arranged in a kind of laissez-faire smorgasbord. Instead, a semiotic glut necessitates the arrangement, even hierarchizing of conflicting discourses by individual subjects at a localized level (1989, 145).

In this musée, subjects are the curators who arrange the semiotic glut. Our goal here is to try to understand the racial and ethnic component of that sorting process. Our trip to these musées is necessarily a problematic one, but it is important that we understand how these curators are arranging this semiotic glut within the context of racial and ethnic relations.

Our questionnaire allowed each student to self-identify his or her racial or ethnic designation by leaving a blank to be filled in, rather than by selecting among predesignated choices. Given this flexibility, we found that four culturally defined categories emerged: Asian/Asian American, Hispanic/Latino(a)/Mexican American, black/African American, and white/Caucasian/European American. Although the use of the term *European American* would not seem to be common, it appeared frequently in the responses, as did the much more common "white, non-Hispanic." It is interesting to note that students who referred to themselves as Caucasian frequently misspelled that term and that none of the Asian/Asian-American students referred to themselves as Orientals.

Within these categories, we found that each group demonstrated a different dominant reading pattern across the videos screened. Although we do not deny that a diversity of responses were gathered within each racial and ethnic group, our focus in this chapter is on the differences among reading patterns given by each group and their relationship to a larger reading formation that we are calling a postmodern mainstream. We will then explain which dominant reading patterns emerged and how they relate to the postmodern mainstream.

Asian/Asian American

The distinction between Asian and Asian American was not clear given the openness of our questionnaire. Though this difference may be important in determining the individual respondent's relationship to U. S. culture, this distinction did not appear to be clearly established in self-identification.

Within this group, the dominant reading pattern seemed to be one of distance or separation from Madonna's popular culture realm. For example, when asked if racial and ethnic differences affected one's reading of the video, one twenty-three-year-old male responded to *Borderline* that "it must have because I have no idea what it was about." Perhaps mockingly, another twenty-three-year-old male wrote: "Unfortunately I have no idea. The only distinguishing relationship was the title and maybe the black and white tile floor or backing." In both cases, we observe a distancing from the politics of the text. The second respondent hints at racial politics, but he refuses to engage the politics by indicating that he has "no idea" what the video is about. This reading strategy reflects a destabilized identity dynamic.

Both of these responses demonstrate important strategies for coping with politically important texts within a white-dominated institution, but we found that Asian/Asian-American students tended to defuse the political potential (at least publicly) of Madonna's videos. Although their refusal to engage the politics of the text were frustrating to us personally, their reactions do point toward important coping tactics for negotiating and surviving within a white-dominated institution. As such, these techniques should not be dismissed easily but instead should be examined for their potential as survival mechanisms within a white-dominated situation. In other words, these tactics seem to reinforce the status quo, yet they do not jeopardize the respondents' position. In this way, the respondents do not explicitly support the status quo, but neither do they challenge it.

We might also see these tactics as a way of refusing to let the "white" voice speak through the Asian/Asian-American respondents on the subject of popular culture products. Chen (1989, 51) observes that "the entire social milieu is always and already in the foreground. Even when an Asian American tries to speak in ways other than 'American,' she or he runs the 'risk' of having a white voice speaking through her or him." Not only was our study conducted entirely in English, it was also given in the context of a white-dominated environment. In this way, evasion, though not oppositional, resists compliance with the status quo. Thus, the Asian/Asian Americans' readings did not mimic the white reading patterns.

Hispanic/Latino(a)/Mexican American

Among Hispanic/Latino(a)/Mexican-American respondents, two different dominant reading patterns emerged, and we found a balance between these reading patterns. The first focused on the universality of conflicts between men and women. For example, one twenty-year-old female noted in response to the lovers' quarrel (between Madonna and her obviously Hispanic boyfriend) in *Borderline* that "this happens in all races, not just whites." Or as one twenty-one-year-old female noted, "The problems of men and women, such as this one, crosses all barriers of ethnic/racial lines." The recognition yet reduced significance of this difference tends to negate the political potential of interracial relationships and their representation in Madonna's videos as well as the politics of separate readings. We believe this reading pattern reflects a Pollyanna identity position.

The other reading formation refers to Hispanic/Latino(a) /Mexican-American culture and serves to ground their readings of Madonna's videos. This example of cultural affirmation privileges ethnic identity in establishing a particular interpretation of the video. Specifically, in response to *Borderline,* one thirty-nine-year-old female noted that "Latinos understand the concept better—not necessarily agree, but understand the machismo. " And a forty-one-year-old male noted that Madonna was "having a hard time understanding it [social and racial difference and also ethnicity] because of her difference." In both these responses, the Latino(a) reading position is privileged in giving insight into what is "really" going on in Madonna's video. As one twenty-three-year-old female observed, "Her message is to hold on to your roots cause you never know what could happen." We see this second reading formation in opposition to the first: It is an affirmation of Hispanic/Latino(a)/Mexican-American culture, yet it is a technique that seems to be successful in surviving in a white-dominated culture.

Black/African American

Among blacks/African Americans, the dominant reading pattern reflects the trend toward de-emphasizing racial and ethnic difference in favor of a universalizing of themes. In this reading pattern, the respondents rejected the importance of race and ethnicity by focusing on the universality of the experience depicted in the video. As one twenty-four-year-old male noted, "This happens in all races." Or as a nineteen-year-old female wrote, "This video is about love." A twenty-five-year-old female observed that "the message is love—something that every individual has experience or are aware of." The universalizing of romantic love defuses the focus on the setting as well as the politics of the representations. These responses are typical of the Pollyanna identity position.

A smaller, although still significant, reading response was the downplaying of race and ethnicity by viewing the actors in the video as members of the same group. One twenty-two-year-old male noted that "everyone is the same race." (This response did not make it clear if everyone was white or Hispanic.) Similarly, a twenty-one-year-old male noted that "everybody's white in this video." We believe these responses fall into the whitewashing reading pattern.

Finally, there was a smattering of responses that did reflect the possibility for resistive reading. For example, one twenty-one-year-old female noted: "Boyfriend is Mexican = lowly, not much money. White man = rich, glamour, power to make girl a star." Her reading incorporates economic class into the power relations. A nineteen-year-old female observed: "I found it odd that all of the breakdancers were white or Mexican, etc. There were no black breakdancers." And a thirty-three-year-old male noted: "I think she is appealing to a Hispanic audience by showing their culture." In each of these responses, there is no whitewashing of the video. However, these scattered responses were numerically marginalized in relation to the black/African-American group's overall reading practices.

The overlooking of racial and ethnic politics, however, was not evident in the responses to *Like a Prayer*. The reading practice that stands out here is the ability to move outside the text and use the video to comment on social life. For example, a thirty-three-year-old female wrote that the video was about "the unfairness in how blacks are being prosecuted in Am. society, and how a white figure, even the second-class white female, has more authority than the black male in our society." A twenty-two-year-old male noted that the video was about "social injustice and prejudice, something that still exists today." Yet another twenty-two-year-old male wrote that the video "showed the kind of racial injustice that goes on in the real world." When asked if race and ethnicity were important in this video, a twenty-five-year-old male simply wrote, in big letters, "Hell yes!" It is interesting to note that this video sparked a move outside the text, whereas the other videos did not. This may have happened because the representation of blacks/African Americans leads more easily to a cultural affirmation identity reading position.

White/Caucasian/European American

Finally, among whites/Caucasians/European Americans, the rejection of racial politics through whitewashing was demonstrated in three ways. First, a large number of responses indicated that there was no racial issue in *Border-*

line. Typical readings included: "There seemed to be no racial issues" (twenty-year-old female); "it doesn't seem to focus on race" (forty-four-year-old female); "I don't see it as an issue" (twenty-one-year-old male); "I didn't see any racial issues" (nineteen-year-old female). To define the importance of race and ethnicity around racial issues is to see racial and ethnic differences in a particular light, perhaps only as a conflict with whites. The dominance of this rejection in the white readings might best be explained by John Fiske (1990, 97), who, in a self-reflexive move, notes that "unlike gender politics they [racial politics] impinge less on the mundanity of my day-to-day existence."

Second, an equally large number of white/Caucasian/European-American respondents saw everyone in the video as white. These students typically responded with readings such as: "All are white" (forty-six-year-old female); "there all whites here" (twenty-two-year-old male); "the people are all cacuasion" (nineteen-year-old female). Others indicated that they did not see any racial differences in the actors, although they did not specifically code them as white.

Third, there was a significant tendency to deny the importance of race and ethnicity by reconfiguring the narrative into the universal theme of relationships. By viewing heterosexual relationships as the same across cultures, racial and ethnic differences are marginalized. Thus, readings such as these were typical: "Relationships are pretty much the same with all cultures" (twenty-year-old male); "the same thing happens whether you're one race or another" (nineteen-year-old male); "relationships such as the one in the video occur within all racial groups" (twenty-two-year-old female); "all races go through this" (twenty-one-year-old female).

When the whites did read the video characters as Hispanic/Latino(a) / Mexican American, either no reading was given or this factor was used to define Hispanic/Latino(a)/Mexican-American culture in the cultural negation process discussed earlier. Typical of the first reading practices were responses such as: "Hispanic neighborhood—I don't know" (eighteen-year-old female); "her boyfriend is Hispanic, but in the plot it doesn't matter that much" (eighteen-year-old male); "the guy looked Hispanic but other than that I don't see ethnicity as important here" (twenty-four-year-old male); "all the girls looked Caucasian and the men looked Mexican" (twenty-one-year-old female).

More importantly, however, was the dominance of cultural negation in reading the Other. These readings tended to evaluate Hispanics/Latino(a)s/Mexican Americans negatively; hence, racial and ethnic difference made a negative difference. Although the focus of this negative evaluation of Hispanic/Latina(o) Mexican-American culture was on sexual politics, this was not the only point of critique: "You need to know something about the Latino male attitude towards women. Women are possessions and should not have any thoughts or initiatives of their own" (forty-four-year-old female); "in Mexican society, the women's identity is her man and the men get very jealous if the women try to go out on their own, and take away support and condemn them" (twenty-one-year-old female); "my friend Doreen tells me that this sort of 'don't go thinking you're better than you are' mentality is very much a part of the Hispanic ethnic. She says this leads to a profile of underachievement" (thirty-nine-year-old female); "Mexican—spray painting. It depicts Mexicans as dancing, spraying while the photographer was trying to change Mad[onna]" (twenty-seven-year-old female); "ethnicity plays a part as it is a gang of Latinos—you wouldn't really associate gangs with whites" (twenty-one-year-old female).

All of the readings, however, were not negative evaluations, but positive readings were clearly fewer in number and tended to focus on the politics of media representations. Thus, there were readings such as: "A white, rich girl finds *true* satisfaction in a poor, ethnic environment. She attempts to show *where* passion for life is" (twenty-seven-year-old male); "this video seems to depict the 'street hoodlum' as the minorities (I saw Mexicans and Orientals) and the 'high society' classy one as the white guy" (twenty-three-year-old female); "the typical imagery of the whites always depicted as wealthy, affluent people always getting their way over others, and the minorities always viewed in ghetto and barrio scenes" (twenty-two-year-old male).

The readings given to *Like a Prayer* demonstrated the ability of the white reading formation to incorporate self-critique. As one twenty-year-old white male noted: "The message seems to be that people that aren't 'white' have all the odds against them but it is ok to stand up for non-white's rights when you are white." More common, however, were generalized statements about racism that did not specify white roles: "Racism. Stop the bullshit. Racism sucks" (twenty-year-old male); "Madonna's message is to not judge people by their race but rather by their action" (forty-four-year-old female); "racism is a theme—the wrongness of it" (eighteen-year-old female); "the message is not to be racist towards people" (twenty-two-year-old male). Perhaps because this video is coded so strongly with racial imagery, it is difficult to avoid social commentary in any reading of it.

BEYOND BINARIES

The responses in each of these four groups demonstrate the problem of trying to understand racial difference through a binary lens. Any attempt to characterize nonwhite readings as unitary or conceptualize racial or ethnic differences based on the experiences of a single racial or ethnic group is problematic. Our responses indicate significant differences within racial or ethnic groups, as well as between them. The refusal of some Asian Americans, on the one hand, to become engaged with the music videos may point to a strategy for evading cultural domination while not resisting it. African Americans, on the other hand, were able to read the video against the back-drop of a white-dominated society that persecutes and sometimes literally prosecutes certain groups.

Here, the Asian Americans are not granting the videos a sense of credibil-ity, whereas the African Americans recognize the verisimilitude between the video and their life experiences. Fiske (1986, 78) writes about this distinc-tion between sense and nonsense: "Not making sense is not resisting the so-cial machine but is denying its presence, asserting its absence. . . . In refusing sense the subject is no longer subjected, for it is sense that subjects." This non-sense making may be done through mocking or refusing to analyze the music video.

Overall, the critical fact here is that there are differences between and within racial or ethnic groups; therefore, it is wrong to attempt to under-stand how race and ethnicity influence cultural processes through a binary framework. The binary racial perspective reduces the world to black and white (or, on occasion, to how white people can conduct business in Tokyo) at the expense of racial and ethnic diversity, whereas the postmodern main-stream is multicultural. The traces of different cultural experiences, how-ever, are not necessarily oppositional or even resistant to the dominant white/European-American readings.

CONCLUSION

Through an analysis of the multiple ways that members of different racial or ethnic groups respond to some of Madonna's music videos, this study makes several important claims about racial and ethnic differences and popular cul-ture. First, such differences cannot be understood through a binary frame-work. Just as there are more than two racial or ethnic groups, there are more than two ways to read Madonna's music videos. Second, our identification of a multiplicity of readings does not mean that readers engage in a semiotic free-for-all. Rather, the reading patterns that emerged pointed to the inclu-siveness of a postmodern mainstream that was dominated by the white read-ing patterns. This mainstream allowed for multiple readings while leaving the dominant position unchallenged. The domination of the white readings is a complex process, and here we return to our trope of the prism to explain how this domination might occur.

The seeming invisibility of white light is undermined when it is refracted through the racial prism, revealing a range of colors. Without the explicit frame of the racial prism, however, white light is difficult to analyze. Rich-ard Dyer (1988, 46) notes: "The colourless multi-colouredness of whiteness secures white power by making it hard, especially for white people and their media, to 'see' whiteness. This, of course, also makes it hard to analyse." In this study, we have seen that the white light gets refracted through a racial prism in which whiteness is the "center" against which other readings take place. Thus, the dominance of the white center creates a tension between inherent whiteness and potential multicultural identification. Except where one's own group is interpellated, the white reading dominates the reading configurations.

The problem here becomes one of losing the center: If whiteness is everything and nothing, if whiteness as a racial category does not exist except in conflict with others, how can we understand racial politics in a social structure that centers whites, yet has no center? This key contradiction—the denial of racial and ethnic differences, yet the importance of them in the white reading formation—creates an enormous problem for those investigating the signifiance of racial or ethnic differences in readings of popular culture.

We have approached this problem in our study, but the complexity of racial or ethnic identity as it crosses other social relations, such as gender, class, age, religion, and sexual orientation, makes this task difficult. Despite these limitations, however, our study has demonstrated the complexity of dealing with racial and ethnic groups and their relationship to popular culture. The rise of former (?) klansman David Duke's popularity, incidences of campus racism, calls for ending affirmative action programs, and hate crimes all point to the continuing persistence, if not increasing importance, of race in U. S. society. However, racial and ethnic conflict is not a uniquely American phenomenon. The popularity of Jean Le Pen in France is indicative of rising xenophobia; the rapid rise of neo-Nazis in Germany and the ethnic conflicts in Eastern Europe underscore the importance of racial and ethnic differences in social formations. As part of the structure of power relations, such differences should be central to the concerns of cultural studies.

We must not make a career of celebrating the *possibility* of progressive, resistive readings. Rather, we must understand how the complexity of race and ethnicity influences cultural processes. It is time for critical communication scholars, faced with increasing racial and ethnic conflicts, to take a sustained and serious look at race and ethnicity, not *in spite of* but *because of* the varied, disparate, multiple forms that racism may take.

APPENDIX A

1. What is this video about? What is Madonna's message?

2. Do you think that sexual difference is important in understanding this video? Explain.

3. Do you think that ethnicity/racial difference is important in understanding this video? Explain.

4. Is there anything about this video that you particularly like? Is there something interesting in this video that you can comment on?

5. Is there anything in this video that you find disturbing? If so, what is it and why does it bother you?

6. Is there anything else that you want to say about this video?

APPENDIX B

The following information will *not* be used to identify anyone. Please answer as accurately as possible.

1. Your age: _____
2. Your sex (circle one): male   female
3. Your racial/ethnic group: _____
4. Your parents' occupations: _____

Thank you for your participation and cooperation. No attempt will be made to connect any answers to anyone. Therefore, please: do *not* write your name on any of the response sheets.

APPENDIX C

Group	Males	Females	Oldest	Youngest	Total
Black/African American	10	15	40	19	25
Asian/Asian American	6	5	27	19	11
Hispanic/Mexican American/Latino(a)	7	13	42	18	20
White/European American/Caucasian	96	83	50	18	179
Multiple heritage	4	9	47	19	13
No answer	4	2	28	18	9*
TOTAL	127	127			257

*includes 3 who did not indicate sex

Acknowledgments

This chapter was completed, in part, with the assistance of an Affirmative Action grant from The California State University. An earlier version of this chapter was presented at the Speech Communication Association national convention, Atlanta, Ga., October 31, 1991.

REFERENCES

Altman, K. E., and Nakayama, T. K. (1991). "Making a Critical Difference: A Difficult Dialogue." *Journal of Communication* 41, no. 4 (Autumn): 116–128.

Brown, J. D., and Campbell, K. (1986). "Race and Gender in Music Videos: The Same Beat but a Different Drummer." *Journal of Communication* 36, no. 1 (Winter): 94–106.

Brown, J. D., and Schulze, L. (1990). "The Effects of Race, Gender, and Fandom on Audience Interpretations of Madonna's Music Videos." *Journal of Communication* 40, no. 2 (Spring): 88–102.

Budd, M., Entman, R. M., and Steinman, C. (1990). "The Affirmative Character of U.S. Cultural Studies." *Critical Studies in Mass Communication* 7, no. 2 (June): 169–184.

Butler, J. (1990). *Gender Trouble: Feminism and the Subversion of Identity*. New York: Routledge.

Chen, K.-H. (1989). "Deterritorializing 'Critical' Studies in 'Mass' Communication: Towards a Theory of 'Minor' Discourses." *Journal of Communication Inquiry* 13, no. 2 (Winter): 43–61.

Collins, J. (1989). *Uncommon Cultures: Popular Culture and Post-Modernism*. New York: Routledge.

Curry, R. (1990). "Madonna from Marilyn to Marlene—Pastiche and/or Parody?" *Journal of Film and Video* 42, no. 2 (Summer): 15–30.

de Certeau, M. (1984). *The Practice of Everyday Life*. S. Rendall (trans.). Berkeley: University of California Press.

Deevoy, A. (1991). "Reveal Yourself!" *Us*, June 13, pp. 16–24.

Devor, Holly. (1989). *Gender Blending: Confronting the Limits of Duality*. Bloomington: Indiana University Press.

Drucker, M. (1991). "Madonna: 'Si ma mère était encore en vie, je ne ferais pas ce que je fais. . . .'" *Paris Match*, May 16, pp. 72, 102.

Dyer, R. (1988). "White." *Screen* 29, no. 4 (Autumn): 44–65.

Ferguson, R. (1990). "Introduction: Invisible Center." In R. Ferguson et al. (eds.), *Out There: Marginalization and Contemporary Cultures*. New York and Cambridge: New Museum of Contemporary Art and MIT Press, pp. 9–14.

Fisher, C. (1991). "True Confessions, Part One: The *Rolling Stone* Interview with Madonna." *Rolling Stone*, June 13, pp. 35–40, 120.

Fiske, J. (1986). "MTV: Post-Structural Post-Modern." *Journal of Communication Inquiry* 10, no. 1 (Winter): 74–79.

———. (1989). *Reading the Popular*. Boston, Mass.: Unwin Hyman.

———. (1990). "Ethnosemiotics: Some Personal and Theoretical Reflections." *Cultural Studies* 4, no. 1 (January): 85–99.

Fougeyrollas, P. (1985). *Les Métamorphoses de la crise: Racismes et révolutions au XXe siècle*. Paris: Hachette.

Franklin, S., Lury, C., and Stacey, J. (1991). "Feminism and Cultural Studies: Pasts, Presents, Futures." *Media, Culture and Society* 13, no. 2 (April): 171–192.

Gilroy, P. (1987). *There Ain't No Black in the Union Jack*. London: Hutchinson.

Goodman, J., and Lavoignat, J.-P. (1990). "Le Pari de Madonna." *Studio Magazine* 40 (June): 62–65, 68–73.

Hayward, P. (1991). "Desire Caught by Its Tale: The Unlikely Return of the Merman in Madonna's *Cherish*." *Cultural Studies* 5, no. 1 (January): 98–106.

Kaplan, E. A. (1987). *Rocking Around the Clock: Music Television, Postmodernism, and Consumer Culture.* New York: Methuen.

Lewis, L. A. (1987). "Female Address in Music Video." *Journal of Communication Inquiry* 11, no. 1 (Winter): 73–84.

McClary, S. (1990). "Living to Tell: Madonna's Resurrection of the Fleshly." *Genders* 7 (Spring): 1–21.

O'Sullivan, T., Hartley, J., Saunders, D., and Fiske, J. (1983) *Key Concepts in Communication.* New York: Methuen.

Rabinowitz, J. (1991). "Madonna—Who's in Control?" *Dynamic,* February–March: 12–13.

Roosens, E. (1990). *Creating Ethnicity: The Process of Ethnogenesis.* Newbury Park, Calif.: Sage.

Rubey, D. (1991). "Voguing at the Carnival: Desire and Pleasure on MTV." *South Atlantic Quarterly* 90, no. 4 (Fall): 871–906.

San Juan, Jr., E. (1991). "The Cult of Ethnicity and the Fetish of Pluralism: A Counterhegemonic Critique." *Cultural Critique* 18 (Spring): 215–229.

Schwichtenberg, C. R. (1991). "Madonna's Postmodern Feminism: Bringing the Margins to the Center." *Southern Communication Journal* 57, no. 2 (Winter): 120–131.

Svetkey, B. (1990). "Some Like It Hot . . . Some Not." *Entertainment Weekly,* December 14, pp. 14–19.

Taguieff, P.-A. (1987). *La force du préjugé: Essai sur le racisme et ses doubles.* Paris: Éditions La Découverte.

Turner, G. (1990). *British Cultural Studies: An Introduction.* Boston, Mass.: Unwin Hyman.

U.S. Bureau of the Census. (1989). "Population Projections." *Statistical Abstract of the United States.* Washington, D.C.: Government Printing Office, Table 17, p. 15.

RONALD B. SCOTT *3*

Images of Race & Religion in Madonna's Video *Like a Prayer:* Prayer & Praise

*M*ADONNA'S *Like a Prayer* music video invites a textually and historically oriented analysis that takes into account the racial themes it contains. *Like a Prayer*, similar to many of Madonna's more recent videos that contain images of people of color, promotes the idea of equality and encourages the viewer to make the right choices. The real significance of *Like a Prayer* and of its reception in and importance to the black community can best be understood by examining the positive social messages imbedded in the text of the video and the black cultural roots of its representations.

This chapter will provide an analysis of the images and narrative in *Like a Prayer* from a black perspective. The intent here is not so much to refute previous perspectives but rather to illustrate how the video's text can be used to provide an understanding of the positive elements of African-American culture as well as the negative impact of racism in white America.

Before discussing the images and themes presented in *Like a Prayer*, it is necessary to understand the significance of the black church and also the role that mass media have played in the presentation of blacks in media culture.

THE BLACK CHURCH/PRE-MADONNA REALITY

Within the confines of the black community, the institution of religion, often referred to as "The Church," continues to be one of the most significant and enduring forces in black America. Christian religious beliefs and ideology (which were frequently forced on African Americans in earlier centuries), the social and cultural organization of the church, and the direct community leadership (which often spilled into the political arenas of America at large)

57

photo by Alberto Tolot, *courtesy of Warner Brothers*

historically have combined to make religion one of the primary organized forms of stability in the African-American community. In our mass-mediated contemporary society, however, that stability faces indirect challenges that may alter the structure, function, and cultural relevance of religion for black people.

One challenge to that stability is the subtle yet consistent depiction of black religion, via visual images, as being practiced far differently from the more sedate, less emotional mainstream religions of whites. Because many people dwell on aspects of black religion that have been reduced to quaint stereotypes and because black religion has often been used as a backdrop for comedic or musical relief in television dramas or music videos, black religion has often been trivialized.[1]

Missing from most of the visual presentations of black religion is an understanding of or sensitivity to the economic, political, and cultural significance of the church for the black community. Also absent from the stereotyped presentations is the knowledge that black religion and religious practices are steeped in African history and culture and that much of contemporary American culture, most notably its musical traditions, has been shaped by and is indebted to that heritage.

As a social force, black religion has served to counter the constant barrage of negative attacks on African Americans and their communities in the United States. In a culture that has suggested, particularly through the agencies of mass media, that African Americans are the wrong color, unattractive, inherently morally defective, and undeserving of the same rights and privileges that all white male citizens acquire at birth, the black church has been the constant, and often sole, voice arguing that in the eyes of God, all men and women are, in fact, equal.

For African Americans, the church has countered negative arguments by showing that African Americans are also created in the image of God, that they are the color God wanted them to be, and that justice and equality are inherent human rights. The black church has countered the racist epithets that have confronted blacks throughout American history, and even more importantly, it has provided an emotional outlet, through its ceremonies and songs, for an embattled people seeking some solace in a hostile world. According to Tony Brown (1988):

> The uncertainty of the black existence in America has historically been expressed in song. Not free—not equal, but here never the less. Booker T. Washington called the songs "spirits that dwell in deep woods." . . . Dr. Wyett T. Walker has dubbed the music "Prayer and Praise Hymns," a music of a people who have been forced to trudge through a history of racism, discrimination, and prejudice while adhering to a belief that it is all a transition to a higher salvation.

This analysis suggests that the contemporary music video *Like a Prayer*, featuring the controversial popular figure Madonna, has come under fire for presenting a view of black salvation that is alien to most white Americans.

Even though the religious, racial, and cultural images and the themes in the *Like a Prayer* video may be foreign to the majority of white Americans, I contend that most members of the black community embrace the social message and representational style present in that visual text. This does not mean that the entire black community agrees with all aspects of the video but that the tenor of the video addresses the universal political and cultural agendas of the community. To understand this point of view, one must first understand the high hopes many in the African-American community have had for mass media as sites for addressing racial issues.

MASS MEDIA: AN UNREALIZED POTENTIAL

Social and political scientists as well as media historians and critics all seem to agree on the potential power of mass media to act as either positive or negative forces for social change. And among those who study and analyze the content of mass media and its potential to affect public and private values, beliefs, and attitudes, no one medium has received as much attention in American culture as television. Despite charges that range from the negative view that television is presently nothing more than "a vast wasteland" or "chewing gum for the eyes" (Gitlin 1986, 3, 4) to the more positive views that affirm the medium's possibilities to effect positive change, all seem to concur on television's potential to address social issues.

Recently, scholars have begun to refocus their attention on mass media audiences and the various ways in which those audiences construct meaning from media texts. Of particular interest is the work of Stuart Hall (1982), who suggests that viewing a media text like a music video involves a cultural struggle, in addition to being an active social process. Hall also suggests that popular media, while reinforcing dominant ideologies,[2] will simultaneously retain relevance for diverse audiences (e.g., African Americans) that remain subordinate and powerless in the culture. Consequently, it is necessary to consider the nature of the subordination and lack of power that has historically confronted blacks and the media's implicit role in the process before one can begin to understand the significance of a media text such as Madonna's *Like a Prayer*.

The potential of television to address social issues was recognized long before the medium became entrenched in the fabric of the culture and long before Madonna began her career. For instance, sociologist Orrin Dunlap, Jr. (1932, 3) concluded:

> Television is a science and an art endowed with incalculable possibilities and countless opportunities. It will enable a large part of the earth's inhabitants to see and to hear one another without leaving their home. . . . Eventually it will bring nations face to face, and make the globe more than a whispering gallery. Radio vision [television] is a new weapon against hatred and fear, suspicion and hostility.

Dunlap's prophecy for television's positive impact on a global scale has, to some extent, proven valid. Indeed, television has been at least partially responsible for reducing the world to what Marshall McLuhan (1967) called the global village. But despite the success of the medium globally, its failures within the United States still point to its unrealized potential.

Some twelve years after Dunlap's statement about the possibilities of television, Lawrence Reddick (1944, 389) assessed the potential power of mass media to alter prevailing social attitudes about blacks, suggesting that:

> it is an old generalization that equality and full democracy will never be achieved this side of basic changes in the objective conditions of life. To this old maxim must be added another: Democracy in race relations will never be achieved until the minds of people are changed. The direct route to these minds is through the great agencies of mass media.

Reddick's claim of mass communication's power, more specifically its possible impact on race relations in the United States, underscores the importance of examining media texts with racial themes. It represents the optimism that has permeated much of the thinking of members of the black community about the inherent power of mass media, particularly television, to affect the application of values like equality and justice for all blacks. But though I believe Reddick's assessment is correct, the mass media (and particularly television) have too often failed to do more than mainstream and perpetuate negative stereotypes that suggest that blacks are neither equal to nor due the same legal, social, and political considerations as whites.

While excluding blacks from the cultural mainstream through visual segregation, the mass media have simultaneously denied blacks direct access to the economic benefits of their industries. This is perhaps best illustrated by the types of commercial music videos that air on Music Television, or MTV.

MTV was the first twenty-four-hour music video cable channel in this country. Even though less than half the nation was wired for cable at the time of MTV's inception—August 1, 1981—the combined American Express and Warner Communications experiment proved to be highly successful. Industry estimates suggest that approximately fifteen million subscribers were regularly tuned to the new format within the first year after its debut (Garofalo 1990).

Unfortunately, MTV, like much of the television before and after it, simply became a forum for the promotion of the status quo. According to Marshall Cohen, the channel's marketing vice president, videos that appeared on the channel were chosen to appeal to a young rock-and-roll audience.[3] Though the creator of MTV, Robert Pittman, could defend the format and its lack of minority images on the basis of target objectives (Garofalo 1990, 108), he failed to recognize that he had simply followed the standard industry practice of using demographics to exclude a substantial portion of the population. In the tradition of the old segregationists, MTV executives argued that the format they had chosen—devoid of minority talent or artists—reflected the public's preferences. The result of MTV programming choices was a virtual exclusion of minority performers and images.[4] Once again, minorities were left without an outlet in a medium that held the promise of including, rather than excluding, their presence.

MTV has subsequently added more minority images to its programming.[5] However, much of the minority talent that appears either has obtained cross-over status or falls within a select group of exceptions to a still restrictive policy based on appealing to a baseline demographic. Consequently, because of the limited number of minority images in music videos, any performer who presents visuals and narratives that highlight the experiences of nonmainstream viewers—as Madonna does in *Like a Prayer*—is significant and worthy of critical exploration. Madonna is, however, relevant for other reasons as well.

Like many of the African-American musical divas who have graced the popular music scene in American history, Madonna has emerged as a controversial figure in popular culture. Similar to those who have gone before her and blazed trails that illustrate the fusion between art and social issues, Madonna has picked up a mantle that many assume is new. But in fact, Madonna is not new in her expressions of her art and her visual style.[6] The recently released HBO special about the life of Josephine Baker (which was, in part, promoted by the slogan "before Madonna there was . . .") illustrates that much of what Madonna brings to music and music videos has already been accomplished by lesser-known artists.[7]

Perhaps the most curious and socially revealing difference between Madonna and the legions of black divas in music history is the amount of attention that she receives. It is also curious that many—both blacks and whites—who attack Madonna have been unable or unwilling to recognize that, in the finest traditions of earlier black divas, she has used her talent to place before the public both the socially relevant issue of racial attitudes and an alternative presentation of black culture that many would choose to exclude from their consciousness. The fact that Madonna, unlike the divas before her, is a white female is irrelevant. What *is* relevant is that Madonna has tapped into images and aspects of black culture that speak to some of the social and political concerns that have long existed in the black community.

Although other white artists have "crossed over"[8] or broken through the artificial barriers that exist between so-called white and black musical genres, Madonna has a clear track record of appealing to black audiences.[9] For instance, her first album, titled *Madonna* and released in 1984, was one of two albums featuring white artists that were listed in *Billboard*'s year-end rankings of the top fifty black albums of the year.[10] Subsequent albums have had mixed reviews, but many of her dance singles have fared well with black audiences, and her popularity remains stable. Although the secret to her popularity may lie in her production choices,[11] that popularity is also due, in part, to Madonna's acknowledgment and celebration of African musical roots and style.[12]

Madonna is not the first artist to utilize minority characters in videos or borrow icons from diverse cultures in her expressions, but she is unique in her consistent presentation of her characters as integral parts of each video's narrative. This use of minorities as central actors in the narratives and the heavy reliance on icons from diverse cultures in her videos is particularly important in understanding her appeal to nonwhite viewers.

The following analysis is designed to accomplish two tasks: first, to explore the issues of religion and race as they are presented in the *Like a Prayer* video and second, to offer an alternative reading and discussion of the text.

RACIAL AND RELIGIOUS IMAGES
IN "LIKE A PRAYER"

Directed by Mary Lambert, *Like a Prayer* was released in March 1989.[13] Despite the fact that much of the direct criticism of this video focused on its so-called sacrilegious imagery and themes, I contend that the real problems posed by the video lie in the manner in which Madonna exposes America's negative and unresolved attitudes about race and racial interaction. The ambiguity of racial interaction and a predisposition to overreact to interracial contact is discussed by Ramona Curry (1990, 26), who states that "in a narrative parallel to that of the murder and false accusation, Madonna worships a statue of a black male saint in the church, who is thus moved to life, and first blesses and later erotically kisses Madonna as she is sprawled on her back on a pew." In a later description of the video, Curry (1990, 27) states that

> the white woman [is] in love with a black man. . . . However, the images of the burning crosses before which Madonna, dress askew, dances wildly, and particularly of a black man lying atop a prone Madonna eager for his kiss, retain the power to shock a racist society. The video's commingling of representation of interracial religious fervor and sexual ecstasy refutes distinctions strenuously maintained by dominant American institutions.

Though Curry's description of the events in the video is relatively accurate, her ultimate reading (which I believe accurately reflects much of the public reaction to the racial elements in the video) is typical of white mainstream interpretations and thus misleading. Such a reading can be readily refuted by examining the narrative and images in the video from a different perspective. Consequently, this segment of my analysis of the racial images presented in *Like a Prayer* will focus on three issues that suggest another reading of the images in the video. The three issues include the stirring to life of the statue, the manner in which Madonna is dressed, and one of the kissing sequences.

Racial Images

From the outset of the video, the viewer knows that the black character has committed no real crime, yet his actions must be explained, justified, and ultimately defended by Madonna's character in the video. But if one looks at the black character's action from the conditioned perspective of the white community (where all racial contact is a potential threat to the well-being of whites, especially females), then the black male character is guilty of a major societal offense: crossing the invisible barrier of race that continues to separate blacks from whites. Through the video characterizations, Madonna is able to bring to light the old fears, myths, and stereotypes that prevent those who are steeped in American cultural prejudices from seeing racial interaction, especially between black men and white women, simply as a positive interpersonal relationship or friendship.

This analysis is not an argument for or against assimilation or interracial relationships. However, some of Curry's phrasing (1990, 26), such as "moved to life" and "erotically kisses," and her descriptions of how Madonna is dressed do hint at Americans' phobias about racial assimilation and interaction and their tendency to see any interaction as sexual in nature.

Clearly, much of what Madonna has done in music videos has had erotic overtones that cannot be ignored; however, a reading that focuses exclusively on this aspect, particularly given the religious and social contexts and setting of *Like a Prayer*, is inappropriate and unfair and only fuels racial controversy and division. Assuming, however, that the most controversial relationships in American culture remain those between black men and white women, [14] one would expect that the manner in which we respond and relate to those relationships might reveal something about the general nature of racial relationships in this country. Specifically, if Americans have truly made progress in terms of accepting racial differences and have come to terms with the concept that all people in the culture are equal and worthy of positive depictions (like those contained in the *Like a Prayer* video), then the most controversial relationships should emerge and be embraced. As such, when a black male character and a white female character are seen sharing a common destiny, one would assume that a more enlightened culture would be free from its own racial assumptions that the relationship was necessarily physical (sexual) and problematic or that it presented a potential for rape or involved some sick psychological game on the couple's part. Instead of old fears and hostilities emerging, an enlightened population that accepted the tenets of equality might simply see it all as positive.

Such, however, is not entirely the case with *Like a Prayer.* Because of our failure to come to grips with any positive depiction of race generally and of interracial interaction specifically, as depicted in *Like a Prayer,* much of what has been written and said and even more of what has not been articulated about the video serves as an elaborate smoke screen, designed to help mask feelings about racial interaction.[15] This is particularly true in discussions about the statue, the dress, and the kiss.

The Black Statue To begin, the statue does come to life but only after Madonna lies down and begins to dream. Prior to this, she prays at the feet of the statue, seeking guidance because of the moral dilemma that faces her. The suggestion that the inanimate black statue is somehow moved to life at the presence of Madonna (a white woman) is indicative of the myth that black men seek and are emotionally and erotically stirred by white females. In the context of the scene, which is both a prelude to and an extension of Madonna's dreaming in the church, it is more plausible to assume that the statue is divinely moved to life by her concerns and prayers for guidance, not by some overwhelmingly innate carnal desire. The fact that the statue, like the falsely accused black male he resembles, has been held behind a cage that suggests a prison is, then, rather significant. For as the video narrative ends, it is only through Madonna's character making the right choice that the statue answers her prayers for guidance and returns to its sacred place, as the black male character is set free.

The video does suggest that race should not be a factor in doing "the right thing." While presenting this positive message, the video does seem to affirm, however, that too often race and the stereotypes attached to it are negative factors in the decision processes of many Americans. Specifically, the black male character is arrested for a crime because institutional authorities believe he assaulted the white woman. Much like the statement that suggests the black statue was "moved to life" by the presence of the white female character, the implication that black men are tempted or moved to aggressively pursue and harm white women reflects underlying beliefs of too many white Americans.[16] As the curtain comes down at the conclusion of the video, the male character stares out at the viewer. Although he is holding Madonna's hand as they bow to the viewer, he is not smiling or leering at Madonna in any manner that suggests a hidden carnal desire for her.

Madonna presents an alternative portrait of black men through this video. Instead of portraying all black males as threats to society, who are often presumed guilty of some criminal activity, she gives us an image of a black man who was moved not by sexually oriented ulterior motives but by compassion to help a person in trouble. The truthful irony, of course, is that as he moves to assist her, his involvement in some crime is presumed by others.

The Dress   Reactions to Madonna's style of dress in the video are curious and revealing in terms of racial perceptions. As the video begins, Madonna is wearing a long black dress coat over the "controversial" dress that she later reveals. It is not until she has entered the church that she finally removes the coat, apparently in a gesture of respect as she approaches the statue to pray.

Despite descriptions and perceptions to the contrary, the dress is not black, nor is it simply a slinky black slip. Madonna is wearing a dark maroon, formfitting dress that is held up by thin shoulder straps. Underneath the dress, she is wearing either a full-length black slip or black bra, also with thin shoulder straps. At various points in the video, the dress straps do fall off her shoulders, but there is no indication that Madonna is using this dress to titillate (or stir to life) the statue or the black character. The straps simply slip down because of her physical movements.

The nature of the dress is important, at least in this particular video, because it belies several misconceptions about the overall erotic nature of this work and, in this case, of Madonna herself. Given the close fit of the dress, it is not possible for Madonna's character to lie "sprawled on her back" (Curry 1990, 26) without raising the dress above her waist. And, in the context and sacred setting of the video, it is difficult to accept any interpretation that alludes to some form of sexual seduction between the characters. What Madonna's dress and viewer reactions to it do suggest, however, is an ingrained sexual response to the black male and white female onscreen.

To substantiate the claim that Madonna's character "worships a statue of a black male saint in the church, who is thus moved to life" (Curry 1990, 26), it is necessary to perceive the dress as a slinky and sexual come-on tool. One must also believe that the black character is so turned on by the "forbidden fruit" in the modestly revealing outfit that nothing else, including his own freedom, matters to him except the sexual conquest. But this mythical belief and stereotypical assumption is not supported by the video. At no point does the statue/man step back, look over her body, or begin to lustfully drool at her appearance in the dress. In fact, for the most part, the male character's neutral facial expressions suggest no emotional reaction to Madonna's character at all.

Interpretations of the dress as being askew or of Madonna's character as parading around in a black slip are demeaning not only to black men but also to white women, who are assumed to be acting as seductresses with low moral fiber or "asking" for trouble. Such interpretations are especially demeaning to black men because they suggest that they are so turned on by women, especially white women (this is apparently compounded if the woman is clothed in anything that hints at or highlights her femininity) that they become lust-filled, sex-crazed animals in their presence. This persistent belief, which initially was part of the slave masters' rationale for keeping white females distant and "in their place" while the masters themselves remained free to lust and rape, is indicative of a culture that steadfastly clings to its own negative racial stereotypes and hang-ups. The strength of the *Like a Prayer* video—and the problem with it—is that it brings to the forefront these old established attitudes and beliefs and forces the viewer to recognize, if not address, them as uncomfortable a process as that may be.

The Kiss   If any one of the images in the *Like a Prayer* video blatantly violates so-called racial taboos and potentially offends viewers, it is the depiction of Madonna's character being kissed by the black male. The power of the image of a black man kissing a white woman is tied to the multitude of media portrayals that traditionally suggest any interactions between black males and white females are based on lust and the related portrayal of black men as rapists who defile white women's virtue. This underlying fear of miscegenation and the loss of racial purity, along with the allegedly brutal and animal nature of black men, have been depicted explicitly in motion pictures, such as D. W. Griffith's *Birth of a Nation* (1915), and indirectly in television dramas, such as the made-for-television drama *A Fight for Jenny* (1986). At the heart of all of the portrayals of interracial relationships is a warning of the dangers facing those involved in them and a hope that such relationships will simply go away.

In *Like a Prayer*, however, Madonna does not allow the viewer to dismiss or ignore the relationship or wish it away. She also does not give in to the racists, whose burning crosses in the background blaze with the rage of fear and hatred that would keep the races polarized. Madonna challenges viewers not by advocating interracial relationships but by presenting images that confront them with their own historically grounded prejudice.

The most controversial kiss in the video occurs when the image of the statue, which was previously seen kissing Madonna's character, is replaced with the image of the black male, who has been arrested for the murder of the white woman in the alley. In fact, the black male is leaning over Madonna, who is lying on a pew, but it is not clear that he is lying atop Madonna's character as Curry (1990) suggests. Neither of the two shots in this scene provide a wide enough angle to allow the viewer to conclude that the black character is, indeed, lying on Madonna. This lack of visual documen-

tation is significant because it raises questions about the popular interpretation of this particular segment of the video.

In the context of the discussion of race, the suggestion is that one kiss is
enough to set off the innate passions and lust of the black male character
(and black people generally). This is not, however, the case. There is no evidence that the characters in the choir, who are celebrating the spirit of God,
are about to throw off their robes and engage in a wild orgy with Madonna's
(white) character as the center of the action. The smiles on all of the characters' faces are not leers of lust; rather, they are smiles of joy at being touched
by a higher power and, as Madonna suggests ("you know I'll take you
there"), at being taken "home" to a higher human and spiritual plane.

Even if the black character *is* lying atop Madonna's character and kissing
her, there is no evidence anywhere in the video that anything more than a
kiss is involved. Certainly, it is possible to make the case that "the lyrics do
bear overtones of carnal love . . . 'In the midnight hour, I can feel your
power, just like a prayer, you know I'll take you there' " (Curry 1990, 27)
and support the notion of a fusion between sexual ecstasy and religious fervor. However, it is also possible to make an entirely different—and less demeaning—case. For example, remembering the setting of the church in
which the video takes place, the lyrics are nothing more than an acknowledgment of the power of God arriving at midnight. The power that is both
felt and demonstrated by the singing and dancing is a celebration of being in
touch with the spirit, not with lust.

Another problem with interpretations of this scene is illustrated in Curry's (1990, 26) description of Madonna's character as being "erotically
kissed" by the black male. As the scene begins, Madonna's character is lying
on her side facing the camera; after a cutaway to the black character who is
looking downward, Madonna rolls over on her back, and the kiss takes
place. Even though Madonna's character does close her eyes while kissing
the black character and raise her hands to gently grasp the sides of his face,
the "erotic" nature of the kiss is unclear. In fact, given the theme of the
video—the concept of a black man being falsely accused of a crime he did
not commit—it is presumptuous to assume anything about the nature of the
kiss.

In the context of the video, for example, it is possible to believe that just
as the black character and black people generally are often accused of crimes
they did not commit, so, too, may this character be accused of erotic passions that, in fact, do not exist. Consequently, the accusations made about
this scene reflect the same accusations that were and are made regarding the
intentions of the black character and of black people. The assumption that
Madonna's character is in love with the black man, that the kiss is erotic, or
that the character is eager for the kiss of this white woman are the racial assumptions that members of a racist society bring to the video.

In the end, the kiss is nothing more than a device that triggers innate reactions: the same reactions that allowed the police to believe the black male was guilty of murder (if not rape as well) and that allowed viewers to see nothing more than a reflection of their own belief that any physical contact between the characters (or between black men and white women specifically) is always based on sexual desire. Thus, while images of crosses burn in the background as a warning to whites to avoid physical contact or getting involved in the causes of blacks, Madonna's character stands before these symbols of the Ku Klux Klan, denying the Klan's power and authority, opting instead for a harmonious resolution.

Religious Issues

Within the confines of the black community, the black church, the collective nondenominational religious experience and practices of black people, has been the most significant and important institution in the community. As a collective experience, the black church has functioned as the ideological basis for religious beliefs (especially Christian), social organization, political leadership, and moral precepts that have provided the primary social structure of stability within the black community. It is true that religion and the black church specifically have confronted changing strategic views articulated in the contradiction of either waiting for a "supreme being" to address the concerns of the community or adopting the belief that God helps those who help themselves. However, the black church has remained a viable force in the worldly concerns of blacks. The real strength of the church may lie in the fact that it has been able to successfully fuse the secular and sacred concerns into a viable working philosophy that touches the lives of virtually every member of the black community.

As such, the black church has been less concerned with religious icons and more focused on the economic, political, and cultural well-being of black people, as well as the direct role that religion can play in the spiritual experience and worldly empowerment of the community. Although Madonna has been criticized by the Catholic church and religious fundamentalists for her use of religious icons (i.e., the burning crosses in the video, the cross she wears, her name, and the stigmata she receives on her hands in the video), there are moral, social, and political icons in the video that have, perhaps, even more significance for blacks. To understand these icons, however, one must keep in mind the secular and sacred nature of black religion, in addition to its role as articulator of the black experience in America.

Though the images presented in *Like a Prayer* can justifiably be considered blasphemous from a strict Eurocentric perspective of religion, they can also be interpreted as a positive and accurate parable of the black experience in America. The following segment of my analysis will focus on this latter perspective.

Religious Images

The fusion between the sacred and secular is perhaps best evidenced in what Curry (1990) labels as Madonna's wild dancing and what others would call her blasphemous behavior in the church. For strict fundamentalist religions, which view dancing and celebration as sinful, the charge of blasphemy is accurate. However, one must remember that this view is not generally held in the black church. Instead of a sign of disrespect, Madonna's actions and the dance of the choir are seen as historical reminders of the fusion of the secular and sacred worlds that exist in the black community. One need only attend, for example, a black Baptist church on any Sunday morning in America to realize that moving to the beat of the music by the choir, minister, and congregation is a vital part of the service. Thus, rather than symbolizing disrespect, the movement or dance in the video demonstrates the power of God and is a means of celebrating the spirit, not sacrilege.

Even though Madonna's movements in the video are slightly faster and more rhythmic than those of the black choir, both she and the choir are in tune and moving in time to the music. Both are celebrating the power ("I can feel your power... just like a prayer I'm gonna take you there") of the spirit to move and uplift the soul, particularly in the overall context of the video (Madonna enters the church with a burden and does not smile until she has encountered the two individuals who show her the way—the black woman who leads the choir and the statue). Thus, Madonna's dancing is direct evidence that the message of the gospel and the power of the black church to provide direction, comfort, and support have reached and touched her persona. The dancing also suggests that the character has become one with both the congregation and the black community. The dance celebrates unity and freedom and, in so doing, affirms the highest moral principals of black religion (truth and unity).

Throughout the video, Madonna presents numerous images that illustrate the power of the black church to function as a positive moral force for both blacks and whites. When Madonna's character first enters the church, she sings, "and it feels like home."[17] This line is sung immediately after her character witnesses the assault and is threatened by one of the white male attackers. Once inside the church, Madonna locks the door, and her journey to a higher moral ground begins.

The video images presented in this initial scene are significant for two reasons. First, the church is presented as a zone of safety, and the function of black religion as a sanctuary from the immoral behavior of the outside world is made manifest. Madonna's articulation of the line "feels like home" underscores the safety that the church provides to all who are in need. Second, the church is seen as a sanctuary for *all* people, regardless of, in this case, race, which underscores the doctrine of the equality of all people that is fundamental to black religion. In effect, Madonna presents a narrative that affirms the comfort and safety provided by the black church by stating that the experience feels like returning to the safety of one's own house.

When Madonna's character is seen freely interacting with members of the choir later in the video, the sequence underscores her acceptance by the church, without question or judgment, and the feeling of safety she experiences. This is particularly important in contrast to the treatment of the black male character. Although the black character is assumed guilty of some crime by the white establishment, the black establishment and the black church assume Madonna's innocence and good faith. As such, she is treated as a member of the congregation and not as a threat to it.

The sequence directly contrasts the real racial attitudes that exist in this country. That is, though many whites either presume that blacks are guilty of offense or are afraid of interaction (or physical contact, such as a kiss), blacks, as depicted in the video, are not so presumptuous or afraid. Thus, Madonna does feel safe, secure, and free to seek guidance within the confines of the community. In her moment of need, she is assisted by the community and not prejudged. This powerful theme, while affirming the moral nature of Madonna's character, is also a direct attack on the less tolerant attitudes (of whites) in American society.

In the video, the church represents a sanctuary from the oppression and racism that exist in the outside world. For blacks, these are depicted in the false arrest of the black character, the intimidation of those who realize the truth (the innocence of the black character in this instance), and the repeated use of images of burning crosses and the racist group (the Ku Klux Klan) they symbolize—images that are universally understood (at least among most blacks). For Madonna's character, oppression appears in the form of physical intimidation should she decide to tell authorities the truth. Like many blacks, Madonna faces a direct threat to her well-being if she decides to stand up to the injustice of racism inflicted on the black character. And like many whites before her, Madonna's character confronts the possibility of a visit from the "knights of darkness" if she decides to take a moral stand against injustice.

Instead of sacrilege, then, the specific images of burning crosses behind Madonna are symbolically both a reminder of the political and social extremes of racism and a tribute to the steadfast and salutatory role the black church has historically played in providing a safe haven from the racist assaults that have threatened blacks throughout their history in this country. Rather than cowering in fear and feeling powerless or silently sanctioning the actions from a distance, Madonna's character is empowered, and, like the church itself, she is free to stand in front of the crosses, refusing to either acknowledge or succumb to racially motivated threats by hiding in the shadows.

The power and significance of the black church is initially affirmed in the video when Madonna's character first prays (for guidance) and then lies on a church pew and begins to dream. In addition to what it reveals about the religious views of members of the black community, the dream sequence is symbolically important because it illustrates the historical debate and unique placement of the dual function of religion within the black experience. Specifically, Madonna's dream state depicts religion as both fantasy and reality, sacred and secular, and it acknowledges and underscores the fusion between the two that has traditionally existed in the black community. As such, religion is depicted not simply as a set of beliefs that one should separate from his or her objective living conditions and only believe in or follow in an abstract, ideal manner; rather, it is represented as a tangible tool that can be utilized to structure and guide one's everyday existence and to empower individuals by providing them with direct control over their own lives. In effect, then, religion can shape and bring to life the dreams and aspirations of those who embrace it.

While in a dream state, Madonna's character falls (presumably descending from truth and grace) but is caught by a black woman before hitting ground. The black woman then whispers in Madonna's ear ("you whisper softly to me") and gently tosses her back to the sky, thus helping her to ascend to a higher level of moral character, integrity, and, presumably, justice. The church and its agents are presented as sources of moral strength and conviction that directly help those they touch to reach the highest moral plane possible.

The fact that a black woman appears in this dream sequence is also significant. She is symbolic of the many unheralded black women in the United States, and it is this agent of the church who provides solace and comfort for Madonna's character. It is the black woman who offers counsel, whispers words of encouragement, and helps Madonna's character return to a higher moral plane. This affirming and vital image of black women as an equal source and intricate part of the moral fiber and strength in the black community is seldom presented in the mass media. Thus, the presentation of a black woman as a positive source of strength and moral conviction, as opposed to a dominant controller or a morally loose individual, is a more reality-based image. Madonna's willingness to present an alternative representation to the overbearing or overly sexualized black women who populate virtually every video, motion picture, and television program is exceptional. Madonna has replaced the stereotypes of black women with a more realistic portrait of them that highlights the role they actually play in the black community.

In an act that further illustrates the fusion of the sacred and secular in the religion of the black community, once Madonna returns to earth (or the secular world) she frees the black statue from its cage. With her exposure to the moral teachings of the church and her interaction with the black woman, she is free to live up to a higher set of principles. This act of freeing represents both the power of black religion to uplift the spirits of the community, raising that community above the outside forces that control it (the empowerment to act), and the more literal and worldly freeing of the black character that follows. Once freed, the statue takes on human form and, like the black woman, whispers encouragement to Madonna's character and kisses her on the forehead. No longer bound by spiritual or sacred confinement, the statue is able to move in the secular world. Now in human form, the statue, like Madonna's character, becomes part of the real world and confronts the viewer with real moral choices, based on the question of racial justice.

Even though the statue returns to its position behind bars at the end of the dream sequence, the principles of justice and moral conviction in the face of violence remain with Madonna's character. Like millions of blacks in America, she has been empowered by the religious institution and the higher principles that it upholds. Although afraid, initially alone, and faced with the prospect of simply allowing the racist status quo to remain unchecked, Madonna's character is taken into a world where moral conviction is more important than personal survival. She is shown that the convictions of one individual can, in the end, make a positive difference. The video itself affirms what many in the black community already understand: that one is never alone, particularly when an institution such as the black church endures.

CONCLUSION

Clearly, one can never know an artist's actual intent or influence on his or her texts, and such is the case with Madonna and the *Like a Prayer* video. But in fact, in the final analysis, it may be irrelevant whether Madonna intended to produce a piece that would advocate the positive role of the black church in the lives of all it touches. And whether she intended to raise questions about the treatment of the black community and black people in this polarized society may prove immaterial. Also irrelevant are questions about whether Madonna, in using the musical rhythms, images, and themes from black culture, has discovered an effective tool for marketing her products at the expense of others. What *is* relevant is the fact that *Like a Prayer,* particularly in comparison with the standard music video fare, is an enlightened work that emphasizes positive aspects of the black community (like the black church) and examines the conditions of black people.

Perhaps most significantly, Madonna's *Like a Prayer* video provides viewers with an opportunity to see facets of black life that are devoid of traditional stereotypes. Madonna exhibits a sensitivity to those stereotypes and then reflexively turns them on the viewers, forcing individuals to question their own attitudes and beliefs. In an age where forthright discussions of race have given way to the old negative depictions of the past, this video is remarkable. It raises questions about the presupposed nature of blacks and their subsequent treatment in the judicial system, and it presents a view of the moral base, the black church, that serves as a foundation for the black community.

Although every black person may not agree with every aspect of the video, Madonna has offered elements of the culture that most blacks can at least understand and relate to. For whites, Madonna has, at the very least, posed an indirect challenge to the negative assertions that permeate most of the mass media and many of the base attitudes and beliefs that affect racial interaction in this country. In the end, Madonna shows a way for blacks and whites to effectively tackle the seemingly impossible task of solving the race problem.

Like Madonna's character in the video, each of us is faced with a choice. We can continue to cling to the negative perceptions about blacks and when faced with obvious wrongs go our own way, or we can seek higher moral ground and confront the forces of darkness that seem to be spreading over the country like the fires that engulf the crosses in the video. In the final analysis, the choice is left to each viewer, but the way home, the way to understanding and harmony, is, as Madonna suggests, just "like a prayer."

NOTES

1. For example, the "Flip Wilson Show" (1970–1974) featured a character named the Right Reverend Leroy of the Church of What's Happenin' Now. The reverend was portrayed as a somewhat shady character and became one of the more popular mainstays on the comedy show. The program "Good Times" (1974–1979), a situation comedy that was a spin-off of "All in the Family," utilized religion as a backdrop condition that affirmed the poverty of the Evans family, who lived in an inner-city tenement.

NBC recently ran a situation comedy titled "Amen," which focused on the "humorous" antics and lives of members of a black congregation in Philadelphia. The principal character, the Reverend Frye, was reminiscent of the Reverend Leroy from the "Flip Wilson Show."

MTV saw a marked increase in videos featuring black choirs in background or backup vocal roles following the release of a video by the group Foreigner (*I Want to Know What Love Is*) and, more recently, Hammer's rap/gospel video *We Pray*.

2. In American culture, the dominant ideologies are reinforced by depicting "others" in negative stereotypes or by excluding images of entire groups of individuals from media texts.

3. This translates to a market strategy that both targets and favors a young, white, male audience between the ages of sixteen and twenty-five. Most demographic figures showed that approximately 85 percent of the viewers were male and between the ages of eighteen and thirty-five.

4. There were several ironies that MTV executives could not explain. For instance, the channel rejected videos from Rick James, whom officials defined as "funk," but included Prince in the video rotation. Later, videos by Donna Summer and Michael Jackson, neither of whom could be classified as rock-and-roll artists, were aired (see Dates and Barlow 1990, 108).

5. MTV currently airs a number of programs that are outside the rock-and-roll format. Although new programs like "Yo MTV Raps" and "Fade to Black" primarily feature black rap artists and talent, the practice of restricting the videos to selected styles and time slots still results in a form of visual and narrative segregation.

A comparison of MTV's competition, VH-1 and BET (Black Entertainment Television) "Video Soul" programs, more clearly illustrates MTV's restrictive play of videos. Although one would expect the selection of videos for the BET network to favor black and minority images, VH-1's popularity does indicate that diverse images can attract broad audiences.

6. For a detailed history of black women in music, see Donald Bogle, *Brown Sugar: Eighty Years of America's Black Female Superstars* (New York: Harmony Books, 1980).

7. Lesser-known does not mean less talented. In some cases, African-American divas were endowed with more natural talent and visual presence than Madonna. Although many people may suggest that Madonna has been more readily accepted by mainstream culture because of her race and her ability to freely use the styles and techniques from African-American culture, they must also grant that much of her work and its social commentary has been critically ignored because it addresses those alternative points of view and voices. In effect, like many divas, Madonna's failure to conform to established rules and commentary have led to her dismissal as a serious artist and fueled attacks on her personal life.

8. "Crossing over" is an industry concept that means an artist, usually black, can appeal to white audiences. Madonna is unique in that she is one of only a few artists who reverse the concept by moving from mainstream, or white, to black audiences.

9. Most discussions of Madonna have ignored the fact that she does have black fans who, in some cases, interpret her music and videos differently than whites do. In addition to studies in this text, see Jane D. Brown and Laurie Schulze, "The Effects of Race, Gender, and Fandom on Audience Interpretations of Madonna's Music Videos," *Journal of Communication* 40, no. 2 (Spring) 1990: 88–102.

10. The only other breakthrough for this year was an album by the group Culture Club, featuring Boy George and titled *Colour by Numbers*. Like Madonna, the group—or more precisely its sexually ambiguous (to many) and flamboyant leader—was also highly controversial. The Culture Club album was ranked thirty-first.

11. The *Madonna* album utilized the talents of black producer Reggie Lucas; her second album, *Like a Virgin*, featured the creative talents of black producer Nile Rogers.

12. Madonna did spend some time studying with the prestigious Alvin Ailey Dance Company, a black modern dance group based in New York City. Of equal note is the fact that, because of the ebb and flow of cultural traditions in America, no American

artist can claim to have avoided the influence of African musical traditions on his or her art.

13. The structurally nonlinear narrative begins with the assault and murder of a young white female (who physically resembles Madonna) by four white male gang members. Responding to the woman's screams, a black male comes to her assistance but is arrested for the murder when the police arrive. As the black male character is taken away, Madonna's character flees the scene after the leader of the white gang spots her and sneers at her.

After fleeing the scene, Madonna seeks refuge and guidance in a black church. Following a dream sequence in which her character encounters a black choir and a black statue that comes to life (the statue physically resembles the young black male who was arrested), Madonna wakes, goes to the police station, and frees the black character.

14. Although interracial relationships between white males and black females are controversial, they have historically drawn less negative criticism and fewer overt attacks. The real point that should be kept in mind, however, is that in a racist society, relationships between individuals with overt physical differences can be held in low esteem by many.

15. Perhaps the biggest irony here (indicative of the real problem with American racial attitudes) is the fact that the video is not actually about an interracial relationship in the conventional sense. However, much of what has been said about the video does suggest that many viewers do, in fact, read the text as if it is presenting an interracial relationship between Madonna's character and the black statue that eventually comes to life.

16. Extensive media coverage of narratives, the Central Park case in New York (a brutal assault and rape), the Charles Stuart case in Boston (an alleged murder of a pregnant white woman by a black male), and the Rodney King verdict in California, along with political ads in the election campaigns of President George Bush (Willie Horton) and Sen. Jesse Helms (reverse discrimination) have all served to keep emotionally charged images and negative beliefs about black males in the public consciousness.

17. All lyrics cited are taken from the *Like a Prayer* video.

REFERENCES

Bogle, D. (1980). *Brown Sugar: Eighty Years of America's Black Female Superstars.* New York: Harmony Books.

Brown, J., and Schulze, L. (1990). "The Effects of Race, Gender, and Fandom on Audience Interpretations of Madonna's Music Videos." *Journal of Communication* 40, no. 2: 88–102.

Brown, T. (1988). "Tony Brown's Journal: Spirits That Dwell in the Deep Woods." Tony Brown Productions, PBS/WNET, N.Y.

Curry, R. (1990). "Madonna from Marilyn to Marlene—Pastiche and/or Parody?" *Journal of Film and Video* 42, no. 2: 15–30.

Dates, J., and Barlow, W. (eds.). (1990). *Split Image: African Americans in the Mass Media.* Washington, D.C.: Howard University Press.

Dunlap, O. (1932). *The Outlook for Television.* New York: Harper.

Fisk, J. (1987). "British Cultural Studies and Television." In R. Allen (ed.), *Channels of Discourse.* Chapel Hill: University of North Carolina Press, pp. 254–289.

Garofalo, R. (1990). "Crossing Over: 1939–1989." In J. Dates and W. Barlow (eds.), *Split Image: African Americans in the Mass Media.* Washington, D.C.: Howard University Press, pp. 57–121.

Genovese, E. (1976). *Roll, Jordan, Roll: The World the Slaves Made.* New York: Vintage Books.

Gitlin, T. (ed.). (1986). *Watching Television.* New York: Pantheon.

Hall, S. (1982). "The Rediscovery of Ideology: Return of the Repressed in Media Studies." In M. Gurevitch et al. (eds.), *Culture, Society, and the Media.* London: Methuen, pp. 55–90.

McClary, S. (1990). "Living to Tell: Madonna's Resurrection of the Fleshly." *Genders* (Spring): 1–21.

MacDonald, F. (1983). *Blacks and White TV: Afro-Americans in Television Since 1948.* Chicago: Nelson-Hall.

McLuhan, M. (1967). *The Medium Is the Message.* New York: Bantam Books.

Morris, A. (1984). *The Origins of the Civil Rights Movement: Black Communities Organizing for Change.* New York: Free Press.

Newcomb, H. (1976). *Television: The Critical View.* New York: Oxford University Press.

Reddick, L. (1944). "Educational Programs for the Improvement of Race Relations: Motion Pictures, Radio, the Press and Libraries." *Journal of Negro Education* 13, no. 3: 367–389.

Part Two

The Sapphic Insurgent: Madonna and Gay Culture

photo by Lorraine Day, *courtesy of Warner Brothers*

CINDY PATTON

4

Embodying Subaltern Memory: Kinesthesia & the Problematics of Gender & Race

Lieux de memoire ["sites of memory"] originate with the sense that there is no spontaneous memory, that we must deliberately create archives, maintain anniversaries, organize celebrations, pronounce eulogies, and notarize bills because such activities no longer occur naturally. . . . We buttress our identities upon such bastions . . . if history did not besiege memory, deforming and transforming it, penetrating and petrifying it, there would be no *lieux de memoire . . .* moments of history torn away from the movement of history, then returned; no longer quite life, not yet death, like shells on the shore when the sea of living memory has receded.
—**Pierre Nora,** "Between Memory and History"

Places are fragmentary and inward-turning histories, pasts that others are not allowed to read, accumulated times that can be unfolded but like stories held in reserve, remaining in an enigmatic state, symbolizations encysted in the pain or pleasure of the body. "I feel good here"; the well-being under-expressed in the language it appears in like a fleeting glimmer is a spatial practice.
—**Michel de Certeau,** *The Practice of Everyday Life*

*T*HE EMERGENCE of lesbian and gay studies in the 1980s was somewhat ironic: Indebted to the political gains of the post-Stonewall (1969) gay movement,[1] lesbian and gay studies were inextricably bound up in the political discourses of both minority rights and liberation, with their opposing assimilationist and nationalist underpinnings. Within the academy, both forms of political analysis promoted and enabled the repositioning of homosexuality from an object of study for sexology or the sociology of deviance

81

to a vantage point for cross-disciplinary interrogation of gender- or sexuality-based subcultures with their own (hidden) histories, social patterns, and political destinies. By the end of the 1980s, however, much of the theoretical work in lesbian and gay studies de-essentialized the once apparently stable "homosexuality" that inquiries had sought to explain, defend, and make visible as a positive life-style choice. Many lesbian and gay scholars came to view same-sex relationships as historically discontinuous, cross-culturally incommensurate, and incoherent in ontological constructions of "gay," "lesbian," or "homosexual," even among culturally similar and historically coincident practitioners.

Critiques of and anxiety about the transience of identity and group membership were never solely academic disputes; poststructuralist work appeared to undercut the claims of the most visible gay and lesbian rights organizations that had, for more than two decades,[7] hitched their wagons to the rhetoric and practices of postwar U.S. minority politics. Serving twin masters of academic rigor (albeit, in disciplines that were already radically questioning their own rhetoric of inquiry) and of community sustenance, lesbian and gay critics were caught between the desire for theoretical clarity and the hope for political and cultural freedom. Every time we thought we had something to say, we seemed to deconstruct the very vantage point that had enabled our speech.

Even the poststructuralist accounts came under attack as gender theorists sought to take the antiessentialist arguments all the way down. Judith Butler (1990), Donna Haraway (1991), and Sandra Harding (1986) have demonstrated that even the supposed biological referents of gender ("sex" in genotype) are themselves socially constructed. Constructionist theories also began to split between cultural studies based in combinations of Marxist and psychoanalytic theories—which I will loosely call ideology critiques—and postmodern theories that disavowed the "underneath" (or "hermeneutic of suspicion") characteristic of the former and also refused the concept of "outside" invoked by minoritizing and nationalistic theories alike.

Although the notion of false consciousness was overtly under assault, at least by Louis Althusser (1969), and the role of consumption was reopened with the Birmingham School view of culture as an increasingly significant domain of class struggle, Marxist criticism continued to cleave the determining material into practices of production and of consumption. The base/superstructure metaphor prevailed with its "last instance," presuming culture as the origin that could, in principle, serve as the reference necessary to speak meaningfully of appropriation and commodification.

Similarly, "minority" analyses of negative stereotypes were a form of critique clearly reliant on notions of ideology, latent content, and signification in the Saussurean sense. The merging of Marxist and liberal pluralist critiques of both figural and democratic modes of representation resulted in critical practices. These practices seemed only to register as resistance production of counterimages by clearly marked oppressed people engaging in successful confrontation with unambiguous personifications of the system. The reading of *Vogue* I will propose in this chapter attempts to understand how critiques of hypostatized rhetorics (discourses that are reified or "raised up" and privileged)—what Marxist critics might now call "hegemony"—can exist within the very surface of the proper of culture.

I use the term *proper* here in the sense used by Jacques Derrida (1981) and Michel de Certeau (1988), referring to the structural place in which strategic engagement means performing critique in (rather than outside of) the rhetorical terms of the hypostatized culture and where tactics, although potentially effective in recircuiting and altering such rhetorics, exist largely as momentary deflections of the hypostatized rhetoric. I will argue that "signifying" in the black cultural sense outlined by Henry Louis Gates, Jr. (1987) is precisely such a tactic of rhetorical alterity. Thus, where some critics have viewed *Vogue* and Madonna's work in general as parasitic on, variously, black and gay culture and even on feminism, I will suggest that she reroutes through mass culture quotidian critiques of dominant culture (in this case, voguing's critique of whiteness and of gender), making them more available as places of resistance, although this may come at some cost. I will argue that it is no longer useful to view recirculation and dislocation of cultural critique as a result of appropriation. Though the full critique embodied in, for example, voguing is necessarily muted when restyled in the *Vogue* video, reembodiment by club dancers unpredictably adds to and reinterprets the critique, retracing or reconnecting memories of resistance.

CRITICAL LIMINALITY

Operating in the space between formal theory and advocacy journalism, lesbian and gay cultural critics are in an awkward position. In our popular and often activist mode, we are asked to thoughtfully evaluate whether particular events of cultural performance are "good" or "bad" for gay liberation. In our theoretical mode, we are searching for a framework that acknowledges the institutional and political constraints and possibilities of our time but also does justice to the amazing capacity within gay and lesbian networks to construct systems of collective self-understanding sufficient to sustain solidarity and resistance even in the bleakest of situations.

This problematic of critical "inbetweenness" occurred again for me in the spring of 1990, when Madonna's music video *Vogue* was released with tremendous fanfare and much popular discourse alluding to but never specifically identifying the "underground" from whence it had diffused into mainstream dance culture. When unveiled on MTV, *Vogue* proposed the dance of the same name as both "new" and "historical, " a postmodern anachronism saturating the video's iconography.

Voguing promised to be the most commercially exploitable dance phenomenon since disco. A casual review of subsequent dance videos by other artists suggests that at least the arm movements of vogue have been incorporated. Even more than disco, as conceived in *Saturday Night Fever* (*SNF*), voguing appears as a quintessentially male response to an urban existence rife with problems for the underclass. But though both *SNF* and *Vogue* engender a style that couples fashion signs with a way of moving (and thus enables the sale of the implicit critiques of masculinity that characterize the dance styles), disco (a barely restylized salsa) references street mobility. Vogue, on the other hand, stands—almost literally—in relation to the ideology of fashion itself. Both dances pastiche the gender roles structured by contemporaneous fashion norms; that they do so in apparently opposite ways suggests that each is a sort of high-water mark of particular gender formations.

Whereas *Saturday Night Fever* suggests that it is okay for men to create themselves as objects of beauty and sexuality—you can be gorgeous and still *move*—*Vogue* suggests that masculine beauty surpasses feminine beauty in its capacity to be an object. In *Saturday Night Fever,* the male dancer's gymnastic competition for differentiation particularizes the collective men-in-motion; individual men stand as metaphors of active beauty and thereby narrowly prevent the male body from hypostatizing into an object. *SNF* presents the dance bar as a utopian space in which male competitiveness (the struggle to be *homme,* not homo) is transcended through variations on a dance: Masculinity here transcends the male body.

By contrast, *Vogue* uses repetition of similarly dressed (though different) men to erase intramasculine (including interrace) distinctions by thematizing the male body as a form. Choreography of the conjunction between body and space incorporates dressing and undressing, which, as in fashion modeling, enables the display of garments under (and even undergarments) but never the model's body as flesh. The persistent dressing and undressing in *Vogue* and the voguing moves that simulate applying makeup and opening the jacket displace the expected play of the male body from body in space to space in body, a traditionally feminine conceptualization. *Vogue* presents a body with neither subjectivity nor depth: Neither masculinity nor the male body is under the clothes; instead, each is constituted by them.[3]

I should not press the similarities and differences of *SNF* and *Vogue* any further: Elements like length, form of consumption (spectacular versus domestic), structure (narrative versus montage), and relation to stardom (actors "act," musicians "perform") mean that film operates quite differently as a cultural nexus than does music video. Nevertheless, I want to note one other characteristic the two share: Both disco dancing and voguing appear to be restylizations of Afro-Caribbean dance forms, informally created within the popular dance practices of urban black and Latin homosexual men. Both constituted a kind of difference and belonging for men who faced racism in the larger white gay male enclaves, as well as varying degrees and types of nonacceptance within their own ethnic or racial communities.

From the vantage point of ideology critique, the dance forms seem to have been co-opted in their passage into mainstream cultural imagery, especially because their relation to the black and Latin homosexual performance is elided. But once we abandon hypostatic notions of culture and subculture and, with them, a message-transfer notion of consumption, there may also be an important way in which the subcultural values (what I will call critique) embedded in the dance forms have perhaps "homosexualized," "Africanized, "[4] and "Latinized" the white, heterosexual urban chic who adopted the moves, fashion, and dance club mores associated with disco and voguing.

Whether it is meaningful to speak of co-optation here divides the ideology critique characteristic of Marxist cultural studies from the rhetorical critique emerging among postmodernists. In the case of *Vogue*, a dance that is, from the outset, a pastiche and critique of white feminine iconization, there can be no question of subcultural ownership of an original form because the texts cannot be separated from each other. Likewise, historicity cannot be separated from kinesthetics; that is, the struggle to make claims to political identity cannot be understood apart from the more corporeal sense of place that actors create in their resistance. Voguing, however much it incorporates moves associated with Afro-Caribbean kick dancing, was always and already a simulation. Unlike black power and gay liberation rhetorics, "negro faggotry"[5] has never made claims to place or history, only to critique and in the rhetorical form of "signifying" in the black cultural sense.[6]

Ideology critiques that rely on notions of a subculture distinguishable by its place or identity or separation from a mainstream cannot capture the subversion of gender that is voguing because they almost inevitably require critique of "negative" images and replacement by "positive" images. Thus, ideology critics can only read voguing as a sadly anachronistic misfire of feminist critiques. In the ideology critique framework, voguing's subversive power and critique of race and gender are annoying because references to the necessary originary subjectivity ("black," "gay," "male") continue to involve a mirror game, a stuttered articulation of a receding community that can never state its name or place.

A rhetorical analysis, enlightened by Gates (1987, 1988) or pried loose from the voguers themselves through some weird form of ethnohermeneutics, would enable us to understand that the critique in voguing still speaks through movement, even when the moves are distorted in the historical elisions that constitute the process of cross-over. Voguing may, in fact, be particularly powerful because it so utterly transforms notions of white femininity already known to and critiqued by the mainstream. To the extent that voguing simultaneously enacts and deconstructs race and gender, it might be that in crossing over, the white, middle-class, heterosexual club dancers are being signified on as they reenact the homoerotic and Afro-Latin resolutions of voguing. That is, they are performing, however noncognitively, the kinesthesia that embodies the problematics of race and gender from the perspective of subalterns.

It is a fact that "straights" always lag behind, but this does not mean that Others possess a culture that has been guarded and kept alive. Straights appear to steal from the subcultures because hypostatic culture has jettisoned its invented Other into a cultural (but ahistorical) future in order to have ever-new routes of escape from the cultural stranglehold it exercises—as boredom. So-called marginal cultures are at the very heart of the dominant culture. Cultural imperialism is simultaneous with a deep recognition of the problems that gender and race also constitute for those in a position to define the terms of oppression.

Such crossings occur not because homosexuals and men of color are uniquely possessed of style and grace but because heterosexual, white, mainstream culture finds its own calculus of gender erotics too troubling. The readability of black gay cultural forms is less a co-optation of subcultural authenticity than the collapse of mainstream culture's lines of difference. A double miscegenation occurs in vogue culture—a double crime that even the elegant disavowals of *Vogue* cannot disguise; not only are the Afro-Latin elements "possessed" by the white middle class but sexualized congress between men is taken up as a gender paradigm.

Retaining or inventing something like culture within the dominant culture—that is, creating and sustaining performances that do not result in Fascist repression or theft—has been the problem of homosexuals since the term homosexual was created to stabilize that other, unnamed, and beleaguered category, *heterosexual* (Katz 1990). It has also been the problem of African Americans since their "emancipation." The question I am proposing in relation to *Vogue*, then, is less whether the video is gay or what the video's relation to gay male culture might be but, rather, what is at stake in the interpretations of the video. As I discussed the video with everyone from long-time gay cultural critics ("isn't it already passé?") to young bar queens whose identities and machismo seemed to be staked on ever-more-elaborate staging of their dance, I discovered that there was more on the line than (another) lost chapter in gay history.

What seemed vital about the diffusion of voguing through release of the video was the battle it sparked over control of the popular memory of homosexuality, for a new generation of queens. Young gay men and women were coming out through their imitation of voguing and Madonna: They were learning to remember their bodies in a critique of gender that is autonomous of gay liberation and feminism. The dominant gay history that situates Stonewall and civil rights politics at the center of gay history is challenged by voguing and the chain of popular memory(ies) that connect the video to earlier, "queer" meanings of modern homosexuality.

RECEIVED WISDOM:
THE PARADOX OF KNOWLEDGE

What we know, as gay and lesbian scholars, about the posited modern homosexual is something of a political paradox.[7] The ambiguous framework of such social and historical analysis (i.e., this knowledge) at once argues against a "homosexual essence" and demands conformity to a humanist ideal of raised consciousness and collective action in order to be counted as gay. By forcing ambiguous homosexual microgroups into the agon of minority politics, only certain performances of same-sex bonds—those that stake political claims *against* the dominant political order—get grouped into the (albeit self-admittedly) socially constructed category. These performances announce gay activists' ambivalent place of engagement with the system.[8] The engagement required to gain minority rights simultaneously bestows identity and constrains marginal difference. Rights come only at the risk of ignoring, willfully misrecognizing, or colonizing the local tactical practices of alternative forms of same-sex bonds.

Still remaining and still embedded in the "proper" (place) of culture are other performances of oppositional identity or, more precisely (and to step away from notions associated with ideology critique), identities that state their difference. These performance identities are not accidental perverts whose private behavior is never recognized as different; they are those who, like de Certeau's city-walkers who refuse the markings of maps, traverse the landscape of heteromasculine discourse only to rearrange the terrain into something in which once comforting signs of gender no longer stand in the same relation to their signifieds or signifiers.

What we know is that twentieth-century Western homosexual subcultures developed elaborate signifiers of membership, which often appear as ordinary clothing or movements to those who are not in the know. Although there is persistent folklore about how homosexuals look, act, or behave, the truth is that one of the problematics—and survival tactics—of homosexuals is to be able to perform and "unperform" ("signify" and "pass") membership: a cluster of tactics homosexuals share in common with African Americans, though perhaps inverted.[9] A major mode of signifying for modern homosexuals has been to subvert or hyperperform signifiers of gender. Likewise, strict attention to gender signifiers (especially those that match one's biological sex signifiers) have constituted a major form of "passing."

This is not to suggest that what we call homosexuality must be or always is constituted in relation to gender; indeed, it is a double construction—of gender and of sexuality—that constitutes the modern category "homosexual." Representations and repressions of homosexuality will vary on two axes and in relation to an unstable object (heteromasculinity) (Sedgwick 1985, 1990). What is most evident in the discourse about homosexual mannerisms is their undecidability and their similarity to the manners or tastes of heterosexual men, even though the homosexuals in question might be men, who ought to look different from "men" because of sexuality, or women, who ought to differ from "men" because of gender.

The strategy of stabilizing the signifiers of homosexuality (that is, constructing stable visible identities available to the political rhetoric of "minorities") may be at odds with the tactic of destabilizing the icons of heterosexual masculinity. The first asserts that constituting and subjectifying the position of "other" can lessen the power of institutional forms of heteromasculinity. The latter proposes a lively, ongoing pastiche of heteromasculinity that constantly subverts the dominant identity's attempts to maintain the illusion of difference in its essence. It is possible that the two can coexist: Homosexuals profess and perform both essentialist and constructivist "native theories" concerning the genesis and meaning of their desires and practices (Sedgwick 1990). But pastiche may be more enduring, even though the *strategy* of identity constitution is more visible and directly engages the liberal plural system constituted through minority politics. Although appearing retrostylistic or reformist, the deployment of difference in the tactical form gender pastiche—the repetition and mixing of masculine and feminine codes—shifts the quality and meaning of resistance to institutionalized heteromasculinity.

The tension between stabilization (the strategy of promoting gay identity, counterposed to heteromasculine identity) and pastiche (the tactic of signifying and passing) threatens heteromasculinity's ability to deploy stable signifiers of masculinity and femininity in order to maintain discursive power. The quest for normalcy sought by mainstream lesbian and gay groups (with emphasis on "positive" and "appropriate" images) results in a perpetual fashion battle: The optimum style is one that loads up heterosexual signifiers but adds just that hint of difference—a handkerchief, a haircut, even a gesture or glance.[10] These fashion battles are traces of historical record that signify heterosexual culture's misrecognition of race and sexuality: difference/performance. Rather, the trace is found on and through the body.

DANCE AND SUBALTERNS

In her "Performing the Memory of Difference in Afro-Caribbean Dance," VeVe Clark (forthcoming) argues that the record of subaltern cultures is often found in dance or, rather, in assessment of the re-production of dance forms that connect environments of cultural performance (a critical operation) with the place of performance. Dance does not operate through the authentic reproduction of "original" dance formats as nostalgic neocolonialists suggest. The attempts to designate or construct the original misunderstands noncanonical dance forms; such efforts view subaltern groups as homeostatic and precultural and consider their creative products as folk art. But Clark argues that the perpetual stylization and restylization of dance by the dancer, the systematic (even if nonformal) teaching of dance forms, and the watching of dance create a structure in which participants and spectators produce cultural memory. Clark contends that interpretation and cultural meaning are embedded in the recognition of the "memory of difference" from performance to performance. For subalterns, who lack cultural and historical capital, this memory of difference (and the sense of dislocation and relocation that underlies diasporal cultures) sustains the trace of subaltern cultural products, even if only in the hermeneutic circle of marginal interpreters at the edges of mainstreamed forms.

Co-optation of locally meaningful forms, then, may highlight the memory of difference as much as it dilutes and commodifies the form and subversiveness of antiestablishment dance. The ability to discern and perform difference in relation to the dominant forms constitutes both the memory of oppression and the repertoire for resistance that define, in part, the coherence of subaltern culture.

THE "PLACE" OF MEMORY

Clark (forthcoming) works from and upends Pierre Nora's (1989) concept of lieux de memoire, making a decisive turn that I would like to follow here. Where Nora argues that forms of national history and the memory of subgroups within the nation have been substantially altered, Clark suggests that, especially among diasporal groups, pockets of "traditional memory" continue to exist and may constitute an important material for the reconstruction of histories for subalterns coming to grips with their place in their new nation.

Nora, in his introduction to his monumental and collaborative work on national memory in France, argues that, increasingly in the twentieth century, history seems to have accelerated and overtaken memory. This seceding of memory to history is related to: (1) the loss of peasant cultures, now lodged within the modern nation, for whom group culture had once constituted the repository of collective memory, (2) the rise of contending histories in postcolonial nations articulated by groups that maintained a reserve of collective memory but lacked "historical capital" under colonialist regimes,

(3) the decline of societies with an ability to marshal all institutions in service of a single ideology that sets the terms for the imaginary of past-present-future relationships that constitute national histories, and (4) the fact that the mode of historical perception is altered due, at least in large part, to the proliferation of mass media.

For Nora, these factors have resulted in a shift from a "real memory"— *milieux de memoire* of a wraparound sort—to a kind of technologized recording and storage of a series of "nows," which is symptomatic of societies that have lost the structures for containing local memories in a national history or metanarrative. The archivist replaces the hero or historian as the truth arbitrator. In this way, local memory becomes a populist genealogical obsession in which imaginary personal histories are reconstructed from traces and, in turn, constitute these traces as miniaturized and personalized appropriations of the dominant historical narrative(s) of the culture. Both archivists and genealogists sift and sort historical traces, replacing what was once perpetual and present memory with a history that is always and only a re-presentation of a simulated past.

Michel Foucault (1989) is also interested in the relation between popular memory, the administration of history, and local resistance. For Foucault, mass media and fragmentation of traditional social units also constitute a new formation; the critical issue is the ways in which popular culture functions as a site of struggle for the control of popular memory. With perhaps typically intellectualist disdain (and little recognition of varying popular interpretive practices), Foucault (1989, 92) argues that "people are shown not what they were, but what they must remember having been."[11]

Foucault (1989) believes that the loss of local control over popular memory occurred after World War II; he cites in particular the labor movement's practices of transmitting a "knowledge" of the struggles and resistances that came before. Writing about a series of films that attempt to present a less romantic view of war through the denial of heroism (which he views as the apparent "reappearance of history" from behind a veil of obvious state history), Foucault argues that the unstated meaning of the films is that there was no resistance to nazism. After France's internal dissention after May 1968, argues Foucault, the existing state history could no longer speak about the history of popular resistance:

> Popular struggles have become for our society, not part of the actual, but part of the possible. So they have to be set at a distance. How? Not by providing a direct interpretation of them, which would be asking to be exposed. But by offering an historical interpretation of those popular struggles which have occurred in France in the past, in order to show that they never really happened! (Foucault 1989, 102).

Both Foucault (1989) and Nora (1989) argue that forms of mass media and changes in the meaning of nation and the loss of microgroups result in the superimposition of two kinds of historical knowledge (in Foucault's terms) or memory—one that builds an edifice from the broken blocks of lost metanarratives and one that resists the totalizing efforts of such a deployment, however ineffective such postmodern populist tales may be.

Both theorists implicitly situate the agon of these memories in mass communication's effect of networking memories that conform to the failing dominant narratives. Foucault in particular laments the loss of sites for the popular, complaining about the lack of analogue for popular-resistance novels about labor history. This is a rare moment in which Foucault's barely excised nostalgia becomes nearly hysterical (a speech form of the "queen," which he must ignore in this and other arguments about performances of resistance); Nora, too, is overwhelmed by the loss of memory. Neither can bring himself to recognize the bricolagelike combination of kinetic moments of resistance, performances of difference, perspectival visions from the margin, and mute recognitions of power effected against the self that continues to form the comic-book story of subaltern place.

"VOGUE" IN PLACE: FORMATIONS OF SUBALTERN MEMORY

MTV is an important new site for the struggle over control of popular memory. Because of their short duration, music videos provide important raw material for the bricolage construction of memory links. The perpetually changing juxtaposition of videos suggests that meaning construction on MTV is more like the montage proposed by Sergei Eisenstein (1975) than the narrative trajectory widely accepted as cinerealism. Although there are not yet any comprehensive studies of MTV-watching behavior, it seems more likely that viewers half-listen for favorite songs or artists and half-watch for visual patterns that signify the style of their favorite musical genres.[12]

Situated in this panoply of meaning units, each with its own internal hermeneutic, *Vogue* exemplifies the transient but pivotal moments in the reconstruction of gay and Afro-Latin history in contemporary popular culture. Especially in its referencing of a certain segment of club culture, *Vogue* becomes the site of struggle over who will "own" the gender or racial problematic evident in the male-male/racialized stylistics of voguing. The voguing that pastiched the haughty white femininity by homosexual men who had a surplus of gender and color must be rewritten by mainstream culture as the province of men who can now attain beauty (a hypermasculine provenance) and "whiteness" (after the emergence of the "beige" model) (Willis 1990). But this rewrite occurs after the construction of double miscegenation that restabilizes race and gender on the shaky grounds of queer style.

Because Madonna reinscribes both "bitch" and "drag" as the province of female masquerade, the beauty of *Vogue* risks repudiating the difference constituted through the performance of femininity by homosexual men. The song blurts out its own confusion when it reverses the regendered "perversions" that voguing constituted: "Ladies with an attitude, fellas who were in the mood" neatly inverts the claims that voguing wished to make about male bitchiness ("attitude") and female desire ("in the mood"). Indeed, this misrecognition of the gender critique of voguing inadvertently restabilizes gender by returning us to what we thought we knew: that women are bitches and that men always "want it."

Madonna also mutely deconstructs race: Her black and Latina backup singers' tones blur into Madonna's, or, rather, they meet in the middle, beige middle ground, and the clothing and movement disperse the men's races. Hue-as-racial-difference is displaced only to reinscribe physiognomy as the more concrete mechanism for "knowing" "race." Although *Vogue* is ambivalent about racial and sexual markers, its coherent allegiance to highly evocative race and gender codes suggests that the video's politic is less a pluralistic vision of the essential humanness beneath race and gender than a postmodern surfacing of signs in a way that produces race and gender as only skin deep. This reconstruction of the gender or race problematic also marks the transition from "preliberation" to Rainbow Coalition culture: Interpreting *Vogue* is a struggle over who will claim the critique constituted through voguing culture.[13] In both its intertextual components and in the hype about the video's subject—voguing—*Vogue* constitutes a site of memory reconstituting Afro-Latin and gay history due to: (1) its prominence and popularity, (2) its self-referential claims to being a kind of history, and (3) its intertextual linkages.

COMMERCIAL "VOGUE"

Vogue was released on MTV with an unusual flourish. The first tease in a spring-through-summer onslaught of Madonna performances, *Vogue* prepared fans for and lured curious new consumers to the visually different, Brechtian, and highly erotic Blond Ambition tour. *Vogue* was the beginning of a complex set of "Madonna-emes," including her film *Dick Tracy* and the *I'm Breathless* album, which contained "Vogue" and "music inspired by" (but not, in fact, the sound track from) *Dick Tracy*. Masterfully orchestrated, the release of each of the major parts of the Madonna onslaught cre-

ated a set of intertextual relations that together and in their sequencing questioned the whole notion of spin-off marketing; indeed, it challenged the
notion of popular memory itself.

Dick Tracy is important in understanding the reconstruction of Madonna
at work here; the film was released after the *Vogue* video but before *I'm
Breathless* and, in some locations, slightly later than the beginning of the
tour. The *Vogue* video was the subject of the initial hype, whetting appetites
for the album and tour. The *Dick Tracy* hype followed almost immediately:
It was difficult for consumers to separate the actual sound track of the movie
from the simulacrum *I'm Breathless* album, which is raunchier and sexier
and which contains strong S/M overtones that formed the core of the Blond
Ambition tour. Together, *I'm Breathless* and *Dick Tracy* serve to reorient
fans to a new Madonna aesthetic: The hypermodernist Blond Ambition
tour, with S/M-esque costuming by Jean Paul Gaultier and lighting, dialogue, and dance recalling Bertolt Brecht and Alla Nazimova, and the nostalgic and morally anachronistic *Dick Tracy* shift Madonna backward in
star history.

The "tragic Marilyn" who emerges in *Material Girl* is transformed into
the more sexually provocative Mae West/Veronica Lake bad girls who preceded Monroe—of whom, indeed, Marilyn was the pastiche and aesthetic
break. Madonna, who was much more popular among African Americans
and especially African-American women at the beginning of her career, is
now fully converted into a gay cultural icon. Early Madonna capitalized on
rhythm and blues and the traditional African-American call and response
structure, with the latter visualized in the video version of the song "Like a
Prayer." The Blond Ambition tour abandoned the carefully constructed,
"womanist"[14] promotion of women strong enough to cope with men, and it
unleashed the queen of gender disorder and racial deconstruction who is so
disturbing to white feminists and white heterosexual men.[15]

HISTORICAL "VOGUE"

Vogue asks to be read as some sort of history in its use of black-and-white
photography and retro costuming and because it thematizes its own beginning and ending through the use of a feather fan to uncover and hide the picture. The fan, which does not appear elsewhere in the video (that is, it does
not take us to a particular place and is not controlled by anyone in the video), may also refer to the coquettishness of eighteenth-century femininity, a
theme picked up in the re-production of *Vogue* as a minuet in hot pants at
the 1990 "MTV Music Video Awards."[16] In the middle of the song, Madonna lists the names of iconic figures from gay male culture: Such hagio-

graphies are both a traditional form of history and a traditional mode of establishing one's lineage and thus one's authority to speak. Importantly, however, the video dehistoricizes itself at the precise moment it creates its history; the evocation of history is not connected to the specific history of voguing. Even the list of names is somewhat perplexing, including Joe Dimaggio, whose only connection to gay male iconography is as the man who married Marilyn Monroe.

In marked contrast is Malcolm McLaren's "Deep in Vogue," released the previous summer with a video featuring the mother of the House of Ninja. With its insistence on retaining the ballroom dance roots of voguing, "Deep in Vogue" received only moderate success in non-vogue-oriented gay clubs—it is undanceable by either disco or neopunk standards—and the video received little play on MTV. Like *Vogue*, McLaren's song deploys a list, but, unlike Madonna's work, it refers to the "real" Houses associated with voguing: "This has got to be a special tribute to the houses of New York / Le Beija, Extravaganza, Magnifique, St. Laurent, Omni, Ebony, Dupree" and, later, "The House of Extravaganza the House of Dupree / Who the hell are they? / They're nobody, except when they're in that little ballroom." This evocation and then apparent dismissal of the "real," of the Houses, underscores but at the same time misunderstands the situatedness of voguing culture. The Houses exist referentially, through membership, but they do more than compete against each other in balls. Although voguing now exists in bars and even on the streets,[17] *Vogue* situates it in a set that resembles a hotel lobby interior.[18] The ball-like, masquerade quality of voguing is represented in *Vogue* through the opening and closing of the feather fan and, like McLaren's "Deep in Vogue," through the promotion of a phenomenologic view of the body. According to a local vogue dancer: "You don't *learn* to vogue."[19]

Although seeing and imitating Madonna's *Vogue* in gay video bars connects two spaces of resistance, dispersing the dance into clubs partially forgets the collective resistance of diasporal queens of color who not only dance but have gangs and help each other learn how to get by in the city. And instead of inventing time, perhaps by evoking the Harlem Renaissance (as in Isaac Julian's earlier and stylistically similar *Looking for Langston*), Madonna's *Vogue* video flattens time by invoking the images of 1930s and 1940s films stars. This rerouting of cultural evocations from *being at* to *looking at* is how memory becomes nostalgia.

In McLaren's song, we learn that "it wasn't easy no 1, 2, 3 / It took a long time to learn to feel free." And in Madonna's *Vogue,* we are told, "Just let your body free." This insistence on freedom of movement confronts the banality of disco dancing transformed from innovation on a basic salsa into that which could be learned in dance classes. It also confronts the realities of intragroup violence among men, especially those who are in some way oppressed. Vogue is a "challenge" dance, as McLaren's lyrics tell us: "Instead of fighting you take it out on the dance floor."[20] In this way, it is remarkably similar to the Afro-Caribbean kick dancing that Katherine Dunham documented and transformed into her Method (Clark, forthcoming).

MADONNA, MADONNA

If the simulation of history in *Vogue* gestures toward but distracts us from a "real" vogue, numerous elements in the text point us to other moments in the later Madonna. This gives *Vogue* the feel of a milieu, a reference that links a set of themes within Madonna's work.

In an early segment, Madonna appears on the same couch and in the same room as in the pseudo-colorized scene in *Express Yourself,* a video that, in turn, draws on the visuals of Fritz Lang's 1926 *Metropolis;* this is a doubled reference because *Metropolis* was colorized and released with a sound track by current new wave and technopop musicians. In addition to its hotel lobbies referring to vogue culture, the video's shots of the male dancers "in pose" and of Madonna being "framed" refer to fashion magazine photography (coextensive with star photography of the same era), which both freezes and references the stylized movements in fashion shows.

The reference to fashion problematizes gender and not only because Madonna and her two female backup signers appear as men (again employing the monocle that Madonna sports in *Express Yourself,* where she masquerades as the industrialist or, rather, as Michael Jackson while performing the industrialist). A chain of memories of fashion history are posed here: Jean Paul Gaultier, one of the most gender-fucking designers of the late twentieth century, displays his fabulous bras, which are ideologically more like the codpiece in their opulent deformation of the underlying secondary sex trait. In the early 1980s, openly gay Gaultier met cries of misogyny with his first set of bra parodies. In 1984, his hugely controversial line of male dresses (historical critiques of contemporary machismo that updated the male skirt of Greek, Roman, and Scottish warriors) was barely reported on outside the fashion world (Ash 1989).

Madonna wears one of the more understated bras in *Express Yourself,* and the male dancers wear some of the most elaborate in the Blond Ambition tour production of "Like a Virgin." Taken together, the gendering of the breast is problematized through the evocation of breast envy ("Like a Virgin")—and, implicitly, men's desire to be lesbians—and breast suppression, in the segment of *Vogue* where three men open their jackets in a tightly cut series of shots, followed by Madonna opening her jacket to reveal not a vest but a Gaultier breast-piece. As Madonna has repeatedly quipped about her two female backup singers and herself, "We're the only real men on stage."

This comment defies being read as homophobic because gender, possession of the accoutrement of gender performance, and "homo"sexuality(ies) are completely destabilized in the latest of Madonna's assaults on postfeminist culture, culminating with *Justify My Love*, as Henderson discusses in this volume.

In its restylization, the vogue of *Vogue* suppresses part of the dance's gender polemic: The extremely feminine moves on the hypermasculine (especially the "black stud") body is lost in the more masculinized moves of the beige dancers in the video. The voguing of *Vogue* desocializes the dance, which is generally performed in pairs, trios, or lines or staged en masse and which contains considerably more aggressiveness than in the video version. In addition, *Vogue* masculinizes a queen's dance by smoothing out the moves and, through intercutting, by focusing much more on the face than one would experience in watching voguing live or in real time. *Vogue* presents itself as a dance video, but it deconstructs dance; unlike the breaking down of dance moves that occurs didactically in rap videos, *Vogue* obscures the dance in order to reproduce it.

POSTMODERN IDENTITY:
MADONNA-GENDER MEETS BEIGE

In *Vogue,* the proclamation that it "makes no difference if you are black or white, if you're a boy or a girl" is politically unsettling to feminists, gay activists, and black activists because it dismisses the "real" to which identity politics pretends an allegiance. On one hand, the libertarian body politic of *Vogue* trivializes the lived experience of black queens in particular, as the ground zero of racial, gender, and sexual oppression. On the other hand, Madonna's increasing use of Brechtian "estrangement effects" (minus the notion of a false consciousness) makes it difficult to dismiss our immersion in her postidentity space as mere nostalgia for a less oppressive world or as a guilty liberal catharsis.

I do not want to overidealize Madonna's work or interpolate a political intention that she might deny or fail to recognize. However, I do want to suggest that, though it may be true that "you can't learn to vogue," Madonna's dismissal of the "deep" truth of gender and racial difference is less a pluralist nostalgia in the service of oppressive color- or gender-blindness than it is an attempt to enlist us in a performance that, in its kinetics, deconstructs gender and race despite its dancer.

Vogue creates a site for the production of memories of difference that capriciously recombines the fragmented and despatialized environment of music/MTV/videos/dance bars into memories to be reembodied and rearticulated to a range of mainstream and subaltern memories. This choreographic—dare I say phenomenologic?—aspect of *Vogue* is a lieux de mem-oire, reconstructing a moment in gay cultural memory in which race and gender were viciously pastiched by the men most in the position to perform that critique.

But textual analysis provides us with only a glimpse of the ways in which popular culture artifacts connect with a wide range of memories and folk knowledges; textual analysis is mute at the moment that we try to under-stand how dancers operate in the lieux de memorie. Though we are likely to be met with resistance and dissimulation to the extent that we try to make cognitive the knowledges embodied in the dance, there are some interesting questions to be addressed through careful ethnographic work: How do peo-ple learn to vogue? What folk knowledges are passed on with the diffusion of the dance? When does voguing cease to be a hermeneutic for participation in and interpretation of mainstream gender ideals? When will voguing be judged by accuracy movements instead of a dancer's ability to "throw shade" or "give face" (that is, articulate "attitude")?

Vogue is stylized and taken to its limit in the Blond Ambition tour: Is it now too stylized, as if vogue were like an ethnic dance that can only be de-rivative and reproducible but not subject to interpretation (by audience or dancer)? What are the effects on subaltern mnemonic processes when some-thing like voguing passes through dominant culture and is situated as a memory of Madonna, rather than a link to the subaltern's invisible past?

DISPLACING MEMORY: TIME WITHOUT PLACE

Vogue creates a memory link—a simultaneity—to specific historical times without constructing a place of memory; that is, we get a "now" disjuncted from its "here." The space of the video and of MTV is doubly connected to a space of dance—both of the body in dance and the dance floor (space) that defines the edges of the body in movement. This dance space simultaneously constructs the body, constructs a situation for the body, and deconstructs the history of that body. The dance space is stretched in a way that elides the social. The embodied response to music and to the video's sound confuses the desire to dance and the desire to dance (and perform the critique consti-tuted through) this *particular* dance. The desire to imitate the video exceeds the desire for the knowledge or critique the dance embodies. Admonished to free ourselves from a painful world by "let[ting] your body move to the mu-sic," *Vogue* provides a stylistic paradigm for freedom of movement. This paradigm elides the sources of repression that the dance means to decon-struct because these sources are disassociated from the particularities of a culture of resistance. The moves of voguing deconstruct gender and race, but *Vogue* makes it difficult to recall why such a deconstruction might be desirable. Thus, in constructing its historicity, *Vogue* alludes to a popular memory of repression that it then anxiously undercuts by atomizing and dequeening the performance of the dance.

As a postmodern critic concerned about lodging arguments that rest on a hypostatized "real" in order to judge co-optation, I am anxious about suggesting that this restylization administers popular memory in the service of dominant culture. As an activist critic, I am being asked to evaluate *Vogue* and its role in perpetuating what many gay people see as a persistent appropriation of gay culture by a parasitic mainstream that cannot think up one of its own. As an incomplete resolution of my anxiety and my task, I would suggest that the particular points of difference, the specific "memories of difference" that are evoked in *Vogue*, invoke particular subject positions: Even if the overt history of black gay male oppression is difficult to find in the video, the critique of race and gender still leaks through. This decoding practice is something like a perverse form of "Jeopardy": Those in a position to know that voguing is the answer will understand that racial and gender oppression is the question. But, in privileging less anxious memories of one set of subject positions—heterosexual male beauty—a marginal history whose only cultural space is on the edge of popular memory is rerouted and a space for performance of cultural critique by queens of color perhaps lost.

Voguing thus becomes a sanitized, post-AIDS solo dance of (masculine) gay men, appropriable by heterosexual men who can learn without remembering, rather than a dance that ritualizes intragroup aggressions among queens and especially migratory queens of color. The roots of voguing in black/Caribbean/Latin homosexual culture and the critique of whiteness and masculinity that voguing contained is neatly evacuated in favor of a more acceptable source: that of chic gay male dance culture. This history of vogue, in which the dance is diffusely about gender and sexual *liberation*, then, is more comfortably situated in its emergence in clubs in the 1970s or 1980s. *Vogue* in part resituates postmodernist voguing, a practice of rhetorical alterity, into a modernist dance that merely liberates dancers from the constraints of a dull, conformist society. The longer chain of memories—to an aesthetic and lived reality of the interwar diaspora that facilitated the Harlem Renaissance—is blocked. This easier circuit of memory stops at the real situation of the contemporary dance bar—that great leveler of difference, place of escape and cultural production for subalterns, and site of cultural neutralization by the radical chic appropriation of underground forms. But this place is neither a utopia nor a narcotic: Postmodernity can have no utopia, no other place, no outside, nor can popular culture be read only as mystification or denial of oppression. Despite the video's effects of truncating memory, voguing may still resist accommodation to the minoritizing politics that must situate the Other somewhere in order to stabilize and mobilize for power under the current political regime. If *Vogue* cannot tell us from whence it came, that is because the lieux de memoire of voguing are not in a time or place but of the body.

NOTES

1. The Stonewall riots occurred in and outside the Stonewall Inn, a small gay bar in New York City, in June 1969, on the evening of gay icon Judy Garland's funeral. Patrons, chiefly Latino queens and butch lesbians, joined by a growing crowd of younger militant homosexuals, fought back against police in what might have been just another harassing raid on a gay bar. Barricaded inside the bar and destroying it and property outside, the patrons fought police for three days. Part folklore, part history, the Stonewall incident, celebrated as Gay and Lesbian Pride Day in June, now stands as an important moment in the popular memory of resistance for those who identify with the lesbian and gay movement. This two-decade-old movement, catalyzed by the riots, combined two long-standing waves of homosexual rights and homosexual libertarian activists with the ideas and rhetoric of the student antiwar and black civil rights movements. Most distinctively, gay liberation absorbed the critique of gender roles from contemporaneous second wave feminism.

2. Although it is always tempting to continue to reference Stonewall as the origin of current gay politics, the present civil rights–oriented groups like the National Lesbian and Gay Task Force and the lesbian and gay community centers in the dozen or so largest cities are quite continuous with the agenda of the early homophile movements, which were employing civil rights rhetoric and strategies by the early 1950s. The House Un-American Activities Committee investigations, which were at least as virulently homophobic as they were anti-Communist, were another catalyzing moment in gay civil rights history. In an interesting sense, the events at the Stonewall Inn were much more anarchistic and liberationistic in form, despite their reconstruction as the genesis of current civil rights activities.

3. This reaches its peak in the constellation of the Jean Paul Gaultier breast-pieces that are worn by Madonna in *Vogue* but by ("male") dancers during the Blond Ambition tour, most daringly in a restylization of the song "Like a Virgin," which features Madonna apparently masturbating in a red velvet bed with two dancers in enormous breast-pieces who fondle and lick her and each other. The phallus/projectile icon is doubled and transformed into either paired, chest-mounted penises or dagger-like breasts.

4. See Robert Stam's use of Bakhtin's ideas to argue that rock Africanized American culture in "Mikhail Bakhtin and Left Cultural Critique" (1989, 116–145).

5. Marlon Riggs's *Tongues Untied* (1989) adopts the term "Negro faggotry" to evade both gay (white) liberation connotations of homosexuality and black power connotations of race.

6. Henry Louis Gates, Jr. (1987, 1988) argues that the unifying aesthetic and formal value in Afro-American literature is the practice of signifying, in which a person of lesser social power indirectly ridicules one of greater social power. This is accomplished in such a way that the person in greater power is unsure of the insult and thus

cannot respond or is made a fool of in front of other marginal people who understand the joke.

7. Following Michel Foucault's ground-breaking work on the history of sexuality, a major current of gay and lesbian history considers homosexuality as we know it to be of recent genesis. Its emergence is situated variously by different scholars between the seventeenth and nineteenth centuries. Against this current is a (perhaps increasingly smaller) group of scholars who view homosexuality as pancultural and transhistorical and only marginally different in its forms. An excellent review of these debates is contained in *Homosexuality, Which Homosexuality?* London: Gay Men's Press, 1989, especially Carole S. Vance's (1989) contribution.

A critical issue in gay and lesbian historiography is, of course, not only what counts as a homosexual but what counts as evidence of homosexuality. In general, those in the latter, transcendental, or essentialist camp are positivist in their orientation, requiring considerable license at times to extrapolate positive evidence of homosexual relations even in times of most resounding silence.

8. I am following de Certeau's (1988, XIX) supplanting of "institution" with the idea of a "proper"—a space in which "force-relationships which becomes possible when a subject of will and power (a proprietor, an enterprise, a city, a scientific institution) can be isolated from an 'environment.' " This space is doubly generative, also creating exteriorities—"competitors, adversaries, 'clienteles,' 'targets,' or 'objects' of research." This set of relations permits "strategies." Alternatively, there are "tactics" that "cannot count on a 'proper' (a spatial or institutional localization), nor thus on a borderline distinguishing the other as a visible totality . . . a tactic insinuates itself into the other's place, fragmentarily, without taking it over in its entirety, without being able to keep it at a distance."

9. It seems to me that though gender-inappropriate significations are hurled at homo and hetero alike in order to police gender, those who intend to signal their homo-sexualities must invoke these gender-transgressions but claim them as completely true. Homosexuals are usually represented as "hiding"; the structure of denial of homosexuality that stabilizes gender makes it paradoxical, even illogical, to claim homosexuality and stable gender. Thus, "passing" by the self-claimed homosexual is more a matter of not failing to conform to gender expectations than of hiding the already hidden "truth" of sexuality.

For African Americans and other marked ethnic, cultural, or national groups, passing is more often represented as actively producing an identity that is not true. What passing means and what it accomplishes is very different within and outside African-American communities. Both gay and racial passing ambivalently invoke a hidden and truer essence.

10. On the battle over images, see Marotta (1982), D'Emilio (1983), Dyer (1982), Newton (1972), Neale (1983), and Duggan (1988).

Signifying and passing include production and interpretation of markers of homosexual membership by both gay and straight men. Thus, production and interpretation occur both among those intending to signify their difference and among those seeking to identify difference in order to shore up their claim to normalcy. Notice that signifiers and passers or episodes of signifying or passing include straight men: They, too, must work within or attempt to avoid the markers that become associated with queerness, must produce and interpret the shifting and nuanced codes that mark difference and their difference from gay difference.

The gay-coded "Marlboro man" models provide an excellent example of this vertiginous preoccupation with choosing the right masculine codes. Both gay and straight men imitate the iconic Marlboro man, though perhaps for different reasons. But what should they adopt? The mustache and haircut that characterized the late 1970s gay "clone" set and appear on the Marlboro man set the most corporeal elements of signification somewhat at odds with the machowear drag, which was part of but not exclusively associated with clone culture. The invocation of a masculine memory of the homosocial world of cowboys, combined with the insertion of a gay-coded model, suggests an explanation for the erotic power of the (all-male) cowboy memory. But at the same time, the association of masculinity with subjectivity and the pretense that all-male social fantasies are bereft of objects are disrupted by the blatant objectification of the Marlboro man. As Dyer (1982) suggests, "we" do not know if we want to be him or have him. That the Marlboro men are so obviously coded gay (and, as it would turn out, one of the most famous would doubly mark his queerness by dying, with considerable publicity, of an AIDS-related illness) squares the gender calculus problem: Do we want to be queer *like* him or queer *for* him?

11. Foucault (1989, 92) goes on to say that "since memory is actually a very important factor in struggle (really, in fact, struggles develop in a kind of conscious moving forward of history), if one controls people's memory, one controls their dynamism."

12. Without conducting any sort of systematic survey, it seems clear to me that there are at least half a dozen visual strategies. The heavy metal videos most stridently criticized for their misogyny are most often concert videos intercut with fantasy sequences or flashbacks of the incidents that inspired the song. Punk/new wave videos are most often surrealist and also include segments of the full band playing but dislocated in nonconcert places. Rhythm and blues videos frequently contain narratives that resemble musicals, with the leader singer playing the role and singing about the drama. Rap has the most complex and varied look, although the basic components are the hypermimetics of classic minstrel, the intercutting of black-and-white historical footage, the Paul Bartel/Pee Wee Herman–like appearance of the lead singer in the settings he or she describes, and facial close-ups to emphasize the physiognomic aspects of rap's wordplay. Madonna, too, has a style of her own; *Like a Prayer* relies on Afro-American storytelling traditions, and the work from *Express Yourself* to *Vogue* is unrelentingly Brechtian in concept. Interestingly, it is rap that most self-consciously debates the status of history and "tellings"; see Burns (1990).

13. Jenny Livingston's recent *Paris Is Burning* (1991), a Wisemanesque documentary about ball culture, is one of the first mass-distributed, sympathetic sets of images of black gay men. However, it avoids the crucial battle over interpretation of voguing by constituting itself as a dictionary of terms and insisting that voguing is about imitating rather than deconstructing gender. Much better is Marlon Riggs's *Tongues Untied* (1989), which disrupts the discourse of "the real" that is shared by documentary film, however self-reflexive, and the dominant culture's inscription of bipolar gender. In an important sense, it is not possible to make a documentary about voguing, especially in the Wisemanesque style that carefully invokes a deep structure of hidden cultures or hidden psychologies that only the most unmediated filmic techniques can begin to reveal. A documentary may only be able to inhabit or construct a modernist world in

which direct cinema may reveal glimpses of that which is behind ideology; see Patton (1982).

14. Alice Walker, in particular, but also other black feminist critics, have chosen the word *womanist* to indicate a form of African-American feminism that existed prior to the white middle-class feminism that emerged in the 1960s. They argue that what white feminists had to learn, black women already knew; womanist politics attempts to critique men and masculinity without splitting racial community along gender lines.

15. See Chapter 1 on Madonna haters.

16. I am indebted to Cathy Schwichtenberg for reminding me of this linkage.

17. Marlon Riggs's *Tongues Untied* (1989) brilliantly and poignantly acts out the conflicts between men of color that result from racism and homophobia, each, in turn, etched through gender strictures. Preferring the term "Negro faggotry," Riggs uses documentary techniques, pastiche, and dissimulation to fashion the story of the men whose style is taken up in *Vogue*. The film contains clips of men voguing in the streets at night in San Francisco, where voguing is now more popular and "less passé" than in New York City.

18. The visuals and interior setting of *Vogue* bear a striking resemblance to those in Isaac Julian's *Looking for Langston*, which was released in the fall of 1989 and addressed similar themes of history, reconstructive narrative, black gay men's oppression, and racial and gender ambiguity.

19. This is according to a devoted voguer. I thank Patty Lau, who interviewed several young men about voguing shortly after the release of Madonna's video and videotaped them performing their vogue to the new Madonna song. I had seen these young men (who "learned" to vogue in New York and later in Springfield, Massachusetts) in a local club and suggested that Lau engage in some "salvage" ethnography and attempt to document this periphery of culture in transition. After discussions with a number of the local voguers, Lau conducted a more formal interview with an especially articulate and knowledgeable young man from this group. I use the interview with her permission.

20. Although the McLaren song was played only in select (probably gay male) clubs, it is my impression that the lyrics provided a more didactic sense of voguing's history for young queens who may have already learned the dance. Lau's (1990) interview with "Billy" contains several sections in which he appears to be appropriating the lyrics in the McLaren song, apparently as "native" explanations of voguing. This provides some preliminary ethnographic evidence for the thesis presented here that popular culture artifacts are crucial spaces for linking memories of resistance to a perceived present.

REFERENCES

Althusser, L. (1969). *Reading Capital*. London: Allen Lane.
Ash, J. (1989). "The Business of Couture." In Angela McRobbie (ed.), *Zoot Suits and Second-Hand Dresses: An Anthology of Fashion and Music*. Boston, Mass.: Unwin and Hyman, pp. 208–214.

Burns, S. (1990). "Black Cultural Politics in 1990." Master's thesis, Amherst College.

Butler, J. (1990). *Gender Trouble: Feminism and the Subversion of Identity.* New York: Routledge.

Clark, V. A. (Forthcoming). "Performing the Memory of Difference in Afro-Caribbean Dance: Katherine Dunham's Choreography, 1938–1987." *History and Memory in Afro-American Culture.* In Genevieve Fabre, Melvin Dixon, and Robert O'Meally (eds.), Memory and History Group of the Dubois Institute, Harvard University.

de Certeau, M. (1988). *The Practice of Everyday Life.* Berkeley: University of California Press.

D'Emilio, J. (1983). *Sexual Politics/Sexual Communities.* Chicago, Ill.: University of Chicago Press.

Derrida, J. (1981). *Positions.* Chicago, Ill.: University of Chicago Press.

Duggan, L. (1988). "The Anguished Cry of an '80s Fem: 'I Want to Be a Drag Queen.'" *Outlook* 1, no. 1 (Spring): 62–65.

Dyer, R. (1982). "Don't Look Now: The Instability of the Male Pin-Up." *Screen* 23, no. 3/4 (September–October): 61–73.

Eisenstein, S. (1975). *The Film Sense.* New York: Harcourt, Brace, and World.

Foucault, M. (1989). "Film and Popular Memory." In Sylvère Lotringer (ed.), *Foucault Live.* Foreign Agent Series. New York: Semiotext(e), pp. 89–106.

Fuss, D. (1989). *Essentially Speaking: Feminism, Nature, and Difference.* New York: Routledge.

Gabriel, T. H. (1988). "Thoughts on Nomadic Aesthetics and Black Independent Cinema: Traces of a Journey." In Mbye B. Cham and Claire Andrade-Watkins (eds.), *Blackframes: Critical Perspectives on Black Independent Cinema.* Cambridge, Mass.: Massachusetts Institute of Technology Press, pp. 62–79.

Garber, E. (1989). "A Spectacle in Color: The Lesbian and Gay Subculture of Jazz Age Harlem." In Martin Bauml Duberman, Martha Vicinus, and George Chauncey, Jr., (eds.), *Hidden from History: Reclaiming the Gay and Lesbian Past.* New York: New American Library, pp. 318–331.

Gates, H. L., Jr. (1987). *Figures in Black: Words, Signs and the "Racial" Self.* Oxford: Oxford University Press.

———. (1988). *The Signifying Monkey.* Oxford: Oxford University Press.

Gledhill, C. (1988). "Pleasurable Negotiations." In E. Deídre Príbram (ed.), *Female Spectators: Looking at Film and Television.* London: Verso, pp. 64–89.

Haraway, D. (1991). *Simians, Cyborgs, and Women: The Reinvention of Nature.* New York: Routledge.

Harding, S. (1986). *The Science Question in Feminism.* Ithaca, N.Y.: Cornell University Press.

hooks, b. (1990). "Marginality as a Site of Resistance." In Russell Ferguson, Martha Gever, Trinh T. Minh-ha, and Cornel West (eds.), *Out There: Marginalization and Contemporary Culture.* Cambridge, Mass.: Massachusetts Institute of Technology Press.

Julian, I. (1989). *Looking for Langston* (film).

Katz, J. N. (1990). "Inventing Heterosexuality." *Socialist Review* 20, no. 1 (January–March): 7–34.

Lau, P. (1990). "The Queen Is Dead." Interview with "Billy."

Livingston, Jenny. (1991). *Paris Is Burning* (documentary film).

McLaren, Malcolm, and The Bootzilla Orchestra. (1989). *Waltz Darling*. CBS Records (Epic).

Marotta, T. (1982). *The Politics of Homosexuality*. Boston, Mass.: Houghton Mifflin Company.

Mercer, K. (1988). "Diaspora Culture and the Dialogic Imagination: The Aesthetics of Black Independent Film in Britain." In Mbye B. Cham and Claire Andrade-Watkins (eds.), *Blackframes: Critical Perspectives on Black Independent Cinema*. Cambridge, Mass.: Massachusetts Institute of Technology Press, pp. 50–61.

———. (1990) . "Black Hair/Style Politics." In Russell Ferguson, Martha Gever, Trinh T. Minh-ha, and Cornel West (eds.), *Out There: Marginalization and Contemporary Culture*. Cambridge, Mass.: Massachusetts Institute of Technology Press, pp. 247–264.

Neale, S. (1983). "Masculinity As Spectacle." *Screen* 24, no. 6 (November–December): 2–16.

Newton, E. (1972). *Mother Camp: Female Impersonators in America*. Chicago, Ill.: University of Chicago Press.

Nora, P. (1989). "Between Memory and History: *Les Lieux de Memoire.* " *Representations* 26 (Spring): 7–25.

Patton, C. (1982). "Creating Fact from Fiction/Creating Fiction from Fact." *Visions* 6, no. 1 (February): 6, 7.

Riggs, M. (1989). *Tongues Untied* (film).

Riviere, J. (1986). "Womanliness as Masquerade." In Victor Burgin, James Donald, and Cora Kaplan (eds.), *Formations of Fantasy*. New York: Methuen, pp. 35–44.

Roach, J., and P. Felix. (1989). "Black Looks." In Lorraine Gamman and Margaret Marshment (eds.), *The Female Gaze*. Seattle, Wash.: Real Comet Press, pp. 130–142.

Sedgwick, E. (1985). *Between Men: English Literature and Male Homosocial Desire*. New York: Columbia University Press.

———. (1990) . *The Epistemology of the Closet*. Berkeley: University of California Press.

Solomon, M. (1979). *Marxism and Art: Essays Classic and Contemporary*. Detroit, Mich.: Wayne State University Press.

Spivak, G. C. (1990). "Explanation and Culture: Marginalia." In Russell Ferguson, Martha Gever, Trinh T. Minh-ha, and Cornel West (eds.), *Out There: Marginalization and Contemporary Culture*. Cambridge, Mass.: Massachusetts Institute of Technology Press, pp. 377–393.

Stam, R. (1989). "Mikhail Bakhtin and Left Cultural Critique." In E. Ann Kaplan (ed.), *Postmodernism and Its Discontents*. New York: Verso, pp. 116–145.

Vance, C. S. (1989). "Social Construction Theory: Problems in the History of Sexuality." *Homosexuality, Which Homosexuality? International Conference on Gay and Lesbian Studies*. London: Gay Men's Press, pp. 13–34.

Wallace, M. (1990). "Modernism, Postmodernism and the Problem of the Visual in Afro-American Culture." In Russell Ferguson, Martha Gever, Trinh T. Minh-ha, and Cornel West (eds.), *Out There: Marginalization and Contemporary Culture.* Cambridge, Mass.: Massachusetts Institute of Technology Press, pp. 39–50.

Williamson, J. (1988). "Two Kinds of Otherness: Black Film and the Avant-Garde." *Black Film/British Cinema.* Document 7. London: Institute of Contemporary Art.

Willis, S. (1990). "I Want the Black One." *New Formations* 10 (Spring): 77–98.

LISA HENDERSON **5**

Justify Our Love: Madonna & the Politics of Queer Sex

ON DECEMBER 3, 1990, ABC's "Nightline" introduced the unedited version of Madonna's new video *Justify My Love* amid promotional fanfare and a controversy at once specific and general. The immediate blow had been dealt by MTV, the music video network that, days earlier, had announced its decision not to show Madonna's latest product. "She makes great videos," noted an official MTV statement, "but this one's not for us" (Holden 1990, C18).

For critics and fans, it was an odd scenario—MTV rejecting its premier pop star, whose stylistic developments had arguably marked (and marketed) the evolution of music television itself. Though the company's statement reportedly did not explain why the network had turned down *Justify My Love*, the video's type and degree of sexual explicitness seemed the likely culprit, ironically so since sexual modesty was hardly MTV's signature position. As Madonna would point out in her "Nightline" interview, she had bent the network's "rules" on nudity once before, baring her breasts in *Vogue*, which MTV had programmed despite her refusal to cut the offending shot. "I guess half of me thought I was going to get away with it, that I was going to convince them," she told Forrest Sawyer on "Nightline," "and the other half thought, well, with the censorship and conservatism that is sort of sweeping over the nation, I thought that there was going to be a problem."

What Madonna called the "conservatism sweeping the nation" inflected the more general controversy surrounding the broadcast release of *Justify My Love*. For over a year, the National Endowment for the Arts had been under fire from Sen. Jesse Helms of North Carolina, among others, for disbursing public funds to organizations that had exhibited the work of photographers Andres Serrano and Robert Mapplethorpe. Helms and others had designated both artists as depraved and immoral—Serrano for blasphemy (his image *Piss Christ* depicted a crucifix submerged in a jar of urine)

107

and Mapplethorpe for homoeroticism. Amid the vocal resurgence of "traditional family values" in the United States and the antigay backlash intensified by the AIDS crisis, the specter of perverse and unbridled sexuality had proven a political gold mine for Helms and an issue that few of his Senate colleagues were prepared to take on.

Though *Justify My Love* was hardly funded by the NEA, the endowment controversy was, indeed, germane to Madonna's (and the video's) appearance on "Nightline."[1] ABC television had advertised the show as a "discussion of art and censorship," precisely the topic animating art world opposition to the Helms amendment. Eight weeks earlier, on October 5, the director of the Cincinnati Contemporary Arts Center had been acquitted of obscenity charges brought against him for exhibiting the Mapplethorpe photographs. But that same week, a Florida record store proprietor had been found guilty of similar charges for selling the 2 Live Crew recording *As Nasty As They Wanna Be.*

Enter Madonna, solicited for her response to the MTV ban and poised between 2 Live Crew and Mapplethorpe as both commercial performer and self-acclaimed and critically praised artiste. Madonna and the "Nightline" producers could have their cake and eat it too with a "public affairs" debut of *Justify My Love* that would attract three overlapping constituencies: the righteously indignant on questions of public morality, those in the liberal establishment piqued by the recent censorship debates, and, most important from a ratings perspective, a huge and heterogeneous ensemble of Madonna fans. Indeed, despite the 1:00 A.M. airtime (following "Monday Night Football") and the threat of war in the Persian Gulf, the Madonna program generated "Nightline's" biggest 1990 audience to date (Cocks 1990, 75).

Included in that audience was a devoted (if unsurveyed) contingent of lesbians and gay men. Unlike Mapplethorpe, Madonna had never identified herself as a gay artist, but also unlike Mapplethorpe, at least prior to the Helms debacle, she had circulated bits and pieces of lesbian and gay subculture in popular genres to popular audiences. Especially for many young gay people in the United States, Madonna came closer than any other contemporary celebrity to being an aboveground queer icon.

In this chapter, I focus on *Justify My Love* and its reception in the mainstream and gay press to consider Madonna's resonance in lesbian and gay culture, particularly her privileged, if ambivalent, position in gay sexual politics. As a popular figure, Madonna speaks to—if not for—lesbian and gay fans and critics amid the oppressions and retrenchments of the sexual counterrevolution. This reactionary tide draws its momentum from a continuing series of legal and cultural initiatives stoked by Helms and his ilk, who recognize and fear changes wrought in the sexual and political landscape by the women's and gay liberation movements of the late 1960s.[2] For some, Madonna is an emblem of sexual resistance, an embodiment of the same in-your-face sexuality evoked by Queer Nation's slogan, "We're here, we're queer, get used to it." Her image reincarnations connote the playful and painful liminalities of lesbian and gay life—always vigilant, always self-conscious, sometimes exposed, sometimes concealed. Unlike other contemporary pop stars, moreover, Madonna seems to want her lesbian and gay fans. Still, she inhabits gay consciousness as a popular guest, despite her status elsewhere as cultural proprietor, and thus her gay presence reveals something about the politics and dynamics of cultural appropriation.

"NIGHTLINE" POLICES THE BOUNDARIES

On "Nightline," however, queer identification was not an angle Forrest Sawyer was inclined to pursue. Instead, *Justify My Love* encountered the standard oppositional news frame: On one side, we saw Madonna as siren and business executive, her red lipstick offset by a black blazer and her peroxide blonde hair pulled back in a corporate sweep. On the other, we saw Sawyer as investigator and everyviewer, his jacket, hairstyle, and tie both serious and familiar. Where Madonna had constructed her persona from metamorphosis, Sawyer had constructed his from tradition and consistency: She was feminine "artifice"; he was masculine "news," the real thing. The satellite image favored this distinction, with Sawyer seated comfortably amid the trappings of the "Nightline" studio and Madonna uncharacteristically pinned in close-up by the on-screen monitor, her awkward address to the camera reminiscent of a "Dating Game" bachelorette on the far side of a studio barrier.

Their exchange was set up by an introductory piece barely decipherable from MTV in its busy pastiche of Madonna video clips and earlier television interviews. "Nightline" correspondent Ken Kashiwahara declared that even Madonna's "serious" endeavors, like the "Rock the Vote" spot, were sexually provocative and concluded that "she had carved a career out of controversy." Sawyer followed with a disclaimer about *Justify My Love*'s graphic nudity and sexuality. "This being late at night, we expect that only adults are watching," he cautioned, a coy gesture given the realities of time shifting (home video recording) and the network's heavy promotion of the video and interview during peak teenage program hours (Beck 1990, A6).

Throughout the interview, Sawyer relied on conventional baiting about sexual propriety. Had not Madonna "pushed the envelope?" he inquired, a question seemingly answered by her presence on the program. Sawyer never asked *why* she had pushed, nor did he take seriously her challenges to sexual double standards. He had apparently decided beforehand that Madonna, not MTV, had gone too far, and he pointedly conveyed that he was wise to her motives; soon to be distributed on the first video single, *Justify My Love* was, he indicated, simply a publicity stunt by one of pop music's "best self-marketers." "In the end, you're going to wind up making more money than you would have," Sawyer declared, as though this were news and also as though his own vehicle, "Nightline," was beyond the defilements of capital. With material-girl alacrity, Madonna exposed Sawyer's pretense—"Yeah," she smiled, "so lucky me."

Later in the interview, in a halting manner more characteristic of her performance throughout the program, Madonna reminded Sawyer that those parents who might object to her version of sex education "weren't doing their job." Teenage pregnancy was at an all-time high, she pointed out, and AIDS was rising at a "frightening rate in the heterosexual community." Here was some real-world thinking rarely displayed by pop stars, which added a facet to Madonna's persona that contradicted Sawyer's intimations about her sexual "irresponsibility." Her reference to the "heterosexual community," moreover, invoked the political discourse of lesbian and gay activism, where talk of *sexually* identified groups had originated and where heterosexuality was routinely denaturalized precisely by being specified: If you meant heterosexual, you had to say heterosexual—it could not longer be presumed. The comment also resisted bigoted illusions about AIDS as a gay affliction, however tragic its consequences in gay communities. Here and elsewhere on "Nightline," Madonna managed to challenge the sexual status quo in spite of Sawyer's concerted evasions. Some gay and lesbian writers would claim a similar victory for *Justify My Love*.

SCENES FROM A VIDEO

Wearing a loosely sashed black coat over lace lingerie, Madonna enters a hotel corridor, her high blond hair barely contrasting the stark walls. She carries a satchel, swaying under its weight as the camera sways with her. Both image and music connote the headiness of arousal, the unsteady camera accompanied by syncopated percussion at once pumping and distant and the continuous, minor-key strains of synthesizer and reverberant vocal. The camera pans across an open doorway to reveal an ambiguously female figure, with heavily made-up white face and slicked black hair, draped in satin and beads, chin dropped through deadened eyes looking to the lens—a prelude to *Justify My Love*'s sexual demimonde and surrealist homage. "I want to kiss you in Paris / I want to hold your hand in Rome," voices a sultry Madonna on sound track and screen.

Tony Ward, former gay porn model and Madonna's lover on camera and off when the video was shot, joins her from the end of the corridor. Disheveled and wanting, he moves slowly but deliberately toward her as she squats against a wall, her coat and legs open to expose stockings and garters and her hand drawn autoerotically across the top of her thigh. She reaches behind Ward's legs and pulls herself up to an open-mouthed kiss: "You put this in me / So now what, so now what / Wanting, needing, waiting / For you to justify my love." Another sequence of doorway figures depict a man and woman standing, laced into leather, she with one hand propped on a wall, turning over her shoulder to watch him behind her; a second woman, alone, in leather bikini and corset, is framed from the neck down as she twists her fleshy hips and pulls the corset against her nipples; finally, the recurring, sylphlike figure of a male dancer in silhouette, his fingers extended by stiletto nails, his long, supple arms stretching away from his body in front and back, his torso arching and curving with erotic grace.

Alternately steamy and campy, *Justify My Love* continues in one of the rooms, Ward and Madonna stripping down to skivvies and lace. He is top to her bottom, then the roles reverse. Crucifixes dangle conspicuously from Ward's neck as the camera tightens on his torso. "Not like that," resists Madonna, pushing him away. Other figures enter the scene, kin to the stylized denizens of the earlier rooms. They, too, are androgynous, made up, and euphoric. Some are black, some Latin, some white. They recline with Madonna, sprawl langorously across Ward, flirt in serious and clever gestures. The face of one enters the top of the frame, descending slowly to meet Madonna's supine body. Is it male or female? It is hard to tell for us or for Ward, who is visible in the background of their open kiss, a voyeur at his lover's bedside: "I don't wanna be your mother / I don't wanna be your sister either / I just wanna be your lover."

A woman enters in low angle through an arched doorway. Strident, barebreasted, and decked in black suspenders and military cap, she turns Ward's mouth to hers with a tight hold on his chin, then reaches across his body harness to grip his crotch: "Tell me your dreams / Am I in them? / Tell me your fears / Are you scared? / Tell me your stories / I'm not afraid of who you are." Two men face each other in close profile, one penciling a moustache on the other. The camera moves through them to Madonna, who looks to the lens and giggles into her hand: "For you to justify my love."

When the scene is over Madonna swans from the room, leaving a spent Ward alone on the couch. She hurries back down the corridor, smiling, shaking her wrist, and rolling her eyes in a burlesque of Parisian ooh-la-la. The video closes with song lyrics keyed on screen: "Poor is the man / Whose pleasures depend / On the permission of another."

In its sexual stances, *Justify My Love* defies some of music video's worst clichés, opening up an aesthetic and political corner for other ways of envisioning sex in popular culture. Unlike most MTV clips (ZZ Top's come to mind), it eroticizes all its characters—female, male, and those in between, black and white—fondly entangling them in a collective fantasy even as it foregrounds its star. Madonna's voice, *her* voice, orchestrates that fantasy, whose polymorphism slips and slides around conventional video images of sensation and arousal.

Absent are the routine degradations of MTV's rough boys, Sam-Kinnison-spits-on-Jessica-Hahn-who-crawls, to paraphrase Madonna on "Nightline." Rigid gender definition, long used to punish masculine women and feminine men as dykes and fags, wavers under the handiwork of drag and with it rigid assignments of sexual attraction. (Is Madonna lip to lip with a woman? Is Ward seduced to the couch by a beautiful beau?) Late in the scene, we are treated to Madonna's giggle, a reflexive frame-break that connotes both fantasy and the occasional silliness of sexual rituals—an instance of her satiric insight, fessing up to the conventionality of both sex and video (cf. Fiske 1989, 104–105). And as always, there are the collusions of desire and faith—Ward's religious pendants gracing bare flesh and the lyrics "poor is the man . . ." first voiced over an oblique image of Christ on the cross behind the undulations of the supple dancer (Layton 1990, A15). It is Madonna's staple comment, perhaps, on the sexual repressions and hypocrisies of Catholicism.

For many lesbian and gay people, the lyrics (and later the epigram) also echo their refusal to await sanction, from Helms or the church, to have sex and to forge their identities through the medium of sexual politics. Joining each other on the dance floors of gay clubs, where *Justify My Love* played as song and video even while it was banned by MTV, lesbian and gay people could (and did) shimmy and sway in sexy solidarity, sparked by the song's rhythmic seductions. Though dismissed by a few unimaginative press critics as not much of a recording, it was, briefly, a queer anthem.

But like most of Madonna's videos, *Justify My Love*'s messages are at least double edged and at once unfamiliar and familiar, liberating and conforming. Madonna remains the essential female spectacle, made up and laced up (à la Monroe) to denote her unambiguous feminity and thus her appeal to heterosexual male fantasy. (Imagine if, instead, she had dressed herself for the video in Annie Lennox's striking version of Elvis Presley or even her own version of Marlon Brando—then where would her audience be?) Many of *Justify My Love*'s sexual gestures depend on dominance and subordination for their effect, overturning the standard of mutuality in much feminist and humanist rethinking of sexual relationships. For some viewers, such images are likely to evoke not erotic choices but real-life sexual coercion and brutality, the experience of huge numbers of girls and women in the United States and abroad. And what are we to think of the hotel? It is an agreeably dramatic and sequestered place for a sexual encounter, and the corridor is a compelling metaphor for Madonna's psychic wanderings. But it is also a brothel, a venue where the sale of sexual services has long benefited men and subjugated women as sexual and economic property, notwithstanding Madonna's coy gender reversals in *Justify My Love*. The sexual ambiguities, finally, are just that—ambiguous. We do not know for sure that Madonna does not kiss a woman, nor do we know for sure that she does. In a pop cultural universe that makes heterosex abundant and abundantly clear, allusions to homosex are nice but not enough. Postmodernism's playful indeterminacy becomes gay activism's short shrift.

ARTICULATING SEX

This critique, however, overlooks the *rearticulation,* under some circumstances, of precisely those signifiers of hetero/sexist oppression. It also overlooks extrinsic sources of Madonna's persona, meaning her performances beyond the video itself. On "Nightline," for example, Madonna stated that *Justify My Love* depicts two people being honest with each other about their sexual fantasies, "regardless of their sex." Wearing his usual blinders, Forrest Sawyer ignored this reference to same-gender eroticism, but lesbian and gay viewers could seize on it, recruit it to the task of interpreting *Justify My Love*'s ambiguous kiss as a statement about sexual fluidity or even lesbianism, rather than Madonna's cleverly finessed evasion. Such appropriations do not seek to resolve the "true" meanings of an image but to fleece the cultural repertoire and ensconce its bits and pieces—here, the kiss scene and Madonna's comment—in new or oppositional discourses and practices. Marilyn Monroe, after all, may have been the quintessential 1950s pinup for straight (white) men, but she also became a staple figure of the gay drag circuit.

In the language of cultural theory, these fleecings may be *articulated* to social movements, creating new political forces. Following Antonio Gramsci, Stuart Hall (1982, 1986) uses the concept of articulation to theorize the relative autonomy of ideology. Unlike classical Marxist thinkers, who see ideology as the necessary outcome of socioeconomic structures and positions, Hall (1982) argues that ideology or the "struggle over meaning" is importantly connected to but not wholly determined by class struggle. In his analysis, articulation means both "expression, " in the conventional sense, and "linking," in the sense implied by the British phrase *an articulated lorry,* a truck whose cab and trailer "can, but need not necessarily, be connected to one another" (Hall 1986, 53). Like trailer and cab, cultural forms can be articulated or connected to specific political meanings and groups, but this is a matter of social process: They do not necessarily or automatically carry those meanings nor reflect those groups. Hall (1986, 55) argues that, indeed, the popular force of any ideology depends on the social groups who engage it, who can be "articulated to and by it."

In the domain of theory, articulation is a construct with no necessary valence. It refers to the process of fusing ideologies and groups to produce social and political forces, whether those forces are dominant or subordinate, progressive or reactionary. But in the contemporary movement for lesbian and gay rights, articulation also plays a central role as a symbolic and political strategy. This is illustrated, for example, by the lesbian and gay community's use of the word *queer*. Long spoken by nongay bigots as a term of indictment (or by gays themselves as one of self-loathing), this word has been reclaimed by lesbians and gay men, along with bisexuals, transvestites, and transsexuals, as a proud declaration of nonconformist sexualities. "Queerness" has thus been articulated to a new group of speakers (queers themselves, rather than homophobes) and a new agenda (queer liberation, rather than heterosexist oppression) in the evolution of the movement as a social force. The process, however, might be better labeled *re*articulation, to emphasize a conscious transformation away from the conventional meanings of dominant groups.[3]

In gay politics, rearticulation as a strategy is also illustrated by the AIDS Coalition to Unleash Power (ACT-UP), whose members have claimed the "power of representation" for the movement (Crimp and Rolston 1990, 13) and have created witty and provocative images in fighting the conservative agendas of business, government, science, and medicine. An example comes from Gran Fury, a radical art collective in ACT-UP New York. One of Gran Fury's posters (pasted conspicuously around the city to announce an ACT-UP demonstration) pairs a caduceus, the traditional symbol of the medical profession, with the boldface statement, **ALL PEOPLE WITH AIDS ARE INNOCENT.** The poster harnesses the idea of medical responsibility to a *refusal* of the mass media's specious distinction between "innocent victims" of AIDS (newborns, blood transfusion recipients) and "guilty" ones (gay men, IV drug users, sex industry workers). It thus demands "the equal and compassionate treatment . . . for all people with AIDS" (Crimp and Rolston 1990, 53).

The Gran Fury poster works within ACT-UP's overall commitment to the sexual and social legitimacy of gay men, IV drug users, and sex industry workers, not despite but *especially* in the grip of the AIDS crisis. To do otherwise would be to surrender to conservative demonizers, who consider AIDS a just dessert for perversion and promiscuity, and to "liberal" apologists (some of them gay), who agree that AIDS is a tragedy but are willing to sell out erotic experience and identity as a means of gaining allies.[4] *Justify My Love* evokes this commitment by presenting sexual, indeed homoerotic, images against the grain of repressive demonizing. Such images are underwritten, moreover, by Madonna's financial and political support in the fight against AIDS.

Questions of legitimacy, sexual freedom, and rearticulation as a political strategy have arisen as well in debates about women's sexuality, debates that have occupied the agendas of both the feminist and gay liberation movements for over a decade and that frame the lesbian reception of *Justify My Love*. Familiarly dubbed the "sex wars," these debates revolve around the political significance of pornography and certain sexual practices (penetration, sadomasochism, lesbian butch/femme roles) and have created, broadly, two opposed feminist positions.[5] In characterizing the antipornography stance, I have noted elsewhere that female subordination in patriarchy is assumed to be both cause and effect of female degradation in pornography (Henderson 1991, 3). Similar charges are leveled against eroticizing dominance and submission in consensual sexual scenarios and the "falsely conscious" use of familiar gender distinctions and hierarchies in butch/femme lesbian relationships.

For *anti*-antiporn feminists, on the other hand, suppressing pornography inevitably becomes part and parcel of a long history of female sexual suppression, including the suppression of lesbian sex in a variety of forms. Proponents of this position take many of their cues from the gay liberation movement of the late 1960s and the 1970s and the explicitly sexual ethos and politics of many gay men's communities (Echols 1991). For those lesbians who align themselves with this stance (and I do, though some do not), Madonna's representation in *Justify My Love* can signify the liberating (versus culpable) "bad girl" who refuses to secure her legitimacy by denying or relinquishing sexual agency, who, indeed, empowers herself, in part, by claiming that agency against the reciprocal threats of homophobia, racism, puritanism, and sexual violence.

A lesbian rearticulation of the bad-girl position comes from the Women's Caucus of ACT-UP Chicago, which recently produced a "Power Breakfast" T-shirt. The shirt features a halftone photograph of two women having sex, one nude and arching back from her knees, the other in jeans and a leather vest going down on the first. The words *power* and *breakfast* appear in bright purple and pink boldface above and below the photograph. The combination subverts both the corporate or yuppie meanings of *power breakfast* (where deals are cut over Belgian waffles and brewed Colombian) and popular athletic ones (where oat bran and protein powder fuel the fitness-obsessed) to the sexual politics of lesbian identity, where sex is sustenance and where power is an enticing part of consensual sex whatever the time of day.

In *Justify My Love*, Madonna's bad-girl repertoire includes her declaratively sexual persona and her acknowledgment of power relations in sexual fantasy and practice. Examples come from the allusion to sadomasochism in the costume and gestures of the barebreasted woman and from Madonna's own hyperfeminine styling, which, in lesbian subculture, connotes the femme position in butch/femme relationships. With earlier songs and videos (e.g., *Open Your Heart, Express Yourself,* and "Hanky Panky"), *Justify My Love* can thus be read from an anti-antiporn position, which separates power and coercion rather than power and sex. From this perspective, the clip signifies desire beyond the negative and threatening meanings of female sexual objectification, though such meanings are not necessarily or entirely displaced.[6]

Finally, though *Justify My Love*'s "lesbian" scene is more ambiguous than clear, the video, for the most part, is available for lesbian reading both because portions of it are *at least* ambiguous (rather than plainly heterosexual) and because lesbians can and do single out what most appeals to them in a strategy now codified as "oppositional reading."[7] For example, I recall a conversation with a lesbian friend for whom cultural analysis was a distant and fairly uninteresting abstraction. We were talking about the movie *The Big Easy* when I asked her if she was ever aroused by straight sex scenes in popular film. "If the women are attractive," she told me (and she included Ellen Barkin, *The Big Easy*'s female lead, in this category). Her comment is a reminder that however gratifying even a glimpse of lesbian eroticism may be, lesbian viewers hardly need to await pop culture's nervous forays into homosexuality in order to produce their own erotic identifications.

Thus far, I have attempted to establish a cultural context of sexual retrenchment and resistance to account for some of the political meanings and lesbian and gay appeals of *Justify My Love*. What should be clear is that this context is created through, not despite, its contradictions and volatilities. "Prosex" gay politics emerges from the struggle between state and oppression and community determination, but the community is itself multiply constituted and strained by divergent interests and analyses. Here, I have dealt with just one example of community struggle—feminist debates on sexual imagery—and even then, only in terms of its primary opposition. Still, my examples suggest how the process of articulation has been consciously brought to bear in a cultural politics that recognizes desire as truly a matter of survival.

In what follows, I briefly examine how the gay press further articulates *Justify My Love* with the imperatives of lesbian and gay politics and identity. It is important to point out, however, that many lesbian and gay (as well as nongay) authors write as cultural critics in both gay-identified and general publications, drawing on some of the same vernaculars and paradigms as academic writers (and many of them are trained and employed at least on a part-time basis by universities). This is a feature of contemporary intellectual practice that softens the boundaries of scholarship and journalism and positions academic critics in some of the same political terms (whether or not they acknowledge them) as the media writers whose work they study. Thus, the axes I have already suggested reappear in this analysis because I am, broadly, a member of the community represented by the writers and journals I cite.

SCENES FROM THE PRESS:
MADONNA AND ''JUSTIFY MY LOVE''

Many writers in the lesbian and gay press (and openly gay writers in more general publications, like Richard Goldstein and Michael Musto of the *Village Voice*) became interested in Madonna well before the MTV brouhaha over *Justify My Love*.[8] They noticed her coyly sexual public appearances with comedian Sandra Bernhard—on "Late Night with David Letterman," at a New York benefit for the Brazilian rain forest, and reportedly in the now-defunct Manhattan lesbian bar called the Cubby Hole. Her gay-styled video *Vogue* and her frequent support of AIDS-related causes, moreover, foregrounded Madonna's connections with gay culture. Those connections have since been extended beyond *Justify My Love* by her performance-film *Truth or Dare*. Thus, much of the current lesbian and gay commentary on Madonna is about more than *Justify My Love* and its controversies, though they provoked some general appraisals of Madonna in the gay press and raised issues that, several writers imply, go to the heart of Madonna's appeal to lesbian and gay audiences. Those issues include her willingness to act as a political figure as well as a popular one and to recognize that such fraught domains as sex, religion, and family are, indeed, political constructions, especially for lesbian and gay people. Like politics, the sex in Madonna's repertoire is conspicuously *there*. In Michael Musto's words (written for the lesbian and gay magazine *Outweek*), it is "on the surface, not in any withering, subliminal message that we can subtly pick up between the lines. It's flagrant, shameless and constant. And a lot of times, thank God—from a distance—it's gay" (1991, 37).[9]

Of course, that the sex is there is hardly an insight restricted to lesbian or gay commentators. Writers in the mainstream press (who, like Forrest Sawyer, may well be gay or lesbian but aren't saying) virtually always remark on Madonna's sexual persona—sometimes approvingly, sometimes ambivalently, and sometimes as evidence of the decline of Western civilization. But virtually none of the thirty-three columns, reports, and features about *Justify My Love* that I have reviewed, from such sources as the *New York Times, Boston Globe, Los Angeles Times, Atlanta Journal-Constitution, People, Wall Street Journal, Chicago Tribune,* and *Time Magazine,* so much as mentioned Madonna's popularity among lesbian and gay audiences or her connection to gay culture and politics. Rather, in terms reminiscent of the "Nightline" interview, they cast Madonna as opportunistic bimbo or financial shark (noting that she is currently the entertainment industry's top-earning woman) or as a sexually liberated gal, a breezy characterization that puts them in her corner if not quite in her politics because it, too, diffuses Madonna's sexual challenges. For example, the following comments come from

New York Times critic Stephen Holden (1990, C18), printed the day of the
"Nightline" broadcast:

> In its overall mood, the video is a titillating but enthusiastic celebration of sexu-
> ality and its varieties, but it includes nothing that comes close to hard-core por-
> nography. . . . Ultimately the video and the commotion it has generated crystal-
> lize what it is about Madonna that fascinates people. More than her beauty, that
> quality is an aggressively free-wheeling, all-inclusive sexuality.

Though Holden is on the verge of acknowledging Madonna's gay audience
with the overstated reference to an "all-inclusive sexuality," he (or his editor)
stops short of the obvious question. If *Justify My Love* is not hard-core pornography and if Madonna's freewheeling sexuality fascinates people, why
did MTV refuse to play the video?

The one group of writers in mainstream publications who do pose this
question are self-identified feminist women who consider where Madonna
and *Justify My Love* fit in contemporary feminist politics. Their critiques reflect the uneasy questions about sexual pleasure and representation mentioned above as the "sex debate," and they suggest that although Madonna
succeeds as "nonvictim" and sexual subject, her messages to young women
are otherwise dubious: As sex symbol and entrepreneur, she represents a
limited gender role reversal in an otherwise unchanged world, a "bimbo in
charge of her own bimboness" (James 1990, H38). Lynne Layton (1990,
A15), Harvard lecturer in women's studies and the author of two *Boston
Globe* features on Madonna, does push the *Justify My Love* controversy a
little further, taking to task her male newspaper colleagues for what she calls
their "Madonna-bashing." Few critics, observes Layton, have anything to
say about censorship as they rail against Madonna's commercialism nor
about the social institutions—family, school, religion—Madonna implicates
in *Justify My Love* and other songs and videos. The fuss, she concludes,
arises because Madonna is a woman who dares to be sexual and to make
money from sexuality. Layton (1990, A15) continues:

> I suggest that what is at issue is her gender, because male stars such as Prince
> have done the same thing as Madonna for years—with not a peep from the
> press. . . .
>   And this brings us back to the question Madonna posed on *Nightline,* which,
> in my view, is the relevant one: Why are images of degradation and violence to-
> ward women OK, almost mainstream, and images of two women or two men
> kissing taboo? Why is it that only Madonna was raising this question, not her
> critics?
>   This is indeed a hypocritical culture, and the hypocrisy has everything to do
> with unequal gender relations and with an open distaste for any version of femi-
> ninity that threatens not to know its place.

Although I agree with Layton's critique, I am again struck by her hesitation on the question of lesbian and gay identity. (Is it self-censorship? Is it an editorial decision?) She refers directly to "two women or two men kissing" but couches this phrase in terms of gender and sexism, never in the closely related dimensions of sexual orientation and homophobia.[10] The flamboyant Prince might also be compared to David Bowie who, his gender notwithstanding, was often bashed in the media—for "faggotry"—in his own glam rock days of the 1970s.[11]

What is important, then, about gay critics' insight that the sex is "there" in Madonna's work is that they articulate it explicitly (if not exclusively) to lesbian and gay politics. However disposed a very few writers in the mainstream press may be to recognizing or even "celebrating" sexual diversity (as Holden does), by ignorance or design (and regardless of who, in fact, is in their audience), they uphold a parallel and straight-identified universe, which leaves gay readers to openly gay writers and most nongay readers complacently in the dark.

In the gay press, conversely, Madonna becomes a queer icon whose very sensibilities are "gay" and whose ironies resonate with particular power in lesbian and gay imaginations. "Hollywood doesn't really get Madonna. She doesn't fit any past models of Hollywood stardom," says Don Shewey (1991, 44), who interviewed Madonna for *The Advocate,* a national lesbian and gay magazine. "The gay world," he continues, "gets Madonna in a big way" (Shewey 1991, 44). Don Baird (1991, 33), columnist for San Francisco's *Bay Times,* a progressive gay paper, described Barry Walter's account of *Justify My Love* in equally essentialist terms: "I read it and got the unmistakable feeling that Madonna does this just for us—us queers, mind you." Baird's feeling was confirmed when he actually saw the clip:

> My, my, my! What a video! I held my head in my hands in utter disbelief, touched myself and said, "Oh my God," about as many times as Madonna does in the intro to "Like a Prayer." Never has a pop star forced so many of the most basic and necessary elements of gayness right into the face of this increasingly uptight nation with power and finesse. Her message is a clear Get Over It, and she's the most popular woman in the world who's talking up our good everything (Baird 1991, 33).

And Sydney Pokorny (1989, 9), writing in *Gay Community News,* a national weekly newspaper from Boston, commented on Madonna's lesbian appeal during her very public stepping out with Sandra Bernhard:

> But what is it about this girl duo that has inspired *such* devotion from lesbians? I think part of the solution lies in the fact that as lesbians, we are all bad girls, we live in a constant state of rebellion. Both Sandra and Madonna adopt the image of the bad girl in the formation of their respective personae. They are tough, in-

dependent rebels (alright, Madonna does slip—Jellybean, Sean and Warren are weaknesses).

Rather than assimilate lesbian and gay people into the cultural mainstream, "the same, only different," Shewey, Baird, and Pokorny set up clear and aggressive us versus them distinctions—between Hollywood and the "gay world," gayness and the uptight nation, or rebel bad girls and nongay women. All three then conscript Madonna across the margins of sexual difference. As hip to our world as we are to hers, they imply, Madonna is one of us. Even her rampant heterosexuality cannot change that. Madonna and Sandra *belong* together in sisterly rebellion, and ex-husband Sean (Penn) and ex-boyfriend Warren (Beatty) are merely "slips."

Of course, Pokorny's final comment and certainly Baird's are tongue-in-cheek remarks, in manner if not in their appraisals of Madonna's lesbian and gay significance. For Pokorny, Madonna (with Sandra) is out for the fun and cachet of an open secret. Baird queens about in a virtual tizzy over *Justify My Love,* adopting a camp voice readily interpretable as gay. But both eventually return to Madonna's more sober import: She brings queerness out of the closet and thus at least some distance away from the closet's tyrannies:

> Just think of the comfort this video could provide for the teen boy who has struggled with hiding his hard-ons in the locker room and thought of himself as a pervert, to finally see that yes, indeed, people do feel a physical attraction for the same sex. Imagine the young girl whose guilt could be alleviated over the wam stirrings she feels while cuddling with her best friend by seeing Madonna enjoy something similar (Baird 1991, 33).

> The root of my obsession with Sandra and Madonna is unbridled lust. I can indulge the pleasure of looking and desiring without guilt. The basis for the formation of lesbian fantasies can easily be found within the context of Madonna's videos, Sandra's work and their friendship. They are truly my favorite post-Stonewall lesbian sex symbols. Together, Sandra and Madonna make lesbianism just a little less invisible and prove that fun (big fun) can be political (Pokorny 1989, 10).

In her dramatic publicness, bolstered by every known mechanism of cultural production and promotion, Madonna stands indirectly (and thus ironically) for outness itself, the crux of lesbian and gay liberation since the 1960s. We may claim our privacy, but we demand our publicity—our right to build communities and to move in the world without having to deny our own self-knowledge (Tucker 1982).

In the mainstream and gay press alike, much is made of Madonna's perpetual transformations. (She is Marilyn, no, Marlon, wrong again, boy toy, wait, gal pal, ah! Marie Antoinette.) But again, the resonances are different.

For Ellen Goodman (1990, 13), liberal columnist from the *Boston Globe*, Madonna's costume changes signal a failure to integrate.

> Multi-Madonna is the survivor of a rough childhood, of religious guilt and a bad marriage. She has purposely become a female with the nerve to be "bad" and the will to be powerful. She is, in short, sexy and hard-nosed, brassy and vulnerable, S and M, victor and victim, dressed in bra and black dress.
>
> But the fight against being "pigeonholed" can also be an excuse for confusion. . . .
>
> In the end, watching the Madonnas pass before us over the years, is a bit like watching the three faces of Eve . . . as a role model. That's not an answer for women trying to integrate their lives.

For Don Shewey (1991, 44), in writing *The Advocate,* those same changes bespeak honesty:

> In true post-modern fashion, [Madonna] is drawn to complexity, contradiction, and ambiguity over harmony, clarity, and simplicity. And she embraces a fragmented wardrobe of personas (Bitch, Little Girl, Vulnerable Love-Seeker) rather than a false, integrated personality.

In the passage quoted earlier, Sydney Pokorny also refers to Madonna's "adoption of personae" as a matter of celebrity strategy, not pathology, and Michael Musto (1991, 37) congratulates her artifice and multiplicity as the bridge between lesbian and gay fans:

> Her pride, flamboyance and glamour reach out to gay guys as much as her butch/fem dichotomy and her refusal to be victimized strike a chord in lesbians. As a result, Madonna—the great leveller, a breath mint and a candy mint—is the first superstar to appeal equally to both camps. It's not the divisive old Judy story, with guys weeping along with the diva as she longs to go over the rainbow and track down the man that got away, while women cringe.

Musto's reference to Judy Garland is telling, though the troubled star of a different era perhaps shares more with Madonna than Musto implies. If to markedly different effect, both Garland and Madonna embody disguise as the flip side of disclosure. These qualities are fused in the practice of passing, one of the central contradictions of lesbian and gay life. To pass—for straight or sometimes for male or female—is to get by in public life, to be out and about, but only at the mercy of detailed and conscious concealment and invention. Garland, profoundly a figure of gay male identification in the 1950s and 1960s, was not passing for straight (would that she had been). But behind her early screen image as the girl next door was another, more tortured, persona, as Richard Dyer (1986, 159) points out in his heartfelt analysis of Garland's gay reception:

> It was the fact, as became clear after 1950, that she was not after all the ordinary girl she appeared to be that suggested a relationship to ordinariness ho-

mologous with that of gay identity. To turn out not-ordinary after being saturated with the values of ordinariness structures Garland's career and the standard gay biography alike.

In her juxtaposition of camp and "authenticity," Garland revealed to gay men a "surface-below-the-surface," a "second nature" that appealed, Dyer (1986, 160) suggests, to an essentialist conception of their own identity—gayness as "a trait that may be repressed but is always there."

Madonna, too, puts forth a disguise but less as a concealment than as a brash revelation of artifice. It is the essence of camp—cracking the mirror, dressing up and acting out to *expose* the constructedness of what in other settings passes as "natural" male, female, or heterosexual. Of course, camp, too, is an act, and Madonna *could* be confused. But her gay and lesbian observers are rightly wary of the sexual naturalisms that villify queers and make up fair game for bigoted legislators and gay-bashing thugs. Perhaps that is what moves us to enjoy her pointed concoctions and sometimes, even, to celebrate them.

CONCLUSION: AMBIVALENT ARTICULATIONS

But amid the reverie, the skepticism endures. Most openly lesbian and gay writers (with the exception of Don Baird, in his commentary on *Justify My Love*) acknowledge the double edge of Madonna's appeal, though they may excuse or dismiss its peril. In his *Outweek* feature, Michael Musto (1991, 36), usually camping and dishing in the *Village Voice* as razor-sharp critic of the New York club scene, pivots around Madonna as both the savior and plunderer of lesbian and gay life:

> She shimmies into our fag imagination, spreads her legs for our dyke approbation, grabs us by the pudenda and makes us face things we didn't think it was possible to learn from pop music. After an hour's private session with her, we're aroused but wearing condoms, mad at her for ripping us off, but somehow thanking her for noticing us, legitimizing us, pulling us by our bootstraps up out of hiding and into the public pleasuredome of scrutiny and success. . . . Deliriously, we imagine we're sitting *with* her in the arena—not cheering from the bleachers, but laughing alongside her onstage and sharing in the kudos from the throngs who recognize that we're a big part of her triumph—even if any real attempt to get near our lady of the poses would have a bouncer dragging us out by the neck as she sang "keep people together" with her usual twisted sense of irony.

Madonna distinguishes herself as queer icon against the ground of commercial pop culture, not the more targeted vernaculars of lesbian and gay representation. She is no Audre Lorde or Dorothy Allison, no Bill T. Jones or

Harvey Fierstein or even Jimmy Sommerville (though she might enjoy the work produced by all of them). But on a different plane, she is also no Andrew Dice Clay. "In her publicity-seeking quest for thrills, isn't she just using us to advance her own notoriety?" asks Musto (1991, 37). "Probably," he answers, "but isn't that infinitely better than a star (Andrew Dice Clay, for example) who uses homophobia to the same end?"

I agree with Musto—Madonna is better than Clay—but with him, I also return to this query: How grateful are lesbian and gay people supposed to be? Though the links or articulations between ideologies and social groups are not necessary ones in the traditional Marxist sense, nor are they free-floating or easily transformed. Madonna's penchant for metamorphosis beckons to us to recognize and toy with our own self-constructions, but ours is a limited universe, bereft of personal trainers, bodyguards, or camera crews, and Madonna's own plasticity retains many of the sedimented, oppressive meanings of consumer society, especially for women: Change yourself (with this cosmetic, that diet plan, that surgery) and maybe you can be happy and worthy (cf. Bordo, this volume).

Such plasticity also retains the greatest audience and thus the greatest profit, a multiple persona and multiple market approach less designed for deconstruction than pop idol diversification. Over this political-economic territory, Madonna reigns supreme. Her plastic repertoire includes gay cultural forms, yes, but appropriated out of their organic venues (like Harlem drag and voguing balls) and into the high-return indifference of corporate cultural production (like the video *Vogue*). Many gay people will recognize the originators, but most others in the audience will not, and Madonna has not gone out of her way to credit (or remunerate) her sources.[12] In Philadelphia, a savvy gay activist and hairstylist named Dominic Bash roller-skated into a recent Gay Pride march, sporting fishnet stockings, plastic nun earrings, and a bleached ponytail like the one Madonna wore in her Blond Ambition tour. "I wasn't doing Madonna on Pride Day," said Bash to a reporter for the local gay press, "I was doing 'Madominic,' and there's a difference. I think of it this way: If anybody is going to imitate anybody, she's gotta be imitating me" (Mallinger 1991, 7). Bash is right, but his insight will not place him—or voguers or drag queens—among the nation's highest-paid entertainers.

It is difficult, finally, to acknowledge the divided self and engage the pleasure of masquerade while at the same time fighting a strikingly antagonistic legal and social system for your health, your safety, your job, your place to live, or the right to raise your children. Indeed, this is the other contradiction of lesbian and gay resistance: to be constructionists in theory, though essentialists as we mobilize politically, demanding that the state comply because this, after all, is *who we are*, not who we are today or who we have become in recent history.[13]

But it is still too much to expect of a pop star that she resolve contradictions not of her own making (or even those that are), and it is unreasonable as well to think that in our fandom or in our critiques we will resolve in Madonna the contradictions that attract us in the first place. Madonna is not queer liberation, nor even radical, necessarily (as a gay friend commented, "I'd really like to see an open queen or dyke do a lot of the same stuff—but more explicit, more raw"). But with vigilance, her work can be articulated to our struggles and our pleasures, offering us a place to play out both construct and essence and to do so, critically, on the captivating and thus politically powerful ground of the popular.

Acknowledgments

Thanks are due to Ronald Bettig, Kathryn Furano, Larry Gross, Leola Johnson, Kevin Patnik, Catherine Preston, Deidre Pribram, Pamela Sankar, Cathy Schwichtenberg, Scott Tucker, and Angharad Valdivia for their critical readings and insightful comments. Special thanks also go to Jeaneen Aldridge for careful and comprehensive research assistance.

NOTES

1. The NEA debates are but one part of the controversy surrounding the MTV ban. Others include the media activism of fundamentalist Donald Wildmon and members of the American Family Association (who have been very effective in targeting commercial sponsors) and the music industry's self-censorship following attacks by the Parents' Music Resource Center. I have placed the Mapplethorpe/NEA discussions in the foreground, given their particular relevance to gay culture and thus to *Justify My Love*. For a terse chronology and a discussion of the political motives involved in the NEA debates, see Vance (1990).

2. See Gross (1990) for a detailed account of the sexual counterrevolution as it has evolved across a variety of cultural, political, and legal sectors in the United States since the 1970s.

3. Not all strategic rearticulations are progressive, however. For example, consider the conservative appropriation of *political correctness*, once a term of approbation among Communist party members, then an ironic and self-critical term among leftists, and now a term of contempt used to forge New Right and neoliberal alliances against progressive academic reform.

4. I do not refer to lesbians in this discussion because they are not typically identified as a high-risk group for HIV and AIDS (though some lesbians are IV drug users, sex-trade workers, and/or sexual partners of such individuals). Though absent from the high-risk list, lesbians, due to their alignments with gay men, are by no means spared the AIDS-related demonizing of antigay forces. At the same time, however, the

low-risk designation has produced virtual inattention, from the medical and social services establishments, toward those lesbians and other women who do have AIDS but who are sluggishly diagnosed (or not diagnosed at all) if the opportunistic infections they suffer do not conform to conventional symptomatology. They are then left out of research protocols and treatment networks. For further discussion, see ACT-UP/New York Women and AIDS Book Group (1991). For an example of liberal gay apologism and a critique of this position, see Shilts (1987) and Crimp (1989), respectively.

5. The antipornography and anti-antipornography literatures are vast. For an introduction to the first position, see Dworkin (1981), Barry (1979, especially chapter 9), Lederer (1980), Cole (1989), and Leidholdt and Raymond (1990). On the second position, see Vance (1984), Snitow, Stansell, and Thompson (1983), Burstyn (1987), Feminist Review (1990), Nestle (1987) and Ellis et al. (1986).

6. For a critique of Madonna as rock *maitresse,* see Goldstein (1990a).

7. Oppositional readings acquire political force especially as they become articulated to social groups, but as the lesbian example suggests, they may also constitute a valuable form of personal resistance even in the absence of a movement. For an interesting example of oppositional reading (and writing) as resistance, see Jenkins (1988).

8. The terms *mainstream* and *gay* hardly exhaust press designations; I use them here as a relevant and convenient contrast. Madonna turns up in other places and amid similar controversies. For an example from the Left press, see Elayne Rapping's (1991a) favorable review of *Truth or Dare* in *The Guardian,* along with the outraged correspondence (and Rapping's response) in subsequent issues.

9. Musto's use of the phrase *from a distance* is a reference to Bette Midler's recent hit song, whose title goes by that phrase. Midler began her cabaret career in gay bathhouses in New York City, though according to Musto, she has long been careful to avoid an "image problem" by not publicly acknowledging her gay fans. Madonna, in contrast, "*wants* an image problem. . . . Her refusals to conform *are* career moves" (Musto 1991, 37).

10. For an analysis of the cultural relationship between gender and sexual orientation, see Williams (1986), who draws from research on sexual diversity in Native American cultures. For a political analysis of the relationship in dominant U.S. society, see Pharr (1989).

11. In mainstream press responses to *Justify My Love,* the only passing reference to Madonna's gay connections comes from a *New York Times* editorial by Camille Paglia (1990), who does not address the gay audience but mentions Madonna's admiration for Stonewall drag queens. Given Paglia's alignment against antiporn feminism (which she simply and disdainfully calls "feminism"), it may appear that I share her notion that only in Madonna do we find a "true" feminist. In fact, I have no use for Paglia's opportunism or for her old-fashioned, sexist essentializing about powerful men and submissive women, a stance that leads her to conclude that in sexual encounters, "no means yes" and that acquaintance rape is therefore a laughable feminist invention. In her contempt, Paglia accepts—indeed, valorizes—sexual coercion. I do not.

12. On cultural appropriation across the lines of race and class, see bell hooks's (1991) review of *Paris Is Burning,* a film about the Harlem drag ball circuit. hooks is

critical of Jenny Livingston, the film's producer/director, for failing to problematize her relationship as a white, middle-class lesbian filmmaker to the predominantly black and poor community she documents. hooks does not recognize any significant difference between Livingston's work in *Paris Is Burning* and Madonna's in *Vogue* as instances in the long history of white producers appropriating black culture.

13. Larry Gross first pointed out to me the constructionist/essentialist tension between sexual identity theorizing and gay political activism. What I think the movement must put forth (as some sectors, notably Queer Nation, are doing) is an uncompromising political agenda that recognizes, rather than nervously eschews, the socially constructed dimensions of sexual identity. For a discussion of essentialism as one subject position among others (in a postmodern analysis that refuses to deny the "real" or give up political activism), see Andrew Ross's introduction (1989) to *Universal Abandon? The Politics of Postmodernism,* especially pp. XI–XII.

REFERENCES

ACT-UP/New York Women and AIDS Book Group. (1991). *Women, AIDS and Activism.* Boston, Mass.: South End Press.

Baird, D. (1991). "Beat This: The Madonna." *San Francisco Bay Times,* January, p. 33.

Barry, K. (1979). *Female Sexual Slavery.* New York: New York University Press.

Beck, J. (1990). "Sex, Hype, Videotape Drown Out Reason" (syndicated column). (State College, Penn.) *Center Daily Times,* December 8, p. A6.

Burstyn, V. (ed.). (1987). *Women Against Censorship.* Vancouver: Douglas McIntyre.

Cocks, J. (1990). "Madonna Draws a Line." *Time Magazine,* December 17, pp. 74–75.

Cole, S. G. (1989). *Pornography and the Sex Crisis.* Toronto: Amanita.

Crimp, D. (ed.). (1988). *AIDS: Cultural Analysis/Cultural Activism.* Cambridge, Mass.: MIT Press.

Crimp, D., and Rolston, A. (1990). *AIDS Demo Graphics.* Seattle, Wash.: Bay Press.

Dworkin, A. (1981). *Pornography: Men Possessing Women.* New York: Perigree.

Dyer, R. (1986). *Heavenly Bodies: Film Stars and Society.* London: St. Martin's.

Echols, A. (1991). "Justifying Our Love? The Evolution of Lesbianism Through Feminism and Gay Male Politics." *The Advocate* 573 (March 26): 48–53.

Ellis, K., Jaker, B., Hunter, N. D., O'Dair, B., and Tallmer, Abby (eds.). (1986). *Caught Looking: Feminism, Pornography and Censorship.* Seattle: Real Comet Press.

Feminist Review. (1990). "Perverse Politics: Lesbian Issues" (special issue) 34 (Spring).

Fiske, J. (1989). "Madonna." In his *Reading the Popular.* Boston, Mass.: Unwin and Hyman.

Goldstein, R. (1990a). "We So Horny: Sado Studs and Super Sluts, America's New Sex 'tude." *Village Voice,* October 16, pp. 35–36, 38, 160.

———. (1990b). "Free MTV! It's Not the Nipple: Madonna's New Clip Threatens the Sexual Order of Music Video." *Village Voice,* December 18, p. 52.

Goodman, E. (1990). "Another Image in the Madonna Rolodex" (syndicated column). *Boston Globe,* December 6, p. 13.

Gross, L. (1990). "The Right to Privacy Vs. the Duty of Sexual Secrecy: Battlefield Sketches from the Sexual Counter-Revolution." Paper presented to the meetings of the International Communication Association, June 24–29, Trinity College, Dublin.

Hall, S. (1982). "The Rediscovery of 'Ideology': Return of the Repressed in Media Studies." In M. Gurevitch et al. (eds.), *Culture, Society and the Media.* London: Methuen, pp. 56–90.

————. (1986). "On Postmodernism and Articulation: An Interview with Stuart Hall" (edited by L. Grossberg). *Journal of Communication Inquiry* 10, no. 2 (Summer): 45–60.

Henderson, L. (1991). "Lesbian Pornography: Cultural Transgression and Sexual Demystification." *Women and Language* 14, no. 1 (Spring): 3–12.

Holden, S. (1990). "That Madonna Video: Realities and Fantasies." *New York Times,* December 3, p. C18.

hooks, b. (1991). "Is Paris Burning?" *Zeta Magazine* 4, no. 6 (June): 60–64.

James, C. (1990). "Beneath All That Black Lace Beats the Heart of a Bimbo . . . and a Feminist." *New York Times,* December 16, pp. H38–44.

Jenkins, H. (1988). "*Star Trek* Rerun, Reread, Rewritten: Fan Writing as Textual Poaching." *Critical Studies in Mass Communication* 5, no. 2 (June): 85–107.

Layton, L. (1990). "What's Really Behind the Madonna-bashing?" *Boston Globe,* December 16, p. A15.

Lederer, L. (ed.). (1980). *Take Back the Night: Women on Pornography.* New York: Morrow.

Leidholdt, D., and Raymond, J. G. (eds.). (1990). *The Sexual Liberals and the Attack on Feminism.* New York: Pergamon.

Mallinger, M. S. (1991). "The Man Behind 'Madominic': An Activist for All Occasions." *Au Courant,* August 12, pp. 7, 16–17, 19.

Musto, M. (1991). "Immaculate Connection." *Outweek,* March 20, pp. 35–42, 62.

Nestle, J. (1987). *A Restricted Country.* New York: Firebrand.

Paglia, C. (1990). "Madonna—Finally, a Real Feminist." *New York Times,* December 14, p. A39.

Pharr, S. (1989). *Homophobia: A Weapon of Sexism.* Inverness, Calif.: Chardon Press.

Pokorny, S. (1989). "Obsess Yourself! The Root of My Obsession with Sandra and Madonna Is Unbridled Lust." *Gay Community News,* July 30–August 5, pp. 9–10.

Rapping, E. (1991a). "Madonna Makes the Media Play Her Game." *The Guardian,* June 5, p. 16.

————. (1991b). Response to Letters to the Editor (appearing June 26 and July 3). *The Guardian,* July 3, p. 2.

Ross, A. (ed.). (1989). *Universal Abandon? The Politics of Postmodernism.* Minneapolis: University of Minnesota Press.

Shewey, D. (1991). "The Saint, the Slut, the Sensation . . . Madonna." *The Advocate,* May 7, pp. 42–51.

Shilts, R. (1987). *And the Band Played On: Politics, People and the AIDS Crisis.* New York: St. Martin's Press.

Snitow, A., Stansell, C., and Thompson, S. (eds.). (1983). *Powers of Desire: The Politics of Sexuality.* New York: New Feminist Library/Monthly Review Press.

Tucker, S. (1982). "Our Right to the World." *The Body Politic,* July/August, pp. 29–33.

Vance, C. (1990). "The War on Culture." *Art in America* 77, no. 9 (September): 39, 41, 43, 45.

Vance, C. (ed.). (1984). *Pleasure and Danger: Exploring Female Sexuality.* New York: Routledge and Kegan Paul.

Williams, W. (1986). *The Spirit and the Flesh.* Boston, Mass.: Beacon Press.

CATHY SCHWICHTENBERG

Madonna's Postmodern Feminism: Bringing the Margins to the Center

> It is precisely at times such as these, when we live with the possibil-
> ity of unthinkable destruction, that people are likely to become
> dangerously crazy about sexuality. . . . Disputes over sexual
> behavior often become the vehicles for displacing social anxieties,
> and discharging their attendant emotional intensity. Consequently,
> sexuality should be treated with special respect in times of great so-
> cial stress.
>
> —**Gayle Rubin**, "Thinking Sex"

ON MONDAY, DECEMBER 3, 1990, the two most current signifiers of sexuality and destruction were coupled on ABC's "Nightline." Although Madonna's defense of her sexually explicit *Justify My Love* video ranked a
newsworthy first, displacing the war in the Persian Gulf, one followed fast
on the other. This pairing was not coincidental. As Gayle Rubin points out,
times of great social stress, such as those created by deficit, recession, and
war, are likely to produce a displacement of anxieties onto sexual values and
erotic conduct. The controversy surrounding Madonna's depiction of diverse sexual practices is, perhaps, symptomatic of the contradictions that
besiege the core of an American value system that polices "deviant"
sexualities but sanctions the violence of war. Madonna, I contend, is involved in a bloodless war. Hers is a "sex war" to be fought on the field of sexual representation.

The episode of "Nightline," with Forrest Sawyer conducting the interview, established such a confrontation. Following a video montage that featured Madonna "pushing the boundaries of sexuality," Sawyer issued a pa-
ternalistic warning to viewers prior to screening *Justify My Love*. Madonna,
as interviewee, spoke nervously from within the television frame—a double

frame established by the normalizing context of the mainstream media. She was forced to justify *Justify* in response to Sawyer's sexual inquisition, which defined the terrain of discussion in terms of moral absolutes. Sawyer appeared patronizing and self-righteous, constantly referring to boundaries, lines, and limits: "Where is that line?"; "First, you have to tell me where *you* draw the line." In Sawyer's "newsworthy" discourse on sexuality "the line" established a zone between a sanctified sexual order and the evil, unspeakable acts on the other side. Madonna, with her polymorphous, gender-blending ménage, had clearly crossed into the "danger zone."

Although Madonna crosses lines between gender polarities and sexual practices in *Justify My Love,* her multiple video incarnations also have been described as a postmodern challenge to aesthetic boundaries. E. Ann Kaplan (1987, 126) notes that Madonna's "postmodern feminism is part of a larger postmodern phenomenon which her videos also embody in their blurring of the hitherto sacrosanct boundaries and polarities such as male/female, high art/pop art, film/TV, fiction/reality, private/public." Madonna's shifting persona and stylistically seductive aesthetic are all hallmarks of a postmodern commodity culture where modernist notions of authenticity surrender to postmodern fabrication.

Madonna's postmodern reinventions are of particular concern for some feminists who view her multiple personae as a threat to women's socialization, which entails the necessary integration of female identity (Goodman 1990). Yet, such displeasure signals an even larger problematic that pits feminism against postmodernism. Here, perhaps most troubling to feminist criticism is Madonna's role as an envoy of a postmodernism that, in its lack of authenticity, unity, and stable categories, challenges the more modernist foundational tenets of feminism itself.

Nancy Fraser and Linda Nicholson (1990) explain that the rift between postmodernism and feminism is the result of two tendencies that have proceeded from opposite directions toward the same objective: to debunk traditional (patriarchal) philosophy in favor of a more politically potent social theory or criticism.

> Postmodernists have focused primarily on the philosophy side of the problem. They have begun by elaborating antifoundational and metaphilosophical perspectives and from there have drawn conclusions about the shape and character of social criticism. For feminists, on the other hand, the question of philosophy has always been subordinated to an interest in social criticism (Fraser and Nicholson 1990, 19–20).

However, though feminists may have willingly subordinated philosophy to social criticism, philosophy as a male preserve has continued to subordinate questions of feminism.

Craig Owens (1983) observes that in the early 1980s, women were excluded from the postmodern debate. This debate, which incited grand theorizing from male philosophers and cultural theorists, focused on the postmodern challenge to modernism and enlightenment philosophy without so much as noting women's absence (Habermas 1983; Jameson 1984; Lyotard 1984). In response, feminists impertinently pointed out that though male philosophers and cultural theorists could freely relinquish mastery, foundational truths, and unified conceptions of self, women had to question such relativisitic thinking because they had yet to establish an adequate foundation for feminism—one that could articulate women's multiple identities to a unified social identity. Such an identity could incite collective political action as well as help forge a social theory responsive to the conditions of all women, oppressed under patriarchy specifically by virtue of gender. Postmodernism called on women to relinquish their foundational goals, and it seemed to undermine earlier feminist theories that moved in that direction.

According to Fraser and Nicholson (1990), feminist thinkers had endeavored throughout the 1970s to produce expansive social theories that could explain the basis for male/female inequities. In the process, feminist thinkers (the authors cite Chodorow [1978] and Gilligan [1983] as representative) often reified female differences through essentialist (or universal) categories that excluded the determinants of race, class, and sexual preference. Postmodernism, by contrast, focused on the differences between women rather than their sameness and emphasized the socially constructed (not to mention fluid and ad hoc) nature of all sex and gender categories.

Feminism's newly emergent foundation, forged as an inclusive, woman-centered basis for social thought and political action, confronted a postmodernism without guarantees for feminism that instead offered a network of potential alliances not necessarily bounded by the category of "woman" and its epistemological entailments. With this as a context, it is easy to see why an alliance between feminism and postmodernism is regarded with skepticism.

Currently, then, postmodernism is thought to be a political liability for feminism, insofar as it challenges a unified conception of feminism. Because feminism attempts to posit a unified identity for the category "woman" as its foundation (as in "women's culture," "feminism writing," or "female discourse"), it is compelled to exclude fragmented or multiple identities from its ranks as disruptive signifiers of postmodernism. Thus, both Christine di Stefano (1988) and Kate Soper (1990) argue that postmodernism, with its emphasis on fragmented identities, runs the risk of destroying or subverting a feminism that, as gender politics, is based on a unified conception of women as social subjects; Seyla Benhabib (1984) notes that postmodernism leads to relativism. Susan Bordo (1990a, 135), however, cautions against "eschewing generalizations about gender a priori on theoretical grounds," and she notes that Madonna's postmodern presentation in a music video like *Open Your Heart* facilitates, rather than deconstructs, her objectification (1990b).

But postmodernism may not be a political liability for feminism. For instance, *simulation,* the key term in Jean Baudrillard's (1983) postmodern theory, is a concept often overlooked in feminist debates. Simulation, which stresses the artificial as "dress-ups," "put-ons," and "make-overs," is not a political liability for a postmodern feminism intent on reclaiming simulation for the "other." In particular, Madonna's political stylistics appeal to lesbians who have long been the "other" as "the skeleton in the closet of feminism" (Case 1988/1989, 57). Madonna's gender-bending, pin-striped suit and crotch grabs in *Express Yourself,* her scene of Sapphic titillation on "Late Night with David Letterman," and her languid French kiss with *l'autre femme* in *Justify* all represent a deconstruction of lines and boundaries that fragment male/female gender polarities and pluralize sexual practices. This is a postmodern, unbounded feminism that unifies *coalitionally* rather than foundationally.

Thus, I read Madonna's figuration against the backdrop of Baudrillardian theory, where simulation is the pivotal term for a postmodern feminism that addresses differences between and among women. Madonna, a postmodern "product," uses simulation strategically in ways that challenge the stable notion of gender as the edifice of sexual difference. Specifically, I analyze Madonna's deconstruction of gender boundaries in the music video *Express Yourself* to illustrate the fragmentation of gender, which is then refashioned through the flux of identities, more conducive to readings of otherness. This, in turn, advances the argument for a radical sexual politics, best exemplified through Madonna's stylistic challenge to an ontological notion of sexuality pluralized in the music video *Justify My Love.* Such an excursion into Madonna's protean persona underscores the need (now more crucial than ever) for feminism to "open its heart" to the radical disjunctures informing gender and sexuality as plural invocations for women under the sign of postmodernism.

DISPERSE YOURSELF:
POSTMODERN GENDER SIMULATIONS

Although Jean Baudrillard's (1983, 1988a, 1988b) bleak postmodern theory may appear from the outset to have nothing in it for women, looks are deceiving. Amid his reified surface world, emblematic of a dead culture, is the concept of simulation. Simulation functions as the conceptual linchpin in Baudrillard's theory of the hyperreal, and it is operationalized at the moment when the poles of the real and of representation contract and collapse into one another. Simulation begins with the liquidation of all referentials, and a new culture of surfaces emerges out of the rubble. This new postmodern culture lacks all reference to a fixed and stable reality. When played out in a postmodern feminist key, this bipolar collapse into fabrication poses a challenge to the male/female polarities of sexual difference, which have by now proved to be an impasse for feminist theory (de Lauretis 1987; Kaplan 1985).

Indeed, sexual difference was erected as a binary structure in which woman's differences were posed in opposition to man's. This reliance on gendered binarisms resulted in woman's separate but equal status or in feminine essentialism, neither of which proved fruitful for theorizing gender beyond the constraints of biological sex. Moreover, the polarities of sexual difference buttressed the edifice of heterosexuality, ostensibly excluding all "others" who did not accede to the male/female couplet (de Lauretis 1986, 1987). Thus, in the effort to collapse this binary opposition, postmodern feminists can seize the moment of simulation and read sexual difference against the backdrop of postmodernism, where gender emerges as a process that must be "worked at" and constructed.

Foremost among constructions of gender is "femininity," which, in light of simulation, can be regarded as artifice or masquerade. For instance, psychoanalyst Joan Riviere (1986) notes that "women who wish for masculinity may put on a mask of womanliness to avert anxiety and retribution feared from men." This, she argues, is especially true of women in male-dominated professions where women disguise themselves as "feminine," as disempowered (Riviere 1986, 35). However, though Riviere contends that femininity is *used* as a masquerade in the form of "protective coloration," she is unwilling to assert that all femininity is a put-on, lacking any essential bipolar foundation in sexual difference. Femininity is marked by the arrangement of signifiers on the body's surface that act in a part-to-whole relationship in the construction of a "look."

The look is key, for women simulate appearances. In this regard, Michele Montrelay (1978, 93) describes femininity as a masquerade that "takes shape in the piling up of crazy things, feathers, hats, and strange baroque constructions which rise up like so many silent insignias." Indeed, Montrelay, Gayatri Spivak (1976, 1983), Mary Russo (1986), Judith Butler (1990b), and Mary Anne Doane (1982) have all suggested the mutable cultural underpinnings of femininity as an exaggeration in which woman "plays" at herself, playing a part. This suggests a reflexive shift to the surface where femininity is in excess of itself as a masquerade. In particular, Doane (1982, 82) notes that "this type of masquerade, an excess of femininity, is aligned with the *femme fatale.*"

The part of the femme fatale has been repeatedly performed by Madonna, who organizes her excess of femininity around the drama of vision.

Her body functions as a "prop" that simulates the excessive femininity of male projections only to turn that vision against herself. For example, *Open Your Heart, Borderline, Material Girl,* and *Express Yourself* are all reflexive commentaries on male "looking" countered by a feminine "look." *Open Your Heart* is structured as a cinematic peep show that frames Madonna's play as stripper; *Borderline* is organized around photography and modeling; *Material Girl* refers to the cinematic construction of Marilyn Monroe, deconstructed by Madonna's feminine double play as a construction of a construction; and *Express Yourself* advances a panopticonlike vision of surveillance, which Madonna underscores in her gyrations against a screen that reduces her figuration to a cartoonlike silhouette.

The exhibitionist knows that the voyeur is watching; thus, Madonna bares the devices of femininity, thereby asserting that femininity is a device. Madonna takes simulation to its limit in a deconstructive maneuver that plays femininity off against itself—a metafemininity that reduces gender to the overplay of style.

If femininity is an excessive performance on one side of the divide, then gender play marks the play of signifiers across the bar. As Wendy Chapkis (1986, 138) notes, "Gender and sex increasingly do appear to be areas of fashion and style rather than biology and identity." Gender play is the mix and match of styles that flirt with the signifiers of sexual difference, cut loose from their moorings. Such inconstancy underscores the fragility of gender itself as pure artifice. Thus, gender play takes shape in a postmodern pastiche of multiple styles: masculinity and femininity fractured and refracted in erotic tension.

Gender play is highlighted, in particular, by the play of differences signifying "drag." Indeed, if masquerade is feminine excess, then drag is the ebb and flow of disengendered and reengendered signifiers that are held in suspension. In the case of female impersonators, Esther Newton (1972, 103) notes this as a "double inversion" in which "appearance is an illusion": "Drag says 'my outside appearance is feminine, but my essence inside [the body] is masculine.' At the same time it symbolizes the opposite inversion: 'My appearance outside [my body, my gender] is masculine but my essence inside [myself] is feminine.' " Drag foregrounds gender as an imitation that lacks an original through a constant shift of contingent signifiers.

Newton's (1972) formulation is relevant to drag insofar as it stresses the double inversion of polarities; however, drag as a performance of gender goes even further. The stylistics of gesture, posture, movement, and pose, as well as the stylization of external adornments, are all signifiers on the loose. They are in process, transiently coded and highlighted in a bricolage of differences that construct an "imagined body" or "provisional identity." Signifiers touch, create friction, and move about in multiple configurations that fragment gender and eroticize play. Drag consists of an energized surrender and retrieval in which parts in flux never designate the whole but rather pose gender as an inherently fractured and easily fragmented construction.

For instance, in Madonna's *Express Yourself* video, drag is a deconstructive performance staged against the futuristic, intertextual backdrop of Fritz Lang's *Metropolis*. This revitalized, postmodern backdrop provides a pastiche of sexually loaded signifiers that reference everything from S/M to gay male pornography, thereby setting the stage for a suited Madonna (Curry 1990). Madonna's performative play has been described approvingly as "a dykey Madonna dancing in a man's suit [and] grabbing her crotch" (Porkorny 1989, 10). Indeed, her drag dance is a decentering vision that highlights the double inversion of drag as a double play on gender. Drag parodies gender, which is fissured through a doubling back on femininity in a masculinity that is feminized: the body multiply figured as gender's autocritique.

Here, Madonna's body is dynamized in a constant conflict and rearrangement of signifiers. Her excessively femme silhouette cuts to a working-class man in silhouette who watches Madonna emerge from the smoke—her monocled and suited transformation, a parodic send-up of "the boss" and the bounds of gendered authority. She throws her body into broad movements—mechanized, abrupt. Madonna's dance freely associates with "masculine" workout moves in a kinetic synchronization that also invokes the dissonantly gendered body of Michael Jackson.

Powerful low-angle shots predominate as Madonna punches the air, grabs her crotch, and spreads her legs. She teasingly opens and closes her jacket, revealing a black lace bra in a dissonant interplay of difference. Here, Madonna's drag dance resonates with postmodern dance, which "directs attention away from any specific image of the body and towards the process of constructing all bodies" (Dempster 1988, 48). Madonna's body, caught in the flux of destabilized identities, deconstructs gender as a put-on, a sex toy. Madonna concludes the sequence with hand on crotch and finger pointed at the viewer. The viewer is compelled to reread her body as the intersection of converging differences.

This imaginary construction of the body as fragments reflects on the artifice of gender. Madonna's disingenuous figuration signifies, through strategies of simulation, a political core at the heart of play. Her strategies are not alien to the lesbian community. As Joan Nestle notes, "On a good bar night, the variety of self-presentation runs the whole gamut from Lesbian Separatist drag to full femme regalia to leather and chains" (Stein and Urla 1988, 18). So, too, Madonna enacts this multiplicity; her postmodern body, in disguise and in process, is "unstable, fleeting, flickering, transient—a subject of multiple representations" (Dempster 1988, 48–49). Two of Madonna's representational strategies have been touched on here as feminine masquerade and drag. Indeed, the surface play of gender suggests plural styles that, under the sign of the postmodern, are made available to multiple discourses.

SEXUALITY: OVER THE LINE
AND BETWEEN THE SHEETS

If gender has gone up in smoke for postmodern feminism in the implosion of sexual difference, then the next step is to deconstruct sex as the basis for identity. Sex must be placed on equally fictive footing with gender for both are mutable and constructed and thus can be deconstructed and refigured. As Butler (1990b, 32) insightfully remarks, "If the regulatory fictions of sex and gender are themselves multiply contested sites of meaning, then the very multiplicity of their construction holds out the possibility of a disruption of their univocal posturing." Indeed, one's biological sex has long been riveted to ontological, essentialist notions of sexuality, with gender as an alibi. Here, Jonathan Ned Katz (1990, 29) notes that "feminists have explained to us that anatomy does not determine our gender destinies (our masculinities and femininities)"; however, he adds, "we've only begun to consider that biology does not settle our erotic fates." Nature has functioned as the basis for culture and its social practices; thus, exposing the artifice of gender is only half the job: Sex still exerts a tenacious hold. It is the last line of defense, harboring "natural," "normal," and "immanent" notions of sexuality.

In this society, in particular, compulsory heterosexuality regulates a normalizing frame, for sex (as biology) and gender (as culture) have long been wedded to produce one acceptable form of sexuality as the "natural" derivation of the two. Sexual essentialism, thus rooted in biology, generates sexual determinism as some immanent proclivity toward "proper" erotic aim, object, choice, and sexual practice. However, as Katz (1990, 29) notes, "The common notion that biology determines the object of sexual desire, or that physiology and society together cause sexual orientation, are determinisms that deny the break existing between our bodies and situation and our desiring."

Thus, I would argue, it is time for a break—a radical break from the impoverished script of a univocal sexuality. Here, the postmodern proliferation of bodies, pleasures, and knowledges advocated by Michel Foucault (1980) deregulates the univocal aim of sexual agency, thereby calling into question the fundamental categories of sex and gender as the basis for a unified identity. As demonstrated earlier, gender can be exposed as artifice through strategies of simulation that collapse binarisms. But sexuality, too, must be derailed from its track, which is locked into a naturalized heterosexual destination.

Once again, the maintenance of gay and straight boundaries categorically reproduces the old dream of symmetry found in the male/female couplet of sexual difference. Although gender succumbs to simulation, sexual practices take refuge in sexed bodies from whence those practices originate as homosexual or heterosexual. Not surprisingly, heterosexuality (like the gender-master-term *male*) is constituted as a monolithic category against which all other practices are defined as other, as deviant. Deviance, though, is necessary to the constitution and invention of heterosexuality (Katz 1990). This tenacious sexual binarism undergirds Forrest Sawyer's compulsion to repeat "lines, limits, and boundaries" in his "Nightline" interview with Madonna. To protect the heterosexual zone, Sawyer tries to stave off sexual plurality through the erection of discursive boundaries, a symptom of his terror. Thus, when Sawyer stutters "and you have . . . apparently group sex," his referent collapses the video with Madonna, her body the finely honed instrument of multiple practices as simultaneously fucker and fuckee with the video's multiple bodies—all detoured from their assigned routes.

Not surprisingly, *Justify My Love* has been characterized with a moralistic litany of charges against nudity, bisexuality, sadomasochism, and multiple partners (group sex). The video opens up a Pandora's box of sexual prohibitions, which are judged as such through the maintenance of a single sexual standard. The kind of sexual morality, whether religious, political, or psychological, that legislates such a standard has, as Rubin (1984, 283) notes, "more in common with ideologies of racism than with true ethics." According to Rubin (1984, 283),

> A democratic morality should judge sexual acts by the way partners treat one another, the level of mutual consideration, the presence or absence of coercion, and the quantity and quality of the pleasures they provide. Whether sex acts are gay or straight, coupled or in groups, naked or in underwear, commercial or free, with or without video, should not be ethical concerns.

Here, one's body (and what one chooses to do with it) may be the last bastion of freedom against those discourses that try to restrict it. Even those discourses associated with the progressive agendas of liberalism, socialism, and feminism, which supposedly pride themselves on a politics of cultural diversity, often deny freedom of expression to alternative sexualities.

Perhaps most alarming is the tactical alliance between antiporn feminists and the right wing, of which Rubin notes that, "stripped of their feminist content, much of the language and many of the tactics of persuasion developed by the feminist anti-porn movement have been assimilated by the right-wing" (Stamps 1990, 9).[1] Thus, feminists concerned with violence against women find themselves strange compatriots with the Moral Majority in a coalition that will not necessarily deter male-perpetrated violence but is likely to place sexual minorities under siege by the state.[2]

Butler (1990a) points out that one way to combat this assault on sexual pluralism is proliferation, a Foucauldian strategy that displaces the binary structure of gay and straight as discursively uncontrollable. Rather than succumb to the ontological identities at the core of this sexual binarism, the task is to efface boundaries by refusing the definitional efficacy of the terms themselves—to build up a range of representations and intensify multiple meanings. Such tactics, which push for a democratic morality, have been implemented unwittingly by the mainstream media. In their eagerness to vilify "deviance," the media continue to be complicitous in proliferating sexual representations that invite viewers to question the very basis of a single-standard morality within public discourse.

In this respect, both Madonna's polymorphic video and Robert Mapplethorpe's S/M photographs have served as vehicles for public controversy. The two have much in common as multidiscursive fragments that have insinuated themselves into our culture's sexual lingua franca as so many loaded signifiers. However, they share even more than representational proliferation and an excess of signification, for Richard Meyer (1990) notes that Mapplethorpe's visual aesthetic relies on the intrinsic theatricality of S/M, a high stylization that also informs the sexual stylistics of Madonna's *Justify My Love* video.

Although *Justify* borrows its mise-en-scène from European art cinema, it duplicates Mapplethorpe's preference for black and white to intensify sexual theatrics, which are visually extended by the video's camera work. Vertiginous camera movement tracks Madonna's dizzying walk through mazelike hotel spaces, a subjective sign of the autoerotic extended to glimpses of bodies in spatial dislocation. Fluid cuts on action shift between Madonna's undulating body in the corridor's exaggerated deep space and the flat, staged spaces where leather- and lace-clad bodies pose between acts. Here, the trope of sadomasochism is complicated through a staged distribution of fetish signifiers that diffuse the typical binary terms of mastery and subordination. Marked by fluidity and dislocation, this dream scene collapses the boundaries inscribed in spatial and sexual relations. As Eric Michaels (1987, 91) notes, "Texts which intend polysemy, which do not police meaning but instead invite it, do not encourage [singular] identification, a psychological response, but displacement, a spatial activity." The polysexual stimulates the polysemic in this dream of dissymmetry where sexual identities are displaced by multiple erotic acts.

Displacement is at the core of the video's transgression where bodies intersect in the infamous bedroom scene. Multiple bodies shift positions in a series of displacements, while camera movement simulates the fluidity of erotic activity as it ranges over bodies, undisturbed by substitutions. Core identities surrender to the assumption of erotic roles in a splitting between dark and light, male and female, gay and straight—differences multiplied and compounded. As Butler (1990a, 110) notes, "Fantasy enacts a splitting or fragmentation or, perhaps better put, a multiplication or proliferation of identifications that puts the very locatability of identity into question."

Thus, at the outset, Madonna draws her lover, Tony Ward, onto the bed in a medium shot. Space is disrupted as a black, sexually stylized figure enters the frame in a close-up, low-angle shot coded as above Madonna, camera, and viewer. A cut reorients space yet again in a medium close-up shot of Madonna prone on the bed, her arms raised in expectation. Splits between spaces break spatiosexual continuity, and Madonna is joined across the divide by a (wo)man coded between male and female, light and dark: a coding split between spaces and identities. S(he) becomes the third term, interceding between Tony and Madonna, as the "top" to Madonna's "bottom." The triangulated erotic action shifts to Tony Ward, now in the revolving third-term position—voyeur to female performers who, as exhibitionists, break the male gaze in two shot-reverse-shot sequences.

Madonna and the complexly figured (wo)man on the bed dislocate and reallocate erotic aims in a polymorphic distribution. As their bodies entwine in a convergence of rhyming black lace, the camera moves horizontally up their bodies toward the locus of categorical rifting, the mouth. Gender and sexuality are placed in question in this crossing of boundaries where a deep, languid kiss is the focal point—a collapse of space and binary terms into the erotic act. As Rosalind Coward (1985, 96) notes, "Sexual relations alone regularly transgress the barrier around each individual, and the kiss seals a crossing into this personal zone, a crossing into the empire of the senses." Close-ups of a muscular back, the flesh between edges of black lace, capture the tactility of Madonna's slow caress, mutually enjoyed.

Justify maintains these structures of splitting, displacement, and the multiplication of erotic aims rerouted into a sexually plural orbit. This extends to top/bottom relations that, though derived from the terminology of gay S/M, more generally refer to sexual exchanges in which power is eroticized in the enactment of fluid erotic roles. Newton and Walton (1984, 246) note that

> in any given sexual exchange, the top is the person who conducts and orchestrates the episode. The bottom is the one who acts out or interprets the sexual initiatives and language of the top. How this exchange takes place is not a given. The top might not move much or the bottom might be expressive and physically active, rather than the inert being conjured up by the word "passive."

Throughout the video, top/bottom relations shift, beginning with the (wo)man on top of Madonna and Madonna as bottom, initiator of the kiss. Later, Ward is top and Madonna bottom as the camera's horizontal movements simulate intercourse, and still later, these movements are rhymed when Madonna tops Ward, the close-up of her black-laced buttocks matching the earlier shot of the (wo)man's black-laced back. Moreover, toward the video's conclusion, the camera moves with Ward down the (wo)man's body in a sensual caress rhymed in a later move upward in which Ward embraces Madonna—black lace doubly matched on the vertical as well as horizontal planes. Thus, the video presents a gridlike structure to represent multiple points of sexual pleasure as split and dispersed across bodies, between bodies, on top of and beneath bodies: a plural assertion of sexualities.

Justify My Love multiplies and proliferates the very terms of sexual identification through top/bottom interchanges and spacial dislocations that refuse to match sex identity with erotic aim and object choice. Indeed, *Justify* issues a challenge to ontological notions implicit in the sex/gender/sexuality triumvirate by producing rifts and breaks between their linkage. As a postmodern vehicle for this insistent rifting. Madonna pries open a space in the mainstream to provide sexual minorities with visibility and confirmation, while provoking feminism to rethink its own lines, limits, and boundaries.

Justify and Madonna's other videos suggest that the answer is not to delimit the spheres of feminism and postmodernism but rather to "push the envelope" toward the postmodern possibilities of multifaceted alliances. Her popularity, which traverses the ranks of cross-dressers, drag queens, Dykes for Madonna, and various gay and lesbian sex-radicals, brings the margins to the center of feminist debate through postmodern representational strategies. Feminism, inflected by postmodernism, may be opened up to more radical possibilities. The gay liberation movement is a case in point, where, as James Darsey (1991, 44) notes, "the rhetoric of gay liberation is unique in being perhaps the most thoroughly postmodern of reform discourses."

Although differentially constituted (and not without internal as well as external conflicts), gay men and lesbians have been at the vanguard of political movements, displacing essentialized notions of identity with "a patchwork of overlapping alliances" (Fraser and Nicholson 1990, 35).[3] Indeed, the material power exerted through postmodern sex and gender representations, as practiced within the gay community and popularized by Madonna, can fracture the notion of "an identity" with a motley pastiche of interests, alignments, and identities that intersect at decisive moments. Such provisional coalitions could present a formidable challenge to patriarchal moralism, which, lacking the presumed immanence of identity categories, would have a more difficult time maintaining social control over others aligned in a disparate unity.

CONCLUSION: TOWARD A POSTMODERN FEMINIST POLITICS OF MOTLEY ALLIANCES

The politics of sex and gender representations as they relate to identity has not been lost on Madonna. One of her more recent guises, recounted without a trace of irony in *Vanity Fair*, has been that of the lonely chanteuse, nostalgic for domestic "pleasures" such as picking lint from lint screens and mating Sean's socks (Hirschberg 1991). This domestic construction provides some rifting with her bold persona in *Truth or Dare*, a confrontational performance-documentary that has, among other things, Madonna declaring that the sight of two men kissing gives her a "hard-on." In each case, Madonna confounds prescribed boundaries by, respectively, playing at femininity and simulating male sexuality. Thus, from her disengendering polysexual display in *Justify* to her drag dance in *Express Yourself* to her representation as space-age dominatrix in the Blond Ambition tour, Madonna will continue to simulate and deconstruct the "truths" of sex and gender.

Through strategies of simulation, she transforms the "truth" of gender into drag, a dialectical fragmentation between two terms, and then fissures this destabilized sex identity further by means of splitting and displacement to advance a prodigious sexual plurality. In more general terms, her disingenuous figuration says much about the political promise of postmodern strategies.

The ungrounded ground of postmodern feminist discourse, in particular, can establish alliances based on an eccentric and disparate mobilization, aimed at concerted political action. As Butler (1990b, 148) insists, "The deconstruction of identity is not the deconstruction of politics; rather, it establishes as political the very terms through which identity is articulated." This reinscription in the plural expands the range for a coalitional politics not determined or fixed by foundationalist frames. Thus, one could "come out" and participate in a range of identities—such as a lesbian heterosexual, a heterosexual lesbian, a male lesbian, a female gay man, or even a feminist sex-radical. As Butler (1990a, 121) notes, "There are structures of psychic homosexuality within heterosexual relations, and structures of psychic heterosexuality within gay and lesbian sexuality and relationships." Once sex and gender are placed on equally fictive footing, the possibilities for multiple identities (and alliances) are enormous.

So, the postmodern era inaugurating simulation and fragmented identities need not be cause for political pessimism—especially in regard to "others" who have lived in the shadows of realist epistemology and sex and gender essentialism. To think otherwise and to entertain multiple styles, surfaces, sexualities, and identities may move us from the margin to the center in coalitional acts of resistance and disruption.

Thus, we return to the center, to the spectacle of Madonna on "Nightline" splitting the seams that attempt to suture her into a seamless interrogation. At the interview's end, Forrest Sawyer asks her what she will do next, rehearsing the media's desire to know and fix this prolific source of multiplicity. To this, Madonna reflexively replies: "So you want me to promote one of my products, one of my up-coming, button-pushing products?" Madonna thus refuses to divulge the ground or location of her future insurrections. A coalitional politics that lacks all truth in appearances can do likewise. So can a strategic postmodern feminism, whose sly deployments multi-Madonna knows only too well.

Acknowledgments

I would like to thank the University of Utah Humanities Center's National Conference on Rewriting the (Post)Modern (March 1990), at which I presented an earlier version of this chapter. I am also indebted to Cindy Patton, Lisa Henderson, Thomas Nakayama, and Harold Schlechtweg. Reprinted with permission from "Madonna's Postmodern Feminism: Bringing the Margins to the Center," *Southern Communication Journal,* 57, no. 2 (Winter 1992): 120–131.

NOTES

1. The specifics of what has been called the "sex wars" or the "sex/porn debates" fall outside the scope of this chapter. However, the debates between antiporn feminists and sex-radicals continue to be a rich area for further research, particularly regarding the defeat of the antipornography ordinances in Minneapolis and Indianapolis, which pitted antiporn feminists against the Feminist Anti-Censorship Task Force (FACT). See Leidholdt and Raymond (1990) and Caught Looking, Inc. (1988) for opposing points of view.

2. An unlikely and unofficial coalition of fundamentalist religious groups and antiporn feminists has created a discursive climate that encourages state repression of sexual minorities. For example, witness the frightening breach of civil rights in recent police raids on gay and lesbian night clubs and gatherings as reported in Boston's *Gay Community News* (Nealon 1990a, 1990b; Yukins 1991).

3. Here, it is important to note that gay males and lesbians respond differently to Madonna. Although the wealth of material in the gay press suggests that she is more popular among gay men (Musto 1991), she has also had a profound impact on the lesbian community (Solomon 1990), whose views have been underrepresented in print (but not in widespread networks of discussion). I recognize differences, to be sure, and do not wish to essentialize gay discourse or lump together others as the same. However, my project here is a first step toward deconstructing sex and gender presumptions and foundations, for which I find the rich and multiple differences represented by gay men, lesbians, and others a lived contestation for what often passes in theory as a given.

REFERENCES

Baudrillard, J. (1983). *Simulations.* P. Foss, P. Patton, and P. Beitchman (trans.). New York: Semiotext(e).
———. (1988a). *America.* C. Turner (trans.). London: Verso.

_____ . (1988b). *The Ecstasy of Communication.* B. and C. Schutze (trans.). New York: Semiotext(e).

Benhabib, S. (1984). "Epistemologies of Postmodernism: A Rejoinder to Jean-François Lyotard." *New German Critique* 33 (Fall): 103–126.

Bordo, S. (1990a). "Feminism, Postmodernism, and Gender-skepticism." In L. Nicholson (ed.), *Feminism/Postmodernism.* New York: Routledge, pp. 133–156.

_____ . (1990b). "Material Girl: The Effacements of Postmodern Culture." *Michigan Quarterly Review* 29, no. 4 (Fall): 653–677.

Butler, J. (1990a). "The Force of Fantasy: Feminism, Mapplethorpe, and Discursive Excess." *Differences* 2, no. 2 (Summer): 105–125.

_____ . (1990b). *Gender Trouble: Feminism and the Subversion of Identity.* New York: Routledge.

Case, S.-E. (1988/1989). "Towards a Butch-femme Aesthetic." *Discourse* 11, no. 1 (Fall–Winter): 55–73.

Chapkis, W. (1986). *Beauty Secrets: Women and the Politics of Appearance.* Boston, Mass.: South End Press.

Chodorow, N. (1978). *The Reproduction of Mothering: Psychoanalysis and the Sociology of Gender.* Berkeley: University of California Press.

Coward, R. (1985). *Female Desires.* New York: Grove Press.

Curry, R. (1990). "Madonna from Marilyn to Marlene—Pastiche and/or Parody?" *Journal of Film and Video* 42, no. 2 (Summer): 15–30.

Darsey, J. (1991). "From 'Gay is Good' to the Scourge of AIDS: The Evolution of Gay Liberation Rhetoric, 1977–1990." *Communication Studies* 42, no. 7 (Spring): 43–66.

de Lauretis, T. (1986). "Feminist Studies/Critical Studies: Issues, Terms, and Contexts." In T. de Lauretis (ed.), *Feminist Studies/Critical Studies.* Bloomington: Indiana University Press, pp. 1–19.

_____ . (1987). "The Technology of Gender." In her *Technologies of Gender: Essays on Theory, Film, and Fiction.* Bloomington: Indiana University Press, pp. 1–30.

Dempster, E. (1988). "Women Writing the Body: Let's Watch a Little How She Dances." In S. Sheridan (ed.), *Grafts: Feminist Cultural Criticism.* London: Verso, pp. 35–54.

di Stefano, C. (1988). "Dilemmas of Difference: Feminism, Modernity, and Postmodernism." *Women and Politics* 8, nos. 3/4 (Spring): 1–24.

Doane, M. A. (1982). "Film and the Masquerade: Theorizing the Female Spectator." *Screen* 23, nos. 3/4 (September–October): 74–87.

Ellis, K., Jaker, B., Hunter, N. D., O'Dair, B., and Tallmer, A. (eds.). (1988). *Caught Looking: Feminism, Pornography & Censorship.* Seattle, Wash.: Real Comet Press.

Foucault, M. (1980). *The History of Sexuality, Vol. I: An Introduction.* R. Hurley (trans.). New York: Vintage Books.

Fraser, N., and Nicholson, L. (1990). "Social Criticism Without Philosophy: An Encounter Between Feminism and Postmodernism." In L. Nicholson (ed.), *Feminism/Postmodernism.* New York: Routledge, pp. 19–38.

Gilligan, C. (1983). *In a Different Voice: Psychological Theory and Women's Development*. Cambridge, Mass.: Harvard University Press.

Goodman, E. (1990). "Multi-Madonna Offers Wrong Answers." (Northampton, Mass.) *Daily Hampshire Gazette*, December 18, p. 8.

Habermas, J. (1983). "Modernity—An Incomplete Project." In H. Foster (ed.), *The Anti-aesthetic: Essays on Postmodern Culture*. Port Townsend, Wash.: Bay Press, pp. 3–15.

Hirschberg, L. (1991). "The Misfit." *Vanity Fair*. April, pp. 158–168, 196–198.

Jameson, F. (1984). "Postmodernism, or the Cultural Logic of Late Capitalism." *New Left Review* 146 (July–August): 53–92.

Kaplan, E. A. (1985). "The Hidden Agenda—Revision: Essays in Feminist Film Criticism." *Camera Obscura* 13/14 (Spring–Summer): 235–249.

——— . (1987). *Rocking Around the Clock: Music Television, Postmodernism, and Consumer Culture*. New York: Methuen.

Katz, J. N. (1990). "The Invention of Heterosexuality." *Socialist Review* 20, no. 1 (January–March): 7–34.

Leidholdt, D., and Raymond, J. (eds.). (1990). *The Sexual Liberals and the Attack on Feminism*. New York: Pergamon Press.

Lyotard, J.-F. (1984). *The Postmodern Condition: A Report on Knowledge*. G. Bennington and B. Massumi (trans.). Minneapolis: University of Minnesota Press.

Meyer, R. (1990). "Imagining Sadomasochism: Robert Mapplethorpe and the Masquerade of Photography." *Qui Parle* 4, no. 1 (Fall): 62–78.

Michaels, E. (1987). "My Essay on Postmodernity." *Art and Text* 25 (June–August): 86–91.

Montrelay, M. (1978). "Inquiry into Femininity." *M/F* 1: 83–101.

Musto, M. (1991). "Immaculate Connection: Madonna and Us." *Outweek*, March 20, pp. 35–41, 62.

Nealon, C. (1990a). "Iowa Gay Fest Raided." *Gay Community News*, September 9–15, pp. 1, 7.

——— . (1990b). "Summer of Gay Raids." *Gay Community News*, September 23–29, pp. 1, 3.

Newton, E. (1972). *Mother Camp: Female Impersonators in America*. Englewood Cliffs, N.J.: Prentice-Hall.

Newton, E., and S. Walton. (1984). "The Misunderstanding: Toward a More Precise Sexual Vocabulary." In C. S. Vance (ed.), *Pleasure and Danger: Exploring Female Sexuality*. Boston, Mass.: Routledge and Kegan Paul, pp. 242–250.

Owens, C. (1983). "The Discourse of Others: Feminists and Postmodernism." In H. Foster (ed.), *The Anti-aesthetic: Essays on Postmodern Culture*. Port Townsend, Wash.: Bay Press, pp. 57–82.

Porkorny, S. (1989). "Obsess Yourself!" *Gay Community News*, July 30–August 5, pp. 8–10.

Riviere, J. (1986). "Womanliness as a Masquerade." In V. Burgin, J. Donald, and C. Kaplan (eds.), *Formations of Fantasy*. London: Methuen, pp. 35–44.

Rubin, G. (1984). "Thinking Sex: Notes for a Radical Theory of the Politics of Sexuality." In C. S. Vance (ed.), *Pleasure and Danger: Exploring Female Sexuality*. Boston, Mass.: Routledge and Kegan Paul, pp. 267–319.

Russo, M. (1986). "Female Grotesques: Carnival and Theory." In T. de Lauretis (ed.), *Feminist Studies/Critical Studies*. Bloomington: Indiana University Press, pp. 213–229.

Solomon, A. (1990). "Dykotomies: Scents and Sensibility in the Lesbian Community." *Village Voice*, June 26, pp. 39–42.

Soper, K. (1990). *Troubled Pleasures: Writings on Politics, Gender, and Hedonism*. London: Verso.

Spivak, G. C. (1976). "Translator's Preface." In J. Derrida, *Of Grammatology*. Baltimore, Md.: Johns Hopkins University Press, pp. IX–XC.

––––––. (1983). "Displacement and the Discourse of Woman." In M. Krupnick (ed.), *Displacement: Derrida and After*. Bloomington: Indiana University Press, pp. 169–195.

Stamps, W. (1990). "On the Edge, Under the Gun: A Boston Symposium Examines the Right-Wing Attack on Radical Sexuality." *Gay Community News*, September 30–October 6, p. 9.

Stein, A., and J. Urla. (1988). "Lesbians of the 80's: A Lesbian Roundtable Discussion." *On Our Backs* 5, no. 2 (Fall): 16–19.

Yukins, E. (1991). "Vice Cops Raid Lesbian Party." *Gay Community News*, March 11–17, pp. 1, 6.

Part Three

Gender Trouble:
Madonna Poses the
Feminist Question

photo by Herb Ritts, *courtesy of Warner Brothers*

E. ANN KAPLAN

7

Madonna Politics: Perversion, Repression, or Subversion? Or Masks and/as Master-y

I wanted people to see that my life isn't so easy, and one step further than that is the movie's not completely me. You could watch it and say, I still don't know Madonna, and good. Because you will never know the real me. Ever.

—Madonna

*I*N THIS STATEMENT and, indeed, in the entire interview in *Vanity Fair* (1991) from which it is taken, Madonna, talking about the new documentary *Truth or Dare* (in Europe, *In Bed with Madonna*), distinguishes her words, her behavior, and her images in the film from what she considers the underlying, "real" Madonna—the "real me," as she puts it. She assumes a split between herself as a subject and the external presentation of "Madonna."[1] Further, she is committed to the idea that we—her fans, her critics, her various audiences—will "never know" that "real" Madonna.

The statement is arresting because, for most of the time, Madonna deliberately plays with surfaces, masks, the masquerade. But the question arises as to which theory of the mask underlies this play. Mikhail Bakhtin's (1968) distinctions may be useful in this regard: He noted that the mask in romanticism was terrifying because it deceived, it hid the "real" subject, it distorted and concealed identity; but the mask in ancient folklore represented play, the recognition of the changeability and nonfixity of the subject. Although Bakhtin carefully locates these differing conceptions of the mask in history, I reintroduce them for a Foucauldian genealogy of the mask—the mask as representing what history, in fact, shows—namely, that there is no stable identity (Foucault 1979).

149

The two theories of the mask will be useful in distinguishing two "subversion" themes that will inform my argument: (1) Madonna as resisting a patriarchal "feminine"—as offering alternative female identification (the patriarchal mask can be abandoned and the "real" woman can step forth) and (2) Madonna as problematizing the bourgeois illusion of "real" individual gendered selves (there is nothing *but* masks).

It is noteworthy that, until recently, Madonna had only rarely flirted with revealing her "real" persona. Her apparently autobiographical *Oh Father* video (1989) and her frankly political "Nightline" interview in 1990 have now, however, been reinscribed in *Truth or Dare:* The film makes clear that the earlier instances of supposed revelation were actually more cases of self-construction—more masks that functioned to *pretend* to reveal, as does the whole documentary.

Fans clearly long for such revelations! And one might well examine just why the "real" Madonna fascinates. Why do fans and audiences want to know her? Why, even, does the public that resents and scorns Madonna want to know about her? Why is selling the real Madonna—in magazine and TV interviews and now in the documentary film and the much-touted unauthorized biography that followed (C. Anderson 1991)—such a commercial success? Why do groupies need to relate to stars through imagining their offstage lives? What can we learn about Western culture's investment in the construct of the "individual" and of a split between inner and outer selves (the real Madonna is inner, the one she shows merely a mask or outer) through fans' needs? Further, why does Madonna want to conceal her real self so adamantly ("Because you will never know the real me. Ever.")?

One might argue, Madonna's quoted statement to the contrary, that there is no real Madonna, at least in any sense that might be useful in a cultural studies context. But addressing those questions approaches what is important about Madonna as real. As a gesture toward such research, my study seeks to understand the investments in a whole series of conflicting constructions of Madonna. The full project is concerned with various discursive constructions of her—by the U.S. media, including teenage consumer culture; by the Parents' Media Resource Center; by women scholars, including feminists; by neo-Marxist critics; by select U.S. teens, distinguished in terms of ethnicity and class, and those in other cultures; and, last but not least, by Madonna herself. For she is the site of a whole series of discourses, many that contradict each other but that together produce the divergent images in circulation. For me, it is not a matter of locating an authentic Madonna core that can be extricated from the various wrappings that enclose her; rather, it is a question of peeling off layer after layer to reveal precisely the absence where a core might be. For fans and audiences, there may be a "real" Madonna that they have chosen to construct to serve their own needs. But, from the perspective of the conflicting discourses, there is nothing but the constitutive layers of differing constructions.

This does *not* mean that the cultural critic must avoid taking any stance toward what I will label the "Madonna phenomenon" (hereafter the MP). In fact, the "Madonna politics" prevalent in the United States and elsewhere arises precisely because of the conflicting positions various constituencies assume. The point, however, is to clarify contestation about the "correct" stance toward Madonna by exploring the investments underlying select Madonna constructions.

The three dominant stances toward the MP may be distinguished as (1) "perversion," alluding to the puritanical characterization of Madonna by U.S. and other cultures, rather than to serious Freudian theories of perversion; (2) repression; and (3) subversion.

PERVERSION

The media have always used Madonna for sensational news and at the same time been quite relentless in their criticism of her. From the start, Madonna caused trouble, challenging prevailing notions of "the proper" in the United States and elsewhere.[2] Her 1985 *Material Girl* video was criticized for encouraging materialism (the reporters misunderstood the video's irony, but in any case, who are the *media* to moralize about materialism?), and *Like a Virgin* was attacked for questioning virginity as a prerequisite for marriage and unnecessarily introducing young children to sexual matters. With each subsequent video (e.g., *Papa Don't Preach, Open Your Heart*), Madonna pushed further and further at the limits of the sexually acceptable; before the Mapplethorpe and 2 Live Crew cases went to court (which Madonna refers to in the "Nightline" interview mentioned earlier), her *Like a Prayer* ad (for which she had already been paid $5 million) was censored by Pepsi-Cola.

Madonna's Blond Ambition tour was also censored in some cities. Evidently, her spectacular parodies of patriarchal male and female sexual icons caused trouble because they revealed the underlying contradictory tensions within dominant U.S. culture vis-à-vis sexuality. Her show violated too many fragile, middle-class sexual codes and boundaries. To take one local example, Wayne Robins, writing in the Long Island, New York, periodical *Newsday,* says: "In 'Like a Virgin,' Madonna acted as anything but. The male dancers, wearing conical brassieres that looked more like phallic symbols than bustiers, engaged in simulated oral sex with her. (Talk about 'Twin Peaks')." Later on, Robins shows his even greater sense of violation in Madonna's siding with Roseanne Barr over the national anthem. He says Madonna has missed the point, namely, that the American public's standards have dropped to zero. "Sooner or later," he says, "we're going to stop making heroes of marginally talented exhibitionists. Madonna was too busy grabbing her crotch to get the point." (The real question, of course, is whether or not Robins himself got the point!)

With *Justify My Love*, MTV did not wait for the Moral Majority: It censored the video itself, leaving it paradoxically to Forrest Sawyer and "Nightline" to show the full video at 11 P.M., with due warnings and careful framings. By and large, the dominant media construct Madonna as a cheap exhibitionist at best, a pervert at worst: They seem blithely unaware of the level of fantasy within which Madonna explicitly works.

REPRESSION

Neo-Marxists with a Frankfurt School bias have been loudest in their representation of this stance toward the MP. For them, the MP is equivalent to the old bread-and-circuses trick: Popular icons function as devices for siphoning off people's unsatisfied social needs and psychic desires. The icon, no matter how outrageous, does not threaten consumer capitalism. On the contrary, she provides ever-new markets and sources of profit for middlemen and women. The icon herself is used by the media as much as she may use them to advance herself and accumulate vast amounts of capital. (Madonna is said to be "worth" $125 million, at latest count: The term *worth* itself exposes the underlying [unconscious] commodity fetishism and the construction of identity and personal status through money.) The actual practices an icon may indulge in are all contained ultimately by the constraints of the international financial elite, the flow of capital, and the various competing market forces.

In this repression theory, Marx's concept of commodity fetishism is relevant. In this theory, as Mulvey (1991) has noted, an abstract quality (eroticism, status, power) is added to a material thing (the object to be consumed), which conceals the labor power involved in the commodity's production. This process accounts for the repressed knowledge of the exploited labor needed to produce the desired commodity: The commodity, as it were, stands in for or covers over the oppressive labor relations.

Meanwhile, Freud's concept of fetishism partly explains the attraction of icons like Madonna, who cover over or stand in for castration anxiety. As Mulvey (1975) has argued, Freud's theory of the fetish was the most semiotic of the perversions because the fetishist focuses on the sign (the shoe, the fur collar) that replaces the actual object—in Freud's case, thinking as he was about the little boy, the object is the castrated woman—with something that the conscious mind can accept. Within the Lacanian framework, men and women alike, if for different reasons, desire the phallus. Stars like Madonna fill this space of desire—this gap that constitutes the subject in desire for an object—and therefore draw everyone in. Many who market products for teenage consumers cynically capitalize on this mechanism and use Madonna to sell objects, as I have discussed elsewhere (Kaplan 1990a).

SUBVERSION

I will return to the political and psychoanalytic issues raised by this hurried summary of the repression thesis because the two subversion positions I now focus on also raise problematic political questions, if of a different kind.

When I first studied Madonna in 1983, my critical task was textual analysis and thematic or formal organization of select MTV videos. At the time, short videos relayed on a twenty-four-hour, nonstop cable station were a new phenomenon. Little in the way of a theoretical apparatus for approaching this phenomenon existed, but I found that some theories of postmodernism circulating at the time illuminated what MTV was doing. Specifically, the concept of the "pastiche" was useful in discussing Madonna's appropriation of Marilyn Monroe in *Material Girl*. My disciplinary constraints made appropriate a textual, rather than either an industry or audience, analysis.

Since then, Madonna has risen to unprecedented fame and was granted her own round-the-clock, nonstop circulation in the 1990 MTV Madonnathon, a unique happening. Thus, Madonna discourses proliferate in an unprecedented series of contexts, warranting a different critical approach that would address the discourses along with specific texts.

One main argument for seeing the MP as subversive has been advanced by scholars working within a strand of British cultural studies that relies on audience research. Popular icons have always generated extensive fandom and the associated magazines and paraphernalia, and such icons have always born the brunt of media focus. With Madonna, the extensive tie-in between media scholars and these other constituencies has produced an exaggerated metacritical level. There are, for example, media scholars interested in Madonna fans, whom they interview in order to reconstruct what meanings viewers derive from Madonna concerts, records, videos, magazine articles, and so forth. Other scholars analyze media-Madonna discourses and representations. Others detail Madonna's business practices, her relations to the record, video, film, and book industries, and her struggle for success within the rock industry. Still others analyze Madonna's rock videos from a variety of perspectives.

One main focus has been on teenage girls because they are interesting to certain feminists in relation to a role-model effect. Researchers in this area work with the "commonsense" category of "real" individual selves and specific cultural identities. Their work exemplifies the romantic notion of the mask as something that conceals the real person, something that deceives, like the patriarchal "feminine." Scholars of this persuasion believe that audiences can see through the false masks in popular materials.

As Fiske (1987, 285) puts it, "Culture is a process of making meanings that people actively participate in. . . . The mass produced text can only be made into a *popular* text by the people, and this transformation occurs when the various subcultures can activate sets of meanings from it and insert these meanings into their daily cultural experience." McRobbie (1980) and McRobbie and Nava (1984) articulated a general theory about "girl culture," which was first applied specifically to Madonna by Williamson (1985), Fiske (1987), and Bradby (1990), followed by Lewis (1990a, 1990b). The approach is best summed up by Fiske, who notes that McRobbie "explored the permeability of the boundary between television and other forms of cultural experience" (1987, 269) and found "among teenage girls a set of meanings for dance and female sexuality that contest and struggle against the patriarchal hegemony" (1987, 270). In relation to Madonna, Fiske (1987, 274) found that "Madonna offers some young girls the opportunity to find meanings of their own feminine sexuality that suit them, meanings that are independent." For Lewis (1990a, 9), "female address videos reclaim style for girls and richly articulate style as a symbolic vehicle for female expression." In relation to Madonna specifically, Lewis (1990b, 123) notes that "at least part of the appeal of Madonna's overtly sexual image for adolescent girls lies in the way it can be used to counter feminine ideals of dependency and reserve."

There are two main problems with the kind of analysis undertaken here. First, there is the shift, without apparent self-consciousness, from the level of discourse analysis (how girls are constituted by male adolescent culture or what female images are in circulation) to the level of lived psychological or social "development," as if such development were not always already discursively constituted. The rock video texts become ethnographic data to prove an a priori theory of female development and of femininity as "expressiveness."

Second, the given gender hierarchies are kept in place, but new values are assigned them. The "discovery signs" approach valorizes a patriarchal femininity hitherto devalorized, scorned, and marginalized. Meanwhile, the "access signs" approach to female musicians offers a way of constructing a female subject as autonomous, independent, and active like the male adolescent subject. Indeed, Lewis (1990b, 171) ends with the following triumphal declaration: "The style imitators push through the symbolic discourse of female culture for the recognition that boys receive. They demand access to male privilege of money, power, and authority, but at the same time they refuse to dispose of the expressive forms provided by female culture."

A final problem, linked to this vision of expressive women in positions of power and authority, has to do with the absence of attention to the overall ideological context for the narratives Lewis develops, whether of female musicians' rise to fame, of the meanings video narratives embody, or of fandom. Lewis (1990b, 161) attempts, for example (quoting Bishop and Hoggett here), to argue that fandom is a subversive activity because it involves "values of reciprocity and interdependence as opposed to self-interest, collectivism as opposed to individualism, the importance of loyalty and a sense of 'identity' or 'belonging' as opposed to the principle of forming ties on the basis of calculation." But these values could all be found equally within Moral Majority groups opposing abortion, arguing against pornography, or even supporting fascism.

For instance, consider a critic like Camille Paglia, who sank Madonna politics to new depths in a *New York Times* op-ed essay on December 14, 1990, apparently inspired by Madonna's "Nightline" interview. In a piece called "Madonna—Finally, a Real Feminist," Paglia lambastes feminists for being "outrageously negative about Madonna from the start." (I have never been able to locate these negative articles.) Her monolithic construction of feminists as puritanical and as having "nerdy, bookworm husbands" was obviously designed to provoke. But her argument that **"Madonna has taught young women to be fully female and sexual while still exercising total control over their lives. She shows girls how to be attractive, sensual, energetic, ambitious, aggressive and funny—all at the same time"** sounds quite like some girl culture research. Yet, her ultimate goals are quite the reverse politically—not having anything to do with subverting dominant gender hierarchies. Paglia ultimately recuperates Madonna not for what I or girl culture scholars would call feminism but for a Nietzschean, Dionysian, and orgiastic sexuality and for a "nature" in which "real" men are ceaselessly driven to lust for women by desire to conquer the unknown. For Paglia, Madonna exemplifies the natural battle of the sexes in her exploration of the "deep recesses" of sexuality that feminists have been unwilling to explore. Paglia sees Madonna as an excellent model for young women in demonstrating what a "shrewd business tycoon" can achieve. She concludes that "through her enormous impact on women around the world, Madonna is the future of feminism."

Paglia's discussion emphasizes how co-optable theories that keep gender binarisms intact are. Any critical method must allow for evaluation of the meanings involved in fandom or in female rock stars rising to power, along with celebration and praise for the potentially subversive processes themselves as they may impact individual women.

Although the very concept of subversion keeps binarisms intact, how the binarisms are theorized is important. One of the values of the audience-centered approach is its concreteness; however, as indicated, this approach leaves untouched the notion of individual subjects. It entails deciding, for example, if Madonna subverts the patriarchal feminine by unmasking it or whether she ultimately reinscribes the patriarchal feminine by allowing her body to be recuperated for voyeurism. This method is appropriate in cultural contexts in which categories of class are dominant and inflected by gender and ethnicity. Madonna's image may be empowering for some young women—this is extremely important, and I do not want to minimize it—but the MP may be far more generally subversive than this if we look at it from a broader perspective that includes both genders and their constitutive elements. A second, more abstract argument for the MP as subversive, to which I now turn, enables a level of discourse in which we can understand the conflicting discursive constitutions of Madonna, including her own, as they function not only politically but also in terms of gender as a sign system not linked to identity. This strategy avoids some of the dangers of the first approach, even though it, too, has problems.

Judith Butler's (1990) theory of parodic performance provides a starting point for such a perspective. In Butler's argument, gender is a particular and prevailing culture sign system that involves subjects repeating gender signs as constitutive of a specific identity. Butler's notion of challenging binary constructs through parodic play with gender stereotypes in gay, transsexual, and carnivalesque reversals is attractive. In many ways, Madonna would seem to precisely embody what Butler believes is the most useful future strategy to avoid oppressive binary "engendering." Having investigated "the political stakes in designating as an *origin* and *cause* those identity categories that are in fact the *effects* of institutions, practices, discourses with multiple and diffuse points of origin," (1990, x–xi), Butler goes on to "think through the possibility of subverting and displacing those naturalized and reified notions of gender that support masculine hegemony and heterosexist power, to make gender trouble . . . through the mobilization, subversive confusion and proliferation of precisely those constitutive categories that seek to keep gender in its place" (1990, 33–34).

Engaged as she is in self-consciously philosophical discourse, Butler does not read cultural texts (fiction, TV, film) and thus is unable to flesh out her abstract argument with concrete examples. But much of what Madonna does can be read, via Butler, as mobilizing for the purposes of subverting the constitutive categories of gender.

I will briefly illustrate what I mean by referring to two videos, *Express Yourself* and *Justify My Love,* and to Alek Keshishian's documentary about Madonna, *Truth or Dare.* All of these materials must be located within Madonna's Blond Ambition phase—her most daring to date and the one that offers the most challenge to the dominant gender sign system. All three texts need to be situated within a network of discourses, including prevailing conservative discourses about Madonna—into which the texts irrupt, deliberately; the fandom constituency that worships the MP and waits expectantly for new developments; the commercial networks constituting the MP and relying on it for profit; the MP's own business enterprise that influences decisions about what is produced, for what audiences, to be exhibited when and where, and so on; and the discourses that move out from the MP's specific texts to other earlier texts.

In the case of both *Express Yourself* and *Justify My Love,* those other texts and contexts are German Expressionist films, directors, and actresses and the decadent Germany of the 1920s immediately preceding the Nazi era. *Express Yourself,* in addition, is specifically modeled on the German director Fritz Lang's 1926 film *Metropolis,* although it also references Josef Von Sternberg's *Blue Angel.* But it rewrites such patriarchal narratives completely. The heroine of the video presides over the text before it begins, heralding it as dedicated to women (in contrast to the male address of both Lang and Von Sternberg's films) and—in the fashion of the circus or vaudeville *metteur en scene*—conjuring up her audience.

The cross-dressing in videos like *Express Yourself,* the shocking violation of conventional sexual representations on prime-time television in *Justify My Love,* the androgny in the video (reminiscent, deliberately, of German Expressionism), the eruption of sexualities into the apparently smooth, unruffled decorum of the eighteenth century in her Academy Award performance, the constant parody through exaggeration of pornographic symbols in *Open Your Heart* and then throughout the Blond Ambition performance—these are just some of the ways in which Madonna has increasingly subverted dominant gender categories. She forces the spectator to question the boundaries of gender constructs and the cultural constraints on sexual themes and sexual fantasies.

That this has long been a key element of the MP is dramatically emphasized in *Truth or Dare.* Daring to pretend to reveal the truth about Madonna, the film, in fact, exemplifies the politics of the signifier. The heroine of the film, "Madonna," is seen in a startlingly diverse array of guises and poses: a grainy black-and-white image of her sitting in bathrobe and shower cap, sipping soup in an awkward position; lush color images of the heroine in performances that themselves challenge gender signs and identities; "surprise" encounters with an old friend (grainy black-and-white footage); the heroine in bed with her gay male dancers or playing a truth-or-dare game in which she performs fellatio on a bottle; the mother/boss-of-the-show figure, who prays before each performance with her group; the boss-who-needs-her-secretary. As the voice-over tells us, she is the "mother" to the group of largely male dancers, being drawn to people who have problems and need her.

This amounts to what can be termed a "politics of the signifier," which must, however, be addressed on two levels. There is the disruption of normative signification on the part of the performer, considered briefly above in relation to Madonna, but there is also the separate, if linked, level of the "receiver" of the text. This is a split that Butler did not have to address, given that she does not use cultural productions in making her argument.

What I find attractive about both Butler's theory and Madonna's textual practices are their apparent challenge to normative processes of identification that, in dominant cultural productions, lead to "denial of one's identity, or having one construct identity based on the model of the other . . . maintaining the illusion that one is actually inhabiting the body of the ego ideal" (Friedberg 1990, 44). Madonna's play with gender categories in recent texts prevents identification with any consistent image, let alone any culturally validated feminine norm, as in the "Mother-Daughter Pageant" or *Cosmopolitan*. Madonna's attraction for some has, in part, been precisely this violation of dominant feminine norms, perhaps too closely linked to the mother or to what the mother desires for the daughter. (Recall how in *Justify My Love*, the heroine destabilizes all such categories by telling her androgynous lover, whom she is kissing on a bed, that she does not want to be the mother and does not want him/her to be her child but rather something beyond these identities.) Adolescents are themselves trying out various identities, and Madonna's constant alteration may well satisfy deep needs for self-experimentation, deep needs to move beyond the constraints of given gender sign systems.

But the issue that now arises, in connection with theorizing the receiver or spectator, concerns how female subjectivity is being conceived. And this, in turn, has political ramifications. In contrast to Butler, critics like Fiske, Bradby, and Lewis function on the concrete level. As noted earlier, their goal is to understand the meanings young people make of Madonna. For this, they assume, with some justice, the construct of subjectivity that predominates in Western culture—that is, of the self as a specific identity. They are interested in how Madonna may help young women contest dominant, oppressive feminine ideals and find ways to assert their sexuality and autonomy.

This politics makes a certain sense, particularly in Britain where class and gender identities and demarcations remain far more salient than within the United States. I can see the *strategic* value of maintaining the categories "woman," "autonomy," and "independence" for women and minorities involved in activist politics of a certain kind. But the sort of politics that Butler advocates and that I see Madonna as performing is not necessarily incompatible with that addressed in works by Fiske and others. Although theorists in this group sometimes criticize theories like Butler's as a form of postmodernism that is not applicable to working-class or ethnic groups (Fiske 1987), such criticism may, in itself, be condescending.

Butler's politics of the signifier sees agency as only meaningful within given gender sign systems, and to this extent, she and members of the first group are in agreement. They differ, it seems, on the question of "depth"; Butler's subject is only a surface constituted through signs that themselves produce varying results in specific social interactions. Her theories mesh more with the concept of the mask in ancient folklore, mentioned earlier, than with that in romanticism on which Fiske and others seem to rely. Butler shows that positing a strong or autonomous female subject leaves intact gender bipolarities and institutional structures (like the nuclear family) that given gender positions sustain. These binarisms, in turn, marginalize the alternative gay and lesbian sexual practices increasingly evident in culture.

Butler's (1990, 147) questions are important: She asks, "How to disrupt the foundations that cover over alternative cultural configurations of gender? How to destabilize and render in their phantasmatic dimension the 'premises' of identity politics?" But her suggested solutions remain unspecific, and they leave her open to the charge that her postmodern politics of the signifier applies mainly to avant-garde and intellectual constituencies. Butler (1990, 149) warns us that if "politics is no longer understood as a set of practices derived from the alleged interests that belong to a set of ready-made subjects, a new configuration of politics would surely emerge from the ruins of the old." But she leaves us without any practical sense of what this new configuration might be.

Let me, then, return to the MP and examine the extent to which what Madonna is doing shows the possibilities and the limits of such a politics of the signifier. Let me return also to the concept of the mask and to its adoption being either in the romantic mode of a real self versus a deceptive self or the antiquity mode of liberation from fixed selves. Further, I will again take up the discussion of fetishism in both the Marxist and Freudian senses. I am interested in how far the systems in play throughout this chapter can be seen to work together—in collaboration with one another—and how far they pull apart. The MP stands as a phenomenon that can be positioned within either a critical system linked to identity politics and focusing on audience research or one linked to a politics of the signifier, focusing on the body as text.

I do not distinguish the systems with any intent to reconcile them dialectically, via some third synthesis. Such a process only creates more problems. I have aimed, rather, to show how each system produces useful Madonna knowledge in relation to specific contexts, specific strategies, and specific social needs.

The basic questions for me remain linked to whose interests the MP most serves. It is here that contradictions proliferate, not least in relation to Madonna's own constructions of herself and to her well-known financial success. So far, three main issues relating to theories of subjectivity and the category of the real have been considered. First, there is the theory that the

Madonna image usefully adopts one mask after another to expose the fact that there is no "essential" self and therefore no essential feminine but only cultural constructions—that is, the mask as *mastery*, as play with the given gender sign system, as, in Freudian terms, deployment and exposure of the oppressive processes of the fetish that rests on fear of castration. Second, there is the theory that the Madonna image self-consciously uses the mask to reproduce patriarchal modes and fantasies—the mask as *deception*. Finally, there is the notion that the Madonna image offers a positive role model for young women in refusing the passive patriarchal feminine, unmasking it, and replacing it with strong and autonomous female images, preeminently in *Truth or Dare*.

What none of these positions offers is an analysis of Madonna as *commodity*, an analysis of how commodity relations interface with an oppositional politics; such an analysis must not only explore how commodity relations interface with an oppositional politics but also must integrate subjectivity and gender issues. Even to raise the question is sometimes seen as moving from postmodernism back to Marxism. My interest in a possible postmodern theory of the subject does not mean abandoning a concept of oppositional politics. But does the politics of the signifier that I have outlined as mobilized by the MP offer such possibilities?

To begin with, let me look briefly at the relevance of such a politics to the majority of the population. I can imagine the dramatic political effects that would be caused by many people playing with gender sign systems: indeed, the fact that such play by masses of people would startle the patriarchal order and would presumably be halted highlights the centrality of the gender sign system we have.

A review of *Truth or Dare* provides an example of the threat that denying a basic, consistent "self" can produce. Writing in *New York Magazine,* David Denby (1991, 60) rebukes Madonna because "when you see her up close . . . and backstage, she has no reserve, no private self or sense of sin, no individual face offered to the people in front of her. . . . Her body is all frame and sinew—mask without expression, will without flesh, temperament without sensuality." Denby goes on to comment on the contrast with Warren Beatty in the film, picking up on Beatty's remark in relation to Madonna only having a "camera" self: "She can just 'be herself' on camera," Denby says, "because she has literally nothing to hide, whereas [Beatty] hides everything. . . . He is an actor with a private life; she is a multimedia image living to be photographed."

Denby obviously works with the depth/surface binarism, in which surface means emptiness, a negative mask because there is nothing underneath. He missed the whole point of the film, which was to challenge precisely the unconscious gender stereotypes and the constructs of private and public selves that prevail in dominant discourse and serve specific ideological purposes. Such a challenge to dominant constructs is basic to the politics of the signifier. But Denby's mistaking the film's ends exposes the limits of such a politics, for the politics is not immediately manifest in a film like *Truth or Dare*. In general, some idea of how those who subvert the gender system would organize any transformation of the patriarchal order in the wake of this politics of the signifier is necessary: The "politics" stops short of the moment of *contestation* that would show people what it could achieve.

In addition, can the politics of the signifier help analyze Madonna as commodity? In Marxist terms, the Madonna image embodies the supreme example of commodity fetishism in that the address to the spectator works to conceal the operations of labor (toil, exploitation) that underlie its production and display. Certainly, it is disingenous to praise Madonna's shrewd business sense, as Paglia (1990) does without recognizing the values involved in marketing oneself for huge profits and querying whether the best or only model for a young woman is that of a successful businesswoman. Must the MP be seen as being in collusion, for its own gain, with an oppressive, late capitalist phenomenon?

Although I am sympathetic to critics who answer in the affirmative, let me offer here another set of arguments. True, consumption is one aspect of her own life that Madonna does not criticize, but that she is sensitive to such a critique is clear, however, in the "Nightline" interview. Pushed by the interviewer, Sawyer, about future videos, she snaps, "You want me to advertise some of my button-pushing products?" Further, her own construction of herself in the "Nightline" interview is precisely one of using her wealth and power for socially conscious ends—promoting safe sex or donating to AIDS research and other needy causes. She also constructs herself not as a low-culture entertainer but as an avant-garde artist, on a level with Mapplethorpe and perhaps also 2 Live Crew, both of whom endured censorship parallel to that which Madonna suffered over the Pepsi-Cola ad and most recently *Justify My Love*. She explicitly attacks censorship in the "Nightline" interview.

Madonna has consistently supported gay and lesbian sex, despite the complaint that her videos and her life (as constituted in interviews and magazine articles) seem predominantly heterosexist and that she rips off gay and lesbian artists like Sandra Bernhard or those involved in Jenny Livingston's documentary about New York gay male underground culture, *Paris Is Burning* (1991). Even *Justify My Love* has been seen as marginalizing gay and lesbian sexual practices because it masks the lesbian scene or makes it a spectacle for the male gaze-in-the-text. There is the further complaint that images perhaps intended to be pastiche (such as those in *Open Your Heart*) are often taken without their irony/critique—as images that patriarchy has long constituted as the "feminine object" and that appeal to an unconscious male objectification of women.

Madonna may well construct herself as merely making use of consumption economies that she did not create and for which she is not responsible. In this sense, the contrast with a star like Sinead O'Connor is striking: O'Connor weepingly declared recently on MTV that she was disgusted with the commodity that she has become, in spite of herself, since winning the MTV awards. Proclaiming her readiness to leave the whole rock scene, O'Connor here addressed the material level of stardom in a way that Madonna never has.

Madonna may believe that her fans and critics will never know the real Madonna, but her whole corpus is constructed as a thinly disguised public confession or autobiography. This may be the real secret of her appeal. Not that she would stand by these constructions as a "true" account of her life, as we saw, but the song lyrics, videos, films, interviews, and performances represent Madonna's public constitution of herself.

It is a story that her fans love because it is so common, so very much an adolescent story in Western cultural terms. Central to it are her repressive Catholic upbringing and her conflicted relationship not only to her literal father but also the symbolic one—the Holy Father, the Law, Patriarchy. If the video *Oh Father* is the most direct construction of this narrative (set, characteristically, within the frame of another narrative, that of the classical film *Citizen Kane*), most of the videos seem driven by the pleasure of sin in the Catholic sense—sins of the flesh or violations of normative sexual boundaries, with Madonna pushing at the limits of the permissible, very much in the mode of the Surrealists and Expressionists on whom so much of her imagination relies.

CONCLUSION

In the end, the questions feminists have been debating and that I have been discussing all arguably have some validity. According to the British cultural studies approach, Madonna, especially in her early phases, has been a useful role model for adolescent women in her self-generating, self-promoting image, in her autonomy and independence, and in her determined creativity. More recently, Madonna has been exploring female sexual fantasies about bondage, group sex, and sadomasochism, as some feminists have discussed (Suleiman 1990). She is, in this respect, if not an artist who should be linked to avant-gardists at least someone pushing the limits of social codes through aesthetic expression in an era of reaction to the challenges of the 1960s in dominant culture.

But what Madonna does is, like most other cultural productions, not transcendent art, for all times and places. Hers is an expression, like others, that is linked to and best discussed within a specific, local, cultural context.

Madonna's version of "no respect" (Ross 1990) has to do with her increasing attention to the constraints of middle-American sexual mores and to the inhibitions and repressions involved, especially in relation to gay and lesbian sexual alternatives and to desires that emerge in sexual fantasies.

The anti-Madonna media discourse serves those threatened by her challenges to patriarchal heterosexual norms, but some feminist overreaction (like Paglia's) in its turn serves dominant patriarchal culture in taking up its antifeminist, clichéd, and archaic discourse. Paglia serves mainstream culture in her stress on individual success and on a sexuality in which men dominate.

But I believe that the level of the politics of the signifier—the second subversion thesis—may make inroads on precisely such oppressive identities over time. The mechanisms of the Marxist and Freudian versions of fetishism—the repression thesis—help account for certain commodity and consumption processes that the politics of the signifier ignores, and therefore, they can usefully complement that politics. That the MP has been able to produce such complex debates—debates that have great implications for cultural studies methods in general—attests to the dramatic impact of the phenomenon itself.

NOTES

1. Although Madonna's subjectivity is multiple and involves Catholicism, class, and ethnicity as well as gender, my main focus here will be on the latter.

2. For example, in Spain during the summer of 1991, I encountered articles about Madonna that evidenced the same kind of horrified reaction as displayed in the U.S. press.

REFERENCES

Anderson, Christopher. (1991). *Madonna, Unauthorized.* New York: Simon and Schuster.

Bakhtin, Mikhail. (1968). *Rabelais and His World.* Cambridge, Mass.; Massachusetts Institute of Technology Press.

Bradby, Barbara. (1990). "Freedom, Feeling, and Dancing." *One Two Three Four* 9 (Autumn): 35–52.

Brown, Jane D., and Campbell, Kenneth C. (1986). "Race and Gender in Music Videos: The Same Beat but a Different Drummer." *Journal of Communication* 36, no. 1 (Winter): 94–106.

Brown, Jane D., Schulze, Laurie, Walsh Childers, Kim, and Nickopolou, Lia. (n.d.). "Race and Gender Differences in Interpretations of Sexuality in Music Videos."

Paper presented at the American Studies Association Conference, Miami, Fla., October 1988.

Brunsdon, Charlotte. (1983). "Crossroads: Notes on Soap Opera." In E. Ann Kaplan (ed.), *Regarding Television: Critical Aproaches—An Anthology*. Los Angeles, Calif.: American Film Institute, pp. 76–82.

Butler, Judith. (1990). *Gender Trouble: Feminism and the Subversion of Identity*. New York: Routledge.

Denby, David. (1991). "Nothing to Hide." *New York Magazine*, May 20, p. 60.

Doane, Mary Ann. (1981). "Woman's Stake: Filming the Female Body." *October* 17 (Summer): 23–36.

———. 1987. *The Desire to Desire: The Woman's Films of the* 1940s. Bloomington: Indiana University Press.

Feuer, Jane. (1989). "Reading *Dynasty:* Television and Reception Theory." *The South Atlantic Quarterly* 88, no. 2 (Spring): 443-460.

Fiske, John. (1987). "British Cultural Studies and Television." In Robert C. Allen (ed.), *Channels of Discourse*. Chapel Hill: University of North Carolina Press, pp. 254–290.

Foucault, Michel. (1971/1984). "Nietszche, Genealogy, History." Reprinted in P. Rabinow (ed.), *Foucault Reader*. New York: Pantheon, pp. 76–100.

———. (1979). *The History of Sexuality*. London: Allen Lane.

Freedberg, David. (1989). *The Power of Images: Studies in the History and Theory of Response*. Chicago and London: University of Chicago Press.

Friedberg, Anne. (1990). "A Denial of Difference: Theories of Cinematic Identification." In E. Ann Kaplan (ed.), *Psychoanalysis and Cinema*. New York: Routledge, pp. 36–45.

Frith, Simon. (1981). *Sound Effects: Youth, Leisure, and the Politics of Rock and Roll*. New York: Pantheon Books.

Hirschberg, L. (1991). "The Misfit." *Vanity Fair*, April, pp. 158–168.

Jameson, Fredric. (1988). "Postmodernism and Consumer Society." Reprinted in E. Ann Kaplan (ed.), *Postmodernism and Its Discontents: Theories and Practices*. London: Verso, 1988, pp. 13–29.

Kaplan, E. Ann (1987). *Rocking Around the Clock: Music Television, Postmodernism and Consumer Culture*. New York and London: Routledge.

———. (1990a). "Consuming Images: Madonna and the 'Look-Alike.'" In *Screen and Monitor: A Critical Investigation of Image Culture*. Taiwan: Fu Jen University, pp. 41–67.

———. (1990b). "The Sacred Image of the Same: Madonna/The Look-Alike/Resistance." In Y. H. Gietma and Frans Haks (eds.), *What a Wonderful World! Music Videos in Architecture*. Groninger, Holland: Groninger Museum, pp. 42–46.

Lewis, Lisa A. (1990a). "Being Discovered: Female Address on Music Television." *Jump Cut* 35 (April): pp. 2–15.

———. (1990b). *Gender Politics and MTV: Voicing the Difference*. Philadelphia, Pa.: Temple University Press.

McRobbie, Angela. (1980). "Settling Accounts with Subcultures: A Feminist Critique." *Screen Education* 34 (Spring): 37–49.

McRobbie, Angela, and Nava, Mica (eds.). (1984). *Gender and Generation.* London: Macmillan.

Modleski, Tania. (1983). "The Rhythms of Reception: Daytime Television and Women's Work." In E. Ann Kaplan (ed.), *Regarding Television: Critical Approaches—An Anthology.* Los Angeles, Calif.: American Film Institute, pp. 65–77.

Mulvey, Laura. (1975). "Visual Pleasure and Narrative Cinema." *Screen* 16, no. 3 (Autumn); 6–18.

————— . (1991). "*Xala* and Fetishism." Unpublished lecture, Humanities Institute, Stony Brook, N.Y., March.

Paglia, Camille. (1990). "Madonna—Finally, a Real Feminist." Op-ed essay, *New York Times,* December 14, p. A39.

Robins, Wayne. "Blonde on the Run." *Newsday,* June 10, part 2, p. 3.

Ross, Andrew. (1990). *No Respect: Intellectuals and Popular Culture.* New York: Routledge.

Suleiman, Susan Rubin. (1990). *Subversive Intent: Gender, Politics, and the Avant-garde.* Cambridge, Mass.: Harvard University Press.

Williamson, Judith. (1985). "The Making of a Material Girl." *New Socialist* 31 (October): 46–47.

ROSEANN M. MANDZIUK

Feminist Politics & Postmodern Seductions: Madonna & the Struggle for Political Articulation

> The only way to control people is to control their sex lives. As for me, I don't like the idea of being controlled.
>
> —Madonna

*A*s AN UNDENIABLY powerful presence in contemporary popular culture, Madonna often is upheld as a model of self-determination and self-expression. She is admired for her constant drive and the intensity with which she pursues her career. Her creativity and business savvy are celebrated; she is the consummate pop icon and self-engineered chameleon. In the apt words of her brother, Christopher Ciccone, "My sister is her own masterpiece" (Hirschberg 1991, 160). All of these characteristics come together in Madonna's film *Truth or Dare*. In the behind-the-scenes sequences of this documentary, we see her alternately preen and cajole, intimidate and gyrate. Madonna orchestrates the people around her—her quasi-family of dancers, her managers, costumers, and makeup staff, even her personal companion at the time, actor Warren Beatty—into a narcissistic song played always in her own key. On stage, Madonna equally controls the musical sequences in an orgy of self-celebration metaphorically captured in her dance of simulated masturbation. The total portrait the film conveys is of a woman who undeniably is her own artist, painting both off- and onstage personas with strong, sensual strokes.

It is important to ask, however, whether accolades for such personal and professional control and success necessarily qualify Madonna for an equally positive reception within feminist theoretical circles. Is sexual expression equivalent to personal freedom? Can pleasure substitute for politics? Precisely what kind of personal and political freedom does Madonna represent? The conflation of power, sexuality, and personal autonomy in the statement quoted above marks Madonna's suitability as a textual point of convergence and departure for a critical reconsideration of such questions. Throughout her history as a pop icon, Madonna's texts insistently equate pleasure with power, sexuality with control. Her assertion that personal freedom and sexuality are intrinsically linked provides an important clue to the terms of the larger debate over political articulation in contemporary feminist theory. Madonna is a fitting representation of feminism's theoretical struggle to come to terms with the intersection of cultural images and political practices.

The problematic of audience, text, and context traditionally has structured theorizing about popular culture and its relationship to political consciousness. Such inquiry began with models that theorized simple linear interactions and hypodermic injections of information into otherwise passive subjects. Alternatively, contemporary lines of inquiry seemingly have brought us far to our current theoretical location that is built on a multitude of "-isms" such as postmodernism, poststructuralism, and deconstructionism. These new vocabularies have opened fresh debates about cultural discourse and popular media, raising new questions about a multidimensional relationship among audiences and cultural texts that is far more complex than simple linearity. From a basis in the works of theorists such as Roland Barthes (1977, 1983) and Jacques Derrida (1976), for example, critics reconceptualize the active role of the reader and the symbolic play possible in textual encounters. From the works of psychoanalytic theorists such as Jacques Lacan (1982), the unidimensional concept of audience is replaced by multiple "subjectivities" that are textually defined. From the dirges of postmodern theorists such as Jean-Franois Lyotard (1985), who proclaim that the "master narratives" of the unified self and progressive course of history are dead, critics now can celebrate the possibility for new identities to be discussed, new stories to be told. From the works of Jean Baudrillard (1981, 1983), who sees not meaning but simulation, critics focus their attention on the shifting play of pseudo identities and abstractions.

As championed by those interested in the politics of minorities, subcultures, and women, these theories have become the cornerstone of a new conceptualization of resistance and opposition as experienced by such traditionally oppressed groups. Pressed into the service of cultural analysis, postmodernism is used to celebrate the political potential in audience responses to cultural discourses such as television or popular music (e.g., Fiske 1986, 1987, 1990; Grossberg 1983/1984, 1984, 1989; Petersen 1987). As proponents of this body of research are likely to argue, there are significant pockets of subcultural resistance to be found in audience readings that interpret texts against the grain of their dominant meanings. These critics find in

postmodernism the promise of liberation through the recognition of pleasure as a significant site of opposition to cultural domination. Politics thus
can be located in the simulated play of images and subjectivities.

For feminist researchers, in particular, the lure of these theories has been
strong, and a consequent turn toward affiliation with postmodernism is under way. The affinities between the feminist theoretical project, with its interest in liberation and critique, and the free space of the postmodern has often been noted (Ferguson 1984; Flax 1986; Fraser and Nicholson 1988;
Meese 1986; Owens 1983). Both share an informed skepticism of universalizing claims to knowledge, and both reject the modernist tendency to recognize a transcendent power in language, science, or the self. For feminism, the
postmodern holds out a theoretical enticement to leave the public space of
reason for the private, localized regions of pleasure. The postmodern promises feminism a symbolic, sensual terrain free of the modernist burdens of
history and unified subjectivity. In a union with postmodernism, feminism
can loosen itself from the binding constraints of materiality and abandon itself instead to the allure of a politics liberated from naive realism. Such are
the temptations of the postmodern—but is feminism too quickly being seduced by these attractive, theoretical promises? Has feminism been fooled
into relinquishing something too precious by celebrating the political potential of images like those projected by Madonna?

The subject of feminist political articulation demands a critical examination of the ways in which much recent feminist analysis has embraced postmodernist theories (e.g., Kaplan 1987; Haraway 1990; M. E. Brown 1990;
Probyn 1990; Butler 1990; W. Brown 1991). The theoretical promises of
politics through symbolic play that characterize this research ring false in
comparison to the complexity of a feminist politics defined according to
praxis. Yet, to a feminist theoretical approach originating from the postmodern landscape, a feminist politics defined as praxis is fraught with
essentializing epistemological traps. Ultimately, the battle for political articulation is fought on the territory of female images and representations. Are
women's images politically subversive? If so, does this subversion benefit the
audience or the artist? What does feminism truly demand when it claims to
be committed to politics? The linguistic and theoretical traps seem endless
within both feminist-realist epistemology and postmodern feminism.

Consequently, a politically rooted enterprise such as feminism must stop
periodically to consider the implications of its theoretical alliances and the
qualifications of its heroines: In the boundaries of this exploration, these are
defined as postmodern theory and the "postmodern feminist heroine" (Kaplan 1987), Madonna. In the previous paragraph, I deliberately invoked the
sexist language of heterosexual seduction, placing feminism in the position
of the woman who is deluded into the act of compromising herself and placing postmodernist theories into the position of the man who promises much

only to take away the woman's power over herself, including her sexual autonomy. Seduction here serves as a powerful metaphor for the relationship between feminism and postmodernism's theoretical enticements: In casting its lot with postmodernism, feminism is, indeed, sleeping with the enemy.

The remainder of this chapter expands on this central argument—that danger lurks in the nexus between feminist theory/praxis and contemporary postmodern theories. Certainly, it is not possible in such a limited format to completely describe postmodernism nor offer a complete critique of its appropriation by feminism. To critique the postmodern means of seduction, however, the major assumptions behind postmodernist theory that have been embraced by some feminist theories will be set out in broad strokes. Explanations of the feminist theoretical positions that emerge on this receptive side of the postmodern debate then can be considered in contrast to the positions of feminist theorists engaged in distancing themselves from these postmodern lures. Much of this comparison rests in the ambiguities in the terms *postmodern* and *politics* as employed in feminist discussions: Understanding such explanatory and definitional moves is necessary in order to evaluate the subsequent paradoxes of affiliation with postmodernism for a feminist politics of praxis. To provide a vantage point from which to view this dance of theory around the question of feminism, I periodically will use Madonna as a point of entry into these theoretical debates.

Three specific Madonna texts reside at the center of my discussion: her 1991 interview on the ABC news program "Nightline," her 1990 "Rock the Vote" television spot, and the 1990 video *Vogue*, which the "Vote" spot mimics. To move from Madonna to the interrogation of the interchange between feminism and postmodernism entails a large but instructive step from praxis back to theory. Central to my invocation of her texts in these three contexts is her emphasis on two elements in all three cases—first, her insistence on the individual ownership of her sexuality and, second, the conflation of sexual expression and political freedom within her discourse. Both elements in Madonna's texts capture, in miniature, the larger conflations that I will argue are being made in feminist defenses of postmodern theory.

FEMINIST THEORY AND
THE DREAM OF SUBSTANCE

As a prelude to my discussion, I will use Madonna's appearance on "Nightline," which nicely illustrates feminism's realist problems and its turn toward postmodernism. Such a choice may seem odd because this particular interview probably stands as Madonna's most fiercely "modernist" appearance on television: She answers the questions put to her directly and care-

fully, she responds to ABC reporter Forrest Sawyer as the typical serious interviewee, with pen in hand, and she is dressed quite conservatively in a
simple black jacket with her hair pulled back from her face. Yet, this is precisely the point of my beginning here: Her appearance on the program raises
several questions central to the problem of feminism, postmodernism, and
political articulation. Madonna's modernist representation exposes many of
the contradictions in the realist approach to representational politics. It is
these theoretical traps that lead feminist theory to abandon a politics of
praxis in favor of postmodern promises.

The "Nightline" program was structured into three parts, with an initial
report from Ken Kashiwahara reviewing Madonna's "controversial" career,
followed by the uncensored, full-length version of the *Justify My Love*
video, and culminating in a live interview between Sawyer in a New York
City studio and Madonna appearing via satellite on a screen to his left. The
overtly stated purpose of the program was to explore the controversy surrounding the *Justify My Love* video, including MTV's refusal to air the tape.
Sawyer asked Madonna a series of questions, first confronting her intentions in the controversy: "A lot of people in the industry are saying, look,
this is one of the best self-promoters in the business . . . it was all, in a sense,
a kind of publicity stunt." He followed this inquiry with several questions
that implied she had crossed the boundaries of acceptability—for example,
"People are saying that there's a kind of trend here, where you are pushing
the limits of what's permissible a little bit further each time . . . where is that
line?" Later in the interview, he questioned whether Madonna was promoting her artistic experimentation at the expense "of the responsibility that
comes along with the kind of prominence that you have, and the fact that
you're a role model for people." Finally, he asked her to respond to charges
that she was promoting the degradation of women in her videos.

What is important to note here is that all of Sawyer's questions originated
from a perspective that assumes images are literally and inescapably linked
to both their artistic origin and their subsequent reception by audiences.
Madonna answered his charges on the same realist epistemological
grounds—hence, my earlier comment that this appearance on "Nightline"
represents a particularly modernist chapter in Madonna's public persona.
Her responses were grounded in a defense of artistic free expression and a
passionate stand against censorship, while her demeanor was that of the
careful college debater. She spoke of herself in the classic sense of a unified,
transcendent subject as she stated, "I do everything by my own volition. I'm
in charge." Especially in her defense against the charges made by "feminists"
that she implies degradation to women in her videos (namely, in the scene in
Express Yourself where she is chained and lying naked on a bed), she again
championed authorial intentionality and unified identity: "I'm chained to
myself, though, there wasn't a man that put that chain on me. I chained my-

self, I was chained to my own desires." Madonna's response here located her in the center of a realist notion of representation—that there is an authorial intent that must be decoded by receivers before they can grasp the "true" meaning of the author's artistic message. She securely positioned herself in the discourse of a liberal pluralist kind of feminism: "Everybody knows—in terms of my image in the public—people don't think of me as a person who's not in charge of my career or my life. And isn't that what feminism is all about, equality for men and women? And aren't I in charge of my life? Doing the things I want to do? Making my own decisions?" The sum of Madonna's appearance on "Nightline" spoke loudly for a feminist realist epistemology, one that argues for a direct relationship between public images and public responsibility as the grounds for feminist politics.

But what does all of this have to do with postmodernism and feminism? I have prolonged this discussion of Madonna's "Nightline" interview in order to use it to set the terms of the feminist debate over postmodern theory. Madonna's statements about artistic control and fighting censorship and her hope that her videos will provoke careful discussions between children and their parents about sexuality seem far removed from the postmodern promise of a politics of subversion and a free play of signifiers. Indeed, she seems here to be the perfect spokeswoman for the "images of women" or "identity politics" brand of feminism that marked much theory and practice in the 1970s and 1980s.[1] The central premise of this body of work is that images are political because when controlled by women authors, they can directly tell a truth about women's experience of oppression that previously had been suppressed under patriarchal control of the mechanisms of representation. Women's cultural expressions, such as those found in literature, art, and film, are celebrated as politically important for feminism because they foreground revolutionary images of women that express power, personal autonomy, and political commitment.

This images of women approach within feminist theory has been critiqued for many reasons by later theorists but primarily because it depends on a naive kind of realist belief in the political efficacy of images. Critics charge that to argue that images can have a direct political effect is to assume an unproblematic relationship between artist, image, and audience, where the meaning is clearly invested in the image, transparently represented, and easily decoded. Moreover, the images of women stance leads feminism dangerously close to the modernist strategy of essentializing women through a limited range of representations that capture the essence of women's true nature. As Linda Alcoff (1988, 414) argues in regard to feminist realist epistemology, "To the extent that it reinforces essentialist explanations of these true attributes, it is in danger of solidifying an important bulwark of sexist oppression: the belief in an innate 'womanhood' to which we must all adhere lest we be deemed either inferior or not 'true' women."

The term *identity politics* also merits attention in the feminist-postmodernist debate, especially because, linked to feminism, it leads to further questions of essentialism and epistemology. That is, the path of feminist theory inevitably leads back to its epistemological beginnings in women's discourse of identity, rooted in the women's liberation rhetoric of the 1960s: "The personal is the political." Politics here is equated with the assertion of and insistence on a discourse of woman's identity held up as different from both dominant cultural definitions of her and from masculine identity. As Elizabeth Weed (1989, XIII) explains, "At the very core of feminism is a struggle against the historical constitution of individual (masculine) identity with its collapse of the female into the biological or into the 'naturally' ordained realm of the functional." Feminist theorists now are quick to admit that a typical identity-based political theory, like that of Nancy Chodorow (1978), which places motherhood as women's foundational experience, overly essentializes the feminist project by finding women's political potential in a single, often biologically determined, characteristic.

The danger in this essentialist definition of politics, however, lies in the erroneous belief in an integrated self in which awareness of a truth about woman's "true identity" beyond patriarchal coding is possible. Kathleen B. Jones (1991) argues convincingly that such simplistic conceptualizations of politics are flawed because they depend on a definition of "personal authority" that is rooted in the notion of authority as sovereignty and control exercised over others. As Jones (1991, 107) characterizes the contradiction in feminist identity politics: "We thought we were telling the stories of our lives, women's lives, in order to uncover the gendered patterns of oppression and resistance that framed those lives. Now we are warned away from giving authoritative readings of other's lives." Feminist politics conceived as cultural intervention in the name of woman seems hopelessly bound up with the discourse of essentialism and epistemology, domination and subjugation. Identity politics appears to lead feminism to the same kind of theoretical impasse as the images of women approach: Both limit and restrain feminism by setting categories, boundaries, and limits.

POSTMODERN PROMISES AND PLEASURES

The discussion of a second Madonna text can assist in setting up the central problematic that comprises the feminist transition from the politics of realism to the politics of the postmodern. If her appearance on "Nightline" invoked the persona of the staid and serious citizen, her presence in her "Rock the Vote" television spot represented the adolescent at play. This text was part of an advertising campaign featured on MTV during the 1990 election season. The various ads featured rock stars in fifteen-second messages that protested censorship and advocated freedom of speech. The series ostensibly was intended to convince the music television audience, presumably young adults, to vote in the current election. All of the advertisements ended with a still shot displaying the "Rock the Vote" slogan, which itself was shadowed by a large check mark signifying the act of checking a choice on a ballot. Madonna's particular text, however, contained a curious mixture of messages, crossing such interventionist politics with a diverse set of articulations of "Americanness." The careful champion of artistic expression from "Nightline" here quite literally wrapped her sexuality in the flag.

Madonna's "Rock the Vote" plays on several levels with notions of democratic politics and public citizenship, and it works off of a self-referential discourse wherein the text mimics Madonna's video *Vogue*. First, the action and appearance of Madonna, in the center of the frame, and the two black male dancers, who stand behind and to the left and right of her, satirize the very discourse of patriotism that the spot ostensibly promotes. All three are costumed to display visual references to prominent discourses of Americanness. The two black males are dressed in dark lace-up boots, navy blue shorts, and plain white T-shirts, and each waves a small flag—a clear invocation of military costuming. Madonna is dressed in a set of bright red lace bikini underwear, a large American flag draped around her shoulders; she also wears military-style combat boots. The combination of the sexually coded gyrations of the male dancers and the final display of Madonna's bikini-clad body serves to subvert the solemn patriotic and military symbols evoked by their dress.

The "Rock the Vote" spot also highlights a curious discourse of race in relationship to its subversive patterns. White, blond Madonna is figured against the background of the black dancers in the spot. This visual organization makes Madonna more prominent by virtue of her whiteness. The contrast between white and black here is further underscored by the obvious playfulness of the two dancers in response to Madonna's mock seriousness. She stops twice to admonish them for singing off key and for being out of rhythm; in several shots, she communicates her exasperation with them through raised eyebrows and looks addressed to the camera. Madonna thus invites the audience to identify with her motherlike position of superiority over the less serious "kids" she has to work with. The effect is disturbing because the spot trades on the racist stereotype that white caretakers must compensate for black immaturity. Americanness seemingly includes a racial hierarchy that remains unsubverted by the text.

The lyrics in the spot further complicate its articulation of Americanness with the discourse of sexuality. Madonna's lyrics juxtapose U.S. political heroes with mixed messages about sex, political freedoms, and nuclear weapons: "Dr. King, Malcolm X, freedom of speech is as good as sex. Abe Lincoln, Jefferson, Tom, they didn't need the atomic bomb. We need beauty, we need art, we need everyone's heart. Don't give up your freedom of speech, power to the people is in our reach. Don't just sit there, let's get to it, speak your mind, there's nothing to it. Vote." Here, the spot foregrounds a curious combination of populist political sentiment and sexual pleasure: The first amendment is equated with sexual gratification. The phrase *freedom of speech is as good as sex* is followed by a shot of one of the black males spanking a willing, bent-over Madonna. Several other phrases in the lyrics dissolve into laughter and mugging for the camera or are accompanied by exaggerated facial or body movements. The spot thus stresses the contradiction between the political sentiment in the message and the overt sexual play and adolescent giggles that accompany the delivery of the lyrics. The purported message about the importance of interventionist politics is undermined by the final statement from Madonna that merges the notions of public freedoms and sexual play: "If you don't vote, you're gonna get a spanking."

The reversal of political priorities associated with Americanness in the "Rock the Vote" spot is revealing. The visual portrayal of Madonna enjoying the gratification from a little playful spanking equates the pursuit of private pleasures with self-determination. Moreover, such pleasures are justified even at the cost of subjugation of others, as in the image here of the black dancer spanking Madonna for her own enjoyment. The promotion of the idea that personal autonomy means having the right to enjoy sexual play in the "Rock the Vote" spot is similar to the message asserted in Madonna's controversial song "Hanky Panky." In this song, she self-assuredly sings about these pleasures and her insistence on them: "Please don't call the doctor, there's nothing wrong with me. I just want things a little rough and you'd better not disagree." Moreover, this same conflation of political freedom and sexuality is evident in the sequence in *Truth or Dare* where Madonna steadfastly defends her right to simulate masturbation on stage in defiance of the Toronto police force. Both "Hanky Panky" and *Truth or Dare* convey the same message as "Rock the Vote": "There's nothing like a good spanking," all things being politically equal.

Madonna's "Rock the Vote" spot underscores questions of feminist realist epistemology and its alternatives. It is a particularly good example of a text where representational politics engages and exposes the liberal pluralist belief in the transparency of images and the serious facade of interventionist politics. Madonna's status as a signifier of femaleness and Americanness does not have one static meaning but moves insistently among several discursive levels. The result is that the text both upholds and undercuts the democratic ideal of free speech by its celebration, in the presence of Madonna, of free play with the symbolic representations of that ideal. She becomes a visual representation of both the impassioned arguer and the giddy adolescent vandal, articulating both individual autonomy and the pleasures of remaining mobile. Such dualities challenge the straightforward image and identity politics of feminist realist epistemology. Madonna's "meaning" cannot be accounted for easily within theoretical boundaries that view representation as an unproblematic process.

These perceived deficits in the realist stance in feminist theory make the postmodern direction in much contemporary critical theory attractive, and they prompt feminist theory to eagerly search for an alternative way to adhere to the persistent refrain of the "Rock the Vote" spot: "Truth is where you find it." Postmodernism seemingly holds out to feminism a means to escape its epistemological traps and adopt an alternative notion of politics. The term *postmodern* references a complex set of associations primarily because it is used in contemporary writings in at least two ways. First, it is used as a noun; *the postmodern* serves as a historical marker that isolates the current period in contemporary culture, characterized by an explosion of technologies and the acceleration of information, mass media access, and cultural change. Second, it is used as an adjective, *postmodern* referring both to cultural manifestations (such as music, television, and clothing) and to theories about the historical period and these cultural artifacts. I will limit my discussion to the major aspects of the theory generally referred to as postmodernism. It is built on three major contentions: the death of "master narratives" in culture, the "death of the author" as a category of inquiry, and an endless play of meanings and surfaces.

The pronouncement on the passing of master narratives in culture is best understood through the work of Jean-Franois Lyotard (1985), whose book *The Postmodern Condition* provides one of the more influential developments of this position. Lyotard sees the postmodern as a designation for a general state in Western civilization in which what he calls "the grand narratives of legitimation" are no longer credible as bases for a philosophical understanding of humankind. Among the narratives that no longer hold sway are the vision of a slow and steady forward progress of history, the belief in the transcendent self, and the Enlightenment belief in reason and freedom. Each is delegitimized in culture because it emphasizes notions of humanity as defined according to essential qualities, to forces of destiny, and to hierarchical relationships between truths and nontruths. In postmodern culture, every discourse is autonomous and is equally subject to the same set of localized criteria for judging its efficacy, wherein attention to language games, localized rules, and the "performativity" of the discourse determine its legitimacy.

Concurrently with the development of postmodern notions about discursive legitimacy, other theorists began to ask questions about the specific category of the author, as again related to notions of the transcendent self and the unproblematic discourse of identity characteristic of much earlier work in philosophy and criticism. Two fundamental statements that announce the "death of the author" come from French theorists Roland Barthes (1977) and Michel Foucault (1979/1980). Both question the set of modernist assumptions typically made about the unified subject or the self. Both argue that the category of "the author" preserves the naive belief that there is an integrated core in individuals from which a piece of discourse unproblematically ensues. According to Barthes, authors do not originate but only translate among various preexisting discourses in the process of textual production. The priority in the struggle over the meaning of texts instead goes to the reader, for in the author's death is the reader's birth. According to Foucault, primary attention should be paid not to the category of the author but to the circulation and appropriation of texts according to established power relations in culture. Authors fade in importance in comparison to the way in which the text takes on a life of its own in its subsequent uses and recontextualizations. What Barthes and Foucault variously describe is a poststructuralist/postmodern assumption that in contemporary culture, the relation between individuals and their discursive products has been severed, thereby opening a space for readers' textual "play" with meanings and power relationships.

Devoid of master narratives and the essentializing presence of the author, the postmodern is a culture of perpetual presents. Culture becomes "fundamentally two-dimensional and lacking in depth, perspective, and time" (Pfeil 1988, 385), a landscape defined by its ever-shifting combinations of images and relationships. The celebrated form of postmodernism is that of a revolutionary pastiche: "a present of hysterical, historical retrospection in which history is fragmented and the subject dispersed in its own representations" (Foster 1984, 72–73). The liberating promise of postmodernism resides in the assumption that from such cultural dispersion can come the opening of spaces for subversion of cultural meanings and consequent play with definitions of power. The concept of "self" yields to recognition of multiple subjectivities, the preponderance of history melts into a series of endless contradictions, and each creation and/or dissolution of meanings and pleasures becomes as significant as the next.

The theoretical promises of the postmodern have been embraced by many feminists for a variety of reasons. First, because it offers the prospect of freedom from the epistemological bonds of the master narratives and the fiction of the unified self, the postmodern is seen as opening endless spaces for the play of multiple selves and meanings. With the world as text and life a series of simulations, feminist theorists envision a landscape that is beyond binary categories of sex or gender, masculine or feminine. Identities are dispersed into what Susan Suleiman calls a multiplied set of narrative and interpretive possibilities, "so that what results is a dizzying accumulation" (1986, 25). Pleasure is found in the confusion of boundaries. As evocatively described by Donna Haraway (1990, 205), the postmodern body becomes that of a cyborg, "the disassembled and reassembled, postmodern collective and personal self" whose mode of expression is "a powerful infidel heteroglossia"

(1990, 223) that replaces a common language. Postmodernist theory promises feminists a means of cultural critique that does not depend on generalizations or categories, a perspective that does not set boundaries but violates them.

Second, postmodernist theory, as a prominent cultural project, pushes feminism to examine its previous alliances and assumptions. Such self-examination is seen as both necessary and healthy for the development of feminist theory. For example, Nancy Fraser and Linda Nicholson (1988) find that the similarities between the two theoretical projects merit attention and cooperation between them. As they note, "feminists and postmodernists have worked independently on a common nexus of problems: They have tried to rethink the relation between philosophy and social criticism so as to develop paradigms of 'criticism without philosophy'" (1988, 83). These authors argue that because feminism and postmodernism have complementary strengths and weaknesses, the two theoretical perspectives have much to learn from each other, regardless of the androcentrism and political naiveté that Fraser and Nicholson find in the postmodern project. For them, postmodernism most importantly highlights the problems of essentialism that plague feminist political theorizing.

The alternative definition of *politics* in postmodernism promises to escape the latent essentialism and consequent exclusion of such traditional feminist invocations of the political. In a postmodern landscape, politics cannot be mapped according to a permanent standpoint such as the category of "women"; rather, politics becomes localized and dispersed into a series of random and unpredictable cultural interruptions. Iris Marion Young (1990, 318) uses the metaphor of the contemporary city to describe the politics of the postmodern: "The temporal and spatial differentiation that mark the physical environment of the city produce an experience of aesthetic *inexhaustibility*. . . . The juxtaposition of incongruous styles and functions that usually emerge after a long time in city places contribute to this pleasure in detail and surprise. This is an experience of difference in the sense of always being inserted." Contrary to the rootedness of what Young calls the modernist dream of community, then, the politics of the postmodern is found in the continual movement across boundaries and into new surroundings. The pleasures of subversion and surprise constitute a kind of postmodern political resistance: The *jouissance* of multiplicities refuses definition and closure as each new emanation will be partial and contradictory.

FEMINISM DANCES INTO THE ABYSS

Such a vision of multiplicity leads to our final excursion into a Madonna text, her 1990 video *Vogue*. The content of the lyrics and the discourse of posing that constitute this video offer the perfect textualization of the postmodern dream of a politics in which subjectivities constantly traverse different forms, all to the movement of music heard in a mythical and safe place removed from the harsh realities of the everyday. *Vogue* is set in an unspecific location resembling a sparsely decorated sound stage or modeling studio backdrop. Scattered icons signifying bourgeois taste and class abound: classically styled statues of the human form, large windows seemingly unattached to walls, columns, pedestals, and high-backed chairs. The video is shot in black and white, an effect that adds to the timelessness of the setting and its inhabitants because it evokes the look of classic Hollywood films from the 1930s. The participants in *Vogue* include Madonna, two female backup singers, and several male dancers/backup singers.

As with the "Rock the Vote" spot, much of the discursive play in *Vogue* is related to the coding of dress and pose. In many of the shots in the video, the camera lingers on individual participants as they "strike a pose." For the males, the different poses evoke the discourse of modeling: They are dressed in vintage suits or smoking jackets, or they are shot in slow-motion sequences with shirttails flowing or twirling. Moreover, the men in *Vogue,* as in "Rock the Vote," are coded as gay. This interpretation of the males can be made both from intertextual evidence, such as the interviews and comments in *Truth or Dare* where the dancers reveal their homosexuality, and from their stylized, almost campy poses and expressions. More importantly, the act of voguing is traceable to the gay subculture in which various personas and identities are enacted in dance and drag as a form of subversion of and opposition to the dominant heterosexual culture.

Madonna's sequence of poses more explicitly references the discourse of Hollywood screen legends such as Greta Garbo, Jean Harlowe, Marilyn Monroe, and Marlene Dietrich. One sequence in particular consists of several shots wherein Madonna reembodies well-known photographs of these stars, mimicking their clothing, gestures, and facial expressions. Madonna and her dancers all move constantly through a series of identities in stylized dance and gestures: It is the culmination of the postmodern subject dissolving into a multitude of symbols and attitudes. In *Vogue,* however, difference and opposition are recuperated only as sources of style. The political content of the act of voguing is appropriated and transformed into a superficial dance of appearances.

The lyrics of the song that accompany the images further extend the postmodern invitation to join in the pleasure of diffusion into interchangeable subjects. The act of voguing is held out as an alternative to the struggles and disappointments facing individuals on the hard road of life. The lyrics instead promote a postmodern subversion through dance: "Look around, everywhere you turn there's heartache, it's everywhere that you go. You will try everything that you can to escape the pain of life that you know. I know a place where you can get away, it's called the dance floor, and here's what it's for. Come on, vogue, let your body move to the music." The song promises that for those who strike a pose, regardless of gender or race, the reward will be elevation to the "superstar" identities of their choice. Even if the moment is fleeting, the enticements of voguing rest in the ability to enter and leave the fantasy of multiple subjectivities at will, gaining sensual pleasure and self-expressive satisfaction. In the timeless, shapeless landscape of the dance floor, all is nondiscriminatory, self-gratifying, and safe.

As Madonna promises, all things are appearances in the postmodern: "Beauty's where you find it." The terrain of postmodern politics is an insular space where the goal is self-aggrandizement and the path to politics is a series of disconnected moments of illusion and play. Yet, the allure of the postmodern vision of *Vogue* obscures a set of insistent questions and absences. Compare the speaking subjects in the three Madonna texts: We have followed a progression that has taken us from the equation of political autonomy with artistic expression, through the association of freedom of speech with sexual expression, to a final diminishment of the distinction between politics and pleasure. From "Nightline" to "Rock the Vote," public argument has given way to speech at play. From "Vote" to *Vogue*, praxis has vanished into the private act of posing; the search for local truths has transformed itself into the fleeting acquisition of beauty. Postmodernism holds out to feminist politics the dream of multiple selves at play, free of the epistemological bonds of authorship, history, and commitment, but at the cost of the ability to stake a claim to power. In a continually changing landscape where gendered subjectivities disappear into aesthetic objects, feminism must relinquish the standpoint of critique. What demands can be made in the name of difference if such categories of social subjects are never anchored?

The alternative postmodern vision of politics is no less problematic than the politics of feminist realist epistemology. Rather than locate politics in a discourse of identity that potentially leads to essentialism and exclusion, the politics of the postmodern refuses responsibility for itself while it reinforces the very power structures and boundaries it promises to violate. The central postmodern promises of an escape from limiting generalizations and the transcendent self into a free play of meanings become for feminist theory only a series of compromising positions. Such a politics predicated on the rewards of pleasure dangerously conflates personal gratifications with cultural liberation. Let me now develop each of these critiques separately.

First, the postmodernist abandonment of both narratives and authorship is premature for feminist political theory, regardless of whether politics is defined as intervention or play. To embrace the postmodern, with its dissolution of the subject and its implosion of meaning, is to ignore the historicity of discourse and the situatedness of the feminist theorist herself. Much femi-

nist identity theory has been critiqued because it falls prey to the essentializing consequences of narrative generalizations and dependence on categories of identity such as "gender" and "woman." Yet, these critiques fail to
recognize a crucial difference between a feminist dependence on the discourse of the personal and the modernist discourse of the transcendent self.
As Susan Bordo (1990, 141) argues: "While in theory, all 'totalizing' narratives may be equal, in the context of Western history and the actual relations
of power characteristic of that history, key differences distinguish the uni-
versalizations of gender theory from the metanarratives arising out of the
propertied, white, male, Western intellectual tradition. . . . Feminist theory—even the work of white, upper-class women—is not located at the *center* of cultural power." When feminism accepts the dehistoricizing tendency
of the postmodern, it loses its specificity as a discourse different from and in
opposition to the historicized power of patriarchal narratives.

What is at stake in the abandonment of standpoints is feminism's ability
to retain its status as a theoretical enterprise motivated by critique. In an-
swering the postmodern call to abandon categories, feminism faces the problem described by Christine di Stefano (1990, 73) as the "postfeminist tendency": "a refusal to privilege any particular form of difference or identity
against the hegemonic mainstream." Without any specificity of reference to
its location in various systems of power and recognition of differences, the
politics of feminism gets lost in the uncharted locales of the postmodern
landscape. Finding joy in the dance of subjectivities, we forget that the music
we move to is manipulated by someone else. No matter how much fun Madonna's notion of voguing may appear to be, posturing cannot be allowed to
replace politics.

Similarly, in substituting the private pleasures of interpretation for the
public intervention of authorship, feminism again has prematurely abdi-
cated its place as an insistent critical pressure within mainstream narratives.
As Nancy K. Miller (1986, 106) argues, "Because women have not had the
same historical relation of identity to origin, institution, production, that
men have had [their] relation to integrity and textuality, desire and authority, is structurally different." The melding of feminism and postmodernism
poses the danger that the death of the author gives birth to nothing more
than a new system of limitations in which all discourse about authorial identity and claims based on it are repressed. At risk is the possibility that the entire discourse of gender might be silenced, with feminism exercising its own
brand of exclusionary control in its refusal to acknowledge the potential for
subjective agency. Such erasure of the author "in favor of an abstract indeterminacy is an act of oppression" (Walker 1990, 571), one that decontex-
tualizes women from the realm of political intervention. In the abstract,
black-and-white landscape of the postmodern, subjectivities are caged into
an endless series of mimetic moves, referencing only an aesthetic of appear-

ances. The postmodern entices us to enjoy nothing more than the free play of our own chains (Pfeil 1988, 385).

Second, because it is located only on surfaces and in simulations, the postmodern politics of personal play relegates woman to the place outside power that patriarchy has always left open for her. Rather than liberating itself from modernist bonds, a postmodern feminism becomes complicit in its own imprisonment once more. In this sense, Madonna's claim that she chained herself to her own bed in her videos does not excuse the historicized meanings of such images. To blithely celebrate such representations as liberating is to reproduce the familiar code of patriarchy that renders women as powerless. Wendy Brown (1987, 15) captures the true irony of the dead end to which postmodernism leads feminism when she asks, "What woman needs to be deconstructed, to know herself as a field of discourse, a 'fiction,' a 'text,' a play of 'free-floating signifiers'? These are the very things woman has been; indeed they constitute a marvelous, if parodied, shorthand for the history of women's oppression."

The elevating promise of postmodernism turns into a bottomless abyss for feminist theory if an alliance with it means an abandonment of any kind of claim to subjective agency. Ephemerality leaves woman precisely where she started, outside discourse and with no place of her own to stand, while postmodernism reworks an old pattern of relationships: "a rerun, in updated garb, of the modernist case of the incredible shrinking woman" (di Stefano 1990, 77). In simply adding itself to the shifting flow of forms and surfaces in the postmodern, feminist politics becomes equated with nothing more than stylistic interruptions of bourgeois sensibilities. The feminist critique that once sought the continued exposure of power mutates into a harmless game of evasion.

Feminism's embrace of postmodernism leads to an ultimate cost: the loss of the space in which to insert the voice of difference into the cultural conversation. If feminism relinquishes the authority of identity in favor of an elided distinction between politics and pleasures, we have gained nothing but an invitation to participate in the endless dance of noncommitment. Rather, as Bordo (1990) argues, feminism must insist on specific locations from which to acclaim generalities as well as explore the subtleties of gendered categories; to turn away from the insistence of critique leads to a trap where feminists "cut ourselves off from the source of feminism's transformative possibilities" (1990, 153). Such a grounded feminist politics, of course, leads back in the direction of feminist realist epistemology but with a new awareness of the limitations of political articulation through the mechanisms of representation. Certainly, an insistence on the discursive intervention of "woman" can never transparently communicate a truth about gender experience, yet feminism must continue to cling to such categorizations regardless of their attendant limitations. A focus on impure concepts such as gender does not doom feminist theory to an essentializing path but rather allows these distinctions to be used strategically to open heuristic spaces for the discussion of the relationship between theory and material reality. A feminist politics does not have to search for a transcendent truth about "woman," but it must continue to seize the spaces to speak in her behalf.

The effacements of postmodern theory result in a closure of these discursive avenues: Pure theory is given an ascendancy that silences the voices of difference that are just beginning to articulate their political demands.[2] Indeed, feminism should be very suspicious of a theoretical agenda that celebrates the dissolution of agency that happens to coincide with critical calls from subcultural communities to move their discourses from margin to center. This is not to say that a feminist politics must insist on rigid boundaries that set these groups apart from each other, but at this point, it is still important to insist on a mapping of locations so that we can travel into different worlds without insisting that we must see all cultural points on our itinerary as interchangeable. It is necessary for a feminist politics to insist on subjective agency in order to preserve the distinction between the critical function of speech and the aesthetic play of style, and it is entirely possible to do so without committing the essentialist error of insisting on a single voice or location for the emanation of such a message.

A feminist politics of praxis, therefore, must hold tightly to a sense of commitment. We must preserve our faith in the ability of feminism to intervene and transform because as a political discourse, it is willing to take responsibility for its voices and presences. To give in to the allure of escape and ephemerality is to become participants in the elimination of the possibility of social change. The alternative path of postmodernism leaves feminism only a kind of passive, private, sexually coded politics of illusion to substitute for its origins in an active, powerful critique of culture. To celebrate the postmodern feminist politics represented by Madonna requires replacing the speech of intervention with the discourse of style. The posturing of "Rock the Vote" and the posing in *Vogue* both promise a subversive alternative to the politics of praxis, but the rewards of such pleasures cannot compensate for what is lost when feminism turns away from its transformative purposes. The feminist theoretical move toward postmodern enticements leads feminism down a slippery path, one that descends from politics through pleasure to erasure.

Distinguishing between postmodern passivity and an authentic interventionist politics must remain an urgent task for feminism, particularly in a consumer culture that equates commodification with choice and sexuality with self-determination. Madonna provides a perfect example of the postmodern feminist heroine, selling the virtues of political indeterminacy in her insistent play with sexual expression. Yet, in her discourse as a postmodern icon, something is all too familiar in her transformation of politics into pleasure: Madonna sounds the same old cultural message that a woman's place is to be sensual, stylish, and self-involved. Feminism must not let itself be persuaded to enter the artificially accelerated scramble toward the newest theoretical fashion of postmodernism,[3] especially if the only place this pursuit leads it to is the sexually coded position of submission always already reserved for it. In its race for a theory purified of the dirt of epistemology, feminism has too quickly embraced in postmodernism a discourse that inevitably will lead it to relinquish its autonomy as the persistent advocate of difference. Ultimately, if feminist theory accepts the postmodern conflation between private sexual play and social intervention, then the forces of patriarchy will have succeeded in closing women out of the public space of discourse and seducing them into the bedroom once more.

NOTES

This chapter was originally presented at the 1991 Speech Communication Association Annual Meeting, October 31–November 3, Atlanta, Ga.

1. Typical of the images of women's literature is feminist literary criticism that focuses on the search for recurring trends in women's writing, art criticism that features the images and icons associated with women and their experiences, and film criticism that sees the representation of women's experience in cinema as an effective political strategy. See, for example, Gilbert and Gubar (1979); Kimball (1981); and Lesage (1978).

2. See hooks's (1990) essay "Postmodern Blackness" and Christian's (1988) analysis for excellent developments of the argument against postmodernism's exclusion of alternative voices.

3. I am indebted to Christian (1988) for the notion of an accelerated and misguided race for theory in contemporary critical studies.

REFERENCES

Alcoff, L. (1988). "Cultural Feminism Versus Post-Structuralism: The Identity Crisis in Feminist Theory." *Signs* 13, no. 3 (Spring): 405–436.

Barthes, R. (1977). "The Death of the Author." *Image, Music, Text.* S. Heath (trans.). New York: Hill and Wang, pp. 142–148.

————. (1983). *Mythologies.* A. Lavers (trans.). New York: Hill and Wang.

Baudrillard, J. (1981). *For a Critique of the Political Economy of the Sign.* C. Levin (trans.). St. Louis, Mo.: Telos.

————. (1983). *In the Shadow of the Silent Majorities ... or the End of the Social.* P. Foss, P. Patton, and J. Johnston (trans.). New York: Semiotext(e).

Bordo, S. (1990). "Feminism, Postmodernism, and Gender-Skepticism." In L. J. Nicholson (ed.), *Feminism/Postmodernism.* New York and London: Routledge, pp. 133–156.

Brown, M. E. (1990). "Motley Moments: Soap Operas, Carnival, Gossip, and the Power of the Utterance." In M. E. Brown (ed.), *Television and Women's Culture.* London: Sage, pp. 183–198.

Brown, W. (1987). "Where Is the Sex in Political Theory?" *Women & Politics* 7, no. 1 (Spring): 3–23.

―――― . (1991). "Feminist Hesitations, Postmodern Exposures." *Differences* 3, no. 1 (Spring): 63–84.

Butler, J. (1990). "Gender Trouble, Feminist Theory, and Psychoanalytic Discourse." In L. J. Nicholson (ed.), *Feminism/Postmodernism.* New York and London: Routledge, pp. 324–340.

Chodorow, N. (1978). *The Reproduction of Mothering: Psychoanalysis and the Sociology of Gender.* Berkeley: University of California Press.

Christian, B. (1988). "The Race for Theory." *Feminist Studies* 14, no. 1 (Spring): 67–79.

Derrida, J. (1976). *Of Grammatology.* G. C. Spivak (trans.). Baltimore, Md.: Johns Hopkins University Press.

di Stefano, C. (1990). "Dilemmas of Difference: Feminism, Modernity, and Postmodernism." In L. J. Nicholson (ed.), *Feminism/Postmodernism.* New York and London: Routledge, pp. 63–82.

Ferguson, K. (1984). *The Feminist Case Against Bureaucracy.* Philadelphia, Pa.: Temple University Press.

Fiske, J. (1986). "Television: Polysemy and Popularity." *Critical Studies in Mass Communication* 3, no. 4 (December): 391–408.

―――― . (1987). *Television Culture.* London: Methuen.

―――― . (1990). "Women and Quiz Shows: Consumerism, Patriarchy, and Resisting Pleasures." In M. E. Brown (ed.), *Television and Women's Culture: The Politics of the Popular.* London: Sage, pp. 134–143.

Flax, J. (1986). "Gender as a Social Problem: In and For Feminist Theory." *Amerikastudien/American Studies* 31, no. 2: 193–213.

Foster, H. (1984). "(Post) Modern Polemics." *New German Critique* 33 (Fall): 72–73.

Foucault, M. (1979/1980). "What Is an Author?" K. Hanet (trans.). *Screen* 20, no. 1 (Spring): 13–33.

Fraser, N., and Nicholson, L. (1988). "Social Criticism Without Philosophy: An Encounter Between Feminism and Postmodernism." In A. Ross (ed.), *Universal Abandon? The Politics of Postmodernism.* Minneapolis: University of Minnesota Press, pp. 83–104.

Gilbert, S., and Gubar, S. (1979). *The Madwoman in the Attic: The Woman Writer and the Nineteenth-Century Imagination.* New Haven, Conn.: Yale University Press.

Grossberg, L. (1983/1984). "The Politics of Youth Culture: Some Observations on Rock and Roll in American Culture." *Social Text* 8, no. 2 (Winter): 104–126.

―――― . (1984). " 'I'd Rather Feel Bad Than Not Feel Anything at All': Rock and Roll, Pleasure and Power." *Enclitic* 8, nos. 1/2 (Spring/Fall): 94–111.

————— . (1989). "Swinging on the (Postmodern) Star." In I. Angus and S. Jhally (eds.), *Cultural Politics in Contemporary America*. New York: Routledge, pp. 254–268.

Haraway, D. (1990). "A Manifesto for Cyborgs: Science, Technology, and Socialist Feminism in the 1980s." in L. J. Nicholson (ed.), *Feminism/Postmodernism*. New York and London: Routledge, pp. 190–233.

Hirschberg, L. (1991). "The Misfit." *Vanity Fair*, April, pp. 158–168, 196–198, 200, 202.

hooks, b. (1990). "Postmodern Blackness." In her *Yearning: Race, Gender, and Cultural Politics*. Boston, Mass.: South End Press, pp. 23–31.

Jones, K. B. (1991). "The Trouble with Authority." *Differences* 3, no. 1 (Spring): 104–127.

Kaplan, E. A. (1987). *Rocking Around the Clock: Music Television, Postmodernism, and Consumer Culture*. New York and London: Routledge.

Kimball, G. (ed.). (1981). *Women's Culture: The Women's Renaissance of the Seventies*. Metuchen, N.J.: Scarecrow Press.

Lacan, J. (1982). *Feminine Sexuality*. J. Mitchell and J. Rose (eds.), J. Rose (trans.). New York: Norton.

Lesage, J. (1978). "The Political Aesthetics of the Feminist Documentary Film." *Quarterly Review of Film Studies* 3, no. 4 (Fall): 507–523.

Lyotard, J.-F. (1985). *The Postmodern Condition: A Report on Knowledge*. G. Bennington and B. Massumi (trans.). Minneapolis: University of Minnesota Press.

Meese, E. (1986). *Crossing the Double-Cross: The Practice of Feminist Criticism*. Chapel Hill and London: University of North Carolina Press.

Miller, N. K. (1986). "Changing the Subject: Authorship, Writing, and the Reader." In T. de Lauretis (ed.), *Feminist Studies/Critical Studies*. Bloomington: Indiana University Press, pp. 102–120.

Owens, C. (1983). "The Discourse of Others: Feminists and Postmodernism." In H. Foster (ed.), *The Anti-aesthetic: Essays on Postmodern Culture*. Port Townsend, Wash.: Bay Press, pp. 57–82.

Petersen, E. E. (1987). "Media Consumption and Girls Who Want to Have Fun." *Critical Studies in Mass Communication* 4, no. 1 (March): 37–50.

Pfeil, F. (1988). "Postmodernism as a Structure of Feeling." in C. Nelson and L. Grossberg (eds.), *Marxism and the Interpretation of Culture*. Urbana: University of Illinois Press, pp. 381–404.

Polunsky, B. (1991). "Madonna Bares All." *San Antonio Express News*, May 12, p. 4-H.

Probyn, E. (1990). "Travels in the Postmodern: Making Sense of the Local." In L. J. Nicholson (ed.), *Feminism/Postmodernism*. New York and London: Routledge, pp. 176–189.

Suleiman, S. (1986). "(Re)Writing the Body: The Politics and Poetics of Female Eroticism." In S. Suleiman (ed.), *The Female Body in Western Culture*. Cambridge, Mass.: Harvard University Press, pp. 7–29.

Walker, C. (1990). "Feminist Literary Criticism and the Author." *Critical Inquiry* 16, no. 3 (Spring): 551–571.

Weed, E. (1989). "Introduction: Terms of Reference." In E. Weed (ed.), *Coming to Terms: Feminism, Theory, Politics*. New York and London: Routledge, pp. IX–XXXI.

Young, I. M. (1990). "The Ideal of Community and the Politics of Difference." In L. J. Nicholson (ed.), *Feminism/Postmodernism*. New York and London: Routledge, pp. 300–323.

photo by Alberto Tolot, *courtesy of Warner Brothers*

photo by Alberto Tolot, *courtesy of Warner Brothers*

photo by Stephane Sednaoui, *courtesy of Warner Brothers*

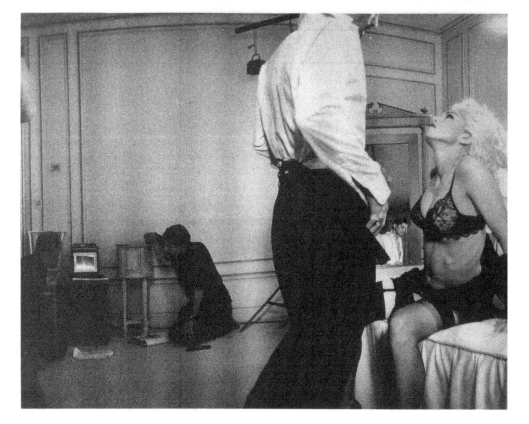

photo by Stephane Sednaoui, *courtesy of Warner Brothers*

E. DEIDRE PRIBRAM

Seduction, Control, & the Search for Authenticity: Madonna's *Truth or Dare*

MADONNA'S 1991 FILM, *Truth or Dare,* based on her 1990 "Blond Ambition" tour—itself a combination of pop music and performance art— defies easy categorization. It is a "docudrama" of sorts: part documentary, part concert film, part dramatic enactment. By combining various filmic styles and traditions, *Truth or Dare* recreates certain long-standing cultural dichotomies between, for instance, onstage and offstage, public and private, reality and appearance, or truth and artifice. The film replicates such oppositions only to then question their continuing validity. Binary distinctions in *Truth or Dare* prove more apparent than real, more fleeting than differentiating. Ultimately, I believe, the film finds such categories irrelevant, at least as far as they concern this particular cultural icon and individual, Madonna.

The collapsing of long-held cultural dichotomies is a central tenet in recent formulations of postmodernism. An examination of *Truth or Dare* within the framework of postmodernist theorizing, in particular Jean Baudrillard's version, indicates that Madonna, in this film, can be viewed as a contemporary application of that body of thought. Moreover, discussion on this topic highlights current and often troubling concerns for feminist film theory, in the face of postmodern formulations, surrounding concepts of subject-object polarity that have played a fundamental role in theorizing the Other.

IS SHE REVEALING, OR ISN'T SHE?: THE RECEPTION & PROMOTION OF "TRUTH OR DARE"

Discussion of *Truth or Dare* most frequently surrounds the question, "Is she revealing, or isn't she?" Do we learn anything "real" about Madonna, and if

189

so, what? This is the debate that frames the film's reception in the popular press. The headline of *Newsweek*'s feature article on her reads: "Madonna Lets It All Hang Out: The Shameless One stages a raunchy, revealing self-portrait." The article goes on to ask, "When a natural-born exhibitionist exhibits herself, is it the 'real' Madonna you are watching or an artful imitation of reality?" (Ansen 1991, 66). *US* magazine prefaces its story with a full two-page color photo of a physically revealed Madonna, accompanied by a quote from her interview, "If you're going to reveal yourself, REVEAL yourself." The article describes *Truth or Dare* as a "touching, vulgar, erotic and revealing documentary" (Deevoy 1991, 18). Janet Maslin (1991, C15) writes in her *New York Times* review, "In the case of Madonna, who is even filmed gossiping in the restroom and visiting her mother's grave, no such sacrosanct territory is shown to exist. Nothing is too private for Madonna to flaunt in public."[1]

This is not to suggest that these questions are raised solely by the film's reception in the press. Madonna and those representing her certainly play along, outside the film's bounds, in the game they have created for the film's revelatory nature. Consider, for instance, the packaging of the film with its slogan, "The Ultimate Dare is to tell the Truth," or the back cover of the video with its image of a barebacked Madonna, "All Access" stamped upon her. Interview comments by the director, Alek Keshishian, adhere to the idea of the film as a search for authenticity around the public *and* private Madonna and its revelations of her "true" being. "Madonna felt a responsibility to let the public in on her truth. Sometimes I think it is more important to be understood than loved" (Heller 1991, 5-E).[2]

Madonna's stance on this varies from interview to interview, and, true to form, she is cagey and elusive. Consider, for example, this excerpt from an interview with Carrie Rickey (1991a, 5-E):

> Does she really believe that she's made a revealing movie? . . . "What's more daring than revealing the truth?" she demands. Excuse me, Madonna, but in the film aren't you revealing only what you choose to reveal? "Yeah," she admits, "I'm revealing what I wanna reveal. . . . While you *can* argue that I chose to show what I wanna show, I can also say that *what* I chose to show is very revealing."

Filmic Signification:
Constructing and Collapsing Distinctions

Truth or Dare is a hybrid of two traditions in concert films. It is a cross between direct cinema practices in its black-and-white segments,[3] recalling films such as *Don't Look Back,* which portrayed Bob Dylan's 1965 tour of England; in its color sequences, it references more recent efforts, such as Jonathan Demme's *Stop Making Sense.*[4] In direct cinema, what is revealed backstage is as critical, if not more so, than what the audience observes through onstage performances in "coming to understand" the personality and cultural importance of a given celebrity or celebrities. In contrast, *Stop Making Sense* occurs entirely in concert. There is no backstage sphere of activity for the Talking Heads, no distinction made between public versus private domains. Diegetically, only onstage exists.[5]

The backstage scenes in *Truth or Dare* make reference to direct cinema, in part because they are shot in black and white, as many of those films were (including *Don't Look Back*). In addition, a number of other signifiers are cited—for instance, it has the gritty look produced by a hand-held camera following action, sometimes too late or off the mark, rather than careful framing and composition. Shots are held longer and edits are less frequent than in the film's color sequences. The black-and-white footage has the feel of a single camera shoot.[6]

By contrast, the color concert segments in the *Stop Making Sense* model are shot with multiple cameras to provide an optimal number of perspectives. Indeed, the editing during the performance scenes is fast-paced: Cuts come with great frequency, while angles and shot distances constantly alter. (This is also influenced by the style of music videos, the medium through which Madonna built much of her career.)

The formal devices and structure of the film establish two broad spaces that together make up Madonna's existence: the public world of performance, of audience and celebrity, and the backstage arena, a more personal, behind-the-scenes space. This backstage arena, although formally unified, can be further distinguished as backstage and offstage. Backstage lies immediately behind the scenes, just as Madonna prepares to go on in front of her audience or comes off after a performance. Offstage is an even more "personal" arena, further removed physically from the stage, and includes time spent with her family and friends such as Sandra Bernhard and Warren Beatty.

The "authenticity" of personal documentary, recording "real" events as they unfold, contrasts the carefully crafted and achieved look and feel of the performance sequences.[7] Two distinct spheres are established in the film, separated formally and spatially: Madonna as public persona, performer, and celebrity versus the more intimate life of Madonna the individual, the human being. The formal strategies surrounding the black-and-white sequences as opposed to those in color are intended to differentiate the two worlds of the film. They are set up, at least initially, in stark opposition to each other.[8]

This is further illustrated by the composition of the film's personnel. The credit sequence indicates that an entirely different crew was used for the documentary footage than for the concert scenes, including the director of photography and the editor, as though two distinct projects were being undertaken side by side.[9] Two different crews, two different traditions, and two different cinematic languages are operating in *Truth or Dare*.

However, though *Truth or Dare* distinguishes between public and private spheres, it does not do so in order to claim them as separable. Instead, having established them in contradistinction, the film works to blur the meanings of those distinctions, to unveil them as more quandary than contradiction. I would like to look in some detail at the transitions between black-and-white and color sequences in order to show how the film structurally manages the oppositional formal and physical spaces it creates and then, ultimately, collapses them.

There are ten color segments, each marking a different song and onstage performance.[10] Seven of the ten numbers are performed in their entirety or near-entirety; three are short clips. With the exception of two numbers, both brief excerpts ("Keep It Together," first version, and "Like a Prayer"), each color segment begins with an extreme wide shot, encompassing the stage and part of the audience.

Transitions surrounding the ten color sequences can be grouped into three categories. In the first, two numbers, "Express Yourself" and "Oh Father," are performed in their entirety. "Express Yourself" is preceded by concert footage in black and white of Madonna and her backup singers performing the same number in Japan, in the rain and out of costume. This is abruptly followed by a straight cut, now in the United States, to an extreme wide shot of the stage occupied by Madonna's dance troupe. (Madonna makes her entrance momentarily, ascending to the stage on a moving lift.) This is also the first instance of color footage. "Express Yourself" ends with a straight cut to a black-and-white image of a plane flying overhead—supposedly, the plane bringing Madonna and her personnel back to the States.

"Oh Father" is framed in a similar manner. The sequence cuts from a black-and-white image of Oliver, one of the dancers, to an extreme wide shot of Madonna on stage. The performance of "Oh Father" also ends in a wide shot of Madonna, although this time there is a quick fade to black before the next black-and-white segment begins. In this first category of transitions, then, the color performances remain intact (that is, without interruption) and are distinctively marked from the preceding and ensuing black-and-white footage.

The middle grouping of transitions encompasses color segments three through six (including two songs only partially performed). In the short version of "Keep It Together," Madonna's performance is hindered by a faulty microphone. Immediately preceding the song's opening, we see her, dressed in appropriate wardrobe for the number, walking out of the backstage area in a medium close shot. This is followed by a straight cut to her, in medium shot, onstage and in color, jumping onto a chair as she performs the barely audible "Keep It Together." This cut looks like matched action. It is a smooth transition from black and white to color, created by the apparent continuity of her movements. This short color sequence ends in the same way: There is a straight cut from Madonna, again in medium shot, jumping down from her chair, to a wide shot, in black and white, of her walking backstage as she says, "Why has it never done this before?" in reference to her sound problems. Again, the continuity of her movements and of the subject matter (the poor sound) give the appearance of a single action. Although the transitions between onstage and backstage are flagged by the changes to or from black and white, the distinction between the two spaces is superseded, at least temporarily, by the (apparent) continuity of Madonna's motions and concerns.

"Like a Virgin" is performed in its entirety and begins with the customary extreme wide shot (cutting from Freddy DeMann, Madonna's manager, placing a bet with two of her bodyguards that her performance will be even more graphic than usual under the threat of arrest). However, this number ends somewhat differently from the previous pattern. There is a cut from the onstage performance to a Toronto TV news report, *still in color,* detailing Madonna's near arrest. This is followed by another cut, this time to black and white, of simulated sex images from *Like a Virgin,* beneath which the audio of the news report continues.

"Like a Prayer" begins with a cut from a black-and-white medium shot of Madonna backstage in prayer, surrounded by her dancers, to a medium wide shot, in color, of Madonna centered in the frame on stage. After a short excerpt of the song, the color sequence cuts from a medium wide shot of Madonna with her dancers to a slightly wider frame, in black and white, of Madonna emerging from a limousine in her bathrobe, with a towel wrapped around her head, as she returns home to have a doctor examine her ailing throat.

The sixth color segment, "Holiday," is performed in its entirety, beginning and ending with extreme wide shots of the stage. However, the performance is preceded by black-and-white footage of Madonna and her two backup singers, standing backstage and singing a portion of "Holiday," then it immediately cuts to the onstage version. In other words, in this middle group of color segments, the transitions are less abrupt and the black-and-white and color portions merge more smoothly, serving to connect, rather than oppose, them to surrounding material.

Until this point, the color performances (and, conversely, the black-and-white segments) have been kept intact. That is, the performance of the song is uninterrupted before the image reverts to black and white. From here on, however, this is no longer the case. The final four color performances (three in their entirety, one in excerpt) intermingle black-and-white footage with color, in varying configurations. "Live to Tell" is preceded by Madonna, in black and white and surrounded by reporters, giving her statement to the press regarding the Vatican's banning of her shows. We then cut to the beginning of "Live to Tell" in color, then back to more of the press conference, and so on. In this instance, the press conference is the foundation of the scene, while the performance acts as cutaway and commentary. Indeed, a good portion of the performance presents Madonna dancing but not singing, while her voice-over of the press statement continues.

The "Vogue" segment also follows a pattern of intercutting between stage performance and black-and-white images—in this case, of fans both with and without Madonna and of Madonna and her troupe at parties, on holiday, and generally having fun, while often making similar physical gestures to those being performed onstage. The cuts back and forth, between color and black-and-white, are frequent and rapid. However, in this instance, the performance serves as the base of the scene, while the black-and-white cutaways act as illustrations or snapshots. "Vogue" ends abruptly with a cut to a medium shot of Madonna, in black and white, playing the game truth or dare with her troupe.

"Causing a Commotion," consisting of Madonna playfighting onstage with her two female backup singers, is only partially performed. We cut to "Commotion" from a conversation, in black and white, between Madonna and the two singers, Donna Delory and Niki Harris, lying in bed. And we return to this conversation several times from further excerpts of the three, in color and onstage.

The final performance number, "Keep It Together" (in its entirety this time), also intercut with black and white, is the most evenly balanced between the film's two opposing stylistic signifiers. The song is performed without black-and-white interruption until all the singers and dancers have left the stage and Madonna remains alone. Then, as she repeatedly sings the chorus, we cut back and forth between her kissing her dancers and personnel good-bye at the tour's end and other images of closure and separation to her, onstage alone. Now, the two aspects of her life and of the film are balanced equally. For instance, the sounds from both arenas—onstage and backstage—occur simultaneously. The color and black-and-white segments and the on- and offstage spaces are no longer locked in struggle for dominance. They do not compete with each other; they coexist until the show, the Blond Ambition tour, and the film end on a close-up of Madonna's hat as it is tossed onto the stage floor.

And so, as the film progresses, the manner in which transitions are managed alters. They evolve not abruptly but gradually. More importantly, their evolution serves to collapse the spaces that the film so carefully defines initially. We are left with one of the most significant questions posed by the film: What, after all, are the differences between onstage and offstage spaces?

A provocative aspect of the film's use of disparate cinematic styles, languages, and traditions is how it then comes to define which incidents and events belong to the onstage world and which to the backstage or offstage arenas. For instance, Madonna's singing of "Happy Birthday" to her father, though occurring onstage, in front of an audience, and in wardrobe, is shot in black and white, clearly denoting it as "personal"—or perhaps questioning it as such?[11]

FEMINIST RECEPTION OF MADONNA AS POSTMODERN PERSONA

The film's use of devices such as black-and-white film stock versus color, concert film versus direct cinema, and public versus private spaces establishes polarities, only to then elide or confuse them. The ultimate goal, I believe, is to raise the validity of the central question of the film: Who is the public persona and who is the "real" Madonna?

Though many of the film's commentators argue that *Truth or Dare* fails to successfully reveal the "real" Madonna, the question, "Is she or isn't she revealing?" remains the framework in which the subject is considered. "While only the gullible would believe that Madonna consciously exposes anything more than her breasts in this film, of which she is the executive producer, *Truth or Dare* is an engaging portrait of the diva as control freak" (Rickey 1991b). Implicit in all the commentary is the acceptance of the terms of the "is she or isn't she?" question. A *New York Times* article by Neal Gabler (1991) makes explicit what is at stake here: "Everywhere the fabricated, the inauthentic and the theatrical have gradually driven out the natural, the genuine and the spontaneous until there is no distinction between real life and stagecraft."[12] Gabler's article—indeed, all the articles quoted here—reference a "real" that is always assumed but never specified.

In contrast, what *Truth or Dare* suggests is that elaborating questions of authenticity around traditional polar opposites is an act of deception. *Truth or Dare*'s provocativeness rests with its ability to question the attempt to understand celebrities within the framework of public performer versus private person. The film offers itself up as evidence of the invalidity of the terms of the question, at least in the face of a (postmodern) performer such as Madonna. It further causes us to ask what the relationship is between this specific performer's ability to fascinate her audiences and her constant reinventions of herself.

At stake here is much more than Madonna's reputation for playfulness—or for playing with her audiences' heads. In a recent essay, which I will quote at some length, E. Ann Kaplan (1988, 153–154) writes:

Feminism, particularly in America, has traditionally relied on a liberal- or left-humanist position. . . . Humanist values, applied specifically to those humans called "women" who often were not included in humanist cultural projections, formed the basis of arguments to improve women's condition of existence. . . . The blurring of distinctions between a "subject" and an "image"—or the reduction of the old notion of "self" to "image"—is something for feminists to explore, even as we fear the coming of Baudrillard's universe of "simulacra". . . .

The new postmodern universe, however, with its celebration of the look, surfaces, textures, the self-as-commodity, produces an array of images/representations/simulacra that co-opts any possible critical position by the very incorporation of what were previously "dissenting" images. . . . As a cultural mode, postmodernism would eliminate gender difference as a significant category, just as it sweeps aside other polarities.

Kaplan's argument is that in a modernist universe, where humanism is the prevailing ideology, individuals can be categorized into those who are granted subjectivity (white, Western bourgois patriarchy) and those who are not. The latter remain the object of someone else's desire and the means by which subjectivity is achieved. In a world defined by humanism, individuals are either "self" or "other," wherein all people of difference, including women, comprise the Other.

The liberal or Left humanist positions that Kaplan refers to are political arguments based on concepts of (in)justice. That is, *all* persons can rightfully lay claim to existences as self-determining subjects, on the basis of individual equality. This, for many years now, has been the fundamental stance of movements struggling for equality of race, class, gender, sexual preference, and so on.

Kaplan suggests that ideological arguments based on the attainment of selfhood for all will be "swept aside" by postmodernism. In this newly forming universe, all are reduced to image, to Other, along with marginalized peoples who were previously defined as "people of difference." In other words, political, economic, and cultural inequalities will remain, but the means by which we have imagined overturning them will have disappeared.

I would suggest that Madonna as the reigning pop icon of postmodernism and *Truth or Dare* in particular are useful models through which to explore some of Kaplan's concerns. This can be done in terms of two broad categories. First, there are the implications *of* postmodernism, using Baudrillard's analyses, without the extreme bleakness of his, or even Kaplan's, views. Second, there are the implications of postmodernism *for* feminism. Here, Madonna has always proven a thorny problem. Many feminists have been reluctant to embrace her, on the one hand, or dismiss her entirely, on the other.

Feminists' ambivalence toward Madonna derives from arguments of whether she works to destroy stereotypes or only confirms traditional roles and representations of women. These contentions are fueled by the difficulties surrounding the Madonna persona, the difficulties of *fixing* her as one set of meanings or another.

In a review of *Truth or Dare* in the leftist journal the *Guardian*, Elayne Rapping (1991a) writes,

> Her sense of humor, irreverent and lusty, is a celebration of female freedom from sexual constraint of all kinds. Her sexual bravado . . . cannot possibly be misunderstood as the behavior of a sexual object. . . . She is so at ease with her sexual power, so fearless of its effects on others, so outrageously candid and open that she stands as a living symbol of the liberating power of breaking social taboos.

Despite Rapping's assertion that Madonna cannot possibly be misunderstood as a sexual object, many of the *Guardian*'s readers did just that, in angry responses to her article. For instance, one reader wrote, "She is part of a continuum of images in our culture that sexually objectifies, degrades and confines women. . . . She makes her millions from the perpetuation of a gender role for women—the sex goddess and beauty queen—that is patriarchal and a thousand years old" (*Guardian* 1991b). Another wrote, "Traditional masculine definitions of sexuality center on power, control, domination and manipulation. We need new visions of sexuality that eroticize sharing, nurturing, communion and love. When a woman such as Madonna appropriates patriarchal attributes of sexuality, she is neither progressive nor feminist" (*Guardian* 1991a).

As Rapping (1991b) quite rightly points out in her response to these letters, a passive and essentializing attitude toward female sexuality is just as potentially regressive as Madonna's aggressive stance:

> A sense of sexual power and a sense of being in control do not strike me as masculine experiences at all. Women have been denied free expression of and control over our desires and pleasures by masculine cultural norms. To portray women as sexually powerful therefore seems to me very exhilarating and positive. . . . Were she to portray herself as passive, powerless and only interested in giving and nurturing, she would indeed be reinforcing sexist notions.

These arguments inevitably become mired in firmly entrenched positions surrounding established definitions of sexual dichotomies: What is progressive female sexuality, and what are regressive, male-imposed representations? Just as *Truth or Dare*'s formal strategies structure two (ultimately false) oppositions around public celebrity versus private individual, discussion around the film and surrounding the figure herself is often polarized, without, however, revealing a similar futility in those oppositional stances.

Whether Madonna is a beneficial or detrimental model for women, whether the image(s) she poses is a "good" or "bad" thing may well be irresolvable for many feminists and, moreover, beside the point. I am not sug-

gesting the dismissal of all value judgments. I will, for instance, affirm that
the goals and concerns of feminism remain, to my mind, "good." But
whether Madonna is good for feminism (or whether she is a feminist) obscures the discussion. Rather, we should ask what she can elucidate (inadvertently or otherwise) about what it means to be feminist in a postmodern
era. At issue here are evolving and tentative formulations of what postmodern feminism is or could be. Utilizing certain key concepts from the work of
Baudrillard, who describes a changing, postmodern world based on new information and mass communications societies, we can begin to explore
what Madonna may have to offer in this regard.

Sexuality, Power, and Gender Ambiguity

Very near the opening of *Truth or Dare,* we see Madonna and her dancers
during a rehearsal of "Papa Don't Preach." The song is disrupted by feed-
back coming from the sound system. Madonna abruptly stops the rehearsal
and, speaking into the microphone, explains that the sound levels are not
high enough to be causing such a problem and that if it cannot be resolved,
she will not do the show. Then, after a moment's pause, too brief to have allowed for a response, she states, "I'm waiting."

Soon after this scene, we cut to the first color performance, "Express
Yourself," in which Madonna ascends to the stage dressed in a pin-striped
business suit. The suit jacket is slit open at the breasts, and the exaggerated
cups of Madonna's bra protrude. As she takes off the jacket, we see that the
bra is actually a corset, with garters, worn over the baggy pants of the suit.
Her backup singers wear similar loose-fitting pants and black bras.

Framed by these two introductory scenes, we are alerted that the film's
treatment of sexuality and power are inextricably linked. Immediately striking is the manner in which Madonna deals with her sound problems during
the "Papa Don't Preach" rehearsal. She speaks calmly and in a low voice,
fully expecting to be given the respect due authority. She does not have to
plead for it, argue about it, or enforce it. It is similar to the way in which
someone like Warren Beatty exudes power—in the quiet, self-assured manner of those accustomed to being listened to. The specific kind of power Madonna exudes is control: control of her performance and how the rehearsal
is conducted and control over those who work for her.

Equally striking are the specifics of the "Express Yourself" wardrobe. She
references both genders simultaneously, signified by the combination of
(male) business suit and (female) corset. That she parodies gender roles is indicated by the stiffness and protrusions of the corset's bra, overdefining female sexuality and thereby neutralizing, altering, or obscuring its meaning
(it is unclear which effect is intended). She is not soft or alluring but sharp
and dangerous. The intentionality of the parody is made clear during the

performance of "Like a Virgin" when her *male* dancers wear and fondle such ridiculously exaggerated bras that they make hers seem diminutive in comparison. The male side of the parody in "Express Yourself" is extended by the old-world (voyeuristic) "charm" of the monocle she sports.

Most notably, the corset worn over baggy suit pants undermines the traditional "sexiness" of the corset itself. Without the pants, the corset might have more strongly resembled the showgirl outfit worn by many women dancers, especially in the classic Hollywood musical. Instead, the departure from the traditional display of legginess is affirmed by the backup singers' similar costuming.

THE WORLD OF SEDUCTION AND APPEARANCE: MADONNA AND BAUDRILLARD

According to Baudrillard's theory of historically changing sexuality, in previous eras sexuality was a set of defined erotic practices that included the hidden, the repressed, and the proscribed. In contemporary society, which has formalized a far greater degree of explicitness, sexuality has come to have different meanings. Douglas Kellner (1989, 135), in his book on the work of Baudrillard, explains: "That is, in a society in which sexuality speaks in advertising, fashion, the media and other popular discourses, it is open and manifest throughout social life."

Baudrillard (1990, 21) defines seduction as a game while sex is a function. Seduction is marked by the attributes of play and defiance:[13] "The ability to turn appearances in on themselves, to play on the body's appearances, rather than with the depths of desire" (Baudrillard 1990, 8).

Combining gender roles and dress *is* Madonna's game of defiance. Her skills as part pop icon and part performance artist are tied to her ability to play on the body's appearances and turn those appearances in on themselves. Is her corset, with its sharpened breasts, an exaggerated parody of women's social function or an example of threatening female sexuality to male psyches? Does her mix-and-match outfit of male business suit and female corset comment on what it means to be male—or female? Or does it address what it might mean to exist in a society not delineated on the basis of gender? Following Baudrillard, it is, indeed, possible to argue that Madonna's displays of sexuality exist on the level of seduction and appearances and not in the realm of sex, at "the depths of desire."

In an earlier age, obscenity was defined as that which was proscribed. But in the world of seduction, the definition of obscenity, too, has changed. "It is no longer the traditional obscenity of what is hidden, repressed, forbidden or obscure; on the contrary, it is the obscenity of the visible, of the all-too-visible, of the more visible-than-the-visible" (Baudrillard 1983, 131). In a culture in which open displays of sexuality are widespread, the obscene is no longer that which is repressed but, instead, that which is too excessively visible. Here, Baudrillard uses the term *obscene* in the sense of "made explicit, fully visible." That is, the obscene is the *excess* of prevailing social attitudes toward sexuality within the cultural context of its use. In a society in which sexuality is severely restricted, the obscene is the exhibition of that which is forbidden. Conversely, in a social context in which sexuality is routinely made apparent, obscenity becomes its unlimited display.

Madonna's performances may shock some people and be banned from time to time. But the numbers of her supporters and their fervor may express, precisely, the recognition of the representation of sexuality as commonplace, even banal, in the postmodern era. This could also be the reason why, despite the supposed sexual extremism of her shows, she commands large and largely mainstream audiences.

Although Baudrillard no doubt plays on the pejorative connotations of the term *obscene,* use of this term is not bound by his limitations. On the contrary, popular usage of the word is socially constructed, based on prevailing notions of morality. That which was defined as obscene in the Victorian era, while referring to what was culturally repressed at the time, may no longer be so, for example, in the expression of women's desires or sexual experiences outside the socially sanctified institution of marriage. Nor is any era's definition of obscenity accepted by all. Quite the contrary: Socially constructed definitions of obscenity that mark repressions or oppressions can rightfully be struggled against, especially by those whose sexual practices are oppressed by that norm (for instance, gays and lesbians). Baudrillard's emphasis on appearances is part of his critique of all theories that search for "truth" beneath the surface. Under attack, then, are virtually all of the "master" theories of Western humanism, including Marxism and psychoanalysis. According to Baudrillard (1988, 149):

> The havoc interpretation wreaks in the domain of appearances is incalculable, and its privileged quest for hidden meanings may be profoundly mistaken. For we needn't search in some beyond, in a *hinterwelt,* or in an unconscious, to find what diverts discourse. What actually displaces it, "seduces" it in the literal sense, and makes it seductive, is its very appearance.[14]

The following conversation between Madonna and Carrie Fisher is excerpted from a two-part *Rolling Stone* interview, under Fisher's byline (1991b, 48):

F: What about your whole spanking thing? I don't get that.

M: It's a joke. I despise being spanked. It's play. I say I want to be spanked, but it's like, "Try it and I'll knock your fucking head off." It's a joke!

F: But I saw you on Arsenio and you said—

M: I was just playing with Arsenio.

F: This is a very important piece of news.

Why Fisher considers this important news or, more importantly, what prompts her to accept Madonna's declaration as more truthful than any other statement Madonna has made in any other context is unclear. It apparently does not occur to Fisher that Madonna might be catering her answers to her immediate audience—whether Arsenio Hall or Fisher herself. What is clear is the absence of any possible barometer for the definitive truth.

This exchange is taken from the same *Rolling Stone* interview (Fisher 1991a, 120):

M: They [men she goes out with] don't tell me I give good head, believe me, because I don't give it.

F: Ever?

M: They just tell me I'm a savage bitch. Who wants to choke? That's the bottom line. I contend that that's part of the whole humiliation thing of men with women. Women cannot choke a guy.

And later (Fisher 1991b, 78), Madonna reiterates: "They're not getting head from me, they're getting gifts from Maxfield."

Once again, we are left wondering, does she or doesn't she? Here is another mystery from the "definitive" source for the rest of us to unravel in our search for the authentic Madonna. Indeed, it is a provocative statement for Madonna to insist she does *not* perform oral sex, especially in conjunction with the now legendary scene in *Truth or Dare* where she gives head, with proficiency, to a water bottle. This inability to "fix" or position Madonna and the indeterminacy of her persona—in both statements and performance—suggest parallels to Baudrillard's concept of simulacra.

Simulation and the Quest for Authenticity

The distinction between appearance and representation, in Baudrillard's view, is that representation refers to an original, a "real," while appearance does not (Baudrillard 1988, 170). Now, in our culture of information and the mass media, we are inundated with an overabundance of images and signs that no longer have referential value but, instead, interact solely with other signs. This marks the advent of simulation. Rather than the previous vertical connection, if you will, between sign and meaning, there is, instead, the horizontal relationship of sign to sign. "All the great humanist criteria of value, all the values of a civilization of moral, aesthetic, and practical judgement, vanish in our system of images and signs. Everything becomes undecideable" (Baudrillard 1988, 128). Moreover, everything becomes exchangeable, one sign for another. There is an uncertainty of meaning, free floating and indeterminate, rather than the stability of a referent tied to meaning.

The process of simulation, the evolution from representation to appearance, is the result of implosion. Rather than the explosion of capitalism and commodification in the modern era, postmodernism is marked by an implosion, a collapsing inward of traditional boundaries and binary distinctions such as elite and popular culture, appearance and reality, and so on (Kellner 1989, 68). Implosion, according to Baudrillard (1988, 210), is caused not by a lack but by an *excess* of information. Here, we arrive at the source of Baudrillard's definition of the obscene as explicit or fully visible. No longer that which is hidden in the sense of "deep structures" of meaning (Baudrillard 1988, 164), the obscene marks the surface confusions of the postmodern information-communication culture: that which is excessively available and made too evident.

Truth or Dare raises the question of the "real"—which is public persona and which private individual?—but refuses to answer it. Or it does answer it by saying that the question itself is absurd and irrelevant. Madonna, this chameleon of appearances who refuses all fixed meanings, may be viewed as simulation in the context of Baudrillard's theories. If one sees her in this way, she can then be received at surface value, confusions and contradictions intact. That is, there is no definitive "real," no authentic Madonna, beyond the person(a) we already know through her various incarnations, guises, and forms. Following Baudrillard, if there is no authentic, then the appearances themselves, by displacing the authentic, become the real (or, to use his term, the hyperreal).

To attempt to distinguish between appearance and reality is, in Madonna's case, misleading. No ground and no means exist to "prove" she is one way in (any) public and different in a separate, private existence. There is no hidden real that she keeps from us like a dark secret, no lie or deception. Ultimately, no distinction exists between her public self and some other concealed self, between the onstage and offstage aspects of her persona.

It is important to distinguish simulation from the "illusion" portion of the reality versus illusion construct. In fact, simulation displaces the entire reality versus illusion equation. Simulation is the map that precedes and displaces the territory it once was intended to describe (Baudrillard 1988, 166). It is of the order of an alternate reality, the hyperreal. As Baudrillard explains (1988, 167–168):

> To dissimulate is to feign not to have what one has. To simulate is to feign to have what one hasn't. One implies a presence, the other an absence. But the

matter is more complicated, since to simulate is not simply to feign: "Someone who feigns an illness can simply go to bed and pretend he is ill. Someone who simulates an illness produces in himself some of the symptoms" (Littre). Thus, feigning or dissimulating leaves the reality principle intact: The difference is always clear, it is only masked; whereas simulation threatens the difference between "true" and "false," between "real" and "imaginary."

To say something or someone is a simulation model does not imply feigning, pretending, or misleading, measured against that which is not feigned, actual, or true. It is, rather, to say that in the postmodern world, simulacra are actualized, self-contained entities, without any measurement against a referent that would then render them representative. Therefore, simulacra displace or threaten the entire dichotomy of true versus false or of reality and its opposite, illusion. Feigning or dissimulation replace only the false or illusory portion of the dichotomy, leaving the *idea* of the equation unharmed.

Madonna's various appearances—her form of seduction—divert others from their path (in the literal sense of seduction) precisely because they search for her authenticity. In both her performances and her comments during interviews, she discloses an awareness, a self-consciousness, that the game is about "revealing" her "true" self. The way to play the game—to win—is by constant renewal. And so, she keeps reinventing herself, sometimes (as in her interviews) from moment to moment. And along the way, she dispenses clues and devises contradictions to keep us guessing. Indeed, her stock in trade (exchange value) depends on never being definitively placed. Once pinned down, fixed, made "real," her persona as it is currently formulated would cease to exist (for, of course, there are many aspects of her life she could easily clarify were she to choose to do so).

And so, in *Truth or Dare,* there is an ironic integrity to her presentation of selves. The secrets given up and the privacies laid bare do not belong to her but to those around her. The moments of genuine vulnerability originate with her brother Marty, her childhood friend Moira, with Oliver waiting for his father or Sharon telling of her rape. There are no equivalent moments for Madonna (certainly not at her mother's grave) where we feel pity or sadness or wish to turn away in order to avoid a moment of intrusion. The dramatic conflicts in *Truth or Dare* arise, for instance, from the animosities between her dancers, not from the specifics of Madonna's life or personality. She is the conflict resolver, the one in charge, which she rather awkwardly conveys through the metaphor of mother.

Performance and Control

This, however, returns us to something else that is absent from Baudrillard's analyses—the issue of control. Although Baudrillard delineates a complex description of the postmodern world, he is far more insightful at critiquing

existing and emerging cultural conditions and much less helpful in identifying alternatives. "Suddenly, there is a curve in the road, a turning point.
Somewhere, the real scene has been lost, the scene where you had rules for
the game and some solid stakes that everyone could rely on" (Baudrillard,
quoted in Kellner 1989, 174). Here, Baudrillard, sounding rather nostalgic,
reads in sharp contrast to Madonna's playful defiance. Her spirited energy
belies the bleakness and desperation of his postmodern view. Despite his disclaimer that postmodernism is neither "optimistic nor pessimistic," Baudrillard paints a bleak picture of what remains for the "survivors" of the demise
of modernity (Baudrillard, quoted in Kellner 1989, 117). Again, his pessimism is in sharp contrast to the vitality Madonna exudes, which seems
linked to her sense of control (the possibility of which, one suspects Baudrillard would argue, has completely vanished in the postmodern era, certainly on any kind of individual level).

The one aspect all parties, including Madonna, seem able to agree on concerning her persona(e) in *Truth or Dare* is that she is in charge. She is the focus of attention. The film presents her controlling the content of her show, as
well as the way the show is run. She controls her life, her people, and even
her image.

It may not make her "nice," but it does make her compelling and, I think,
makes aspects of her life enviable to others. Those are the sentiments one
hears in Carrie Fisher's (1991a, 35) introduction to their interview: "Madonna has no equal in getting attention. She often seems to behave like
someone who has been under severe restraint and can now say and do whatever she likes without fear of reprisal." A similar euphoria surfaces in Elayne
Rapping's review of *Truth or Dare* (1991a): "I left this film almost walking
on air, so exhilarating was its sense of female pride, power and progress."

Madonna is a complex of controlled performance mixed with total abandon. We hold in awe someone who, with such audacity, can call Warren
Beatty an asshole, gag on Kevin Costner's description of her show as "neat,"
give head to a bottle, and then retain them all in her film. Approval and dis-
approval within the bounds of *Truth or Dare* belong to her. What Madonna
as public persona appears to want and to represent, in contrast perhaps to
Marilyn Monroe (the other cultural icon she most frequently references), is
to be in charge of her own life without exchanging control over her career,
her body, or her image.

In this postmodern era, Madonna has succeeded in maintaining some degree of control over her existence—a good deal, by contemporary standards—precisely because she functions as simulation. Here is someone who
lives as pure sign, who *chooses* to live as pure sign. She is an entirely public
figure, a persona in and of the world, who more than willingly renders herself an image and an icon. Her whole life consists of performance. Apart
from the issue of whether this is a beneficial or detrimental choice as an indi-

vidual life-style (or how many others would—or could—choose it), what it has provided Madonna is, precisely, this level of control, especially over her own image.

And so, as Madonna stays at least one step ahead of her audiences, reinventing herself and expressing herself in what are received as ever more daring appearances and all the while evading definition, we finally return to the question of the "assumed real" that is so often implied, though unspecified, and against which Madonna is measured, as people ask, "Yes, but is this the real Madonna?"

THE ROLE OF THE "REAL"
IN THE PRODUCTION OF MEANING

The two most frequently cited scenes from *Truth or Dare* are those in which Madonna gives head to a water bottle and converses with Warren Beatty while being examined by the throat specialist. Lost in Beatty's always quoted line "Turn the camera off? She doesn't want to live off-camera, much less talk," is the tenor of the entire conversation, including Madonna's responses.[15]

Madonna often "wins points" in various press accounts for not editing this scene out of the film, given the general consensus that Beatty gains the upper hand. But it could equally be argued that, within the bounds of the film, Madonna possesses him. He is reluctantly drawn into the film and becomes the property of her image. She, for instance, refused his request to be deleted from the film. Instead of Madonna being his status symbol, after all the press describing her as another one of Beatty's women, he ends up being a postscript in her story. She shows him off hanging around backstage, calls him "asshole," and calls him to her ("And don't hide back there, Warren. Get over here.") like a recalcitrant child or one of her attendants. He becomes her boy toy. She retains control of the image of their respective personae and the presentation of their relationship.

More important is the context of this scene, both within and beyond the bounds of the film. Warren Beatty, who more than any other Hollywood star understands the publicity value and therefore the box-office value of having an offscreen affair with his onscreen love interest,[16] suddenly turns camera-shy in *Truth or Dare*. In early scenes of the film, he is edgy, he paces and avoids the camera. Although accustomed to being a celebrity whose existence is frequently lived in front of cameras, here he jealously guards his privacy, his "real" life.

Madonna is contantly aware of the camera, but, then, so is Warren. He just wants it turned off—occasionally and selectively. She doesn't.

Something about the shooting of this particular scene, while Madonna is being examined by the doctor for a fairly serious throat problem that will result in the cancellation of some of her shows, offends Beatty's sense of propriety (assuming he hasn't been set off by any number of other instances that were edited out of the film). For him, a line has been crossed between public and private, and he seems genuinely angered. It is Madonna who asks what the difference is between this and any other instance: "Why should I stop here?"

In her interview in *US* magazine (Deevoy 1991, 20), responding to a question about this scene, Madonna states:

I think what Warren was *trying* to say is that he is very shy and private and he doesn't understand my lack of inhibition because he's the opposite of me. What's so intimate about my throat? I mean, my God, everyone knows when I'm having an abortion, when I'm getting married, when I'm getting divorced, who I'm breaking up with. My throat is now intimate? Anyway, the cameras didn't follow me around 24 hours a day. They weren't in the room when I was *fucking!*

Madonna poses a good question here. What is it about this particular scenario that sets Beatty off, that offends his sensibilities, despite any number of other incidents that could be considered more intimate? Does it have something to do with the fact that what is at stake here is her livelihood, the business side of her existence? Perhaps it is the use to which the camera is put. When it is furthering her (or his) career by garnering publicity, for instance, it is not threatening. However, when her ability to work is on the line and the camera is recording that, it becomes intrusive.

At issue in the encounter with Beatty is the crux of the search for authenticity and of the implied real. In a column on *Truth or Dare,* Ellen Goodman (1991) writes,

But suddenly the voice of reason and sanity passed to none other than Warren Beatty. . . . But poor Warren was dating himself. There he was, tagged forever, as a member of a generation that actually draws a line, however often violated, however egotistically crossed, between life and art, between the private and the public self.

Here, Beatty is cast as the old-style star—more noble, less tarnished because he retains a sense of traditional values based on drawing lines between concepts such as life or art and public or private.

Madonna, on the other hand, represents the opposing tendency, as Goodman (1991) argues:

In *Truth or Dare*, the director makes a visual line between person and performer. He uses black-and-white film for backstage, color for onstage. But Madonna crosses that line, playacting real life. In the strikingly narrow world that she rules as a superstar, the projection of her personality is her greatest artistic achievement.

This is opposed, one assumes, to "real" artistic achievement. What concerns me is how Goodman knows Madonna crosses the line if all we are presented with is the star playacting at real life. How would Goodman recognize Madonna's "real life" in contrast to the playacting? Does her real life ever surface, no matter how briefly, in the film? Or is the implication that reality is simply something we would all immediately recognize?

Goodman's concern—and Beatty's—reflect more of their own perspectives than Madonna's. Beatty, as representative of the old-style star, relies on notions of authenticity; Madonna denies them. The collapse of distinctions, based on binary opposites, may remain troubling for Madonna's audiences and her press, but they do not bother her. Her work, as evidenced in *Truth or Dare*, does not attempt to resolve the collapse of distinctions such as public versus private, appearance versus reality; it only asks the audience to question the ongoing meaning and validity of such distinctions. It is not Madonna's discomfort that the film confronts; it is Beatty's, the press's, and our own—the audience's. *Truth or Dare* recalls clear distinctions of the past and summons a longed-for authenticity.

As Baudrillard (1988, 153–154) warns, "The alternative is unbearable (precisely because *truth does not exist*). We must not wish to destroy appearances (the seduction of images). This project must fail if we are to prevent the absence of truth from exploding in our faces." By the destruction of appearances, Baudrillard means simply recognizing them for what they are: the displacements of old truths and old values that we are accustomed to and that have given shape and sense to our lives. Revealing the disappearance of those distinctions, of the ability to "fix" authenticity and its replacement with the seduction of images, is perhaps the ultimate dare with which *Truth or Dare* challenges us and the risk that Madonna poses.

MADONNA'S POSTMODERN REPRESENTATIONS: RETHINKING FEMINIST EQUATIONS

Although I agree with Ann Kaplan that subject-object categories may no longer be applicable in a postmodern universe, I would question the degree to which this, through the demise of humanism, eliminates a feminist position. In an article entitled "The Economy of Desire," Mary Ann Doane (1989, 24) speaks of "rethinking the absoluteness of the dichotomy between subject and object which informs much feminist thinking." Doane refers to recent theorizations that delineate individuals as either subject or object, wherein women are inevitably "object." Her argument is that there are instances in which women take up identifiable positions of subjectivity and that to relegate women to only object reaffirms their existing polarized and marginalized cultural positioning. Doane's is a position that has been held by many feminists, myself included. However, in light of current theorizations around postmodernism, I would suggest that it is the categorization of all individuals based on subject-object distinctions (that is, the equation itself) that needs rethinking.

"There is and there always will be major difficulties in analyzing the media and the whole sphere of information through the traditional categories of the philosophy of the subject: will, representation, choice, liberty, deliberation, knowledge, and desire" (Baudrillard 1988, 214). The postmodern culture of mass media and information excess overturns and reshapes the relationship between subject and object in two important ways, according to Baudrillard. First, the simulated object that seduces takes precedence over the previously defined subject that believed itself in the sovereign position of power in the equation. Second, following poststructuralist theory, the subject position is eliminated entirely. As distinctions between public and private, interior and exterior are replaced by nonbinary media space, the subject itself becomes an object within the realm of information and communication technologies and practices (Kellner 1989, 71). This newly defined object, then, is not the old presence of the subject-object dichotomy but an altogether different entity that displaces the entire previous equation.

There are serious limitations to Baudrillard's work, including his all-encompassing generalizations and frequent theoretical excesses. In addition, I have here considered only one public figure, Madonna, as a model for current configurations of personae. Much work needs to be done, vis-à-vis postmodernism, in the sphere of nonpublic, especially political, constructs of the individual. I would suggest, however, that many of these still early postmodern formulations merit exploration, while guarding against a view of postmodernism as antithetical to feminism. If Madonna is a model of seduction, of the succession of the simulated object's primacy, then her striking ability to seduce with some measure of control over the dissemination of her image(s) may be a point of departure in the articulation of postmodern feminism.

PUBLISHER'S NOTE

The publisher regrets that the first printing of *The Madonna Connection* included alterations to Deidre Pribram's essay that were incorrect. The original language of the essay has been restored for this and subsequent printings.

Acknowledgments

I would like to thank Lisa Henderson for her helpful comments over several conversations.

NOTES

1. Maslin (1991, C15) goes on to add, "True, perhaps, to the spirit of the times, *Truth or Dare* turns commerce and real intimacy into those rare subjects that are off limits, and it exhibits calculatingly full abandon about confessions of any other kind." Other examples abound. In *Entertainment,* James Kaplan (1991, 18) writes, "Is this an intimate meeting between friends or a movie scene [between Madonna and Sandra Bernhard]? If it's a movie, where is the script? If it's a documentary, where's the reality?" In the British magazine *The Face,* James Ryan (1991, 59) notes, "If indeed, as the movie implies, Madonna's career can be boiled down to a series of rising dares, giving up her privacy to the unblinking eye of Keshishian's 16mm camera may have been the toughest gauntlet to accept."

2. I deliberately avoid the issue of authorial intentionality. Besides the difficulty of establishing it with any certainty in any instance or the question of its relevancy in an analysis such as this, there is the particular difficulty in this case of determining whether we are discussing Madonna's intent or that of the director, Keshishian—a subject much debated in the press on the film. "Evidence" in this regard is unclear and—not surprisingly from this source—contradictory. Early in the film, for example, during Madonna's "adjustment" scene, she is reluctant to allow the camera's presence, but Keshishian prevails. On the other hand, preceding this scene, as she is about to discuss business with her manager, Freddy DeMann, Madonna, with no apparent concern or hesitation, slams the door of her trailer in the camera's face, so to speak.

3. Direct cinema, the American version of cinema verité, was formulated around the belief that the camera could function as neutral observer, recording dramatic events as they naturally unfolded. Cinema verité, in contrast, used the camera to provoke events and thereby bring truths to light. The major proponents of direct cinema include Robert Drew, Richard Leacock, Don Pennebaker, and Albert and David Maysles. Among their most notable films are *Primary* (1960, Drew Associates), *Happy Mother's Day* (1964, Leacock), *Don't Look Back* (1966, Pennebaker), and *Salesman* (1969, the Maysles).

4. *Don't Look Back,* directed by Don Pennebaker, applied "behind the scenes" techniques to a pop culture figure. These strategies were used successfully in earlier films focusing on political subjects, such as *Primary* and *Crisis: Behind a Presidential Commitment* (1963). *Stop Making Sense* (1984), directed by Jonathan Demme, is a concert film on the Talking Heads. Stylistically similar is Martin Scorses's 1978 film of The Band, *The Last Waltz.*

5. Although I have stated that *Stop Making Sense* describes a more recent tradition in concert film, due to its focus on public performance and persona only, it is possible to argue that *Woodstock* (1970), directed by Michael Wadleigh, is the precedent here.

6. I say the "feel" because it is clear in many sequences that more than one camera was used. For instance, the scene with Madonna and the doctor, which cuts back and forth as each say, "Aah," is achieved by two cameras filming simultaneously.

7. Indeed, the concert sequences are expertly shot and edited. On initial viewing, the concert segments seem equally balanced with the documentary footage. Only on repeated viewings does it become evident that the documentary footage takes up proportionately more screen time.

8. It is for these reasons that I make a distinction between the traditions represented by *Truth or Dare* and *Don't Look Back,* although both utilize onstage and offstage spaces. Elayne Rapping (1991a), for instance, uses *Don't Look Back* to compare and contrast Dylan and Madonna, but she does not differentiate the uses made of public performance versus private existence in the two films. In *Don't Look Back,* the on- and offstage segments are stylistically more unified. They are not set up in opposition to each other or used to elaborate the film's issues in the same way as in *Truth or Dare.* The two spaces are more of a piece in *Don't Look Back,* functioning as a continuum in the compilation or creation of its portrait of the artist-individual. *Truth or Dare,* on the other hand, establishes its arenas in contradiction to each other precisely to iden- tify a quandary in the activity of celebrity-individual portraiture.

9. The credits are as follows: Robert Leacock: director of photography—documen- tary for the U.S. and Europe; Doug Nichol: director of photography—documentary for New York footage; Toby Phillips: director of photography—concerts; Barry Alex- ander Brown: editor; John Murray: editor—musical sequences.

Robert Leacock and Doug Nichol are credited as camera operators—but not direc- tors of photography—along with eight others for the concert footage. Robert Leacock is the son of Richard Leacock, one of the original and most prominent members of the direct cinema movement.

10. The color segments, in order of performance, are:

1. "Express Yourself"	6. "Holiday"
2. "Oh Father"	7. "Live to Tell"
3. "Keep It Together"	8. "Vogue"
4. "Like a Virgin"	9. "Causing a Commotion"
5. "Like a Prayer"	10. "Keep It Together"

Though I have stated that each of the color segments parallels a different song, there is, in fact, a repetition. Number 3, "Keep It Together" is a brief version that, at the film's finale, is performed in its entirety (number 10). I am most concerned, for the sake of my discussion, in giving priority to the color segments, rather than the song represented by each.

11. Although I have limited my discussion to the songs differentiated by their color performances, in a number of other instances (in addition to *Happy Birthday*), the songs are marked by black-and-white performance. These include: a brief excerpt of "Papa Don't Preach" in rehearsal; a short clip of "Express Yourself," performed in the rain in Japan; an excerpt of "Holiday" as Madonna and her backup singers walk to the stage, hand in hand, under threat of arrest in Toronto; "Promise to Try" in its entirety, accompanied solely by black-and-white images, principally of Madonna at her mother's grave; a glimpse of "Causing a Commotion"; and a brief excerpt of "Holiday" as Madonna and her singers prepare to go onstage, which I have discussed in the text.

12. *Truth or Dare* is one of a number of examples cited to illustrate Gabler's points.

13. I introduce Baudrillard's concept of seduction although I am fully aware of his extremely essentializing discussion of sexuality, wherein sex is masculine and seduc- tion is feminine. I make no apology for him, nor could I think of any that would suffice.

14. In *Seduction,* Baudrillard (1990, 22) defines seduction, "in the literal sense," as "to take aside, to divert from one's path."

15. The transcript of the entire conversation between the doctor, Madonna, and Beatty is as follows:

B: This is crazy. Nobody talks about this on film.

M: Talks about what?

B: The insanity of doing this all in a documentary.

M: Why?

B: Well this is a serious matter, your throat. Yes?

M: Why should I stop here?

B: But does anyone say it?

M: Who's anyone?

B: Well anyone that comes into this insane atmosphere. You realize they all feel it when they come into this atmosphere. When they come into your dressing room, when they come wherever you are, they feel crazy. Now, do they talk about it?

M: No. They accept it.

B: Well, why don't they talk about it?

M: Cause.

B: Well you want to think about that, don't you?

M: No I don't. So let's get back to my throat.

There is a cut here that marks a jump in time. Madonna no longer speaks but is writing notes to communicate, per instructions from the doctor.

D: Do you want to talk at all off-camera? You have nothing to say? [M. shakes her head no.]

B: [laughs] She doesn't want to live off-camera, much less talk.

D: Yeah, I think that's what it is.

B: There's nothing to say off-camera. Why would you say something if it's off-camera? What point is there of existing?

Beatty apparently addresses this last comment directly to the camera (his sunglasses mask his eyeline) because we can hear a voice from offscreen, presumably that of the doctor talking to Madonna.

16. The latest is Annette Bening, his costar in *Bugsy.* Their baby, we are told at the time of this writing, is due at the same time the film is scheduled for release. The presence of a child "renews" what could otherwise have been a tired tale of yet another Beatty involvement.

REFERENCES

Ansen, David. (1991). "Madonna Lets It All Hang Out." *Newsweek,* May 13, pp. 66–67.

Baudrillard, Jean. (1983). "The Ecstacy of Communication." In Hal Foster (ed.), *The Anti-aesthetic: Essays on Postmodern Culture.* Port Townsend, Wash.: Bay Press, pp. 126–134.

———. (1988). *Jean Baudrillard: Selected Writings*. M. Poster (ed.). Stanford, Calif.: Stanford University Press.

———. (1990). *Seduction*. London: Macmillan Press. First published in France by Éditions Galilée (1979).

Deevoy, Adrian. (1991). "Madonna Talks" (interview). *US*, June 13, pp. 16–20, 23–24.

Doane, Mary Ann. (1989). "The Economy of Desire: The Commodity Form in/of the Cinema." *Quarterly Review of Film and Video* 11, no. 1: 23–33.

Fisher, Carrie. (1991a). "True Confessions: Part One." *Rolling Stone*, June 13, pp. 35–36, 39–40, 120.

———. (1991b). "True Confessions: Part Two." *Rolling Stone*, June 27, 45–49, 78.

Gabler, Neal. (1991). "Now Playing Across America: Real Life, the Movie." *New York Times*, October 20, sec. 2, pp. 1, 32–33.

Goodman, Ellen. (1991). "Madonna and Letting It All Hang Out" (syndicated column from the *Boston Globe*). *Philadelphia Inquirer*, June 11, p. 15 A.

Guardian. (1991a). "Letters from Our Readers." June 26, p. 2.

———. (1991b). "Letter from Our Readers." July 3, p. 2.

Heller, Karen. (1991). "Filmmaker Shies from Celebrity." *Philadelphia Inquirer*, May 16, pp. 1-E, 5-E.

Kaplan, E. Ann. (1988). "Whose Imaginary? The Televisual Apparatus, The Female Body and Textual Strategies in Select Rock Videos on MTV." In E. D. Pribram (ed.), *Female Spectators: Looking at Film and Television*. London: Verso, pp.132–156.

Kaplan, James. (1991). "Madonna: The Naked Truth." *Entertainment*, May 17, pp. 14–21.

Kellner, Douglas. (1989). *Jean Baudrillard: From Marxism to Postmodernism and Beyond*. Cambridge, Mass.: Polity Press.

Lovell, Glenn. (1991). "Madonna Taunts, Teases and Talks About Her 'Truth or Dare'" (interview). Knight-Ridder newspapers in the State College, Penn. *Center Daily Times Sampler*, May 7, pp. 1–2.

Maslin, Janet. (1991). "No One Ever Called Her Shy." *New York Times*, May 10, pp. C1, C15.

Rapping, Elayne. (1991a). "Madonna Makes the Media Play Her Game." *Guardian*, June 5, p. 16.

———. (1991b). Response to "Letters from Our Readers." *Guardian*, June 26, p. 2.

Rickey, Carrie. (1991a). "Madonna on Madonna." *Philadelphia Inquirer*, May 16, pp. 1E, 5E.

———. (1991b). "Onstage and Backstage with Madonna, That Dazzling Creature of the Spotlight." *Philadelphia Inquirer*, May 17, weekend section, p. 5-W.

Ryan, James. (1991). "Madonna!" *The Face*, June, pp. 56–59.

MELANIE MORTON *10*

Don't Go for Second Sex, Baby!

> We carry out little rebellions every day. As soon as we make a little
> disorder—otherwise stated, as soon as we make our own order, an
> order that is particular, individual to us—we carry out a revolt.
> —Jean Genet

*A*T THE OPENING OF HER 1989 music video *Express Yourself,* Madonna calls out to her audience, "Come on girls, do you believe in love? Well I've got something to say about it and it goes like this." As she urges us to put our "love to the test," she does not restrict her homily to a romantic or a domestic context. Instead, *Express Yourself* takes as its object the general logic and various practices of domination most prevalent in Western culture. In so doing, Madonna purposefully re-presents and revises both visual and plot fragments from Fritz Lang's 1926 film *Metropolis.* This intervention calls attention to the film's strategies of domination. In addition, the scope of her critique also includes an intervention into the *musical* practices that similarly participate in discursive constructions of domination.

These interventions offer Madonna an opportunity to interrogate our peculiar cultural understanding of difference as a wild alterity to be subdued or expunged. In terms of representational practices, standard narrative conventions position difference within a hierarchy, so that anything understood to be Other is cognized in a subordinate position or only in reference to a position defined in a politically questionable manner as the norm or the center. These strategies of subordination are perpetuated by the narrative conventions that regulate formal storytelling practices in visual, literary, and sonorous media. It seems we must account for the power and effects of these conventions in order to thoroughly criticize how this hierarchical compulsion participates in the construction of not only gender, as one might easily suspect, but also of subjectivity. I come to this discussion with a sensitivity toward the feminist maxim that states that "the personal is political," stressing

213

that the maxim is also reversible, that is, "the political is personal." Thus, we must also direct our attention to the construction of the personal and to the political effects of these two arguably oedipal categories.

Even to pose this kind of critique violates a set of assumptions that are foundational to liberal humanism, the dominant modern ideology. Recent feminist and poststructuralist theorists have advanced this critique, focusing on the politics of representation. Counter to humanists, proponents of these critiques refuse to view representation in any form (be it linguistic, pictorial, sonorous, etc.) as innocent or capable of merely reflecting the world in a transparent manner. In particular, they focus their attacks on the representational practices that present the centrality and *naturalness* of the masterful bourgeois subject. In a like manner, Madonna's disruption of representational norms also subverts these liberal humanist conventions. Specifically, Madonna presents semiotic collages in her music videos that rewrite the fate of sexual women, and she rejects any kind of representation that would call forth the kind of subject posited by liberal humanist ideology and constructed in *Metropolis*.

Thus, the first question is: What if we read *Metropolis* as an exemplar of bourgeois ideology that most explicitly reveals the continuity of the liberal humanist project with fascism? Notice both how Madonna makes this argument and the turf on which she engages in struggle. She does not ascribe to the ascetic ideal of a humorless warrior, nor does she claim to speak with the pure voice of a victim. How can we understand this as political combat, and why would we care to? Her questioning of conventional bourgeois definitions of the political may seem to abandon or to mutate beyond recognition any critique of oppression, but it is my argument that she has strategically brought this critique onto new and productive ground. As such, some of her analysis is more radical than the usual analyses that place sexism or the class struggle at the heart of all political economy as ultimate signifieds. This is partly true because Madonna's strategies engage in an ideological critique of the standard fare of liberal humanist truisms. This brings to the fore a question of effective strategy.

A simple condemnation, destruction, or attempt at censorship of the patriarchal, racist, and capitalist constructions established in *Metropolis* would have to operate on two contradictory levels. In content, a confrontation would identify Madonna with the powerless victims of a dangerous discourse and praxis, and in rhetoric on the formal level, Madonna would be aligned with the authoritative voice of the master. What I find interesting about this kind of analysis is not that it denies that there are real victims in this world but that it forces intellectuals and artists to avoid the bad political conscience of claiming to be powerless. To speak is to exercise power. This emphasizes Foucauldian definitions of power figured not in terms of absolutes like domination but as anything that moves or has effects. This is a shift from the victor of a contest to the process of participating in a fight. When Madonna displays the repressed and brutal maxims of liberal humanism and stages both their construction and deconstruction, she imaginatively brings the struggle onto a more fruitful and conscious terrain. It is my aim in this chapter to show a few examples of this and to offer an argument for why we might care. Furthermore, I will briefly mention how her work is influenced by the historical avant-garde, which she manages to both address and outdistance by refusing to reject pleasure as a source of power, lending support to her arguments. As Michel Foucault (1983, XIII–XIV) insists, "Do not think that one has to be sad in order to be militant, even though the thing one is fighting is abominable. It is the connection of desire to reality . . . that possesses revolutionary force."

MODERNITY

As it is articulated in the liberal humanist thought of the Enlightenment and as it continues in contemporary bourgeois, capitalist, and patriarchal society, modernity is characterized by a near-religious faith in the possibility of objectivity as a standard for truth claims, a concomitant belief in the individual as a free, unified, and autonomous subjectivity, and a fervent insistence on the innocence and neutrality of artistic practices as distinct from politics. Together, these form a tripartite system of mutually reinforcing foundational norms on which the smooth operation of our political system depends.

Objectivity is an impossibility because, as Immanuel Kant argued (1965, 22), all sensation is necessarily bound up with understanding as it is mediated and enacted through concepts or language—a representational process. Given the material conditions for the possibility of cognition, then, our access to some metaphysical totality must be regarded as fantasy. This is not an argument against the possibility of truth but against the idea that there can be a single or ultimate truth. Interpretations and truths are plural because any use of language or format requires a choice of perspective, tone, and mode through which any expression is mediated. Various modes are inflected with the politics that inform these choices. This contradicts the favored liberal humanist myth that art and politics can be absolutely distinguished, as well as the myth that it is possible to speak neutrally. What counts as neutral merely agrees with dominant epistemes. Thus, one should, instead, watch for *which* politics are endorsed by those engaged in discourse. Who is talking, what are they saying, and how? If we have no choice but to speak ideologically, our attention must shift from a focus on objectivity to the effects of various discourses.

Further, to endorse a faith in objectivity is to profoundly fail to account for the material effects of representational mediums. To speak of this materiality is to question how style and form affect content. This requires that we attend to the not-so-small details like the plot devices that sustain our narratives. In addition, the political force of our representations must be taken seriously for it is in the aesthetic realm that we test, explore, and imagine our reality. This is important if the selves we imagine are disciplined, critical, submissive, or brutal.

"METROPOLIS": EXEMPLAR OF BOURGEOIS IDEOLOGY

At heart, this discussion critiques a core metaphysical stance that regards difference in terms of hierarchy. This stance is actually intolerant of difference because it seeks to reduce all terms to a dichotomous, binary relation that effectively erases and annihilates the abjectified term as it establishes the superordinance of the privileged term. As Donna Haraway (1990, 219) explains, "Certain dualisms have been persistent in Western traditions; they have all been systemic to the logics and practices of domination of women, people of color, nature, workers, animals—in short, domination of all constituted as others, whose task is to mirror the self."

The film *Metropolis* is obsessed with exploring and underwriting a variety of dualisms ranging from mind and body, rational and emotional, up and down, male and female, virgin and whore, human and machine, master and slave, order and chaos, and good and evil. But the music video *Express Yourself* explicitly calls attention to the dialectics of domination by refusing to repeat the rule of these oppositions. This differs from a standard political strategy that would respect the oppositions while trying to seize the moral high ground with a simple inversion substituting, for example, sisterhood for patriarchy or black power for white supremacy, leaving intact the same reductionist logic of domination that operates within a fantasy framework opposing evil with virtue.

In *Metropolis,* when Maria, a daughter of a worker, takes a group of ragged children to the Eternal Gardens, her presence and her words ("Look—these are your brothers" [Lang 1989, 28]) wreak havoc on the order of the day. Located in the Club of the Sons, the Eternal Gardens are described in the film script as the epitome of privilege: "For fathers, for whom every revolution of a machine-wheel spelt gold, had presented this house to their sons. It was more a district than a house. It embraced theatres, picture-palaces, lecture-rooms and a library . . . race tracks and stadium and the famous 'Eternal Gardens' " (Lang 1989, 22). Like points on a fulcrum, a film title explains, the Eternal Gardens are located as high above Metropolis as the workers' tenements are located below the city, as if the metaphor of a balance justified the workers' degradation. The balance metaphor masks injustice by evoking a common symbol of justice. The decadent playground, filled with a "bevy of girls in erotic, sequined costumes" (Lang 1989, 22) roaming peacocks, the film's only greenery, and ubiquitous servants, is, of course, reserved for the sons of the city's elite, who are far removed from the worlds of commerce and labor below them. The workers are restricted to the subterranean factory or to the tenement houses below the factory level. Maria's trespass sets in motion a narrative drive that could either take seriously this challenge to the established norms or use it as an occasion to reaffirm the dominant ideology. Not surprisingly, the latter strategy is pursued as it absorbs the apparent disruptions of filial and working-class rebellion against the film's patriarch and industrialist, who is explicitly titled "John Fredersen, the Master of Metropolis" (Lang 1989, 36).

Further, what is crucial about the rebellions staged in *Metropolis* is the fact that we witness not their success but their suppression. Fredersen's son Freder violates taboos by identifying himself with the workers, whom he calls his brothers, and by his amorous pursuit of a working-class woman. After catching sight of Maria in the Eternal Gardens, Freder makes his way to the underground factories in search of her. Witnessing an explosion that kills several workers, Freder is shocked to learn of their degraded state. When he runs to report this to his all-powerful father, he is even more shocked to learn of his father's knowledge and indifference. Freder returns to the subterranean world of the underclass, where he passes himself off as a worker and meets up again with Maria in a secret, quasi-religious meeting deep in the catacombs, the lowest physical location in the film. Maria preaches patience to the workers and counsels them that they can be saved if the heart mediates between the hand and the brain. They must await the arrival of a mediator who will surely come.

With the help of Rotwang, a sort of magician-scientist, Fredersen spies on this meeting and instructs the scientist to replace Maria with an identical cyborg. I call this a cyborg and not a robot because it is explicitly given a sexualized female form and is characterized by irrationality and recklessness—hardly features of a machine. The cyborg is charged with inciting the workers to riot to provide Fredersen with an excuse to crush the workers' critical instincts. The workers destroy the machines in the factory and inadvertently flood their homes, nearly drowning their own children. Freder and Maria, with the help of Joseph, a knowledgeable assistant, lead the children above ground to safety. Filled with remorse at the near loss of their children, the workers turn on the cyborg as an angry mob and burn her at the stake, shouting, "Kill the witch!" As she burns, the cyborg loses Maria's physical features and regains the appearance of a machine, restoring the good name of Maria. Freder is credited with saving the children, thereby securing the workers' trust. Rotwang, who inexplicably has chased Maria up to a rooftop, struggles briefly with Freder before falling to his death, while a horrified Fredersen watches below, fearing for his own son's life. A victorious Freder returns to street level with Maria by his side and is met by his relieved father.

No longer an angry mob, the workers approach in a tight pyramidal formation headed by their foreman, Grot, who is the only worker named in the script. Along with their bowed heads and regimented gaits, every detail of the workers' disciplined bodies expresses their total submission. Why do the workers just fall back into their old places at the end of the film? The force of guilt and shame for abandoning their children hardly seems persuasive enough to explain this total submission, especially because they do not "assume the position" of disciplined bodies until after the witch-burning and Rotwang's death. Such absolute surrender is illogical, but the film pays no mind to it.

As a bashful Grot, seeking rapprochement, hesitates a few feet away from him, Fredersen sternly stands his ground. Maria prompts Freder, and the film's last title appears: "There can be no understanding between the hands and the brain unless the heart acts as mediator" (Lang 1989, 130). Freder joins hands with his father and urges him to welcome the foreman. They shake hands, everyone smiles happily, and the film ends with Freder firmly in place at the dawn of a new era in labor relations.

Why are these people smiling? With his son established as a mediator, Fredersen is the only person who stands to gain. Freder has usurped Maria's role as the workers' spokesperson and mediator (Lang 1989, 63), and he is one who firmly respects the paternal authority of the capitalist. Fredersen now has access to the hearts of the people. I would use the phrase *hearts and minds,* but the film claims that the workers do not have any minds. It is their emotional, animal status as purely irrational brutes and manual laborers that is supposed to justify their subservience to the pure rationality of the minds of those who just happen to also profit from the workers' oppression; Fredersen is called the "Brain of Metropolis" (Land 1989, 35). The workers have not won anything, nor will any of the obvious social injustices be addressed. Why do they apologize to "Dad"? The automatic and total surrender of the workers lends a surreal serenity to what must be considered a brutal scene.

The foreman, Grot, also has a questionable status. He is the only worker who does not revolt. In fact, he spies and informs on the other workers on Fredersen's behalf. He refuses to leave his post during the rebellion. He tries to warn Fredersen that the machines will flood the workers' city, an outcome desired by Fredersen. And Grot berates the workers to return to their posts, accusing them of child neglect and blaming them for an outcome that he knew had been within management's control. His only fraternal participation with the workers amounts to seizing the cyborg and tying her up. He is more of a flunky than a member of the rank and file. And this underscores the type of handshake deal we see performed in front of a docile crowd at the film's end.

There are two other points I would like to mention in reference to the qualities that make *Metropolis* an exemplar of bourgeois ideology. The first is that the dualisms described earlier are also represented in the style of the visual layout of the film itself. Each frame is composed with exacting attention to the balance of objects within it, so that there is a thorough presentation of order and control communicated in every detail. This attention to compositional elements is directed to the depiction of towering shots of massive expressionist cityscapes throughout and the stylized presentation of rigidly ordered geometric ranks of workers at the change of shift or in the conduct of their labors. (Apparently, the workers have no leisure.) These details signify precise order and absolute control, representing disturbingly Fascist displays of docile, disciplined bodies. Order dissolves during the workers' rebellion, when they are, instead, presented as an anarchic mob, running around in a destructive panic. However, as the film draws to a close, the workers' bodies once more display rigid pyramidal order. And this is one of the elements that makes the abrupt return to formation both so stark and shocking.

The other aspect I wish to broach involves a second strategy of subordination through the insistence of a teleology. This is a question of narrative strategy, which imposes a pattern on the events of a story. This follows predictable and familiar lines from an initial disruption to an orderly environment through to a resolution. Catherine Belsey (1985, 53) argues that in narrative, "stories move inevitably towards closure which is also disclosure, the dissolution of enigma through the reestablishment of order, recognizable as a re=instatement or a development of the order which is understood to have preceded the events of the story itself." Thus, narrative promotes a conservative affirmation of the status quo.

REPRESENTATIONAL POLITICS: NARRATIVITY AND SUBJECTIVITY

What is crucial about the kinds of resistance and transgression enacted in the so-called aesthetic realm is that these strategies of representation have a material and political impact that is frequently all the more potent because it is not examined; that is, the ideology of liberal humanism insists that art has nothing to do with politics. But, as I said earlier, it is within the aesthetic realm that we represent, question, explore, and imagine social reality. How we imagine ourselves has a direct bearing on our behavior and our expectations, so we must attend to the kinds of party lines our discourses are obliged to mouth. To attempt to protect our pleasures from hard questions disables any understanding of the kinds of services such aesthetic practices perform. Susan McClary (1991, 4) states this problem nicely in reference to classical music: "To be sure, music's beauty is often overwhelming, its formal order magisterial. But the structures graphed by theorists and the beauty celebrated by aestheticians are often stained with such things as violence, misogyny, and racism." Our frameworks for *making* sense are necessarily ideological. However, Belsey (1985, 53) explains that ideology "is not, therefore, to be thought of as a system of ideas in people's heads, nor as the expression at a higher level of real material relationships, but as the necessary condition of action within the social formation." Dominant ideologies appear to be invisible. The more firmly entrenched a particular ideology is, the more seamless and natural its framework appears, which masks its limits, silences, and contradictions. According to Louis Althusser (1971), ideology constitutes concrete individuals as subjects. Thus, subjectivity can be understood as a function of power.

Madonna's work is informed by a keen insight into the connection between subjectivity, power, and ideology. As Foucault (1984, 66–67) describes it, "The political significance of the problem of sex is due to the fact that sex is located at the point of intersection of the discipline of the body and the control of the population." Thus, the intimate conduct and our very understandings of our personal identities are subject to the interests of state that require docile bodies for a governable populace. And this is precisely why Madonna's displays of sexuality can be understood as politically subversive. To speak of her work as a threat makes conscious this connection between sex and power. Madonna says, "It has nothing to do with whether I am a man or a woman. I think I am a sexual threat, and I think, if anything, there is a prejudice against that. I think that it is easier for people to embrace people who don't poke at their insides and make them think about their own sexuality" (Sessums 1990, 48).

AVANT-GARDE IDEOLOGICAL CRITIQUE

With the discomfort that she arouses, Madonna's meditations on sexuality and gender have much in common with the thematic concerns of Jean Genet, another avant-garde avatar. He writes,

> If I examine my work, I now perceive in it, patiently pursued, a will to rehabilitate persons, objects and feelings *reputedly* vile. . . . Not that I want to transform them or bring them around to your kind of life, or that I look upon them with indulgence or pity: I recognize in thieves, traitors and murderers, in the truthless and the cunning, a deep beauty—a sunken beauty (Genet 1964, 109, emphasis added).

Genet examines the mutual interdependence of binary oppositions. For example, there is no sensible concept of the clean without the dirty or of order without chaos. Each concept functions as the limit and exclusion of the other. Genet attempts to address the dualisms mentioned earlier to criticize the structural role of the abject, as well as to change the value of these degraded terms. Rather than submit to this scheme, he questions the legitimacy of the social formation that creates masters and slaves and victors and victims.

Like Genet, Madonna is also preoccupied by what he would call "the underside of our values" (1964, 109). She takes as her guide our pressure points. As she said in a November 1990 "Nightline" television interview, "I'm gonna keep pushing buttons." Rather than comply with the inevitability of prevailing customs, Madonna reshapes the art form to tell a different story. However, despite the similarity of their goals, Madonna's strategies differ from Genet's in some important ways. This question of artistic practice and strategy resonates with the old program of the historical avantgarde.

To sum up the dilemma, artists began questioning how one might effectively negate the order of the world when this will to negate is the most clichéd of modern artistic and intellectual gestures. If our art is irreverent and critical of the status quo as a matter of course, then that particular stance belies the possibility of effective critique. What chance do we have of actually negating anything? We seem to be stuck. When the avant-garde reflected on this dilemma, they shifted their attention away from mere critique to a focus on "the extent to which art comprehended the mode in which it functioned in bourgeois society, its comprehension of its own social status" (Schulte-Sasse 1984, XIV).

However, no one could persuasively argue that the avant-garde successfully altered the modes in which the institution of art functions. Because their aim was to call attention to modes of reception, their method involved disrupting pleasure to interrupt the habitual modes of unconscious consumption. This was very unpopular. Also, their strategies for breaking the codes were vulnerable to either co-optation or illegibility. Critic Una Chaudhuri (1986, 127–129) writes,

> Genet's drama escapes these two kinds of failure. It does so by a method, or stance, that is *genuinely* dialectical, one that entertains oppositions *without* privileging one of their terms. This method is one of remarkable ideological *restraint*, for it does not, as is usual with dialectical reasoning, oppose thesis to antithesis in order to arrive at a (predetermined) synthesis. Genet's drama, contrary to most interpretations, does not *go anywhere*. Instead it creates and maintains a static dynamic, a paradox reflected in its simultaneous affirmation and denial of all signs.

Genet's deconstructive strategy enabled him to address avant-garde concerns to produce political art without bogging him down in its traditional failures.

OUTDISTANCING THE AVANT-GARDE

Madonna's approach is similarly deconstructive, refusing to restrain the play of signifiers through an insistence on foregrounding the partial and constructed nature of the signs she employs. *Express Yourself* is an ambiguous text, which resists appropriation by modern modes of reception and rejects core bourgeois epistemes. However, it must be added, Madonna lacks Genet's "ideological restraint." Despite her deconstructive arsenal and frequent use of parody, she really does indicate where her story should go. Her instructions are clearly emphatic and nearly testimonial. Consider the number of her song titles constructed with the imperative voice, such as "Papa Don't Preach," "Express Yourself," and "Justify My Love." This advocacy contradicts a purely deconstructive interpretation, although some of the more shocking signs in "Express Yourself," such as the masochist, the Nazis, and the racists, do perform such a service when they undermine the fresh-scrubbed presentation of the film's brutality.

In addition to deconstructive techniques, Madonna uses a variety of other disruptive strategies. Sometimes, she simply violates assumptions or clichés. For example, in *Express Yourself,* vision is not used as a metaphor for knowledge, as is frequently the case; we commonly describe knowledge in terms of visual metaphors: "Do you see?" In the music video, however, vision is not transparent, fully meaningful, or sufficient. In fact, the video is chaotic on the visual level. Turn the sound off and *Express Yourself* makes no sense because the image track is purposefully constructed incoherently. This is vastly different from the emphasis placed on the image track in *Metropolis,* which was, after all, a silent film. The movie constantly equates vision with knowledge. Characters never overhear information. Communication is face to face, inscribed, or obtained through visual surveillance. The cyborg-Maria has to be unveiled to the city's elite in order to convince them that she is real: Seeing is believing. This scene requires that we examine its own bizarre illogic. If the cyborg is supposed to replace all the workers, why is a striptease or a masquerade as a "real" woman at all desirable? This logic is as weird as the gap that fails to account for the workers' sudden submission, mentioned earlier.

Another of Madonna's subversive strategies involves ambiguously positioning the audience and the characters by eliciting multiple and contradictory subject positions. For example, Madonna seems to draw on the character of the preaching woman to direct attention to the terms of women's oppression. But unlike *Metropolis*'s Maria, Madonna does not counsel patience when she speaks of oppression; instead, she directs us to engage in struggle. She calls—in one of the most overt hailings in music video—"Come on girls! Do you believe in love? Well I've got something to say about it and it goes something like this." Condensing reproduction and production, her perky lyrics advise us to put our "love to the test." However, the visual images do not follow a conventional "privatizing" of love in an intimate, domestic, or romantic setting. Instead, we "girls" are located on a factory floor in the bowels of Metropolis with a bunch of sweaty, sexy men enslaved to fearsome machines. This invites us as spectators to either identify with the exploited workers who are hard at work complying with a system of oppression or to desire these shirtless hunks. As identification and desire flow in opposite directions, any attempt to determine one or the other contradicts. A radical ambiguity remains, which frustrates any search for the constitution of a pure bourgeois subject, even as it deconstructs the notion that our identifications must not be partial, multiple, or contradictory.

In the same way, Madonna says, "I guess I just have a sense of mischievousness. I never want to hit something on the head. I never want to present A as A. You can take what I do at surface value or you can go underneath the surface" (Sessums 1990, 208). Because her aim is not annihilation but contestation, she cannot afford to deconstruct every ground of articulation, to unravel the medium, because she needs room and tools with which to fight. The music video's last peopled frame is emblematic of this leitmotiv: It shows two men fighting or dancing in a boxing ring, a stark contrast from *Metropolis*'s resolution.

OEDIPUS: NARRATIVE AND SEXUAL DIFFERENCE

In addition to constructing subjectivity, feminist theorists such as Teresa de Lauretis (1984), Kaja Silverman (1983), and Catherine Belsey (1985) argue that narrative is also obsessed with sexual difference. The technologies of cinema that construct the experience of unity for the essentially voyeuristic spectators center around the apparatus of the "look." What the camera records becomes associated with the perspective of a particular subject. And in most cinema, even in supposedly "female" genres like the melodrama or the romance, that subject is gendered and coded as masculine. *Metropolis* offers a special example of this activity because the apparatus structuring the look is so overt; it is considered to be imperfectly hidden, imperfectly self-evident, and therefore not seamlessly naturalized. I would make one last point about that (masculine) subject position constituted by the cinematic apparatus: The question of who is doing the looking is very crucial, especially if there is only one, unified position established, because that position is invested with authority and, therefore, functions to determine the meanings. This position, called the "maker of meaning," is a point around which all the details and elements of a story are organized.

De Lauretis notes that narrative form and function are also obsessed with the establishment of an always already prevailing male perspective that denies the limits of its own articulation by pretending to hide its specificity. Part of the attempts at fixing this configuration of power are aimed at earning the complicity of the woman it represses. She questions how

> narrative cinema in particular must be aimed, like desire, towards seducing women into femininity. What manner of seduction operates in cinema to procure that consent, to engage the female subject's identification in the narrative movement, and so fulfill the cinematic contract? What manner of seduction operates in cinema to solicit the complicity of women spectators in a desire whose terms are those of the Oedipus? (de Lauretis 1984, 137).

In other words, what can identification have to do with one's own subjugation?

Exploring how the concept of narrative necessarily implies a reference to the oedipal narrative, de Lauretis reworks Laura Mulvey's question—"Does sadism demand a story?"—to ask whether a story demands sadism. In other words, how does our form of narrative organization insist on an oedipal economy of domination? This resonates with a similar question posed by Gilles Deleuze and Félix Guattari (1983) in their analysis of the repressive nature of oedipal subjectivity. Within Freud's theory, it is through the work of the oedipal complex that children form their egos, relinquishing desire for the mother in obedience to the Law of the Father. It is at this moment that they simultaneously learn to recognize themselves as both individual and gendered. Deleuze and Guattari regard this recognition as an unfortunate *misrecognition* with grave political consequences. In his introduction to the English translation of Deleuze and Guattari's *Anti-Oedipus,* Mark Seem explains the anti-oedipalists' analysis of the ego (or Oedipus), which they call an agency of the State: "Oedipus is belief injected into the unconscious, it is what gives us faith as it robs us of power, *it* is what teaches us to desire our own repression" (1983, xx).

In regard to the question of subjectivity, compare *Express Yourself* with *Metropolis.* In the music video, as discussed earlier, the plausibility of establishing any stable subject or a "maker of meaning" is impossible. And the fact that Madonna masquerades as a number of the film's characters calls attention to their fragmentary status. It makes no sense to even speak of a subject. Consider the opening moment again when she hails us from the pinnacle of Metropolis. In detective fashion, the speaking woman in *Express Yourself* sends her audience on an intelligence mission both similar to and different from Freder's. Pursuing what it is she has to say about love, the camera sweeps down to the steamy subterranean factory, similar to Freder's passage through the factory in smitten and agitated pursuit of Maria.

As girls, the spectators might be positioned as Maria, the film's leading lady and the only woman with any substantial dialogue, but as detectives, our journey repeats Freder's search for (his) love. And whom might Madonna be portraying at this moment? Partly she assumes Maria's position as prophet and guide, even while her sparse athletic garb and physical location high above the city call to mind Freder's white silk outfit worn for the race in the opening scenes set in the Eternal Gardens. However, Madonna is wearing black. There is no ultimate determination because the fragments contradict. And because the video establishes no ultimate "maker of meaning," attempting to make identifications is to miss her point. Her multiple masquerades assert her presence, as elsewhere, to underscore the limits of the representation rather than repeat the totalizing fantasy *Metropolis* manipulates.

SIMILITUDE AND DECONSTRUCTION:
A NEW POLITICS OF DIFFERENCE

And what is the relationship between *Express Yourself* and *Metropolis*? Is it a copy of an original, if it does not tell the same tale? To borrow Foucault's (1982) terminology, the video does not resemble the film; rather, it simulates it. He defines the two modes:

> Resemblance has a "model," an original element that orders and hierarchizes the increasingly less faithful copies that can be struck from it. Resemblance presupposes a primary reference that prescribes and classes. The similar develops in series that have neither beginning nor end, that can be followed in one direction as easily as in another, that obey no hierarchy, but propagate themselves from small differences among small differences.... Similitude multiplies different affirmations, which dance together, tilting and tumbling over one another (Foucault 1982, 44–46).

Madonna celebrates these different affirmations and interpretations because what she stresses is not a particular meaning but the reductive norm that demands a single meaning. Similitude subversively manifests itself against identity as it refuses to mirror the perfect whole to demonstrate the inexorability of narrative. Moving from resemblance to similitude is a rejection of the rule of an original. This explores the arbitrariness of our discursive constructions, so that our names and identities, our categories, and our modes can be examined.

The combination of several kinds of signification in music video provides an excellent deconstructive mise-en-scène. *Express Yourself* is loaded with a profusion of signification as manipulated by costume, film genre (expressionist, musical comedy, Socialist realism, gospel, etc.), lighting, tonic procedures, rhythm, melody, manner of presentation (ironic, parodic, sardonic, sincere), characterization, plot, image, music, text, point of view, and so on. Each element is capable of inflection, of insinuating a tone or a mood. Madonna's deft and complex manipulation of each medium of expression exploits relations in and among them. At times, a visual image will contradict, parody, or affirm the words or the music without establishing any hierarchy between them. At other times, the nonsimilarity or the gaps between media are alternately stressed and sutured.

By marshaling the forces available to the various types of signification (I am reminded that even the cassette tape package of "Like a Prayer"—which included the song "Express Yourself"—was scented with patchouli, reminiscent of incense and the smell of a Catholic church), Madonna paradoxically disrupts the order of representation because she does not force the different sign systems to repeat and underline each other. This lack of synchronicity violates another rule of bourgeois discourse strictly observed in *Metropolis*. The dispersion of conflations denies a single or ultimate relation between elements and, instead, felicitously estranges them into odd juxtapositions, emphasizing their alterity and the gaps between them. No narrative form of order can emerge on this type of field. This allows Madonna to break rules.

Yet, her discourse breaks free of a purely negative adversarial posture. That is, she avoids nihilism by presenting alternatives. This makes her homily more forceful. As Foucault (1984, 61) writes, "What makes power hold good, what makes it accepted, is simply the fact that it doesn't only weigh on us as a force that says no, but that it traverses and produces things, it induces pleasures, forms knowledge, produces discourse."

MUSIC AND THE POLITICS OF REPRESENTATION

A strategic analysis of narrative also applies to the musical semiotics that motivate tonic closure through the arousal of narrative expectations. In her musical analysis of Bizet's opera *Carmen*, McClary (1988) describes how the instrumental introduction to the "Habañera" positions Carmen as a violator of tonic categories by employing chromaticism. These half-tones slip between the opera's musical order, established by its tonic structure. Because the opera adheres to a convention that demands diatonic closure, Carmen (through her association with chromaticism) represents a troublesome element to be put in place. Consequently, it is telling that the opera maintains a tension between its tonic structure and the disruptive chromatic intrusions until the diatonic closure coincident with Carmen's death. As Don José plunges the knife into Carmen's body, the orchestra fleshes out a full cadence marking the triumphant, final expulsion of chromaticism as the suppression of the Other. McClary (1988, XIV) points out, "Music is not an innocent accompaniment—ignoring the text does not mean that one avoids the potentially questionable dimensions of the (musical) pieces."

"Express Yourself's" combat against the norms of representation is nuanced by this discussion of narrativity and subjectivity. This is as evident in the music as it is in other media. Here, Madonna and coauthor Stephen Bray gesture toward conventional tonal procedures only to destabilize them. McClary (1991) argues that narrative conventions organize both Western classical music and popular music as each are regulated by tonality. "Tonality, then, is not merely a matter of using just the tones of a particular scale. It is more a process of setting forth the organized relationship of these tones to one among them which is to be the tonal center" (Piston 1978, 49). It is the inexorability of this organized relation among tones, along with the requirement to establish a unified center, that "Express Yourself" compositionally rejects. The opening bars of "Express Yourself" are recognizable as elements of a G-major scale, but, despite the force of convention, G major is not established as a tonic (a "home key"). Rather, it is constructed as one part of a relation negotiated with F major. The harmonic structure of the song is more complex, maintaining a tension between two tonalities, G major and F major, that reflects similar struggles for control apparent on the textual and cinematic levels. The second key is not defined as either subordinate or dominant, so neither is positioned as the home key. Specifically, G major ought to have a B natural and an F sharp, but the very first melodic note (corresponding to the first word in the song—"don't") is reflected as a blues tone down to B flat, which would seem to signal instead an F-major tonality. And when the F sonority is present, Madonna keeps singing B natural, leading us back to G. Neither area finally is privileged because each implies the other. Even as "Express Yourself" abuses tonal conventions by refusing to indicate a principal tonal center, it constructs a different kind of story that speaks from partial and temporary positions, none of which attempts to master. This is a new kind of relation to difference, which rejects hierarchy.

For example, there is an ascending scale in measure sixty-five that does not sound incomplete, even though it should. In the treble clef, the scale starts at G and ascends, stopping at F instead of the G that would be expected to affirm a final tonality in G. Hum a scale to test this: do-re-mi-fa-so-la-ti-do. If you stop before the second *do,* you will arouse an expectation for that next note. To speak of tonality does not necessarily imply a linear progression of notes. Properly speaking, we cannot define cadence in diachronous terms of melody because cadence applies to the synchronous terms of harmony. Tonality is used to create narrative motivation by creating an order, then compositions disturb that order through the manipulation of a desire for an element of that particular organization. The incomplete ascending scale you just hummed demonstrates one crude method of adding narrative interest by withholding fulfillment of a tonality. Traditionally, that incompleteness arouses a kind of anxiety in the listener that stands as a problem in need of resolution. One can find an excellent example of this kind of disturbance in the sound track of nearly any horror movie. Incompletion is what makes music sound suspenseful.

As is proper to Madonna's strategies, the fact that her ascending scale does not make it to the last note of a G-major scale functions to prevent what we would call, in narrative terms, an ideological closure. There is no recapitulation that fixes power and establishes (or reestablishes) any element as the dominant one. This is disjunctively coordinated with the visual image. At this point in the video, we see the Teutonic master wearing a monocle while he gazes at a group of black horn players, imprisoned in a life-sized, rotating glass music box. There is a diegetic relation when we hear horns. They are playing a scale definitely in the key of G, but the presence of a B flat in the bass line hints to a sonority in F (with an F natural) establishing an F-major tonality. So, the treble line suggests one tonality as the bass line subverts it with another. If we were talking about piano music, we might say that the left hand is not coordinated with the right. Through this unsettled tonality (or polytonality), the composition points to the negotiations between the two keys.

Without a mastering subject defined musically by a home key or a tonal center, a different kind of coherence is constructed elsewhere, using other elements. These two tonalities negotiate their differences, while a common ground is also articulated between them. A tonality in C serves this purpose, taking advantage of a certain equidistant relationship between C and the other two tonalities because the C is a fifth above the F and the G is a fifth above the C. The C allows for smooth transitions between the tonalities. Beyond the use of this C chord, the piece also relies on a very steady beat. Further, intermittent lip-synching binds the image to the sound track.

These cohesive grounds enable innovations to be legible, instead of wreaking pure chaos. For example, looking at the sheet music, the word *self* clues us in on some of these mediations on the constitution of a decentered· subjectivity. *Self* is first sung on G, then on F sharp, moving to F natural, then on G, moving back to F sharp, and lastly (not counting repeated bars), *self* is sung on F sharp to F. The word as well as the concept gets divided and put in motion, articulating agency through positions that remain partial and temporary.

Another innovation includes the convention of the upbeat. In a musical piece written in 4/4 time, the second beat (or the upbeat) is usually designated as the weak beat. But when Madonna comes in singing on this upbeat throughout most of the song, it is as if she is daring her audience to ignore her. By starting on the "less important" beat, she interrogates how this convention becomes assigned.

CINEMATIC APPARATUS AND THE
POLITICS OF REPRESENTATION

Homologous to the functions of both literary and musical narrative, the "cinematic apparatus . . . binds affect and meaning to images by establishing terms of identification, orienting the movement of desire, and positioning the spectator in relation to them" (de Lauretis 1984, 137). When *Express Yourself* makes reference to vision, it pays less attention to the camera and plays more with the monocle as a condensed symbol of mastery, the gaze, and the cinematic apparatus. Recall the scene described above, where the master gazes through his monocle at the black horn players. This is the only scene in the video with black people, and suggests a similar reference in *Metropolis,* which also was the only scene with black people: the cyborg-Maria's striptease. Wearing a large headdress and surrounded by serpentine appendages, the cyborg emerges out of some sort of elaborate urn. This is supported by a group of black slaves—the only nonwhites in the film, used to highlight her exotic and colonized alterity—who are then replaced by a set of characters introduced to us as the Seven Deadly Sins.

Express Yourself seems to present a similar display of domination in the scene between the master and the horn players. But the music undermines the stability of domination. The video scene, as well as the same musical accompaniment, are repeated a second time. However, in its re-presentation, the "master" is standing and peering through his raised monocle into the music box from which he seems excluded. Does he want in? Or is the monocle raised in the appreciative gesture of a connoisseur? Madonna does not like to say A is A. So, we can read it both ways. This ambiguity deconstructs the master. But one thing is certain: For the white man to represent a master, he must be dominant. Because dominance is not clear or stable, we have a different kind of paradigm, wherein our attention is directed to the process of the struggle for power instead of to the maintenance of a particular regime.

Other deconstructions occur on the cinematic level. For example, Madonna seems to offer herself as the "object of the gaze" in *Express Yourself.* After all, in one scene she does sort of strip, and in another, there is an explicit moment when she assumes the masochist's position. She lies naked on a bed, wearing an iron collar attached to a heavy chain. Despite these elements, which would suggest vulnerability and victimization, she appears to be enjoying herself. Madonna's self-possessed gaze is directed straight into the camera, as if aroused by and desiring her spectators—us, her voyeurs.

This is not the way the script usually reads. Who is the object of whose gaze? Her gaze undermines the spectator's access to illusions of control and mastery developed by the apparatus of classic cinema. Her posture seems to position the spectators as masters, while her gaze does the opposite.

The force of this apparent contradiction causes the representation to implode. The object that creates the subject is not an object. This is her point: to reveal the not-so-secret relation between subjectivity and mastery. By denying the illusion of control to the spectator, who is conventionally constituted as the "bearer of the gaze" and therefore positioned by the apparatus as the subject of this transaction, Madonna reveals this transaction by positioning herself as an unruly object.

Also, Madonna draws out the investments associated with the vamp as an object of the gaze. In *Metropolis,* the cyborg is constituted as an object of the gaze during the striptease scene repeatedly invoked throughout *Express Yourself.* Claiming to want to prove that nobody will be able to tell his robot apart from the human workers it is designed to replace, Rotwang arranges a gathering of the city's elite. Provided with Maria's features, the cyborg "performs a seductive strip-tease attracting the lustful gaze of the assembled male guests. This gaze is effectively filmed as an agitated montage of their eyes staring into the camera" (Huyssen 1986, 74). Lang monstrously depicts this gaze, suggesting that erotic desire is ugly. It is the cyborg's "job" to satisfy the men's voyeuristic and dominating desires to see, to know, and to possess. Spliced in with this action are scenes of a hallucinating Freder at home in bed, a distraught witness to the spectacle. The serpents surrounding the cyborg and her capacity to fascinate the male gaze suggest the figure of Medusa, a well-known symbol of castration. The scene becomes more explicit. When the serpents appear, the black slaves are replaced by the Seven Deadly Sins. As the men converge on the dancing cyborg, a steam whistle roars and ejaculates a head of steam, then the figure of Death swings his scythe. Freder grabs his crotch, cries out, and faints. The presence of this symbol bears witness to the anxiety and vulnerability inscribed in this exercise of mastery. Even as the gazing men construct their phantasm as an object for their desires, they express a fear of seeing what they dare not recognize.

Referencing the photo montage of gazing male eyes in *Metropolis,* Madonna adds a twist by establishing the bearer of the gaze as female. Even though she plays with the representations of the vamp and the masochist, she also stays in constant control of the gaze. Instead of a montage of monstrous and agitated male eyes gazing at a naked woman, the video returns to the scene of the dreaming man. Overlooking him, superimposed over the top half of the frame, Madonna's eyes gaze down on him. Supplementing rather than replacing the male gaze, she disengages the exclusive dominance of the male gaze. She expresses desire as well as control as she watches him dream. Her superimposed gaze also returns in the last moments of the video, before the screen fades to the closing text. Her eyes gaze down on the city of Metropolis—another male dream?

Attention is directed to the cinematic apparatus in *Express Yourself* when it deviates from established conventions because vision is frustrated and the camera does not show. The eye of the camera is not at all omnipresent. Madonna's bathroom striptease takes place behind a screen. We see and know only ourselves wanting to see more and wanting to know, wanting to know how the narrative ends to suppress the story. We see our own habitual gestures of appropriation—or at least their trace—indicated by the discomfort aroused in the spectator when scopophilic desire is solicited but not fulfilled.

All these disruptions call attention to a twofold procedure that constructs a center by privileging one term and denigrating or marginalizing another. Hélène Cixous (1986, 71) remarks on this gesture, "With the dreadful simplicity that orders the movement Hegel erected as a system, society trots along before my eyes reproducing to perfection the mechanism of the death struggle: the reduction of a 'person' to a 'nobody' to the position of 'other.'" Cixous's analysis connects many of the themes developed in *Express Yourself* to an explicit critique of the ideology that demands a center constructed on the back (so to speak) of an exclusion. Madonna urges us to express ourselves, to join the discussion, in order to not "go for second best." Cixous's discussion merits a long citation:

> And one becomes aware that the Empire of the Selfsame is erected from a fear that, in fact, is typically masculine: the fear of expropriation, of separation, of losing the attribute. In other words, the threat of castration has an impact. Thus, there is a relationship between the problematic of the not-selfsame . . . and the constitution of a subjectivity that experiences itself only when it makes its law, its strength, and its mastery felt, and it can all be understood on the basis of masculinity because this subjectivity is structured around a loss (1986, 80).

This explains why I call the subjectivity of liberal humanism "masterful."

There are a few other revised items in *Express Yourself* to which I would like to call attention. First, the loudspeaker is a densely coded sign. A propaganda tool and Nazi icon purportedly responsible for much of the successful mobilization of Adolf Hitler's popular support, the loudspeaker resonates with the film's slogan: "Without the heart, / there can be / no understanding / between the hand / and the mind," which Madonna uses in the last frame of the music video. Roger Dadoun (1986, 140) observes that "Lang's wife, Thea von Harbou, approved of the Nazis' ideas; after Lang's departure in 1933, she remained active, making films for the Nazis." Further, Siegfried Kracauer (1989) reports that when Joseph Goebbels addressed the Nuremberg Party Convention of 1934, he praised the "creative art of propaganda." Goebbels said, "Rising from the depths of the people, this art must always descend back to it and find its power there. Power based on guns might be a good thing; it is, however, better and more gratifying to win the heart of a people and to keep it" (Kracauer, 1989, 17). Kracauer adds, "In the case of *Metropolis*, Goebbel's own words bear out the conclusion drawn from this film. Lang relates that immediately after Hitler's rise to power Goebbels sent for him: ' . . . he told me that, many years before, he and the Führer had seen my picture *Metropolis* in a small town, and Hitler had said at that time that he wanted me to make the Nazi pictures' " (1989, 17). With reference to totalitarian regimes and both the icons and the slogans with which popular support was obtained, Madonna explores the persuasive techniques that make domination possible. That her Teutonic master and his assistant look at this device with apparent alarm instructs us to consider its revolutionary power.

Elsewhere in *Express Yourself,* dressed in a bizarre combination of masculine business suit and her trademark feminine lingerie with bra and garter straps, Madonna struts in front of Moloch. In another switch from *Metropolis,* the suit would indicate that the master is dancing here, not the cyborg. According to Huyssen (1986, 79) the *Metropolis* scene condenses fears of both technology and woman:

> The narrative links Freder's first exposure to the great machines with his sexual desire. . . . In his vision, the aperture high up in the belly of the great machine, in which we can see revolving cranks, changes into a grotesque mask-like face with a gaping mouth equipped with two rows of teeth. . . . Of course, the meaning of Freder's nightmarish hallucination is quite clear: technology as moloch demanding the sacrifice of human lives. But that is not all. If we assume that Freder in pursuit of Maria is still sexually aroused, and if we remember that his second hallucination in the film deals explicitly with sexuality (that of the machine-vamp Maria), we may want to see the imagery in this sequence as a first indication of the vagina dentata theme, of castration anxiety, of the male fear of uncontrolled female potency displaced to technology.

In contrast, as Madonna dances something like a phallic swagger at the consuming mouth of Moloch, she might (or might not) be playfully impersonating the master. But she solicits no paranoid fear of an overwhelming opponent. She flexes her biceps with her hands curled into fists, and she peers through her monocle. This one-eyed gaze focuses the metaphoric content as it imposes a frame. The monocle underscores the partial nature of the elite's gaze and an enactment of mastery. "The gaze . . . both historically and theoretically is the representation of the phallus and the figure of the male's desire" (de Lauretis 1984, 143). Madonna's playful show of strength elegantly reworks the scene of sexual horror and repudiation. However, the signs are again ambiguous. Madonna may not only be pretending to be a man. When she opens her jacket, she is displaying her bra. And when she caresses her breasts and crotch, perhaps there is no pretended allusion to a penis, even though the gesture mimics the phallic swagger of crotch-grabbing male rock stars. Her parody of the phallic swagger is also sincere. As she grasps her crotch and sings, "What you need is a big strong hand to lift you to your higher ground," she emphasizes her own specific adequacy. This challenges Freudian and cultural conventions that ground women's identity around a lack of a penis and a consequent penis envy. McClary (1991, 33) notes that "Madonna's cheeky modes of self-representation habitually greet the anxieties so often ascribed to women's bodies by 'mooning' them: She flaunts as critique her own unmistakably feminine ending." This challenges a myth of female lack. What women have been lacking is not a sexual organ or a libido of their own but the power that comes from discursive participation in culture.

As Madonna plays with the limits and capacities of representation, she examines its connection with domination in other visual puns. This occurs in the scenes where her disembodied face appears superimposed on a frame sitting on a vanity table, a clever personification of the trope "representation." Significantly, the portrayed face is not contained by the mirror or picture frame; it exceeds the borders. Like the loudspeaker, the black cat that appears throughout *Express Yourself* does not appear overtly in the film. Perhaps the cat can also be read as a visual pun: a black pussy that represents condensed and overdetermined notions of the object of white supremacy and of the sexual, animal, and female elements so rigorously repressed in the rational world of Metropolis. The importance of the cat as a figure is underscored by Madonna's cat masquerade. Elsewhere, Madonna appears as a member of the elite, standing in a tower in a slinky green gown and holding the black cat. One might say that this elite status alludes to a metaphorical wielding of the phallus, although here the phallus is a pussy.

CONCLUSION

Against the petrified images of a metropolis, Madonna sketches a world in struggle and in motion, with a beat you can dance to. Hers is not a serene view but one that instructs us to negotiate from a fluid stance. Unlike *Metropolis*'s laborers, Madonna insists that we not be conquered by the power relations to which we are subject. We can produce "talking cures" if we express ourselves, resist the seductions to complicity, and do not posit our power in domination over others. In this view, sexuality and contestation reside at the core of the struggle, but in her hands, they take on positive new meanings and values. The imaginary invoked by Madonna does not merely reverse the power relations established in *Metropolis;* rather, it attempts to subvert subjugation.

Acknowledgments

I thank Susan McClary and Isabelle Deconinck for extensive help with technical aspects of the musical analysis and to Catherine Schwichtenberg for her helpful editorial comments.

REFERENCES

Althusser, L. (1971). *Lenin and Philosophy and Other Essays*. B. Brewster (trans.). London: New Left Books.

Belsey, C. (1985). "Constructing the Subject: Deconstructing the Text." In J. Newton and D. Rosenfelt (eds.), *Feminist Criticism and Social Change*. New York: Methuen, pp. 45–63.

Chaudhuri, U. (1986). *No Man's Stage: A Semiotic Study of Jean Genet's Major Plays*. Ann Arbor, Mich.: UMI Research Press.

Ciccone, M., and Bray, S. (1989). "Express Yourself" (words and music). Secaucus, N.J.: Warner Brothers Publications.

Cixous, H., and Clément, C. ([1975] translated 1986). *The Newly Born Woman*. B. Wing (trans.). Minneapolis: University of Minnesota Press.

Dadoun, R. (1986). "*Metropolis*: Mother-City-'Mitler'-Hitler." *Camera Obscura* 15: 137–164.

de Lauretis, T. (1984). *Alice Doesn't*. Bloomington: University of Indiana Press.

Deleuze, G., and Guattari, F. ([1977] 1983). *Anti-Oedipus: Capitalism and Schizophrenia*. R. Hurley et al. (trans.), preface by M. Foucault, and introduction by M. Seem. Minneapolis: University of Minnesota Press.

Foucault, M. (1982). *This Is Not a Pipe*. J. Harkness (trans.). Berkeley and Los Angeles: University of California Press.

———. ([1977] 1983). "Preface." In G. Deleuze and F. Guattari, *Anti-Oedipus: Capitalism and Schizophrenia*. Minneapolis: University of Minnesota Press, pp. XI–XIV.

———. (1984). "Truth and Power." In P. Rabinow (ed.), *The Foucault Reader*. New York: Pantheon, pp. 51–75.

Genet, J. (1964). *The Thief's Journal*. New York: Grove Press.

———. (1987). "Affirmation of Existence Through Rebellion." *Journal of Palestine Studies* 62 (Winter): 64–84.

Haraway, D. (1990). "A Manifesto for Cyborgs: Science, Technology, and Socialist Feminism in the 1980s." In L. Nicholson (ed.), *Feminism/Postmodernism*. New York: Routledge, Chapman & Hall, pp. 190–233.

Huyssen, A. (1986). *After the Great Divide: Modernism, Mass Culture, Postmodernism*. Bloomington: University of Indiana Press.

Kant, I. ([1781] 1965). *Critique of Pure Reason*. N. Kemp Smith (trans.). New York: St. Martin's Press.

Kracauer, S. (1989). "Industrialism and Totalitarianism." In F. Lang, *Metropolis.* Boston, Mass.: Faber & Faber Limited, pp. 15–17.

Lang, F. (1989). *Metropolis.* Boston, Mass.: Faber & Faber Limited. Criticism and original 1926 screenplay interspersed with extracts from the English translation of the original novel (of the same name) by Thea Von Harbou.

McClary, S. (1988). "The Undoing of Opera: Toward a Feminist Criticism of Music." Foreword to C. Clément, *Opera, or the Undoing of Women.* B. Wing (trans.). Minneapolis: University of Minnesota Press.

———— . (1991). *Feminine Endings: Music, Gender and Sexuality.* Minneapolis: University of Minnesota Press.

Piston, W. (1978). *Harmony.* New York: W. W. Norton.

Schulte-Sasse, J. (1984). "Foreword." In P. Bürger, *Theory of the Avant-Garde.* Minneapolis: University of Minnesota Press, pp. VII–XLVII.

Seem, M. (1983). "Introduction." In G. Deleuze and F. Guattari, *Anti-Oedipus: Capitalism and Schizophrenia.* Minneapolis: University of Minnesota Press, pp. XIV–XV.

Sessums, K. (1990). "White Heat: Interview with Madonna." *Vanity Fair,* April, pp. 142–148, 208–214.

Silverman, K. (1983). *The Subject of Semiotics.* Oxford and New York: Oxford University Press.

Part Four

The Political Economy of Postmodernism: Madonna as Star-Commodity

photo by Just Loomis, *courtesy of Warner Brothers*

DAVID TETZLAFF **11**

Metatextual Girl: —▶ patriarchy —▶ postmodernism —▶ power —▶ money —▶ Madonna

O NE OF THE THINGS I usually do when attempting to gain a better understanding of a cultural product is to read up on who or whatever it is in newspapers and magazines. This generally gives me a pretty good idea of how other people have reacted to the subject in question. So, when I began to contemplate the social significance of Madonna, I thought I should make a thorough examination of Madonna coverage in the popular press. I gave up this idea very quickly. One might as well contemplate mapping the vastness of the cosmos as attempt to collect, let alone read, everything that has been written about Madonna. She is ubiquitous at the newsstand and on the TV set, unavoidable for anyone but cultural hermits. Announcing that no less than three unauthorized biographies of Ms. Ciccone are now scheduled to be published simultaneously, with still more in the works, *Time* noted, "Cut Madonna, and ink comes out" (Tresniowski 1991). Or, as one entertainment news voice-over put it, Madonna continues to "push the envelope of overexposure" (Tresniowski 1991).

This alone makes Madonna a phenomenon worthy of analysis. Never before has a popular performer survived so much hype for so long and continued to attract the fascination of a broad public while staying completely contemporary. The cultural longevity of Liz Taylor or even Elvis Presley has been largely based in nostalgia; the Rolling Stones have been around forever, but they have only occasionally, if ever, been associated with the level of publicity that constantly envelops Madonna. The Beatles provide the only comparable example of a long-term stay in the center of the pop culture spotlight, and they broke up seven years after they hit it big. The Madonna phenomenon has now been with us for a similar length of time, yet neither Madonna nor the legions who follow her show signs of calling it quits anytime soon.

The media's appetite for Madonna items is insatiable, but Madonna fascination is potent enough to ensure that anything even loosely related to her will attract enough interest to make it a bankable product. "Inside Edition" even did a story on college professors who study Madonna or discuss her work in class. When tabloid journalists start presenting the activities of academics to their sensation-seeking audiences, it is obvious that some very large cultural power is at hand.

THE SECRET OF HER SUCCESS

> "I don't know whether or not she's talented, but I like the way she's in control of her life."
> —Monica Seles, tennis champion and wanna-be (quoted by Dick Enberg during NBC's telecast of the French Open)

So, I ask myself, what is it about Madonna that commands such long-standing and intense public attention? I begin by the process of elimination.

Is it her musical abilities? Financially, Madonna's success has come primarily as a recording artist. And most recording stars have been celebrated for exceptional musical talents. Fans consider them to be possessed of unique or powerful singing voices, particularly expressive or innovative vocal interpretive skills, extraordinary songwriting ability and studio wizardry, or special performance skills. Yet, one does not encounter similar remarks about Madonna. Musicologist Susan McClary (1991, 148) protests, "What most reactions to Madonna share is an automatic dismissal of her music as irrelevant." She says, "The scorn with which her ostensible artistic focus has been trivialized, treated as a conventional backdrop to her visual appearance, often is breathtaking." McClary wants to claim Madonna's music for progressive politics on the basis of its supposedly disruptive form (the "denial of narrative closure" argument so familiar from film studies). Music critic Robert Christgau (1991, 33) also sees Madonna's music as something special—he refers to her greatest hits compilation as "stunning, and as likely to remain stunning as *Blonde on Blonde*"—and he, too, has unkind words for "eye-oriented" Madonna critics. However, whether McClary and Christgau like it or not, *irrelevant* is quite a good word to describe the role musical values play in the Madonna phenomenon. Her music may be as radical as McClary claims or as artistically exceptional as Christgau asserts—or not. Regardless, there is no evidence that the mass of Madonna fans really care. It's not that they don't like Madonna's singing or songwriting; they do. It's just that they don't think about it or talk about it much. Madonna doesn't present herself as a great musical talent, either. In fact, for all the plethora of published pages of Madonna quotes and interviews, one almost never finds the Material Girl actually discussing the musical aspects of her material. As John Fiske (1989, 95)—one of the image-conscious Madonna scholars McClary dismisses—notes, "Her fans and her publicity materials, along with journalistic reports and critiques, pay far more attention to what she looks like, who she is, and what she stands for than to what she sounds like." It is Madonna culture itself, not its analysts, that have reduced the music to irrelevancy.

Is Fiske right, then, that Madonna's appeal is based on "who she is and what she stands for"? Is her audience attracted by the sort of charismatic, symbolic personality possessed by old-time Hollywood film stars, the Kennedys, or even talk show hosts? I don't think this is it either. Madonna has retooled her screen persona frequently, leaving no consistent point for fan attachment. Nor do the countless interviews or articles construct a detailed, memorable character. I have plunged into these texts in search of the "real" author, and I have come away with very little sense of Madonna as a person. Even as she exposes intimate details of her life, as she has done with great frequency lately, she still comes off as shallow or blank. Her interview with Carrie Fisher (1991) in *Rolling Stone* gives us a definite impression of who Carrie Fisher is, but Madonna's contributions emerge as merely a collection of provocative statements. As a number of film reviewers have noted, the revelations in *Truth or Dare* are essentially devoid of emotional resonance (cf. Denby 1991; Sragow 1991; Kaufman 1991). They fail to penetrate the spectacle and connect with an everyday human life, which Madonna ultimately seems not to have. To the extent that she has personal characteristics, they are defined by words like *success, media savvy, manipulation*—terms that describe what she has and what she does rather than who she is.

Madonna's film career testifies that something other than her personality must be the source of her success. Film stars are generally required to project a three-dimensional humanity and certain unique individual characteristics on screen. The public has repeatedly shown that it will flock to see such charismatic performers (Eddie Murphy, for example) even in mediocre pictures. Yet, Madonna's film appearances since *Desperately Seeking Susan* have all fallen curiously flat. Her film presence doesn't measure up: There's nothing there. She's a marvelous icon, but icons don't hold our interest over the length of a dramatic narrative. Madonna has wisely moved into cartoonish films (*Who's That Girl, Dick Tracy*) designed to contain their appeals on the surface, to make icons shine brightly. Yet, even here, in what amount to exaggerated versions of the music video form of which she is an acknowledged master, she has failed to capture the public imagination. The "odd lots" closeout stores were overflowing with unsold Breathless Mahoney merchandise while *Dick Tracy* was still in the theaters.

Is the Madonna phenomenon just a case of plain old sex appeal? After all, she has certainly rolled around on the floor more than most celebrities. But though a certain sleaze factor was undoubtedly an important element of Madonna's initial rise to fame, it simply cannot account for her continued superstardom. For one thing, being the sex symbol of the moment has always been a job with high turnover—male sexual fantasies are more likely to be fueled by iconic variety than by iconic fidelity. Besides, a fair portion of the male audience seems to dislike Madonna, having discerned a mocking tone in her sexual displays. Even at her most suggestive, there has always been an exaggerated flamboyance, a little ironic wink at the camera suggesting that she is putting us on. Moreover, Madonna dropped her Boy Toy image quite a while ago, and since then, she has presented herself in a variety of images. The sex-object Madonna now appears to have been merely one of a wardrobe of theatrical guises. Yet, she is now even more famous. Finally, we probably need to look past sex appeal to account for the fact that the majority of Madonna's fans have always been heterosexual young women.

If Madonna's phenomenal popularity can't be accounted for by her music, her personality, or even her sexuality, where does it come from? I suggest that the core of Madonna's appeal lies in her aura of power. This isn't exactly an original observation: I got it out of *People* magazine. Actually, the issue of power comes up again and again in the way almost everyone discusses Madonna—from profiles in fashion magazines to rarefied academic theory to Madonna's own talk about herself. Here's Madonna on the cover of *US* proclaiming, "Power is a great aphrodisiac, and I'm a very powerful person." Madonna holds down the anchor position on *Glamour*'s list of "women of the year" in December 1990, where she is cited "for personifying women's power of self-determination." *Glamour,* typically, praises Madonna not for her talent but for her success: "While other media stars come and go, Madonna remains as hot as ever—and we admire her for it." A quote from Madonna ends the feature—"It's a great feeling to be powerful. I've been striving for it all my life" (*Glamour* 1990, 101). And *People* (summer 1991 "extra," 109) puts Madonna on the final page of its "50 most beautiful people" issue, and while all the other beautiful folk are identified conventionally by occupation—actor, singer, politician—Madonna is listed as "superstar." *People* asks, "But is she really beautiful?" and answers, "Of course she's beautiful. That comes with the territory, with the power."

Scholars in the field of cultural studies have also focused on issues of power in their analyses of the Madonna phenomenon. Most notably, John Fiske (1989) has argued that Madonna's image (Boy Toy phase) generally and her videos specifically offer her young female fans the semiotic tools to create self-understandings that break from the limiting models presented by patriarchal culture. Madonna's image of personal autonomy is thus actually transferred to her fans as well.

> Madonna offers her fans access to semiotic and social power; at the basic level this operates through fantasy, which, in turn, may empower the fan's sense of self and thus affect her behavior in social situations. . . . Madonna's popularity

is a complexity of power and resistances, of meanings and countermeanings, of pleasures and the struggle for control (Fiske 1989, 112–113).

The analysts all generally agree that Madonna's power derives from her success at manipulating her own image. *Manipulation* is probably the key term in Madonna criticism. Whether critics approve or disapprove of the Material Girl breaks largely along the edge of how they identify, interpret, and evaluate this manipulation. On the one hand, when she is attacked, the charge is usually that she coldly manipulates her audience, that she is power hungry. On the other hand, when she is praised, the claim is that her successful manipulation of the media culture system shows admirable spirit, independence, and self-determination. The audience, too, whether pro or con, has focused not so much on her singing, dancing, and acting or even her sexuality per se as on how she has constructed and managed her fame. As Christgau (1991, 31) says, "There can no longer be much doubt that Madonna now regards celebrity itself as her art," which is what her fans have recognized, at least intuitively, all along. In the world of Madonna, celebrity, success, manipulation, and power are all more or less exchangeable quantities.

I want to examine Madonna power—how she displays it and how she gets it. In doing so, I will divide her celebrity-art into two periods. First came the Boy Toy phase, in which she presented a relatively consistent image of self-conscious trashiness and excess. We are still in phase two—Chameleon Madonna, where she presents herself in an ever-changing series of roles and settings, occasionally straightforward and minus trash and excess (*Live to Tell, Papa Don't Preach, Cherish*), occasionally with the trash or excess accompanied by tones of high seriousness (*Like a Prayer, Justify My Love*), and occasionally with the trash and excess almost absurdly amplified into expressionist aestheticism (*Open Your Heart*, the Blond Ambition tour version of "Like a Virgin"). Both phases, though, are marked by continuing themes—the appropriation and decontextualization of discourses of sexuality and morality and the commodification and exploitation of the realm of the personal in exchange for public power. These themes are not articulated within the texts of her videos and songs themselves but within the metatextual narrative of her management of her own career quest for fame, fortune, and independence. That is, Madonna's texts carry as much or more resonance as signs of her ability to create them than as references to their manifest subject matter.

SEX AND MONEY

"At first I thought Madonna was just a slut. But she wins. She's happy."

— professional woman and wanna-be, age 27

At first I thought she was just a slut, too. In early 1985, I was working on an essay about MTV, and I was watching videos, making little telegraphic notes describing each one, in case I decided to put some sort of crude content analysis into the paper. *Lucky Star* came on. I had never seen Madonna before and had heard little or nothing about her. I watched her wink suggestively, bite her lip, and roll on the floor while the director fragmented her body into a series of fetishized parts via a montage of close-ups, and this is what I wrote on the note card: "the world's oldest profession."

Of course, I soon discovered that there were other readings of Madonna in circulation. Apparently, a lot of female fans had taken what I saw as a straightforward, if calculated, come-on as more of a playful put-on. The idea that all of Madonna's early pouting and navel wiggling was only a form of irony has become the standard line of pro-Madonna rhetoric, reaching its zenith (or nadir, depending on how you look at it) in Fiske's analysis. Fiske (1989) goes to great lengths to explicate a close reading that locates feminist content in the *Burning Up* video (where Madonna wears a choke chain around her neck), and he includes part of a student essay on *Lucky Star* as an example of typically antipatriarchal fan interpretation:

> In *Lucky Star* at one point in the dance sequence Madonna dances side on to the camera, looking provocative. For an instant we glimpse her tongue: The expectation is that she is about lick her lips in a sexual invitation. The expectation is denied and Madonna appears to tuck her tongue back into her cheek. This, it seems, is how most of her dancing and grovelling in front of the camera is meant to be taken. She is setting up the sexual idolization of women. For a woman who has experienced this victimization, this setup is most enjoyable and pleasurable, while the male position of voyeur is displaced into uncertainty [Robyn Blair, nineteen-year-old fan] (Fiske 1989, 112).

Ultimately, Fiske implies that any viewer who comes away from *Lucky Star* with a different impression is just either too dumb or too ideologically incorporated to get the joke.

In fact, at the moment Blair refers to in *Lucky Star,* Madonna actually *does* lick her lips, albeit rather quickly. She is in close-up, looking back over her shoulder, peek-a-boo style, her face almost in profile but her eyes still fixed on the lens. She opens her mouth into a little pout, sticks her tongue toward the viewer, and licks the corner of her mouth exposed to the camera. This shot is one of six points in the video where lip synch is interrupted to present close-up poses of Madonna. Thus, she is able to strike facial expressions without having to mouth the accompanying words of the song. Three of these shots specifically emphasize her mouth—in addition to the lick shot, she also bites her lower lip suggestively and slowly inserts her finger into her mouth. Taken by itself, the tongue movement in question is relatively ambiguous, and Blair's interpretation does not seem out of line. But in the context of the video as a whole and especially in relation to the other shots to which it is structurally tied, the idea that Madonna's tongue is intended as a put-on rather than a come-on hardly seems likely.

In the terms of traditional criticism, we would have to say that interpretations of *Burning Up* and *Lucky Star* as parodic critiques of voyeurism are simply not supported by the text. Yet, such misreadings of Madonna videos seem to be common. The interpretations put forth by Fiske and Blair are not idiosyncratic by any means. They fit right in with a general view of Madonna and her work that appears to be widely held among her fans. But if the fans are not drawing the meanings of the videos from the universe of the text itself, where do their interpretations come from?

From the beginning, Madonna's self-representation in promotion and publicity material portrayed her as defiantly independent, a woman who challenged and overcame gender restrictions. This representation was greatly bolstered by Madonna's role in the popular Hollywood feminist film *Desperately Seeking Susan*. In contrast to the image of woman as nurturer, the metatextual Madonna was plainly focused on success in her own career. She clearly articulated that she was out only for herself, that stardom and its perks of money, power, and respect were her goals. In contrast to the image of woman as keeper of decency and morals, the metatextual Madonna was clearly thumbing her nose at the traditional discourse of femininity. She also expressed that she would reject the bounds of others' discourses as well and that she felt she had the right to use imagery from the crucifix to the camisole in any way that suited her. None of this was articulated in vengeful or vindictive terms, just as a means to self-actualization. Madonna was a "bad" girl only in a performative sense.

The nuances of this position are demonstrated by the video *Material Girl* and by its reception. The opening shots of the video introduce us to a male character (played by Keith Carradine) of considerable power, as evidenced by the nervous, doting attention he receives from his assistant (Robert Wuhl). They are watching the rushes of a musical film starring an up-and-coming actress (Madonna). The Carradine character seems to be the producer of the film, and his costume and hairstyle evoke the image of Howard Hughes. He is enthralled with the image of the actress he sees in the rushes and begins to pursue her surreptitiously. The musical number of the film is a pastiche of the "Diamonds Are a Girl's Best Friend" number from *Gentlemen Prefer Blondes*. In it, the character played by the actress (who is, in turn, played by Madonna) sings that she is only interested in wealthy men who will support her in a lavish style. However, the producer observes the actress backstage rejecting upscale gifts from upper-class suitors. He casually tosses the expensive gift he had brought for her into the trash, and we then see him paying a large sum of money to acquire the trappings of "sincerity" in a calculated attempt to impress her. It works. She is charmed by his apparent earthiness and goes off with him in the end.

The discourses activated by the text of the *Material Girl* video are complex and contradictory. The independent woman is unwittingly manipulated by a powerful male, yet she is also controlling his actions in a way, via the obsession her image has aroused in him. The actress devalues wealth, yet she winds up attaining the doting attention of a rich man (a traditional image of female success), achieving by happy accident the material aims expressed by the character she plays. Yet, Madonna herself has claimed that the actress in *Material Girl* rejects wealthy suitors in favor of a "sensitive" guy "with no money," and Fiske (1987), among others, has reiterated this interpretation, all as supposed evidence that the video indicates the sentiments of greed in the lyrics of *Material Girl* should be read ironically. Again, I think many fans probably had similar interpretations.

At first, these readings may seem contradictory to the metatextual narrative of Madonna's self-interest, arguing that Madonna is just a nice, simple girl looking only for romance after all. However, neither Madonna, Fiske, nor the fans are claiming that the romantic Madonna is the *real* Madonna. The purpose of *Material Girl* is for Madonna's audience to witness her playing with her own persona, to indicate that she is the author of her image, that she constructs it to suit her own desires, and that she can change it as she likes. *Material Girl* shows us that Madonna has not been trapped by her Boy Toy image or by her success. Because she is a heroine of self-actualization, it is important for her fans to distinguish her desire for money and power as a means toward that end from simple greed as an end in itself. Money *isn't* really important to Madonna; success and control are. Madonna is certainly shown to be successful in *Material Girl*. She gets everything—career, love, and the money, too. Ah, but the control element in the video *is* a problem. Even though the issue ultimately works out in Madonna's favor because the producer's manipulative actions occur under the spell of her image, the presence of the contradictions apparently constitutes too much of a blemish on our perfect goddess of self-help, and so the contradictions are resolved by repressing the true identity of Carradine's character.

All of Madonna's early videos are constructed primarily around codes that clearly contradict the "spunky gal" narrative of the Madonna metatext, especially the patriarchal codes of sexual objectification activated in *Lucky Star, Burning Up,* and *Like a Virgin.* However, the techniques used in the videos also act in certain ways to assist viewers who wish to reject the surface meanings of the texts and interpret them in the light of Madonna's career quest for independence and control. At the very least, the highly presentational performance—the great camera awareness Madonna always shows—can support an "it's all just a show, she doesn't really *mean* it" sort of response. More importantly, although seductive imagery may dominate the early videos, these videos also contain a consistent subtheme of Madonna as an object of public attention, representing her emergence and perfection as a media icon. *Borderline* shows Madonna moving from the wrong side of the tracks to become a successful cover-girl fashion model who nevertheless maintains her independence by blowing off the photographer who discovered her once he impinges on her individual style. The conventional clips-from-the-film structure of *Gambler* is framed by shots of the film slate entering the frame and being clapped in front of Madonna as she pauses before and after the song, emphasizing that she is performing in a Hollywood movie. *Into the Groove* (which, being a plotless compendium of shots of Madonna from *Desperately Seeking Susan,* is sort of a visual ode to Madonna as icon anyway) reinforces the point by employing the device of using a close-up of a photoflash going off (repeated thirteen times in the piece) as the recurring visual motif that graphically ties together the loose assemblage of images. As E. Ann Kaplan (1987) has noted, *Material Girl* subordinates its plot to the moments when Madonna is performing "on screen" in the pastiche of "Diamonds Are a Girl's Best Friend." The "nice girl" actress is given less screen time and less compelling images than the seductive star performance in the movie within the video. And as I just noted, the framing narrative itself can serve as a testament to the power of the star image. Thus, these videos have characteristics that invite viewers not aroused and absorbed by the conventional sexual seductiveness that dominates the imagery to view it as merely a strategy in Madonna's quest for success—the prick tease is not the purpose of the work, stardom and adoration are, and the naughty stuff is just a convenient vehicle. The self-referentiality to media frames gives this moral to the story: Make of thyself a spectacle and ye shall be rewarded.

Now, it seems unlikely that the primary appeal of a major cultural phenomenon would spring merely from a certain correspondence between narratives articulated by promotional materials and second-level textual elements in a series of music videos. If Madonna fans were attracted to her because, in Kaplan's (1987, 126) words, she was "the postmodern feminist heroine" who combined "unabashed seductiveness with a sort of gutsy independence," we still have to ask, first, how and why the audience could reject the unabashed patriarchal surfaces of the texts to reach the idea of gutsy independent womanhood in the metatext beyond, and, second, what would make something as compromised as postmodern feminism broadly appealing to begin with.

Kaplan's label is apt because the readings of Madonna's early work as feminist depend exactly on cultural practices that have become habitual within postmodernity. Madonna arrived into a cultural scene dominated by spectacle, where textual meaning was already all but irrelevant. As Jean Baudrillard (1980, 1983), Fredric Jameson (1984), and a host of other theorists have observed, depthlessness and fragmentation characterize the texts of postmodern culture. If we seek meaningful stories, we certainly don't look to the surface of the text. In fact, we can assume that whatever *is* on the surface of the text is *not* meaningful but exists only for its ability to stimulate the senses. Madonna videos were born into the broad context of a youth culture dependent on sequels, special effects, and other forms of simulacra and into the specific context of mid-1980s MTV. The "concept videos" that dominated MTV routinely plundered the entire history of Western culture for visual material, ripping images away from their historically or socially situated meanings and transforming them into visual tricks to jazz up the presentation of the star. If none of the signs used on MTV or for that matter in most of popular film and television were actually meant to refer to anything, to invoke the master narratives from whence they were plucked, why should young women read Madonna's navel twirls, pursed lips, hair flips, and writhing on the floor as enactments of patriarchy or as anything but spectacular performance?

However, for all of its hermeneutic vandalism, postmodernism has not meant the death of narrative, as some commentators have argued. Narrative is no longer *necessary,* and it has largely been kicked out of the text, but it has found new, though more restrictive, quarters in the economic system. The vicissitudes of the market and the glitter of wealth have become more reliable sources of narrative spectacle than anything inherent in the work itself. Ubiquitous entertainment news features have popularized the dramatic stories of cultural products struggling in the marketplace. Space that was once devoted to movie reviews is now filled by box office reports and estimates of studio profit and loss. Instead of getting critics who tell us whether the new TV shows are artful, now we get analysts from giant ad agencies like Saatchi and Saatchi, gauging the program's chances for success in the Nielsen ratings. The function of these pieces has not changed, only the methodology has. The point is still to give the culture consumer a guide to the good, but good has been redefined almost exclusively in terms that make cultural success and marketplace success indistinguishable (anything that conquers the mass market must be good, right?).

Postmodernism applies commodity fetishism to aesthetics, emptying the use value of symbols in the search for exchange value, but it also aesthetizes the realm of commodities, turning economic exchange into spectacle for mass consumption. A similar phenomenon has infected political discourse, which no longer tells stories of the clash of policies or social philosophies but reduces everything to the level of horserace reports: Who's ahead and by how much, who won the debate or the floor fight and who lost, how the wagers of the power brokers turn on these events. Narrative has found a home in the instrumental metatext of money and power overriding all cultural production, and this is increasingly the only source of drama that mass-produced culture will accommodate. Articulate feminism within these conditions and you wind up with Madonna.

Much has been made of Madonna as an example of "oppositional" tendencies within popular culture. Now, her status as an oppositional figure in any sense as well as her status as a success symbol are based in understandings of how she addresses her gender position. That is, her achievements and attitudes stand for defiance or independence because she is a woman making her way in a man's world. Yet, if postmodern feminism is oppositional, I think we need to be more specific about what exactly it opposes and how this opposition is situated historically.

If we take the Madonna metatext in gender-neutral terms, we would have to say that it is antiestablishment in the sense of *moral* values, while presenting establishment values *economically*. On the one hand, we have overt sexuality freed from the bonds of marriage or commitment to any single partner, a self-centered sensuality in which the partner actually becomes irrelevant. On the other hand, we have rugged individualism, the ends justifying the means, and a philosophy of win at all costs.

However, both sets of values in Madonna's metatext run counter to the traditional patriarchal address to middle-class women. This discourse directs women to be romantic objects and moral beacons. It trains them to eschew self-interest, to be nurturing and other-directed, often to the point of servitude. Thus, women are directed to steer clear of the dirty business of the marketplace. They are not, however, led to reject the questionable values of commerce in absolute terms, just to leave them to their menfolk, whose breadwinning struggles they are expected to support. This position promises rewards of respect—"behind every successful man stands a woman"—and even of a form of power (of which Nancy Reagan has become a caricature). Of course, this model of womanhood, what Kaplan (1987) refers to as the "patriarchal feminine," is not the only one promoted within the discourses of patriarchy. It represents only one half of the "virgin-whore dichotomy." This term, of course, describes the tendency of men to envision women only in one of these extreme categories, allowing little space for accommodating the complexities of actual women. This, in turn, has a limiting effect on how women are able to understand or envision themselves. On both ends of the dichotomy, women are represented as if their proper role is to serve as objects of male desire, and the dichotomy as a whole can be seen as articulating alternate strategies for women to get or please men.

I think it is important to note that, in practice, the poles of the virgin-whore dichotomy have tended to be correlated with different groups of women. It is a class dichotomy as well. The "virgin" address is primarily bourgeois. The phrase *nice girl* indicates not only a set of values but a certain social standing. The "whore" address is primarily reserved for women who wind up on the short end of power relationships—from prostitutes forced to sell themselves to survive to secretaries having illicit trysts with their bosses to the blonde sex bombs of old Hollywood films, too dumb and dependent to get by without their leading men. The "bad girl" is usually from the bad side of town. Witness the familiar story of the preppie college boy sowing his wild oats among a series of disposable townies ("just don't get 'em pregnant, son") before settling down to marry a well-connected sorority woman after graduation (though he'll still have affairs with his secretaries on the side, heh, heh).

Recently, however, the terms of the traditional class and gender patriarchal discourse have changed. The entire system was dependent on certain economic conditions that allowed middle- and upper-class women to avoid work outside of the home. However, Western economies have slackened as conservative governments allow the wealthy to fatten up at the expense of the middle class, and the First World worker no longer finds Third World labor an exploitable source of cheap consumer goods but part of a competitive world market for his or her once secure job, keeping wages low. Middle-class couples find that the women must work in order to maintain the lifestyle to which they are accustomed. At the same time, the divorce rate has risen dramatically. Single women, especially single mothers, need to work to support themselves. All of this comes in the wake of the development of virtually universal college education for the middle class that followed World War II. As such, many of the women entering the marketplace are highly skilled for jobs in an economy in transition from manufacturing to information processing.

What has happened, then, as a result is that capitalist imperatives have displaced many of the traditional practices and discourses of patriarchy. Capitalism cannot afford the old forms of sexism anymore. In tight economic times, corporations take their profit maximization from wherever they can get it, and if a woman can outperform a man on the sales floor or in the boardroom, more power to her. The new economic conditions are not compatible with the old idea of the patriarchal feminine, and a new cultural address to the female work force must be created.

I submit that the metatextual readings of Madonna as the postmodern feminist heroine and, subsequently, a large part of Madonna's phenomenal popularity are artifacts of a historical shift from patriarchy to capitalism as the dominant discourse for middle-class women. Madonna is not the first cultural product to articulate and exploit these changes. We might view Madonna as the *Cosmo* girl having taken a few more steps away from patriarchy toward capital along the path of postmodern irony. Nevertheless, Madonna meanings are teeming with contradictions because the transition is still in process—the patriarchal discourses are still well in evidence. Yet, all the old verities have been destabilized, and amid the scramble for new positions on the ideological hierarchy, it is no accident that the audience has focused on texts that play out the contradictions and indicate economic imperatives as the direction for (happy) resolution.

In the old virgin-whore dichotomy, both men and women tended to identify the two poles along the same characteristic lines. But where does the new
postmodern feminist fit? Capital's displacement of patriarchal discourse has
fractured the unity of the virgin-whore dichotomy, and the postmodern feminist is read with different inflections, breaking along lines of gender and
class. The interpretations of bourgeois women and petit bourgeois men are
affected the most. These two groups are now, in effect, competing for employment—if not for the same jobs, then for the same limited sources of job
funding. Economic terms dominate sexual representation. The women look
at (metatextual) Madonna and see that the trappings of whoredom can be
used for economic gain and then discarded without actually entering the position of the whore. The true whore is defined by powerlessness, by being
herself used and discarded. However much Madonna may grovel in front of
the camera, she is anything but powerless; she is the user. She wins. Winning
elevates seductiveness up from sluttiness. For men who are economically
threatened by the changing status of women, once they catch the Madonna
metatext, her come-ons are no longer turn-ons but signs of the guys' declin-
ing power. They, too, recognize that she is not a whore, that seductive posture no longer necessarily signifies availability beyond the proliferation of
the image, no longer stands as a ratification of the old social order. Thus, the
sexy postmodern feminist may face as much male resentment from these
quarters as would a radical lesbian. For both more subordinate women and
more privileged men, the accommodation of the postmodern feminist to the
virgin-whore dichotomy is less of a drastic departure from patriarchal tradition.

Well-to-do men are not threatened economically by the changing status
of women, but they are threatened sexually. Both their romantic objects and
their economically dependent bimbos are disappearing into the job market.
Suddenly, here is a new category: women who are not bound by the confines
of monogamous coupling but who are also economically independent, even
powerful. The privileged male responds by having his consciousness raised
far enough to upgrade the power relations of the whore category to equality—an even market exchange replaces the leveraged buyout. Now, the prospect of ready sexual excitement lies not with the dependent woman but with
the woman who has no use for virginity and its obligations because of her
career. There is a mutual agreement on the disposability of the liaison. Thus,
when the virgin-whore dichotomy appears these days, it is often in the form
represented in the popular film *Nothing in Common,* in which the male protagonist is an advertising executive torn between two women—sweet love
and hot sex; the good girl is, following tradition, an elementary school-
teacher, but the bad girl is a powerful corporate executive who has con-
tracted the protagonist's firm. To men like the hero of *Nothing in Common,*
power is aphrodisiac, not threat. To these guys, Madonna's metatext just

makes her sexier. She is still a whore, but whoredom had become kinder and gentler. The flip side of this economic egalitarianism is the new address to the subordinate woman. Becoming a sex object is still the prescribed mode of behavior, but Madonna's metatext indicates that this position promises more than temporary reward or comfortable dependence. It promises a route to independence, upward mobility, an escape from powerlessness.

Although middle-class women, lower-class women, and upper-class men working through the new gender relations of the capitalist economy certainly have conflicting material interests and very different uses for their readings of representations of female sexuality, the postmodern feminist articulation of the Boy Toy appealed to them all. Yet, however powerful these readings turned out to be, they did not invalidate the meanings preferred by the texts themselves. Not everyone was hip to the metatext. A lot of people who encountered Madonna were neither prone to postmodern interpretive habits (still seeking meaning at the manifest level of the work) nor immediately involved in negotiating an understanding of the new economic role of women. For this audience, from "traditional" feminists to porn hounds, the traditional patriarchal context of the sexual symbols Madonna employed was activated.

Madonna's Boy Toy phase was doubled coded. Although career narrative and video subtext created the postmodern feminist appeal, the manifest content of the videos also had strong appeal in traditional patriarchal terms. It is simply wishful thinking to imagine that anyone who comes up with a good old-fashioned sexist interpretation of these texts is misreading them. Madonna and her creative cohorts are not stupid. However they may have conceived her presentation as coding a form of female independence, they also knew damn well that when she ground her belly button, slithered on the floor, and stuck that coy finger between those pouty lips that a lot of men were going to be aroused and that these men would start talking about her, circulating her fame; a fair number of them would probably even buy a record or two. After all, the media industry is still controlled by men, and men compose a large part of the mass market. The patriarchal presence in both media production and consumption is strong enough that the presentation of a purely female-addressed set of codes is not going to make anyone an international superstar.

Of course, Madonna's core audience, around which the larger sphere of her celebrity would be spun, consisted of dance music fans, a group that is predominantly female. Boy Toy double-coding had the commercial advantage of appealing to two different conditions within this audience: the subject of patriarchy, interested in attracting the attention of men, and the subject of capital, interested in locating pragmatic means to individual gain. An added benefit of this double-coding (perhaps intentional, perhaps not, it really doesn't matter) was that by activating contradictory discourses, it

helped make Madonna a continuing subject of public controversy and debate, enhancing her fame and her status. Conversely, for the segment of the
audience most immersed in postmodern fragmentation, the conflict between
text and metatext could be resolved by reading neither as credible, so that
the referential aspects of the codes cancel each other out yet still leave a resi-
due of emotional intensity that amplifies the spectacle of detached signs that
remains.

Anyway, the idea that Boy Toy Madonna didn't stroke the male audience
and that she and everyone else didn't know it just doesn't wash. Virtually all
pro-Madonna statements from this period are of the "yes, but . . ." variety.
Her defenders recognized that her presentations would activate some nasty
sexist discourses, but they begged us to look at the other branch of the code,
too, to find the female independence and determination that the fans understood as the "real" Madonna. I think most wanna-bes understood, implicitly at least, the contradictions inherent in the Boy Toy image and resolved
the equation by determining that the increase in personal power and control
outweighed any loss from the general perpetuation of patriarchy.

Now, political purity is only possible in the realm of the idea. In the material world, no meaningful gain comes without compromise, without cost.
There is always some sort of trade-off involved. Yet, some deals are better
than others, and some stink altogether. I want to identify four points I think
we need to consider when we total up the bottom line for the Boy Toy's postmodern feminism.

The first problem is postmodernism itself. A culture dominated by superficial spectacle and the play of free-floating signifiers offers great political
advantages to the status quo. The cultural chaos has little effect on the material control mechanisms of the state—economic policy, bureaucratic regula-
tion, the police—but any would-be political opposition faces great problems—first, in merely identifying where the effects of subjugation actually
come from and, second, in reconstituting a meaningful language for organizing resistance into a political force. By appropriating powerful symbols
and stripping away their historically and socially situated meanings,
Madonnaism contributes to this general condition.

Second, although there is no question that participating in a sort of guer-
rilla warfare with symbols can feel very liberating, access to any particular
instance of such affective liberation is seldom, if ever, universally available.
Rather, it is dependent on a certain social and cultural position. Symbols
that have been appropriated in one context may still be doing business as
usual in another. If you walk down North Halstead Street in Chicago,
among the boutiques that cater to the hip, upwardly mobile young professionals that overpopulate the area, you will find a couple of shops specializ-
ing in sexual paraphernalia, with items related to *S/M* practices prominently
displayed. The atmosphere in these shops retains the hip ambience of the

rest of the street. The various leather appliances and giant dildos do not seem threatening here. Pornography is offered as fashion statement, and icons of bondage become signs of youthful rejection of the bounds of middle-class morality. Yet, one suspects that somewhere across town, the same icons are being employed with a more historically rooted and less friendly purpose. Unlike the shops on Halstead, the Boy Toy is not limited to a localized context. As massive as mass culture gets, Madonna's fame has proliferated her signs throughout society. In some quarters, they certainly were received as liberating appropriations, but in others, they just as certainly served to distribute and legitimate symbols that still stood as testaments to patriarchal power. Thus, middle-class "empowerment" may rest on the back of continued oppression across town.

Third, even for its middle-class subjects, postmodern feminism hardly constitutes the taming of patriarchy. The virginal ideal of the patriarchal feminine has been displaced, and capitalist imperatives now drive the discourses through which young women are directed to model their lives, but the other half of sexism's favorite dichotomy has snuck around into the backseat. As I write these words, Clarence Thomas has just been confirmed to the U.S. Supreme Court. In the last few weeks, *sexual harassment* has become a household phrase, and the U.S. Senate and the public opinion polls have educated us to its terms: The man charged will be considered the most likely victim; he may refuse to deal with the accusations while the woman who accuses him is put on trial, and most people don't think a few dirty words around the office are really that big of a deal anyway. And so the message to the career woman is: Business comes first, but we still might call on you to be a sex object on the side. And for all of Madonna's independence, for all of her power, she still offers her image as an object of the gaze—looking hot, tantalizingly cosmetized and costumed, ready and waiting for whatever use her audience may wish to make of her. Boy Toy feminism rests on a cynical calculation—sexual autonomy is a lost cause anyway and the female body is always already a token for male exchange, so we might as well try to get control of the transaction and attempt to get some cultural and economic independence out of the deal. Perhaps, as a male, it's not my place to judge, but having just watched Anita Hill being savaged on national TV, I think feminism ought to set its sights a little higher.

Fourth, in conclusion, postmodern feminism is simply not oppositional to the relevant powers that be—which, in case anyone hasn't noticed the entirety of Eastern Europe kissing the feet of Milton Friedman and the IMF, are the ever more hegemonic forces of transnational capital. The Boy Toy offers no challenge to the bottom-line market ideologies now directed at working women, nor to the patriarchal qualifier that getting ahead may require that the corporate female play along with the sexual imaginations of the boys in the boardroom. We are not witnessing a resistant subculture appropriating the dominant discourse here but the displacement of one dominant discourse by another and the enlistment of the subjugated population in question to help transform the cultural backstock from the old regime into liquid assets for the profit of the new masters.

IMAGES AND POWER

> I want to conquer the world. —Madonna

Shortly after her marriage to Sean Penn, Madonna dropped her Boy Toy persona and entered her Chameleon phase. Her more recent videos and shows have shed much of the troublesome gender politics of her early works—the sexuality in *Open Your Heart, Express Yourself,* and *Justify My Love* seems designed to shock, not titillate. Madonna's performances are increasingly arty, self-conscious, issue-oriented *statements*. The change is most apparent in the visual presentations of "Like a Virgin." In *Truth or Dare,* the song is presented onstage in a surreal context amid androgynous images and backstage as a blow against prudish repression of free speech. The image has moved light-years away from the teasing sex object representation of the original video.

Yet, Madonna has not simply dropped one (disreputable) image and taken on another (more legit) one. Instead, she has offered the audience a constantly shifting series of screen personas. Her appearance, performance style, genre references, thematic concerns, and attitude seem to change with each new hit tune and video. Yet, for all her imagistic instability, Madonna is even more popular and more talked about than before. It has really only been in this phase of her career that she has gained the exceptional celebrity and ubiquity that I noted at the beginning of this chapter.

Madonna is not the first pop artist to continually reappear in a variety of identities, to reinvent herself on a regular basis. In a way, she follows in the footsteps of such image-changers as Bob Dylan and David Bowie. Yet, Madonna's metamorphoses are different. Previous pop star reinventions of self are best interpreted in modernist terms, serving as signs of the performers' creative powers and aesthetic genius. Bowie creates a new identity much as an author creates a fictional character. We understand him as a cool, detached artiste, holding his private life away from his aestheticized creations. His poses are not so much reflections of himself as his studied reflections on culture and society. In contrast, Dylan fills his persona of the moment more completely. It extends beyond his performance, making his daily life into his work of art. Although Bowie and Dylan have assumed multiple personalities, their fans continue to view them as "authentic" performers, which, in the terms of rock philosophy, means that they are following a path of personal inspiration, rather than the dictates of the market. There is a form of romanticism in how fans understand the transformations undergone by these performers. The changes are the proof of "artistic vision."

However, this does not seem to be the case with the Material Girl. There seems to be no sense of an authentic Madonna behind all those changes of image, and she certainly isn't pursuing any sort of visionary aesthetic quest. Her context is purely postmodern, and she, like her milieu, is devoid of romantic aura. It is tempting, though, to view Chameleon Madonna as a mass market Cindy Sherman, offering our received images of women back to the media culture that spawned them but decontextualized and piled on top of one another in a way that reveals their constructedness, that subverts their hold on us. There are certainly textual similarities between Sherman's photos and Madonna's videos. However, the semiotic process through which Sherman's images acquire their status as feminist critique is dependent on their location within the world of high art. The fact that her photos are labeled as "art" and placed in galleries or museums instructs us to approach them with critical distance, to seek motive and hermeneutic depth within them. Yet, put the same images on a promotional calendar for a tool-supply firm and they would certainly inspire no such contemplation. They would simply constitute a smorgasbord of cheesecake with various flavor toppings. Postmodernist style signifies different things in the realms of high culture and mass culture, or perhaps it is more accurate to say that, in high culture, its fragmentations and pastiches of popular symbols signify a challenge to the modernist canon of the establishment, and in popular culture, they don't really signify anything at all.

Madonna does not maintain the sort of distance from her images that Sherman does. The audience knows that none of the star's presentations are the "real" Madonna Ciccone, that each is an affectation that results from a certain amount of calculation. Yet, the poses are not held at arm's length for the purpose of promoting critical reflection; they are embraced for the purpose of promoting consumption. Madonna's images are all presented as amplifications of her star status; they are all clothed in desire. A Cindy Sherman image says, "Interrogate me." A Madonna image says, "Buy Me!" Madonna is still an icon of glamor, still a cover girl. Her image transformations move with the rhythm of seasonal style changes in the world of high fashion because that is more or less what they are. Each provides a reinvigoration of the commodity cycle. "Have you got the new Madonna yet?"

If we simply read the surface texts of Madonna's changing image, we might see something like the poststructuralist vision of the decentered subject, a personal position defined not by an individual uniqueness but by a chaotic clash of intersecting and competing discourses—a sort of cultural schizophrenia. However, Madonna herself is not schizo because none of the discourses get inside her. Instead of different voices colliding *inside* the subject, Madonna selects a series of discourses to drape *outside* her subjectivity. The discourses pass in order, never really clashing because they're never in the same place at the same time.

Yet, Madonna still has an identity. It is located where it has always been located, at the point where the postmodern audience finds meaning—not in the manifest content of surface, not in the historical discourses beneath the surface, but *above* the surface, in the arena of exchange and wager in the pursuit of privilege and power. Madonna's fans are still tuned to the metatext, though its capitalist imperatives are inflected a bit differently in this new phase. In terms of the overt meanings in the texts themselves, Chameleon Madonna is simultaneously everywhere and nowhere, blithely and anarchically dabbling with a host of discourses, reducing them to surfaces and mixing them all together. There are few points of semiotic stability for the masses to grab hold of, few hooks on which to hang long-term interest. Metatextually, though, it's a different story. All the image changes, all the gaudy superficial displays are testaments to her clever saleswomanship in marketing herself, her adaptability to the late capitalist marketplace, and her power in the realm of the image.

Buying and selling have always figured heavily in Madonna's metatextual narrative, but her periodic metamorphoses make it easier to see exactly what is being bought and sold, what commodity is being exchanged for autonomy and adulation. In the Boy Toy phase, we might have understood Madonna as operating through the commodification of sexuality or street culture or even Catholic rebelliousness. Now, as the attitudes and subcultural references change from one video to the next, we can see that all these things are disposable. She still commodifies sexuality and subcultural style, but now these appear as merely particular marketing features adopted for each new issue of the product. None is essential to her appeal. The discourses she employs are but mere tools in the self-promotion through which she achieves self-determination. The one continuing, dominating presence in the sales pitch is Madonna herself. As superstar, as icon of adulation, as repository of power—*she* is the commodity.

Now, neither the commodification of entertainment personalities nor our awareness of it is anything new. To say that Madonna is a pure commodity figure and that all her poses are superficial and offered only for the sake of consumption is a limp (albeit true) critique that doesn't get to the heart of the matter. The important point here is that Madonna is seen to have made a *conscious* attempt to adopt this mode as a means of acquiring fame, fortune, and power, and she is seen to have been successful in doing so. What is interesting here is not that she is so thoroughly a self-promoter—this is not uncommon for a big star—but that she is openly so and that this is simply accepted by her fans. A number of commentators have pointed to her calculated manipulations and self-saleswomanship as if they have leveled a meaningful attack against her in the process. But the critics who assume that a charge of "sellout" is a cutting critique may as well be speaking a forgotten language from a bygone age. The audience replies, "So what's wrong with that?" Madonna tells Forrest Sawyer, "I crawled under my own table, OK?" and the fans know that it *is* OK because she knew what she was doing and she got what she wanted out of the deal—and, hey, Forrest, get with the program!

The truly remarkable thing here is that Madonna's conscious self-commodification may be the primary trait for which she is admired by her mainstream audience. This is a frightening indication of how deeply late capitalist values have been absorbed into our popular culture. Commodity values are more precious than human values. Our culture validates success no matter what is sacrificed to achieve it.

Actually, I suspect that at least a small part of Madonna's audience recognizes at some level that there is something frightening about what she has done, which makes her all the more fascinating. She has taken a Faustian gamble, seeming to have traded away her human soul for her success, but the moral of the story isn't in yet—maybe it's a reasonable deal after all! Madonna seems to be but one step ahead of the devil waiting to take his due, but she's still holding that lead. There may be no *truth* in Madonna, but there is one hell of a *dare*. This gives her an air of the sublime, of beauty wrapped within terror. This is not the hysterical sublime that Jameson (1984) describes as characterizing postmodernism, where semiotic fragmentation obscures the processes of capitalism and we experience the effects of capitalist relations with dread and awe precisely because we cannot locate their origins. This is more like the sublime of Colonel Kurtz in *Apocalypse Now*, of knowing full well that the path to desire leads through the Heart of Darkness and plunging into the jungle of commodity fetishism anyway.

But whether fans see Madonna as besting Mephistopheles or just male privilege, whether they wanna be Madonna or just wanna watch, their gaze is drawn by her power. And it is her ability to convert any substance at hand, from her own subjectivity to social controversy, into fuel for her quest for adulation and control that is the primary source of this power. Chameleon Madonna has taken on a succession of potent social and personal issues, incorporating into her videos a series of strong discourses aimed at contested cultural terrain. Her great triumph is to appropriate the signs of these struggles and to exploit them for their value as attention-getting display, to reduce deep psychology to the level of a Pepsi-Cola commercial, to subvert the symbols of struggle to the construction of her own celebrity. Her videos have regularly involved her in high traumas and dramas—pornographic exploitation in *Open Your Heart*, teen pregnancy in *Papa Don't Preach*, religion and racism in *Like a Prayer*, desire for a racial or cultural Other in *La Isla Bonita*, and

Cherish, sex, power, and cross-dressing in *Express Yourself*, gay flamboyance in *Vogue*, androgyny and public masturbation in the updated *Like a Virgin*, and bisexuality and S/M in *Justify My Love*. All of this is fairly heavy stuff, yet, interestingly enough, it has only generated a limited amount of controversy. Madonna has identified herself with all sorts of socially marginal groups or practices in these videos, the sorts of associations we would normally expect the mass audience to balk at, yet she remains hugely popular.

She is the Teflon idol, nothing sticks to her. The sleaze, the blasphemy, the perversity all slide off. Perhaps the audience recognizes that Madonna only inhabits these positions as if she were modeling a collection of fashions. She dresses up in them, prances around on the runway, then changes to a new one, unaffected for having worn them for a while. This is represented in the videos themselves, which always end with Madonna seemingly unfazed by the cultures and struggles she has encountered, dancing off screen to the perky disco bounce of the dance-pop audio track. Look, she puts herself on display for geeks in a peep show, then she bounces into the sunset. She conjures up a passionate Hispanic alter ego, then bounces happily down a Third World street. She confronts racial violence with the stigmata on her hands, then bounces joyfully in front of a smiling gospel choir. She hangs out with some seriously kinky sex outlaws, French-kisses another woman even—and then bounces away down the hall.

The discourses engaged by Chameleon Madonna have no claim on her. How could she be free for her ultimate self-actualization if she were bound to the historically rooted struggles of the subaltern groups who populate her videos? Thus, on the contrary, she demonstrates her autonomy over culture by showing herself unfazed by its most tempestuous conflicts, by transforming them into a fuel that makes the aura of her celebrity glow ever brighter. The fashion industry has long expropriated images of the exotic other in order to extract exchange value from their affective charge of mystery and danger. Madonna has translated and mastered this technique in terms of domestic subculture. She has won for herself an unlimited ticket for subcultural tourism—she can visit any exotic locale she likes, but she doesn't have to live there. The metatext remains unchanged, its message of upward mobility reinforced by her ability to bend the discourses of oppositional subcultures to the celebration of her own stardom. Behold Madonna, the bohemian from Dale Carnegie! Postmodern culture has not become depthless of its own accord; depth has been purposefully sucked out of it. To flatten culture is to deny its power and to assert power over it in return. Postmodernism may signal the death of ideology but not the death of cultural power, which has been reincarnated in the cut-and-paste blade of the mass-mediated bricoleur.

Regardless of what Madonna does to realize her own narrative of personal power, we are still with the question of what all this means for her audience. What about the claims that Madonna provides a cultural foundation for empowerment and resistance? How does Madonna's power figure in relation to the power of her fans?

Madonna's core audience is composed primarily of people belonging to subordinate social groups of varying degrees of marginality: from teenage girls to transvestite voguers. There are currently different aspects of Madonna's presentation that have specific appeals to different sorts of people, that are interpreted in different specific ways and have different specific cultural uses. I do not want to suggest that there is any sort of homogeneity among Madonna fans, yet I can't help but imagine that attraction to Madonna's image of seductive, semiotically unfettered power is a common thread that runs between them, an essential aspect of her appeal that cuts across other cultural boundaries.

The powerless are, quite logically, drawn to sources of power. They desire to be in its presence, hoping perhaps that some of it will rub off. Yet, if we observe this phenomenon generally, we see that it often has negative consequences. Too often the readily available icons of power represent nothing but an alternative set of traps. The subordinate face a cultural double whammy. The dominant system aims first of all to deny them any power whatsoever. To this end, the system barrages them with discourses promoting apathy, resignation, passivity: "Stay where you belong. Shut up. Accept your fate." Of course, this doesn't work all the time. The entire subject population can't be beaten down. Rebellion against the dictates of powerless passivity is inevitable, so the system has evolved ways to channel and redirect this energy to its own benefit. After all, the forces of the status quo have a strong hand in deciding which forms of resistance to powerlessness will be materially rewarded and which will not. It is no accident, I think, that the paths to empowerment that offer the biggest payoffs—from the lottery to crack dealing to becoming a token minority official in the Reagan/Bush administration—support institutions or practices that prey on the rest of the subaltern and act to keep them in their place. On the other hand, effective organizing for serious political opposition among the dominated just gets you permanently locked up or killed. Drug outlaws cruise the street in BMWs. Clarence Thomas is nominated to the Supreme Court. Leonard Peltier is in prison for life, framed for murder by the FBI, and Fred Hampton is dead, ambushed in his sleep by the police.

And for those who do not get the message from the consequences, there is always mass-produced culture. The culture industry specializes in popularizing and validating forms of escape from oppression that double back and create more of the same. In fact, the entertainment media hardly support the discourses of submissiveness at all anymore, ceding almost all responsibility for this ideological imperative to the institutions that always carried the bulk of it anyway: politics, education, and the personal cultures of family and work. Instead, the media present the subordinate with an endless procession of romanticized outlaws and Horatio Alger success stories. Once rebellious subordinates attain the escape velocity needed to break away from abject powerlessness, they are not going to pause, reflect, and philosophize on where that energy might be best directed; they are going to head for the first exit sign they see, which will probably have been placed there by the mass media.

And here is Madonna, outlaw and Horatio Alger all rolled into one. She seems to have found the best of all possible paths to empowerment by focusing different addresses on the realms of culture and the economy. As long as her rebelliousness is merely cultural and poses no threat to the established economic order (which, on the contrary, it aids rather nicely), she need only fend off a few outraged moralists. These opponents have only minor influence on the powers of police action and judicial enforcement, and their attempts at suppression are easily ducked (if you have Madonna's money and connections, that is). On the other hand, as long as her complicity with the establishment is merely economic, she can maintain a rebellious image that allows for identification by the subordinate audience. This position has enormous commercial value because its mixed mythology appeals to people in a wide variety of sociocultural positions, addressing wish fulfillments of everyone from street kids who want to believe that cultural rebellion might actually take them someplace to yuppie women who want to believe that their corporate upward mobility isn't really a sellout and that they can still maintain an expressive nonconformist independence.

Of course, the problem is that, for the most part, the street rebels aren't going anywhere and the yuppies *have* sold out. Madonna culture can be a means for all of us to kid ourselves that things are actually better than they are. After all, the historical political function of the Horatio Alger myth is to justify the fact that a majority of citizens receive a raw deal from society by saying, "But look, the path to success *is* open. To anyone!" and by enlisting the seekers in the promotion of the very values and practices that created the inequalities and injustices in the first place.

Yet, I don't think that most of the mass audience believes that the Horatio Alger myth is directly relevant to them anymore. We have become a people who imagine ourselves powerless. Citizens are totally disinterested in politics, believing, not without cause, that they have no influence on public affairs. Fatalistic slogans abound. "Shit Happens" is the philosophy of the day. Power may be still be desired, but we no longer believe it can actually be held. It is no longer, in fact, real. It is truly comprehensible only as a dream or, rather, a story on the evening news. And so the masses, eternally apart from their desire, worship its image at the nineteen-inch altar. In this, marginal subcultures and mainstream wanna-bes find oneness in their fandom of Madonna.

Power is, ultimately, a material issue. Feeling empowered and being empowered are not the same thing. For Madonna to be truly empowering to her fans, her recordings and videos would need to do more than help them feel good by allowing them to join the celebration of her successful quest for attention and control. Her work would need to present the fans with some sort of blueprint adaptable to their own struggle for self-determination. She would need, indeed, to be a role model. The only guidance available from the Madonna metatext follows the basic precepts of Reaganism: Be selfish, competitive, use whatever you can to reach the material position on which self-actualization depends and to hell with anyone or anything that stands in your way. History has shown that this is hardly a plan for the liberation of the masses. At best, it offers a means for the plucky few to climb to success on the backs of their brothers and sisters—call it the "Clarence Thomas strategy."

More importantly, the only tools Madonnaism identifies for realizing its quest are the ones Madonna herself has employed, the capture and manipulation of images. Ultimately, Madonna's power is tied to her ability to have her image reproduced and distributed. Each image dispersed throughout the culture is another validation of worth. In postmodern culture, only a picture can testify that we exist, that we matter. The twenty-seven-year-old Madonna fan I quoted earlier is a part-time photographic model. She tells me that she went into modeling because she suffers from low self-esteem, and if she has attractive and interesting pictures of herself, then she can feel attractive and interesting rather than hopelessly inadequate. She doesn't make much money modeling. Mostly she poses free for photographers building their portfolio, who provide her with prints in return. Her own portfolio book is probably her most prized possession, even though she rarely has call to show it to clients. Her hopes and even her will seem to be stored between its covers. In *Truth or Dare,* Madonna is asked, "Do you want to talk at all off-camera?" She shakes her head. Then Warren Beatty interjects, "She doesn't want to live off-camera. . . . There's nothing to say off-camera. Why would you say something if it's off-camera. What point is there of existing?" Madonna herself says: "People think that being a star is about being fabulous, being in the spotlight, having your picture taken all the time, and having everyone worship and adore you. . . . And you know what? They're absolutely right" (voiceover in MTV's "Breakfast with Madonna").

"America's Funniest Home Videos" notwithstanding, the masses cannot follow Madonna's path to empowerment because they cannot disseminate mediated images of themselves throughout the world. The gates to the dream world of the screen open only to the few who are useful to cultural industry's search for maximized profit. Madonna can be idolized but not really emulated. Her power exists only in the hyperreality of the postmodern media spectacle, which is available to regular folks only as something to sit and watch, something to buy.

REFERENCES

Baudrillard, Jean. (1980). "The Implosion of Meaning in the Media and the Implosion of the Social in the Masses." In K. Woodward (ed.), *The Myths of Information: Technology and Postindustrial Culture.* Madison, Wis.: Coda Press, pp. 137–148.

———. (1983). "The Ecstasy of Communication." In H. Foster (ed.), *The Anti-aesthetic.* Port Townsend, Wash.: Bay Press, pp. 131–132.

Christgau, Robert. (1991). "Madonnathinking, Madonnabout, Madonnamusic." *Village Voice,* May 28, pp. 31–33.

Denby, David. (1991). "Nothing to Hide." *New York,* May 20, p. 58.

Fisher, Carrie. (1991). "True Confessions: The *Rolling Stone* Interview with Madonna." *Rolling Stone,* June 13, pp. 35–39, 120 (part one); June 27, pp. 45–49, 78 (part two).

Fiske, John. (1987). "British Cultural Studies and Television." In R. Allen (ed.), *Channels of Discourse.* Chapel Hill: University of North Carolina Press, pp. 254–289.

———. (1989). *Reading the Popular.* Boston, Mass.: Unwin Hyman.

Glamour. (1990). "Women of the Year." December, pp. 96–101.

Jameson, Fredric. (1984). "Postmodernism, or The Cultural Logic of Late Capitalism." *New Left Review* 146 (July–August): 53–92.

Kaplan, E. Ann. (1987). *Rocking Around the Clock.* New York: Methuen.

Kaufman, Stanley. (1991). "Naked Truths." *The New Republic,* June 10, pp. 26–27.

McClary, Susan. (1991). *Feminine Endings: Music, Gender and Sexuality.* Minneapolis: University of Minnesota Press.

People. (1991). "Fifty Most Beautiful People," Extra edition. Summer, p. 109.

Sragow, Michael. (1991). Capsule review of *Truth or Dare. Time,* June 10, p. 29.

Tresniowski, Alexander. (1991). "A Look at the Books on Madonna." *Time,* September 16, p. 75.

US. (1991). Cover. June 13.

12

"Material Girl": The Effacements of Postmodern Culture

PLASTICITY AS POSTMODERN PARADIGM

In a culture in which organ transplants, life-extension machinery, microsurgery and artificial organs have entered everyday medicine, we seem on the verge of practical realization of the seventeenth-century imagination of the body as machine. But if we seem to have technically and technologically realized that conception, it can also be argued that metaphysically we have deconstructed it. In the early modern era, machine imagery helped to articulate a totally determined human body whose basic functionings the human being was helpless to alter. The then dominant metaphors for this body—clocks, watches, collections of springs—imagined a system that is set, wound up, whether by nature or God the watchmaker, ticking away in predictable, orderly manner, regulated by laws over which the human being has no control. Understanding the system, we can help it to perform efficiently, and intervene when it malfunctions. But we cannot radically alter the configuration of things.

Pursuing this modern, determinist fantasy to its limits, fed by the currents of consumer capitalism, modern ideologies of the self, and their crystallization in the dominance of "American" mass culture, Western science and technology have now arrived, paradoxically but predictably (for it was a submerged, illicit element in the mechanist conception all along) at a new, "postmodern" imagination of human freedom from bodily determination. Gradually and surely, a technology that was first aimed at the replacement of malfunctioning parts has generated an industry and an ideology fueled by

Reprinted with permission from *Michigan Quarterly Review* and Susan Bordo from "'Material Girl': The Effacements of Postmodern Culture," *Michigan Quarterly Review*, 29, no. 4 (Fall 1990): 653–677.

fantasies of re-arranging, transforming, and correcting, an ideology of limit-less improvement and change, defying the historicity, the mortality, and in-deed the very materiality of the body. In place of that materiality, we now have what I will call "cultural plastic." In place of God the watchmaker, we now have ourselves, the master sculptors of that plastic. This disdain for ma-terial limits, and intoxication with freedom, change, and self-determination, is enacted not only on the level of the contemporary technology of the body but in a wide range of contexts, including much of contemporary discourse on the body, both casual and theoretical, popular and academic. In this es-say, looking at a variety of these discursive contexts, I will attempt to de-scribe key elements of this paradigm of plasticity, and expose some of its ef-facements—the material and social realities that it denies or renders invisible.

FIGURE I

PLASTIC BODIES

"Create a masterpiece, sculpt your body into a work of art," urges *Fit* magazine (FIG. 1). "You visualize what you want to look like, and then you create that form." "The challenge presents itself: to rearrange things." "It's up to you to do the chiseling. You become the master sculptress."[1] The preciartsion technology of body-sculpting, once the secret of the Arnold Schwarzeneggers and Rachel McLishes of the professional body-building world, has now become available to anyone who can afford the price of membership in a gym. "I now look at bodies," (says John Travolta, after training for the movie *Staying Alive*) "almost like pieces of clay that can be molded."[2] On the medical front, plastic surgery, whose repeated and purely cosmetic employment has been legitimated by Michael Jackson, Cher and others, has become a fabulously expanding industry, extending its domain from nose jobs, face lifts, tummy tucks and breast augmentations to collagen-plumped lips and liposuction-shaped ankles, calves and buttocks. In 1989, 681,000 procedures were done, up 80% over 1981; over half of these were performed on patients between the ages of eighteen and thirty-five.[3] The trendy *Details* magazine describes "surgical stretching, tucking and sucking [as] another fabulous [fashion] accessory," and invites readers to share their cosmetic surgery experiences in their monthly column "Knifestyles of the Rich and Famous" (FIG. 2). In that column, the transportation of fat from one part of the body to another is described as breezily as changing hats:

> Dr. Brown is an artist. He doesn't just pull and tuck and forget about you. . . .
> He did liposuction on my neck, did the nose job and tightened up my forehead
> to give it a better line. Then he took some fat from the side of my waist and in-
> jected it into my hands. It goes in as a lump, and then he smooths it out with his
> hands to where it looks good. I'll tell you something, the nose and neck made a
> big change, but nothing in comparison to how fabulous my hands look. The fat
> just smoothed out all the lines, the veins don't stick up anymore, the skin actu-
> ally looks soft and great. [But] you have to be careful not to bang your hands.[4]

Popular culture does not apply any brakes to these fantasies of rearrangement and self-transformation. Rather, we are constantly told that we can "choose" our own bodies (FIG. 3). "The proper diet, the right amount of exercise and you can have, pretty much, any body you desire," claims Evian. Of course, the rhetoric of choice and self-determination and the breezy analogies comparing cosmetic surgery to fashion accessorizing are deeply mystifying. They efface, not only the inequalities of privilege, money, and time that prohibit most people from indulging in these practices, but the desperation that characterizes the lives of those who do. "I will do anything, *anything,* to make myself look and feel better" says Tina Lizardi (whose "Knifestyle" experience I quoted from above). Medical science has now des-

FIGURE 2

Phyllis Diller's Resumé

- Hard contact lenses. 1960.
- Soft contact lenses. 1970.
- Teeth straightened. 1970. Dr. Budd Rubin (San Diego)
- Complete face-lift: nose job (rhinoplasty), eyes (above and below), neck job. 1971. Dr. Franklin L. Ashley (Los Angeles)
- Breast reduction. 1974. Dr. Franklin L. Ashley
- Tummy tuck. 1976. Dr. Franklin L. Ashley
- Teeth bonded. 1980. Dr. Ronald Goldstein (Atlanta)
- Mini-lift (face). 1981. Dr. Franklin L. Ashley
- Teeth bonded. 1984. Dr. Alfred Menzies (Los Angeles)
- Teeth bonded. 1985. Dr. John Lake (Palm Springs)
- Brow-lift. 1985. Dr. Michael Elam, Dr. Frederick Berkowitz (Newport Beach)
- Nose job. 1985. Dr. Michael Elam, Dr. Frederick Berkowitz
- Under-eye lift. 1985. Dr. Michael Elam, Dr. Frederick Berkowitz
- Cheek implants. 1985. Dr. Michael Elam, Dr. Frederick Berkowitz
- Eyeliner tattoo. 1985. Dr. Warren Katz (Dallas)
- Chemical peel. 1986. Dr. Michael Elam, Dr. Frederick Berkowitz
- Fat liposuctioned from stomach and injected into deep vertical wrinkles around mouth. 1987. Dr. Steven M. Hoefflin, F.A.C.S. (Santa Monica)

FIGURE 3

FIGURE 4

ignated a new category of "polysurgical addicts" (or, as more casually referred to, "scalpel slaves") who return for operation after operation, in perpetual quest of the elusive yet ruthlessly normalizing goal, the "perfect" body.[5] The dark underside of the practices of body transformation and rearrangement reveals botched and sometimes fatal operations, exercise addictions, eating disorders. And of course, despite the claims of the Evian ad, one cannot have *any* body that one wants—for not every body will *do*. The very advertisements whose copy speaks of choice and self-determination visually legislate the effacement of individual and cultural difference and circumscribe our choices (FIG. 4).

That we are surrounded by homogenizing and normalizing images—images whose content is far from arbitrary, but instead suffused with the dominance of gendered, racial, class, and other cultural iconography—seems so obvious as to be almost embarrassing to be arguing here. Yet contemporary understandings of the behaviors I have been describing not only construct the situation very differently, but in terms that preempt precisely such a critique of cultural imagery. Moreover, they reproduce, on the level of discourse and interpretation, the same conditions which postmodern bodies enact on the level of cultural practice: a construction of life as plastic possibility and weightless choice, undetermined by history, social location, or even individual biography. A recent "Donahue" show offers my first illustration.

The show's focus was a series of television commercials for DuraSoft colored contact lenses. In these commercials (as they were originally aired), a woman was shown in a dreamlike, romantic fantasy—for example, parachuting slowly and gracefully from the heavens. The male voiceover then described the woman in soft, lush terms: "If I believed in angels, I'd say that's what she was—an angel, dropped from the sky like an answer to a prayer, with eyes as brown as bark." [significant pause] "No . . . I *don't think so.*"

FIGURE 5

[At this point, the tape would be rewound to return us to:] "With eyes as violet as the colors of a child's imagination." The commercial concludes: "DuraSoft colored contact lenses. Get brown eyes a second look" (FIG. 5).

The question posed by Donahue: Is this ad racist? Donahue clearly thought there was controversy to be stirred up here, for he stocked his audience full of women of color and white women to discuss the implications of the ad. But Donahue, apparently, was living in a different decade than most of his audience, who found nothing "wrong" with the ad, and everything "wrong" with any inclinations to "make it a political question." Here are some comments taken from the transcript of the show:

"Why does it have to be a political question? I mean, people perm their hair. It's just because they like the way it looks. It's not something sociological. Maybe black women like the way they look with green contacts. It's to be more attractive. It's not something that makes them—I mean, why do punk rockers have purple hair? Because they feel it makes them feel better." [white woman]

"What's the fuss? When I put on my blue lenses, it makes me feel good. It makes me feel sexy, different, the other woman, so to speak, which is like fun." [black woman]

"I perm my hair, you're wearing makeup, what's the difference?" [ww]

"I want to be versatile . . . having different looks, being able to change from one look to the other." [bw model]

"We all do the same thing, when we're feeling good we wear new makeup, hairstyles, we buy new clothes. So now it's contact lenses. What difference does it make?" [ww]

"It goes both ways . . . Bo Derek puts her hair in cornstalks, or corn . . . or whatever that thing is called. White women try to get tan." [ww]

"She's not trying to be white, she's trying to be different." [about a black woman with blue contact lenses]

"It's fashion, women are never happy with themselves."

"I put them in as toys, just for fun, change. Nothing too serious, and I really enjoy them." [bw][6]

Some things to note here: First, making up, fixing one's hair and so forth are conceived only as free *play*, fun, a matter of creative expression. The one comment that hints at women's (by now depressingly well-documented) dissatisfaction with their appearance trivializes that dissatisfaction and puts it beyond the pale of cultural critique: "It's fashion." What she means is: "It's *only* fashion," whose whimsical and politically neutral vicissitudes supply endless amusement for woman's eternally superficial values. ("Women are never happy with themselves.") If we are never happy with ourselves, it is implied, that is due to our female nature, not to be taken too seriously or made into a "political question." Second, the "contents" of fashion, the specific ideals that women are drawn to embody (ideals that vary historically, racially, and along class and other lines) are seen as arbitrary, without meaning; interpretation is neither required nor even appropriate. Rather, all motivation and value comes from the interest and allure—the "sexiness"—of change and difference itself. Blue contact lenses for black women, it is admitted, make one "other" ("the other woman"). But that "other" is not a racial or cultural "other"; she is "sexy" because of the piquancy, the novelty, the erotics of putting on a different self. *Any* different self would do, it is implied. Closely connected to this is the construction of *all* cosmetic changes as the same: perms for white women, corn rows on Bo Derek, tanning, makeup, changing hairstyles, blue contacts for black women—all are seen as having equal political valance (which is to say *no* political valance) and the same cultural meaning (which is to say *no* cultural meaning) in the heterogeneous yet undifferentiated context of "the things women do" "to look better, be more attractive." The one woman in the audience who offered a different construction of things, who insisted that the styles we aspire to do not simply reflect the free play of fashion or female nature—who went as far, indeed, as to claim that we "are brainwashed to think blond hair and blue eyes is the most beautiful of all," was regarded with hostile silence. Then, a few moments later, someone challenged: "Is there anything *wrong* with blue eyes and blond hair?" The audience enthusiastically applauded this defender of democratic values.

This "conversation"—a paradigmatically postmodern conversation, as I will argue shortly—effaces the same general elements as the rhetoric of body-transformation discussed earlier. First, it effaces the inequalities of social position and the historical origins which, for example, render Bo Derek's corn rows and black women's hair-straightening utterly non-commensurate. On the one hand we have Bo Derek's privilege, not only as so unimpeachably white as to afford an exotic touch of Otherness with no danger of racial contamination, but her trend-setting position as a famous movie star. Contrasting to this, and mediating a black woman's "choice" to straighten her hair, is a cultural history of racist body-discriminations such as the nineteenth-century comb-test, which allowed admission to churches and clubs only to those blacks who could pass through their hair without snagging a fine-tooth comb hanging outside the door. (A variety of comparable tests—the pine-slab test, the brown bag test—determined whether or not one's skin was adequately light to pass muster.)[7]

Second, and following from these historical practices, there is a "disciplinary" reality that is effaced in the construction of all self-transformation as equally arbitrary, all variants of the same trivial game, without differing cultural valance. I use the term "disciplinary" here in the Foucauldian sense, as pointing to practices which do not merely transform, but *normalize* the subject. That is, and to repeat a point made earlier, not every body will do. A recent poll of *Essence* magazine readers revealed that 68% of those who responded wear their hair straightened chemically or by hot comb.[8] "Just 'for fun'?" The kick of being "different"? Looking at the pursuit of beauty as a normalizing discipline, it is clear that not all body-transformations are "the same." The general tyranny of fashion—perpetual, elusive, and instructing the female body in a pedagogy of personal inadequacy and lack—is a powerful discipline for the normalization of *all* women in this culture. But even as we are all normalized to the requirements of appropriate feminine insecurity and preoccupation with appearance, more specific requirements emerge in different cultural and historical contexts, and for different groups. When Bo Derek put her hair in corn rows, she was engaging in normalizing feminine practice. But when Oprah Winfrey admitted on her show that all her life she has desperately longed to have "hair that swings from side to side" when she shakes her head (FIG. 6), she revealed the power of racial as well as gender normalization, normalization not only to "femininity," but to the Caucasian standards of beauty that still dominate on television, in movies, in popular magazines. Neither Oprah nor the *Essence* readers have creatively or playfully invented themselves here.

DuraSoft knows this, even if Donahue's audience does not. Since the campaign first began, the company has replaced the original, upfront magazine advertisement with a more euphemistic variant, from which the word "brown" has been tastefully effaced. (In case it had become too subtle for the average reader, the model now is black.) [FIG. 7] In the television commercial, a comparable "brownwash" was affected; here "eyes as brown as . . ." was retained, but the derogatory nouns—"brown as boots," "brown as bark"—were eliminated. The announcer simply was left speechless: "eyes as brown as . . . brown as . . ." and then, presumably having been unable to come up with a enticing simile, shifted to "violet." As in the expurgated magazine ad, the television commercial ended: "Get *your* eyes a second look."

When I showed my students these ads, many of them were as dismissive as the Donahue audience, convinced that I was once again turning innocent images and practices into "political issues." I persisted: if racial standards of beauty are not at work here, then why no brown contacts for blue-eyed people? A month later, two of my students triumphantly produced a DuraSoft ad for brown contacts (FIG. 8), from *Essence* magazine, and with an advertising campaign directed solely at black consumers, offering the promise *not* of "getting blue eyes a second look" by becoming excitingly darker, but of "subtly enhancing" already dark eyes, by making them *lighter* brown. The creators of the DuraSoft campaign clearly know that not all "differences" are the same in our culture, and they continue, albeit in ever more mystified form, to exploit and perpetuate that fact.

FIGURE 6

FIGURE 7

FIGURE 8

PLASTIC DISCOURSE

The Donahue-DuraSoft show (and indeed, any talk show one might happen to tune to) provides a perfect example of what we might call a postmodern conversation. All sense of history and all ability (or inclination) to sustain cultural criticism, to make the distinctions and discriminations which would permit such criticism, have disappeared. Rather, in this conversation, "anything goes"—and any positioned social critique (for example, the woman who, speaking clearly from consciousness of racial oppression, insisted that the attraction of blond hair and blue eyes has a cultural meaning significantly different from that of purple hair) is immediately de-stabilized. Instead of distinctions, endless *differences* reign—an undifferentiated pastiche of differences, a grab-bag in which no items are assigned any more importance or centrality than any others. Television is, of course, the great teacher here, our prime modeler of plastic pluralism: if one Donahue show features a feminist talking about battered wives, the next day a show will feature mistreated husbands. Incest, exercise addictions, women who love too much, the sex habits of priests, disturbed children of psychiatrists, male strippers—all have their day, all are given equal weight by the great leveler: the frame of the television screen.

This spectacle of difference defeats the ability to sustain coherent political critique. Everything is the same in its unvalanced difference. ("I perm my hair. You're wearing makeup. What's the difference?") Particulars reign, and generality—which collects, organizes and prioritizes, suspending attention to particularity in the interests of connection, emphasis and criticism—is suspect. So, whenever some critically charged generalization was suggested on the Donahue-DuraSoft show, someone else would invariably offer a counter-example—e.g., "I have blue eyes, and I'm a black woman," "Bo Derek wears corn rows"—to fragment the critique. What is remarkable is that people accept these examples *as* "refutations" of social critique. They almost invariably back down, utterly confused as to how to maintain their critical generalization in the face of the de-stabilizing example. Sometimes they qualify, claiming they meant "some" people, not all. But of course, they neither meant all, nor some. They meant *most*—that is, they were trying to make a claim about social or cultural *patterns*—and that is a stance that is increasingly difficult to sustain in a postmodern context, where we are surrounded by endlessly displaced images and no orienting context to make discriminations.

Those who insist on an orienting context (and who therefore do not permit particulars to reign in all their absolute "difference") are seen as "totalizing," that is, as constructing a falsely coherent and morally coercive universe that marginalizes and effaces the experiences and values of others. ("What's *wrong* with blond hair and blue eyes?") As someone who is frequently interviewed by local television and newspaper reporters, I have often found my feminist arguments framed in this way, as they were in a recent article on breast augmentation surgery. After several pages of "expert" recommendations from plastic surgeons, my cautions about the politics of female body transformation (none of them directed against individuals contemplating plastic surgery, all of them of a "cultural" nature) were briefly quoted by the reporter, who then went on to end the piece with a comment on *my* critique—from the director of communications for the American Society of Plastic and Reconstructive Surgery:

> Those not considering plastic surgery shouldn't be too critical of those who do. It's the hardest thing for people to understand. What's important is if it's a problem to that person. We're all different, but we all want to look better. We're just different in what extent we'll go to. But none of us can say we don't want to look the best we can.[9]

With this tolerant, egalitarian stroke, the media liaison of the most powerful plastic surgery lobby in the country presents herself as the protector of "difference" against the homogenizing and stifling regime of the feminist dictator.

*   *   *

Academics do not usually like to think of themselves as embodying the values and preoccupations of popular culture on the plane of high theory or intellectual discourse. We prefer to see ourselves as the de-mystifyers of popular discourse, bringers-to-consciousness-and-clarity rather than unconscious reproducers of culture. Despite what we would *like* to believe of ourselves, however, we are always within the society that we criticize, and never so strikingly as at the present postmodern moment. All the elements of what I have here called "postmodern conversation"—intoxication with individual choice and creative *jouissance,* delight with the piquancy of particularity and mistrust of pattern and seeming coherence, celebration of "difference" along with an absence of critical perspective differentiating and weighting "differences," suspicion of the totalitarian nature of generalization along with a rush to protect difference from its homogenizing abuses—all have become recognizable and familiar elements of much of contemporary intellectual discourse. Within this theoretically self-conscious universe, moreover, these elements are not merely embodied (as in the Donahue/DuraSoft conversation) but are explicitly thematized and *celebrated*—as inaugurating new constructions of the self, no longer caught in the mythology of the unified subject, embracing of multiplicity, challenging the dreary and moralizing generalizations about gender, race, and so forth that have so preoccupied liberal and left humanism.

For this celebratory, academic postmodernism, it has become highly un-fashionable—and "totalizing"—to talk about the grip of culture on the body. Such a perspective, it is argued, casts active and creative subjects as "cultural dopes," "passive dupes" of ideology; it gives too much to domi-nant ideology, imagining it as seamless and univocal, overlooking both the gaps which are continually allowing for the eruption of "difference" and the polysemous, unstable, open nature of all cultural texts. To talk about the grip of culture on the body (as, for example, in "old" feminist discourse about the objectification and sexualization of the female body) is to fail to acknowledge, as one theorist put it, "the cultural work by which nomadic, fragmented, active subjects confound dominant discourse."[10]

So, for example, contemporary culture critic John Fiske is harshly critical of what he describes as the view of television as a "dominating monster" with "homogenizing power" over the perceptions of viewers. Such a view, he argues, imagines the audience as "powerless and undiscriminating," and overlooks the fact that:

Pleasure results from a particular relationship between meanings and power. . . . There is no pleasure in being a "cultural dope." . . . Pleasure results from the production of meanings of the world and of self that are felt to serve the inter-ests of the reader rather than those of the dominant. The subordinate may be disempowered, but they are not powerless. There is a power in resisting power, there is a power in maintaining one's social identity in opposition to that pro-posed by the dominant ideology, there is a power in asserting one's own subcul-tural values against the dominant ones. There is, in short, a power in being dif-ferent.[11]

Fiske then goes on to produce numerous examples of how *Dallas, Hart to Hart,* and so forth have been read (or so he argues) by various subcultures to make their own "socially pertinent" and empowering meanings out of "the semiotic resources provided by television."

Note, in Fiske's insistent, repetitive invocation of the category of "power," a characteristically postmodern flattening of the terrain of power-relations, a lack of differentiation between, for example, the "power" in-volved in creative *reading* in the isolation of one's own home and the "power" held by those who control the material production of television shows, or the "power" involved in public protest and action against the con-ditions of that production, or the dominant meanings—e.g., racist and sex-ist images and messages—therein produced. For Fiske, of course, there *are* no such dominant meanings, that is, no elements whose ability to grip the imagination of the viewer is greater than the viewer's ability to "just say no," through resistant reading of the text. That ethnic and subcultural meaning *may* be wrested from *Dallas* and *Hart to Hart* becomes proof that dominat-ing images and messages are only in the mind of those totalitarian critics who would condescendingly "rescue" the disempowered from those forces that are in fact the very medium of their creative freedom and resistance ("the semiotic resources of television").

Fiske's conception of "power"—a terrain without hills and valleys, where all "forces" have become "resources"—reflects a very common postmodern misappropriation of Foucault. Fiske conceives of power as the *possession* of individuals or groups, something they "have"—a conception Foucault takes great pains to criticize—rather than (as in Foucault's reconstruction) a dynamic of non-centralized forces, its dominant historical forms attaining their hegemony, not from magisterial design or decree, but through multiple "processes, of different origin and scattered location," regulating and normalizing the most intimate and minute elements of the construction of time, space, desire, embodiment.[12] This conception of power does *not* entail that there are no dominant positions, social structures or ideologies emerging from the play of forces; the fact that power is not held by any *one* does not entail that it is equally held by *all*. It is "held" by no one; rather, people and groups are positioned differentially within it. This model is particularly useful to the analysis of male dominance and female subordination, so much of which is reproduced "voluntarily," through our self-normalization to everyday habits of masculinity and femininity. (Fiske calls this being a "cultural dope.") Within such a model, one can acknowledge that women may indeed contribute to the perpetuation of female subordination (for example, by embracing, taking "pleasure" in, and even feeling empowered by the cultural objectification and sexualization of the female body) without this entailing that they have "power" in the production and reproduction of sexist culture.

Foucault does insist on the *instability* of modern power relations—that is, that resistance is perpetual and unpredictable, and hegemony precarious. This notion is transformed by Fiske (perhaps under the influence of a more deconstructionist brand of postmodernism) into a notion of resistance as *jouissance,* a creative and pleasurable eruption of cultural "difference" through the "seams" of the text. What this celebration of creative-reading-as-resistance effaces is the arduous and frequently frustrated historical struggle that is required for the subordinate to articulate and assert the value of their "difference" in the face of dominant meanings—meanings which often offer a pedagogy directed at the reinforcement of feelings of inferiority, marginality, ugliness. During the *Brown v. the Board of Education* trials, as a demonstration of the destructive psychological effects of segregation, black children were asked to look at two baby dolls, identical in all respects except color. The children were asked a series of questions: which is the nice doll? which is the bad doll? which doll would you like to play with? The majority of black children, Kenneth Clark reports, attributed the positive characteristics to the white doll, and negative characteristics to the black. When Clark asked one final question—"which doll is like you?"—they looked at

FIGURE 9

him, as he says, "as though he were the devil himself" for putting them in that predicament, for forcing them to face the inexorable and hideous logical implications of their situation. Northern children often ran out of the room; southern children tended to answer the question in shamed embarrassment. Clark recalls one little boy who laughed, "Who am I like? That doll! It's a nigger and I'm a nigger!"[13]

Not acknowledging the hegemonic power of normalizing imagery can be just as effacing of people's experiences as lack of attentiveness to cultural and ethnic differences, and just as implicated in racial bias—as postmodern critics sometimes seem to forget. A recent article in *Essence* described the experience of a young black woman who had struggled with compulsive overeating and dieting for years and who had finally gone to seek advice from her high-school guidance counselor, only to be told that she didn't have to

FIGURE 10   FIGURE 11

worry about managing her weight because "black women can go beyond the stereotype of woman as sex object" and "fat is more acceptable in the black community." Saddled with the white woman's projection onto her of the stereotype of the asexual, material Mammy, the young woman was left to struggle with an eating disorder that she wasn't "supposed" to have.[14]

. None of this is to *deny* what Fiske calls "the power of being different," but rather to insist that it is won through ongoing political *struggle* rather than through an act of creative interpretation. Here, once again, although many postmodern academics may claim Foucault as their guiding light, they differ from him in significant and revealing ways. For Foucault, the metaphorical terrain of resistance is explicitly that of the "battle"; the "points of confrontation" may be "innumerable" and "instable," but they involve a serious, often deadly struggle of embodied (that is, historically situated and shaped) forces.[15] Barbara Kruger exemplifies this conception of resistance in a poster which represents the contemporary contest over reproductive control via the metaphor of the body as battleground (FIG. 9). The metaphor of the body as battleground (rather than postmodern playground) more adequately captures, as well, the *practical* difficulties involved in the political struggle to empower "difference." *Essence* magazine consciously and strenuously has tried to promote images of black strength, beauty, and self-acceptance. Beauty features celebrate the glory of black skin and lush lips; other departments feature interviews with accomplished black women writers, activists, teachers, many of whom model styles of body and dress that challenge the hegemony of white Anglo-Saxon standards. The magazine's advertisers, however, continually elicit and perpetuate consumers' feelings of inadequacy and insecurity over their racial bodies. They insist that hair must be straightened (and eyes lightened) in order to be beautiful; they almost always employ models with fair skin, Anglo-Saxon features and "hair that moves," ensuring associations of their products with fantasies of becoming what white culture most prizes and rewards. This ongoing battle over the black woman's body and the "power" of its "difference" is made manifest in the recent 20th anniversary issue, where a feature celebrating "The beauty of black" *faced* an advertisement visually legislating virtually the opposite (and offering, significantly, "escape") [FIGS. 10 AND 11]. This invitation to cognitive dissonance reveals what *Essence* must grapple with, in every issue, as it tries to keep its message clear and dominant, while submitting to economic necessities on which its survival depends. It also reveals the conditions which make it difficult for black women (particularly dark-skinned black women) to *believe* that they are beautiful. This terrain, clearly, is not a playground, but a field of dangerous mines threatening to *literally* (and not merely literarily) deconstruct "difference" at every turn.

"MATERIAL GIRL": MADONNA AS POSTMODERN HEROINE

John Fiske's conception of "difference," in the section quoted above, at least imagines resistance as challenging specifiable historical forms of dominance (FIG. 12). Women, he argues, connect with subversive "feminine" values leaking through the patriarchal plot of soap operas; blacks laugh to themselves at the glossy, materialist-cowboy culture of "Dallas." Such examples suggest a resistance directed against *particular* historical forms of power and subjectivity. For some postmodern theorists, however, resistance is imagined as the refusal to embody *any* positioned subjectivity at all; what is celebrated is continual creative escape from location, containment and definition. So, as Susan Rubin Suleiman advises, we must move beyond the valorization of historically suppressed values (for example, those values that have been culturally constructed as belonging to an inferior, female domain and generally expunged from Western science, philosophy, religion), and toward "endless complication" and a "dizzying accumulation of narratives."[16] She appreciatively (and perhaps misleadingly) invokes Derrida's metaphor of "incalculable choreographies" to capture the dancing, elusive, continually changing subjectivity that she envisions, a subjectivity without gender, without history, without location. From this perspective, the truly resistant female body

FIGURE 12

ou can have sex, but...use your imagination.
Be *creative."*

is not the body that wages war against feminine sexualization and objectification, but the body that, as Cathy Schwichtenberg has put it, "uses simulation strategically in ways that challenge the stable notion of gender as the edifice of sexual difference . . . [in] an erotic politics in which the female body
can be refashioned in the flux of identities that speak in plural styles."[17] For
this erotic politics, the new postmodern heroine is Madonna.

The celebration of Madonna as postmodern heroine is not the first time
that Madonna has been portrayed as a subversive culture-figure. Until recently, however, Madonna's resistance has been seen along "Body as Battleground" lines, as deriving from her refusal to allow herself to be constructed
as an object of patriarchal desire. John Fiske, for example, argues that this
was a large part of Madonna's original appeal to her "wanna-bes"—those
hoards of largely white, middle-class sub-teeners who emulated and mim-
icked Madonna's moves and costumes. For the "wanna-bes," Madonna
modeled the possibility of a female heterosexuality that was independent of

patriarchal control, a sexuality that defied rather than rejected the male gaze, teasing it with her *own* gaze, deliberately trashy and vulgar, challenging anyone to call her a whore, and ultimately not giving a damn what judgements might be made of her. Madonna's rebellious sexuality, in this reading, offered itself, not as coming into being through the look of the Other, but as self-defining and in love with, happy with itself—something that is rather difficult for women to achieve in this culture—and which helps to explain, as Fiske argues, her enormous appeal to teenage girls.[18] "I like the way she handles herself, sort of take it or leave it; she's sexy but she doesn't need men . . . she's kind of there all by herself," says one. "She gives us ideas. It's really women's lib, not being afraid of what guys think," says another.[19]

Madonna herself, significantly and unlike most "sex symbols," has never advertised herself as disdainful of feminism, or constructed feminists as "man-haters." Rather, in a 1985 *Time* interview, she suggests that her lack of inhibition in "being herself," and her "luxuriant" expression of "strong" sexuality, is her *own* brand of feminist celebration.[20] Some feminist theorists would agree: Molly Hite, for example, argues that ". . . asserting female desire in a culture in which female sexuality is viewed as so inextricably conjoined with passivity" is "transgressive":

> Implied in this strategy is the old paradox of the speaking statue, the created thing that magically begins to create, for when a woman writes—self-consciously from her muted position as a woman and not as an honorary man—about female desire, female sexuality, female sensuous experience generally, her performance has the effect of giving voice to pure corporeality, of turning a product of the dominant meaning-system into a producer of meanings. A woman, conventionally identified with her body, writes about that identification, and as a consequence, femininity—silent and inert by definition—erupts into patriarchy as an impossible discourse.[21]

Not all feminists would agree with this, of course. For the sake of the contrast I want to draw here, however, let us grant it, and note, as well, that a similar argument to Fiske's can be made concerning Madonna's refusal to be obedient to dominant and normalizing standards of female *beauty*. I'm now talking, of course, about Madonna in her more fleshy days. In those days, Madonna saw herself as willfully out-of-step with the times. "Back in the fifties [she says in the *Time* interview] women weren't ashamed of their bodies." (The fact that she is dead wrong is not relevant here.) Identifying herself with that time and what she calls its lack of "suppression" of femininity, she turns her nose down at the "androgynous" clothes of our own time, and speaks warmly of her own stomach, "not really flat" but "round and the skin is smooth and I like it." Contrasting herself to anorexics, whom she sees as self-denying and self-hating, completely in the thrall of externally im-

FIGURE 13

posed standards of worthiness, Madonna (as she saw herself) stood for self-definition through the assertion of her own (traditionally "female" and now anachronistic) body type (FIG. 13).

Of course, this is no longer Madonna's body type. Over the last year or so she has gone on a strenuous reducing and exercise program, runs several miles a day, lifts weights and now has developed, in obedience to dominant contemporary norms, a tight, slender, muscular body. Why did she decide to shape up? "I didn't have a flat stomach anymore," she has said. "I had become well-rounded." Please note the sharp about-face here, from pride to embarrassment. My point, however, is not to construct Madonna's formerly voluptuous body as a non-alienated, freely expressive body, in contrast with the constricted, culturally-imposed ideal that she now strives for. The voluptuous female body is a cultural form, too (as are all bodies), and was a coercive ideal in the '50s. It seems clear, however, that in terms of Madonna's *own* former lexicon of meanings—within which feminine volup-

FIGURE 14

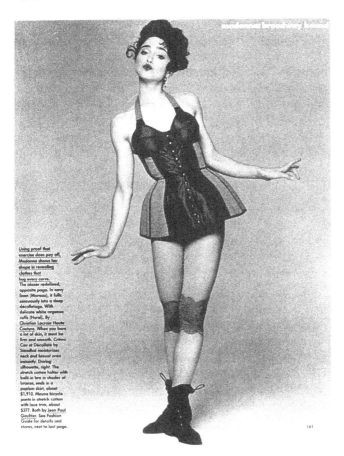

Living proof that exercise does pay off, Madonna shows her shape in revealing clothes that hug every curve. The blazer redefined, opposite page. In navy linen (Moreau), it falls sensuously into a deep décolletage. With delicate white organza cuffs (Hurel). By Christian Lacroix Haute Couture. When you bare a lot of skin, it must be firm and smooth. Crème Cao et Décolleté by Stendhal moisturizes neck and breast area instantly. During silhouette, right. The stretch cotton halter with built-in bra in shades of bronze, ends in a peplum skirt, about $1,910. Mauve bicycle pants in stretch cotton with lace trim, about $377. Both by Jean Paul Gaultier. See Fashion Guide for details and stores, next to last page.

tuousness and the choice to be round in a culture of the lean was clearly connected to spontaneity, self-definition, and defiance of the cultural gaze—the terms set by that gaze have now triumphed. Madonna has been normalized; more precisely, she has self-normalized (FIG. 14). Her "wanna-bes" are following suit. Studies suggest that as many as 80% of nine-year-old suburban girls (the majority of whom are far from overweight) are making rigorous dieting and exercise the organizing discipline of their lives.[22] They don't require Madonna's example, of course, to believe that they must be thin to be acceptable. But Madonna clearly no longer provides a model of resistance or "difference" for them.

None of this "materiality"—that is, the obsessive body-praxis that regulates and disciplines Madonna's life and the lives of the young (and not-so-young) women who emulate her—makes its way into the representation of Madonna as postmodern heroine. In the terms of this representation (in both its popular and scholarly instantiations) Madonna is "in control of her image, not trapped by it"; the proof is her ironic and chameleon-like approach to the construction of her identity, her ability to "slip in and out of character at will,"[23] to defy definition, to keep them guessing. In this coding of things, as in the fantasies of the polysurgical addict (and, as I have argued elsewhere, the eating-disordered woman[24]) "control" and "power"—words that are invoked over and over in discussions of Madonna—have become equivalent to "self-creation." Madonna's new body has no material history; it conceals its praxis, it does not reveal its pain. It is merely another creative transformation of an ever-elusive subjectivity. "More Dazzling and Determined Not to Stop Changing," *Cosmopolitan* describes Madonna: ". . . whether in looks or career, this multitalented dazzler will never be trapped in *any* mold!"[25] The plasticity of Madonna's subjectivity is emphasized again and again in the popular press, particularly by Madonna herself. It is how she tells the story of her "power" in the industry. "In pop music, generally, people have one image. You get pigeonholed. I'm lucky enough to be able to change and still be accepted . . . play a part, change characters, looks, attitudes."[26]

Madonna claims that her creative work, too, is meant to escape definition. "Everything I do is meant to have several meanings, to be ambiguous," she says. She resists, however (and in true postmodern fashion), the attribution of serious artistic intent; rather (as she recently told *Cosmo*) she favors irony and ambiguity "to entertain myself" and (as she told *Vanity Fair*) out of "rebelliousness and a desire to fuck with people."[27] It is the postmodern nature of her music and videos that has most entranced academic critics, whose accolades reproduce in highly theoretical language the same notions emphasized in the popular press. Susan McClary writes:

> Madonna's art itself repeatedly deconstructs the traditional notion of the unified subject with finite ego boundaries. Her pieces explore . . . various ways of constituting identities that refuse stability, that remain fluid, that resist definition. This tendency in her work has become increasingly pronounced; for instance, in her recent controversial video 'Express Yourself' . . . she slips in and out of every subject position offered within the video's narrative context . . . refusing more than ever to deliver the security of a clear, unambiguous message or an 'authentic' self.[28]

Later in the same piece, McClary describes "Open Your Heart," which features Madonna as a porn star in a peep-show, as creating "an image of open-ended *jouissance*—an erotic energy that continually escapes containment."[29] Now, to many feminist viewers, this particular video may be quite disturbing, for a number of reasons. First, unlike many of Madonna's older videos, and like most of her more recent ones, "Open Your Heart" does not visually emphasize Madonna's subjectivity or desire—through, for example, frequent shots of Madonna's face and eyes, flirting with and controlling the reactions of the viewer. Rather, it places the viewer in the position of the voyeur, by presenting Madonna's body-as-object, now perfectly, plasticly taut and tightly managed, for display. To be sure, we do not identify with the slimy men depicted *in* the video, drooling over Madonna's performance; but, as E. Ann Kaplan has pointed out, the way men view women *in* the filmic world is only one species of objectifying "gaze." There is also *our* (that is, the viewer's) gaze, which may be encouraged by the director to be either more or less objectifying.[30] In *Open Your Heart*, as in virtually all rock videos, the female body is offered to the viewer purely as a spectacle, an object of sight, a visual commodity to be consumed. Madonna's weight loss and dazzling shaping-up job make the spectacle of her body all the more compelling; we are riveted to her body, fascinated by it. Many men and women may experience the primary reality of the video as the elicitation of desire *for* that perfect body; women, however, may also be gripped by the desire (and likely impossibility) of *becoming* that perfect body.

These elements can be effaced, of course, by a deliberate abstraction of the video from the cultural context in which it is historically embedded (the continuing containment, sexualization and objectification of the female body) and in which the viewer is implicated as well, and by treating the video as a purely formal "text." Taken as such, *Open Your Heart* presents itself (along with most of Madonna's recent videos) as what E. Ann Kaplan calls "postmodern video": it refuses to "take a clear position *vis-à-vis* its images" and similarly refuses a "clear position for the spectator within the filmic world . . . leaving him/her decentered, confused."[31] McClary's reading of *Open Your Heart* emphasizes precisely these postmodern elements, insisting on the ambiguous and unstable nature of the relationships depicted in the narrative of the video, and the frequent elements of parody and play. "The usual power relationship between the voyeuristic male gaze and object" is "destabilized," she claims, by the portrayal of the male patrons of the porno house as leering and pathetic. At the same time, the portrayal of Madonna as porno-queen-object is deconstructed, McClary argues, by the end of the video, which has Madonna changing her clothes to those of a little boy and tripping off playfully, leaving the manager of the house sputtering behind her. McClary reads this as an "escape to androgyny," which "refuses essentialist gender categories and turns sexual identity into a kind of play." As to the gaze of the viewer, she admits that it is "risky" to "invoke the image of porn queen in order to perform its deconstruction," but concludes that the deconstruction is successful: "In this video, Madonna confronts the most pernicious of her stereotypes and attempts to channel it into a very different realm: a realm where the feminine object need not be the object of the patriarchal gaze, where its energy can motivate play and nonsexual pleasure."[32]

I would argue, however, that despite the video's "hedging along the lines of not communicating a clear signified," there *is* a dominant position in this video and it is that of the objectifying gaze. One is not *really* decentered and confused by this video, despite the "ambiguities" it formally contains. Indeed, the video's postmodern conceits, I would suggest, facilitate rather than deconstruct the presentation of Madonna's body as an object on display. For in the absence of a coherent critical position *on* the images, the individual images themselves become preeminent, hypnotic, fixating. Indeed, I would say that ultimately this video is entirely about Madonna's body, the narrative context virtually irrelevant, an excuse to showcase the physical achievements of the star, a video centerfold. On this level, any parodic or de-stabilizing element appears as utterly, cynically, mechanically tacked on, in bad faith, a way of claiming trendy status for what is really just cheesecake—or, perhaps, pornography.

Indeed, it may be worse than that. If the playful "tag" ending of *Open Your Heart* is successful in deconstructing the notion that the objectification and sexualization of women's bodies is a serious business, then Madonna's *jouissance* may be "fucking with" her youthful viewer's perceptions in a dangerous way. Judging from the proliferation of rock lyrics celebrating the rape, abuse and humiliation of women, the message—not Madonna's responsibility alone, of course, but hers among others, surely—is getting through. The artists who perform these misogynist songs also claim to be speaking playfully, tongue-in-cheek, and to be daring and resistant transgressors of cultural structures that contain and define. Ice T, whose rap lyrics gleefully describe the gang rape of a woman—with a flashlight, to "make her tits light up"—claims that he is only "telling it like it is" among black street youth (he compares himself to Richard Wright), and scoffs at feminist humorlessness, implying, as well, that it is racist and repressive for feminists to try to deny him his indigenous "style." The fact that Richard Wright embedded his depiction of Bigger Thomas within a critique of the racist culture that shaped him, and that *Native Son* is meant to be a *tragedy,* was not, apparently, noticed in Ice T's "postmodern" reading of the book, whose critical point of view he utterly ignores. Nor does he seem concerned about what appears to be a growing fad—not only among street gangs, but in fraternity houses as well—for gang rape, often with an unconscious woman, and surrounded by male spectators. (Some of the terms popularly used to describe these rapes include "beaching"—the woman being likened to a "beached whale"—and "spectoring," to emphasize how integral a role the onlookers play.)

Turning to Madonna and the liberating postmodern subjectivity that McClary and others claim she is offering: the notion that one can play a porno house by night and regain one's androgynous innocence by day does not seem to me to be a refusal of essentialist categories about gender, but rather a new inscription of mind/body dualism. What the body does is immaterial, so long as the imagination is free. This abstract, unsituated, disembodied freedom, I have argued in this chapter, celebrates itself only through the effacement of the material praxis of people's lives, the normalizing power of cultural images, and the sadly continuing social realities of dominance and subordination.

NOTES

1. Quotations from Trix Rosen, *Strong and Sexy* (New York: Putnam, 1983), pp. 72, 61.

2. "Travolta: 'You Really Can Make Yourself Over,' " *Syracuse Herald,* Jan. 13, 1985.

3. "Popular Plastic Surgery," *Cosmopolitan,* May 1990, p. 96.

4. Tina Lizardi and Martha Frankel, "Hand Job," *Details,* February 1990, p. 38.

5. Jennet Conant, Jeanne Gordon and Jennifer Donovan, "Scalpel Slaves Just Can't Quit," *Newsweek,* January 11, 1988, pp. 58–59.

6. Donahue Transcript #05257, Multimedia Entertainment, Inc.

7. Dahleen Glanton, "Racism Within a Race," *Syracuse Herald American,* September 19, 1989.

8. *Essence* reader opinion poll, June 1989, p. 71.

9. Linda Bien, "Building a Better Bust," *Syracuse Herald,* March 4, 1990.

10. This was said by Janice Radway in an oral presentation of her work, Duke University, Spring 1989.

11. John Fiske, *Television Culture* (New York: Methuen, 1987), p. 19.

12. Michel Foucault, *Discipline and Punish* (New York: Vintage, 1979), p. 138.

13. Related in Bill Moyers, "A Walk Through the Twentieth Century: The Second American Revolution," PBS Boston.

14. Retha Powers, "Fat Is a Black Women's Issue," *Essence,* October 1989.

15. *Discipline and Punish,* pp. 26–27.

16. Susan Rubin Suleiman, "(Re)Writing the Body: The Politics and Poetics of Female Eroticism," in *The Female Body in Western Culture,* ed. Susan Rubin Suleiman (Cambridge: Harvard University Press, 1986), p. 24.

17. Cathy Schwichtenberg, "Postmodern Feminism and Madonna: Toward an Erotic Politics of the Female Body," paper presented at the University of Utah Humanities Center, National Conference on "Rewriting the (Post) Modern: (Post) Colonialism/Feminism/Late Capitalism," March 30/31, 1990.

18. John Fiske, "British Cultural Studies and Television," in *Channels of Discourse,* ed. Robert C. Allen (Chapel Hill: The University of North Carolina Press, 1987), pp. 254–290.

19. Quoted in John Skow, "Madonna Rocks the Land," *Time,* May 27, 1985, p. 77.

20. Ibid., p. 81.

21. Molly Hite, "Writing—and Reading—the Body: Female Sexuality and Recent Feminist Fiction," in *Feminist Studies,* 14; 1, Spring 1988, pp. 121–122.

22. "Fat or Not, 4th Grade Girls Diet Lest They Be Teased or Unloved," *Wall Street Journal,* February 11, 1986.

23. Catherine Texier, "Have Women Surrendered in MTV's Battle of the Sexes?" *New York Times,* April 22, 1990.

24. Susan Bordo, "Anorexia Nervosa: Psychopathology as the Crystallization of Culture," *The Philosphical Forum,* 17; 2, Winter 1985, pp. 73–103.

25. *Cosmopolitan,* July 1987.

26. David Ansen, "Magnificent Maverick," *Cosmopolitan,* May 1990, p. 311.

27. Kevin Sessums, "White Heat," *Vanity Fair,* April 1990, p. 208.

28. Susan McClary, "Living to Tell: Madonna's Resurrection of the Fleshly," *Genders,* Number 7, Spring 1990, p. 2.

29. Ibid., p. 12.

30. E. Ann Kaplan, "Is the Gaze Male," in *Power of Desire,* eds. Ann Snitow, Christine Stansell and Sharon Thompson (New York: Monthly Review Press, 1983), pp. 309–327.

31. E. Ann Kaplan, *Rocking Around the Clock: Music Television, Postmodernism and Consumer Culture* (New York: Methuen, 1987), p. 63.

32. McClary, p. 13.

13

The Distance Between Me & You: Madonna & Celestial Navigation (or You Can Be My *Lucky Star*)

> It's flattering to me that people take the time to analyze me and that I've so infiltrated their psyches that they have to intellectualize my very being. I'd rather be on their minds than off.
>
> —Madonna

MAPS OF THE STARS: CELESTIAL NAVIGATION AND POSTMODERNISM

> We are describing subjects which think about themselves in the presence of objects which think about themselves without any necessary presumption of a denotative imperative linking one to the other. We now have a label for this kind of activity: postmodernism.
>
> —Eric Michaels, "My Essay on Postmodernity"

> I think I've met everybody.   —Madonna

When Elvis Presley died in August 1977, Lester Bangs (1987, 216) concluded his eloquent *Village Voice* obituary with the following words:

> If love is truly going out of fashion, which I do not believe, then along with our nurtured indifference to each other will be an even more contemptuous indifference to each other's objects of reverence. . . . We will continue to fragment in this manner, because solipsism holds all of the cards at present; it is a king whose domain engulfs even Elvis's. But I can guarantee you one thing; we will never again agree on anything as we agreed on Elvis. So I won't bother saying goodbye to his corpse. I will say goodbye to you.

photo by Steven Meisel, *courtesy of Warner Brothers*

In almost every regard here, Bangs seems to have gotten it right. The 1970s was a decade of fragmentation: of and within generational audiences, of popular culture, of political sensibilities and emotional investments. (Or, at the very least, it was a time when this fracturing was made immediately palpable.) Solipsism, it appeared, had won. But what if Lester Bangs got one minor detail wrong? What if, as it turns out, solipsism isn't a king but a queen?[1]

Whether Madonna now looms as large over the cultural landscape as Elvis once did is a question that, in a lot of ways, could probably be better debated by stargazers and statisticians, impresarios and ideologues. And though it would be dishonest to say that such notions won't be entertained (at least, peripherally), this chapter will be more centrally concerned with Madonna in relation to the changing nature of our cultural geography and the ever-problematic but increasingly sophisticated methods for mapping its terrain. Although it was almost certainly not Bangs's intention to initiate a charting of late 1970s popular culture (especially because he saw it as irretrievably scattered), his remarks help to shape and define the thematics, the articulations, and many of the questions that will be raised herein. His Elvis eulogy serves here both as an important historical marker and as one way to limit the bounds of this analysis. For a variety of reasons that I hope will soon be apparent, taking the time to analyze (and "intellectualize") Madonna—if only because she seems to have infiltrated more psyches than any other pop star of recent memory—offers the best opportunity to consider some of what has transpired in popular culture in the last decade and a half.

There was, Lester Bangs realized, something even more significant about the death of Elvis Presley than the passing of one of this century's most important cultural figures. His death raised broader questions that needed to be framed in contemporary American pop culture at large—questions about the configurations of its stars, about our increasingly "nurtured indifference," about the extent of our continued fragmentation, about the real difficulty of making meaningful connections among the debris of a fractionated popular culture. In the time since then, these queries haven't become any less pertinent; if anything, they now only reverberate more loudly.

In his expository essay on the popular music of the past decade, Robert Christgau (1990, 65) simply put it this way: "The '80s were when '70s fragmentation went kerblooey." Simon Frith (1988c) has also paid notice to this fragmentation refrain (with its attendant verses) and draws special attention to how it has been sounded with some regularity—from the late 1970s onward—in a great deal of music journalism and academic discourse. Referring to this as "the pop-world version of the 'postmodern condition,' " Frith (1988c, 5) notes that these arguments have centered around the notion (the realization of Bangs's nightmare) that "no single pop taste, no particular rock fragment, seems any weightier, any *truer* than any other." If, in any way, these dominant themes from "the pop-world" are metonymic of changes on a more pronounced scale in our culture as a whole, what sort of "maps" might be appropriate in an attempt to read and respond to these newly emergent sensibilities?

Would they be star maps, perhaps, or celestial charts? The 1980s may have been the time when the fragments further fragmented, but it was also the decade, as Christgau (1990, 65) notes, "when stars replaced artists as bearers of significance." Albeit of a slightly different sort, the "stars" play a key role in what one of America's foremost scholars of the postmodern, Fredric Jameson (1991), calls *cognitive mapping*. Jameson's chief claim for his particular critical and aesthetic maneuver of mapping is that it serves as the best means for negotiating our way and (temporarily) finding our place in a dispersed and decentered world. The cognitive map, he asserts, will have to be adopted by any political form of postmodernism that wants to "begin to grasp our positioning as individual and collective subjects and regain a capacity to act and struggle which is at present neutralized by our spatial as well as our social confusion" (Jameson 1991, 54). This kind of totalizing social theory follows in a long line of Marxist theoretical models (Hegel, Lukács, Sartre, Althusser; see Kellner 1989, 35)—each attempting, in its own way, to paint, as completely as possible, a representational portrait of our present moment in history.

Although Fredric Jameson probably never intended the cognitive map to be used in the following fashion, I will consider his "homeopathic" strategy for managing the postmodern condition in relation to Marxist accounts of the (Hollywood) star system. This conjunction first requires a slight rearticulation of "the stars" to which Jameson refers in his cartographic metaphor.[2] To illustrate the degrees of ontological complexity that separate a cognitive map from more commonly recognized forms of cartography, Jameson draws a quick comparison between the narrowly situated, flat, gridlike itinerary of the city traveler and the advancements that have led to the more highly developed nautical itinerary of the ocean navigator.

> The new instruments—compass, sextant, and theodolite—correspond not merely to new geographic and navigational problems . . . they also introduce a whole new coordinate: the relationship of the totality, particularly as it is mediated by the stars and by new operations like that of triangulation. At this point, cognitive mapping in the broader sense comes to require the coordination of existential data (the empirical position of the subject) with the unlived, abstract conceptions of the geographic totality (Jameson 1991, 52).

Though the efficaciousness of such totalizing, metatheoretical models has been increasingly called into question (see, e.g., Morris 1992) and though Jameson's map is not without similar problems (Young 1991; Zuidervaart 1989), what I wish to leave unproblematized is the possibility that "objectivistic accounts of Marxism" and "subjectivistic accounts of existentialism and psychoanalysis" (Best 1989, 349)—that is, the two sides of the cognitive mapping equation—can be mediated by the stars.

It is this same sort of "mediation" that has informed recent work on theories of stardom by Barry King (1987). His project has focused on extending discussions of the star system beyond (or perhaps, more properly, below) the traditional, predominant emphasis on the regime of signification. Although not denying the very real effectivity of the symbolic, King's "performance theory of stardom" is an attempt to offer a ground for those approaches that "wish to explain the 'meaning' of stardom [by simply cataloging] the presence of existential themes in its discourses" (1987, 145).

Critical readings that are preoccupied only with the star as transcendent subject, as text, as mythic construct need to be complemented, King contends, by an (objectivistic) account that pays "attention to the particularities of performance as a labour process, and the relations of production in which such a process occurs" (1987, 145). The star is to be understood as unique within the realm of commodities; at once labor in process *and* the product of labor. Thus, although there will always be a fair amount of mystification, the star displays—as an inevitable part of the performance itself—the effort that goes into his or her own making. Taking the materiality of performance into account means that the form of agency embodied by the star arises from the site of production, and, given this, the star might allow insight into the nature of labor power in general (King 1987, 148, 153). King's specific assertion is that "the star, *before all contents,* can function as a metonymy for labour power and for what stands behind this connection—that is, the sensuous, creative capacity of human labour power" (1987, 158). In this case, the critical work on stardom concerns itself with the connections forged (which can never be guaranteed beforehand) between the spheres of production and consumption—connections where the star serves as a highly visible intermediary.

The inherent risk involved with Barry King's performance theory of stardom, like Fredric Jameson's cognitive map, is that it must be continually protected against the slide from metonymy to metaphor, from mediation to expressive causality. That is, one must avoid the temptation of falling into those tacit sorts of base-superstructure arguments that produce a simple reflection model of culture by "prioritizing economic relations and economic determinations over cultural and political relations" (McRobbie 1992, 719). Jameson is certainly not entirely immune from such criticism (see, e.g., Bennett 1990), and King, likewise, skirts along the very edge of this danger.[3] This chapter will look at certain broad changes in the organization and functions of global entertainment industries, and a critical understanding of these changes provides important mapping coordinates. However, they should not be perceived as the sole (or even necessarily the decisive) determinants of Madonna's success.

Finally, what both Jameson and King agree on—and what is particularly crucial about their arguments for this present work—is that a triangulation of the objective (the "unlived" structures of the social formation), the subjective (individual experience), and "the stars" might offer a certain unique access into popular consciousness. For Jameson (1991, 418), the cognitive map is really just another way to speak of class consciousness, "only it proposed the need for class consciousness of a new and hitherto undreamed of kind, while it also inflect[s] the account in the direction of that new spatiality implicit in the postmodern." Meanwhile, King's (1987, 159) attempt to reconceptualize the star as a performance commodity offers, he believes, one path toward a deeper understanding of "the anonymous subjects of this [type of] analysis, the lower middle class and working class of Western capitalism and beyond." In short, stars speak to the sense of crisis over what it means to be "a subject" (Dyer 1982, 183).

Although I am reluctant to hold to some of the more expansive mapping claims (especially in the case of Jameson) about grasping the "totality," it may be more than wishful thinking that sustains the belief that turning our attention toward the stars can help rescue us from whatever place we find ourselves mired. No one—the cartographer or cultural critic especially—can pretend to adopt an omniscient perspective on the current situation as if somehow afforded a sort of privileged view from outside or above the milieu. It is a context in which we are all inextricably (and, on occasion, pleasurably) a part, even if, as Lester Bangs noted, we seem unfortunately and increasingly *apart* as well.

Still, establishing our location via the stars might offer one of the best means for finding and charting a course that would help narrow the distance—no matter how close, no matter how far—that separates us one from the other. Although it could be either premature or audacious to argue that Madonna provides us with the chance to say "hello" again, she has been, unquestionably, among the most consistently lucky and brightest of stars in the past decade. On a map that might register the distance of popular culture's continued fragmentation and the quality of our indifference through the 1980s and into the 1990s, Madonna's star could be an invaluable first coordinate.

TRUTH OR DARE: (READING CULTURAL STUDIES) IN BED WITH MADONNA

> Madonna snags vanguard attention while pitching critics into fierce Barthesian discussions about her belt buckles.
>
> —Steve Anderson, "Forgive Me, Father"

> What you have to understand with Madonna is that she has substance. People forget that. Since she reinvents herself all the time and does these provocative things, people tend to concentrate on her image of the moment. But there is substance there.
> —Freddy DeMann, Madonna's personal manager

Simply *finding* Madonna's star might not be an easy task; there's a lot of cloud cover. If ever a particular convergence has cried out for delimiting, it is the intersection of Madonna with cultural theory and pop commentary. The nature of this critical surfeit is neatly pointed up by a photograph of Madonna from a recent issue of *Time* magazine (Arrington 1991, 57). As usual, Madonna is at least one step ahead of her commentators. Posed topless, facing away from the camera, there is a door painted on her back. Two words are inscribed on the door: "ALL ACCESS." With Madonna, there is a constant danger—especially within the realm of critique or commentary—of quickly passing through this door, of saying too much (with her) and too little (about her).

It is this sort of peril—especially acute in those instances when one is also a fan of whatever is being examined—that is nearly always present whenever theorizing culture. As a forewarning against any such critical pitfall, Simon Frith (1988a, 461) maintains that "rather than using cultural theory to illuminate critical practice, [it is best] to examine certain cultural practices and suggest ways in which they can help us refine cultural theory." Start the other way around and the critic quite often ends up simply (or, sometimes, *complexly*) validating cultural theory through the clever manipulation of a textually malleable example. In the case of Madonna, she has frequently come to serve as both the fully functional surrogate for the critic's feats of derring-do while also providing an "all access" site for the convenient superimposition of critical discourse.

The consequences of such self-fulfilling critical prophecies help contribute to what Meaghan Morris (1990, 23) has termed "banality in cultural studies"—a disciplinary malady that arises whenever the subject(s) of theoretical discourse become "also the textually delegated, allegorical emblem of the critic's own activity." With Madonna, the stakes are even higher: A cultural studies analysis that already runs the risk of lapsing into banality is suddenly confronted by a subject considered by many to be the utmost in banality herself.

For instance, declaring Madonna to be far *too* decipherable to warrant serious critical contemplation for very long, Frith (1991b) has suggested that writers should look elsewhere in the popular underbrush for much more elusive game. "Cultural studies theorists have been misled . . . by Madonna, a deliberate artificer, whose moves are so obvious that it sometimes seems like she's running a semiotics course for beginners—it would be more challenging to pin down the sexual politics of, say, Sheena Easton" (Frith 1991b, 74). And, in a review of Madonna's documentary *Truth or Dare*, J. Hoberman (1991, 56) has concurred: "She even directs her critics, the millions of sociologists, psychologists, and students of semiotics who have made her the world's biggest pop star. . . . What is there to say about Madonna that her clothes, accessories, hairstyle, and historical references don't already explain?" Thus, although it is perhaps a disheartening realization for anyone trying to eke out an existence doing such things, there is a real sense that—despite the flattering pleasures of being analyzed that Madonna expresses in this chapter's opening quote—she doesn't exactly need any of us all that much.[4]

But then, this has stopped very few writers from plunging forward anyway (and the irony isn't lost here, but if you're going to write about Madonna, you should at least be fairly self-conscious). Echoing the words of Frith and Morris, while chiding "Madonna scholars" in particular, Robert Christgau (1991, 31) believes that

> their Madonnathink tends to be about mass culture itself—usually not mass culture as it is experienced, though that is a noble aim, but mass culture as a site of theory. Much of it feels translated . . . and sometimes you get the feeling that their subject's incomparable fame relieves interpreters of the need to truck with lesser cynosures. In short, Madonna is honored less as an artist than as a cultural force.

Perhaps it is almost inevitable that whenever academicians attempted to shed more light on Madonna's mass cultural multiaccentuality, they have invariably cast their own long shadows across the text (obscuring the object of their desire) or ended up with results that hint at overly ambitious cross-purposes. Madonna, as the subject of critical analysis, seems to require the elaborate conjuncture of a whole host of grandiose themes.

Maybe the best magic trick that cultural studies (in some of its more poststructuralist guises) has to offer is not the one that conjures Madonna up out of thin air; instead, it's that stunning combination of feverish, theoretical sleight of hand and incantation where Madonna herself (though *not* really "herself" but rather a subject under heavy textual construction) dissolves into her surroundings. See, for example, John Fiske (1989, 124), who writes: "Madonna is only the intertextual circulation of her meanings and pleasures; she is neither a text or a person, but a set of meanings in process." In theory, this is true enough. But, then, this same statement could be made about anyone who is mediated through the industries of popular culture and its accompanying discourses. It tells us very little about what makes Madonna unique, special—at once an artist and an undeniable cultural force.[5]

Cultural studies need not plead guilty, however, to all the misdemeanors committed in its name. Examining cultural practices and locations of power, attempting to understand and explain the significance of particular artists and cultural actors, working through the problems and insights of cultural theory are just some of the broader concerns that come with the territory. The more arduous but rewarding task lies in the attempt to move beyond the textual, to trace out the ways in which the subject under analysis operates within a variety of different sites or "planes of effectivity" (Grossberg 1986, 73) and, then, to begin to map out the points at which these planes might intersect (or articulate) and diverge. There is never any certainty (no guarantee in advance) that one can chart any or all of the possibilities by which these different "moments" might speak to one another. In the end, the linkage of these articulations produces a kind of "cartography of daily life" (Grossberg 1992)—not wholly unlike Jameson's cognitive map, minus some of its grander assertions—that provides the cultural analyst with an always provisional context in which specific cultural practices, identities, socioeconomic relations, and so forth might illuminate each other in ways that can only be discovered as the map is drawn.

The terrain covered by such a map should represent more than just an effort to understand Madonna at the level of audience response or as the locus point of myriad, critical-textual analyses (although it would need to include each of these and more). A cultural studies analysis needs to also take into account the simple, empirical fact that Madonna is a *real* person—who will always exceed and impinge on the field of textual representation—operating within an undeniably intricate matrix of corporeal and corporate relations; she is a self-proclaimed material girl living in a material world. To paraphrase her manager, Freddy DeMann, what you have to understand is that *Madonna has substance.*

Or, to put it slightly differently, as much as Madonna might be differentially deployed within cultural theory—seemingly able to transcend "ordinary" social relations as a star or, conversely, tied to a variety of entertainment industries as another dreary product of exchange—she also "speaks" for herself (without any assistance from her analysts), producing real material effects across and within whatever conjuncture she finds herself. Morris (1990, 41) writes, "When the voice of that which academic discourses—including cultural studies—constitute *as* popular begins to theorize its speech, then you have an interesting possibility." This is one way, Morris hypothesizes, that cultural studies might find itself extricated from its own banality. I would argue that Madonna possesses such a voice.

In significant ways, this sort of voice—*voice* meant here as a shorthand way to refer to the subjects of analysis and the effectivity of their signifying practices—has long existed; it's just seldom been recognized. As a result of a cultivated neglect from scholarly discourse, Simon Frith (1988a) contends, something that he calls "low theory" exists. It's the kind of theory generated out of "the day-to-day practices of pop itself, out of people's need to bring some sort of order and justification to the continuing processes of musical [or cultural] evaluation, choice and commitment" (Frith 1988a, 461). This low theory is "confused, inconsistent, full of hyperbole and silence, but still theory, and theory that is compelled by necessity to draw key terms and assumptions from high theory, from the more systematic accounts of art, commerce, pleasure, and class that are available" (Frith 1988a, 461–462). This could be one reason why Christgau believes so much of the academic writing on Madonna *feels* translated. Sometimes in presuming to speak for (or in the place of) low theory, rather than acknowledging its own necessary, dialectical relationship with it, high theory silences the voices that it seeks to understand. Or, it simply gets them wrong.

Perhaps, then, it would be more advantageous to explore the means by which Madonna's knowingly ironic presentational style, her seeming omnipresence, and her agility with the cultural vernacular seem to preempt almost all commentary by rendering it always already redundant or banal. In other words, Madonna has proven remarkably capable at taking the silence traditionally assumed in the space where the subject is supposed to be and turning it back on her analysts. If Madonna has not actually reduced all of her interpreters to silence, she has led many of them to reflect on their own practice or, at least, caused them to look for an explanation for what feels like an eerie experience of déjà vu. Consider, for example, how musicologist Susan McClary (1991, 161) describes the interaction of Madonna's music with certain cultural problematics:

> The fact that some of Madonna's music enacts models of organization that correspond to formulations of critics such as Teresa de Lauretis need not suggest that Madonna is a connoisseur of critical theory. Yet to the extent that de Lauretis and Madonna inhabit the same historical world and grapple with the same kinds of problems with respect to feminine identity, their similarities are not entirely coincidental either. And Madonna is as much an expert in the arena of musical signification as de Lauretis is in theoretical discourse. It seems clear that she has grasped the assumptions embedded within these basic musical mechanisms and is audaciously redirecting them.

Why the confluence of Madonna and critical theory? For McClary, it's partly shared environment, partly gender-related, partly intuitive, and partly magic.

In one of this chapter's opening quotes, Eric Michaels (1987) remarked that postmodernism is really just a convenient label for the kind of intellectual crisis that ensues when subjects think (and, for Morris, speak) for themselves in the presence of objects that are doing the same and when no one can really be sure how these two might be related. With this description, Michaels was acknowledging how any commitment to the firm distinctions between high and low theory had begun to break down. Interestingly, these remarks were prompted by his viewing of Madonna's *Open Your Heart* video. Michaels (1987, 91) noted that although he usually saw the video in a fairly mundane location—not "at a seminar by Fredric Jameson at Yale, or Jonathan Culler at Oxford"—he could not help but feel jolted by how neatly Madonna had anticipated his week's reading list.

> We watch the videoclip looking for clues about the relationship between the director and the star. Instead, we get Madonna playing to a gallery of voyeurs. In passing, we can't help but notice suspiciously academic references to Lacan's essays about "the Gaze," Deleuze and Guattari's *Anti-Oedipus,* the feminist critique of woman's film image, and other citations too scholarly to be believed but too precise to dismiss (Michaels 1987, 90).

"Madonna's videoclip asserts," Michaels (1987, 87) writes, "[that] the distinction between artist and critic has collapsed." Madonna thus presents a voice that has clearly—if not without a fair amount of controversy—theorized its own speech, becoming one of those "pained and disgruntled subjects, who are also joyous and inventive practitioners [beginning] to articulate our critique of everyday life" (Morris 1990, 41).

As a (fortunate) consequence of all this, a critical account of Madonna *does* need to rethink the manner by which such an analysis should proceed, the kind of problematics that need to be addressed, and the most effective manner in which to frame the results. The guidelines for such a critical activity could be thought of as a modified, theoretical version of the rules for "truth or dare." Because games of truth or dare do not depend on epistemological questions of truth versus falsity, the contest inherently invokes the directive, " 'Take my word for it' " (Probyn 1989, 18). Thus, the response given to any challenge should not be met with the question, Is it true? but, rather, Is it revealing or effective?—Does it work?[6] But, of course, this issue of truth or dare is necessarily complicated in cultural theory because, even as much as one is sometimes implicated within the stories told, we must almost inevitably speak of and contextualize others as well. The sufficiency of the results, then, are intimately bound up with another—an other who is not silent, an other who is also engaged in his/her/their own form of theorizing (no matter how it's characterized), an other who can generally evaluate the effectiveness of what has been said or done by the analyst. If truth lies in the ability to tell effective stories, the dare that guides us is the imperative to construct coherent narratives that aren't built on the exclusion of these others, others who can perhaps no longer be understood quite so easily—following Meaghan Morris and Eric Michaels—as the compliant, silent "subjects" of our critical practice.

As Cathy Schwichtenberg (1990, 8) has said of Madonna, "Whether or not truth resides in her representation is less important than that she poses the question of otherness for others to read." This particular critical strategy (which doesn't worry about "unmasking" but considers, instead, the *real* effectivity of signifying practices) seems a well-suited response to the theoretical-cultural problematics that I've outlined here. In the next section, I'll attempt to coordinate the various ways in which Madonna, as star, has been read and represented in popular and theoretical discourse and look, as well, to how these different accounts and descriptions open up the possibilities for enacting (and melding) some of the cartographic strategies outlined in these first two sections.

MYTHOLOGIES: SHOOTING STARS (FALLING TO EARTH)

> As it grew more heated and intensive, the Elvis myth burst into a final brilliant luminosity, exploded inwards with a fantastic density of energy, and then settled down through the '70s and '80s as a steadily-flashing cultural pulsar.
> — Arthur Kroker, Marilouise Kroker, and David Cook,
> *Panic Encyclopedia*
> Madonna is the biggest star in the universe. And she likes the view.
> — Freddy DeMann, Madonna's personal manager

In a scene from Jim Jarmusch's film *Mystery Train*, a young Japanese couple—who've traveled to America to visit Sun Studios and the home of the departed King—settle into a drab Memphis hotel room. The walls of their room are adorned only by a huge picture of Elvis that looks down on them from above the bed. The young woman sits on the floor at the foot of the bed, cutting pictures from magazines and pasting them into a photo album. She shows her boyfriend what she calls her "important discoveries." In the album, she has placed photographs of Elvis opposite snapshots of other well-known figures or landmarks. First, Elvis looks just like a Middle Eastern king, then the Buddha, then the Statue of Liberty. Her boyfriend is bemused and accepting, dispassionately replying at one point: "Elvis is even more influential than I thought." But when the final photo comparison is Elvis and Madonna, the boyfriend reacts—for the first time—with total incredulity: "Oh no, not Madonna! Give me a break."

But it *does* seem instructive for, at least, a preliminary understanding of the breadth of Madonna's stardom—in popular music, film and video, checkout line tabloids, and contemporary iconography—to consider her alongside one of the last people to have achieved a similar sort of boundless, universal circulation. Instead of carefully clipped magazine headshots, let's begin in a more suitably academic manner by juxtaposing three quotes:

> It is extremely difficult to vanquish myth from the inside: for the very effort one makes in order to escape its stranglehold becomes in its turn the prey of myth: myth can always, as a last resort, signify the resistance which is brought to bear against it (Barthes 1972, 135).

> It is as if there is nothing Elvis could do to overshadow a performance of his myth. And so he performs from a distance, laughing at his myth, throwing it away only to see it roar back and trap him once again (Marcus 1982, 143).

> At some level she [Madonna] clearly wanted to humanize and perhaps even debunk herself, yet as the most self-aware celebrity in history, she knew it was impossible—that every revelation would only reinforce a myth she spends half her career shaping and the other half hanging onto for dear life (Christgau 1991, 33).

In the first quote here, one can see how living within a myth is—as Roland Barthes chose to describe it—akin to wrestling with an almost unbeatable opponent. The only strategy that Barthes (1972, 135) believed could successfully defeat a myth was to turn it back on itself, mythify the myth, and thus produce an "artificial myth" in its place.

Next the words of Marcus and Christgau mirror rather widely held, commensensical perceptions of Elvis and Madonna. That is, one way in which Madonna and Elvis's public personae differ most significantly is in terms of the direct control each exerts (or exerted) over their careers, public images, personal mythos, and so forth. Or, to put it another way, these two stars perhaps diverge most when we consider—even if rather abstractly for the moment—their individual relations to power. As Jeff Ayeroff, copresident of the Virgin America record company, summed it up in a recent *Rolling Stone* interview, Madonna is "better than Elvis was, because Elvis was manipulated as opposed to being a manipulator. Madonna pulled all of *our* strings. *She* was the puppeteer, you see" (Pond 1990, 114).

Theories on Elvis's downfall have been written, rehearsed, and rehashed often enough that a virtual "critical canon" has been established to categorize the slew of plausible fatal moments and wrongheaded choices. The logic tends to follow one of several predictable paths; it could be that "Elvis's folk purity, and therefore his talent, was ruined by (a) his transmogrification from naive country boy into corrupt pop star (he sold his soul to Colonel Tom, or Parker just stole it), (b) Hollywood, (c) the army, (d) money and soft living, (e) all of the above" (Marcus 1982, 189). In response to this critical canon, Lynn Spigel (1990, 186) finds—in her study of Elvis impersonators—that as

their own life stories become intertwined with their recountings of the Elvis
myth [the impersonators] affirm their own life experiences by promising to correct Elvis's fatal flaw—his inability to take care of his own business. . . . They
want to exact the King's ransom by liberating his memory from the mass-cul-
ture industry that stole his fortune.

But whereas Elvis's story seemingly begs for a corrective retelling because
somewhere along the line it went drastically, tragically off course, Madonna
has presented herself as very much in control of her own popularizing narrative almost from the beginning—consciously building it, continually recast-
ing it.[7] Counter to Elvis's lack of business acumen, "it may be that Madonna
is best understood as head of a corporation that produces images of her self-
representation, rather than as the spontaneous, 'authentic' artist of rock mythology. But a puppet she's not" (McClary 1991, 149). After two votes now,
for Madonna as the puppeteer and *definitely not* the puppet, it might be useful to look at some possible reasons why such statements should ring true.

Though hardly charting an entirely original course on the road to fortune
and fame—she follows in the irony-laden, time-honored tradition of many
post-Beatles pop and film stars like David Bowie—Madonna *does* engage in
a very active, seams-showing construction of her own popular persona (she
pulls her own strings). "Within each image, far from deconstructing the eli-
sion of image and identity, she very smartly leads the viewer to *construct* it;
by presenting a whole lexicon of feminine identities, all of them played by
'her,' she undermines your little constructions as fast as you can build them
up" (Williamson 1986, 92). Although artist-photographer Cindy Sherman's
work is actually the subject of the preceding quote, its words apply equally
well to the way in which Madonna has slipped in and out of a wide variety
of roles (in different media) throughout her career. Thus, it seems that with
the consecutive release of each new album, movie, single, video, *Vogue* or
Rolling Stone cover and photo spread, television appearance, and on and
on, Madonna's star has only become all the more flexible, assuming a kind
of "postmodern plasticity," as Susan Bordo (this volume) calls it.

The opportunity to produce this proliferation of identities has been partly
due to the introduction of MTV and to changes within the music industry
since the late 1970s—especially the changing emphases in the way that the
music business is both internally organized and outwardly directed (Frith
1988b, 88–130) . One of the most significant effects of the industry's structural reorganization is a transformation in the methods by which talent is
now discovered, produced, and marketed. Stars rarely appear and ascend in
the ways that they once did (on that long and difficult ladder of success).
"There are no longer gatekeepers regulating the flow of stardom, but multinationals 'fishing' for material, pulling ideas, sounds, styles, performers
from the talent pool and dressing them up for worldwide consumption"

(Frith 1988b, 113). These alterations have had a profound effect on the boundaries that were previously known to the pop star.

> While stars have always been produced and promoted, and in some cases (like Elvis Presley) have moved across media and genres, there have always been limits to this mobility. These limits have not only disappeared in the contemporary forms of the production of stardom, but it is their absence which defines the star (Grossberg 1989, 261).

With the removal of many of the production, distribution, and cross-promotional barriers within the music industry, stars are—more than ever before—able to concentrate more fully on the work of being a star.

Madonna's recent contract negotiations with Time-Warner clearly point to some of these reformations within the music business, particularly in the industry's deal-making with artists and the continued streamlining of different kinds of production within a single entertainment conglomerate. Although at the time of this writing only a few of the details about Madonna's contract demands are known,[8] chief among them is apparently the formation of her own music label and film production company (Michael Jackson has received a similar deal with Sony Music). If Time-Warner cannot come through with the goods, *Musician* magazine states that there is no shortage of multinationals waiting in the wings.

> There are plenty of companies who can give Madonna the kind of deal she is believed to want: Sony, Matsushita (which owns MCA) and Thorn/EMI all cover music and films, while PolyGram—whose Propaganda Films co-produced *Truth or Dare*—recently announced it will invest $200 million in increasing its Hollywood presence and would have to be considered the company with the most to gain from an association with Madonna (Goodman 1992, 97).

If granted a contract that met her demands, Madonna could obviously take greater advantage of the mobility available inside the industry, as well as assume much greater control over her own image-making.

By generating—over the course of her career—more than $500 million in worldwide music sales for Time-Warner, Madonna has lent a certain added resonance to the notion that she's like the head of a corporation overseeing her own image control. Having attained this sort of enormity, flexibility, and mastery, Madonna—as "a corporation in the form of flesh" (Sessums 1990, 148)—becomes a valuable property in the world of international capital. With increasing frequency, multinational entertainment industries have been looking to (and acquiring) software companies as a means to ensure the success of their hardware divisions, particularly those software companies that already possess artists with bankable, recognizable names and images. For example, a 1990 article in *Forbes* magazine reports:

When Sony bought CBS Records for $2 billion in 1988, it wasn't just looking
for profits from Bruce "Born in the U.S.A." Springsteen, Billy Joel, and Michael
Jackson. It was also buying market entree for its digital audio tape, or DAT, format, against a rival format developed by giant Philips of the Netherlands (Huey
1990, 51).

Although this kind of investment practice is not at all a recent phenomenon
(see, e.g., Frith 1988c, 11–23), the high degree of business concentration in
the music industry (dominated by six record companies—EMI, Warner,
Polygram, BMG, CBS, and MCA), their expansion into all corners of the
globe, and their total market share have reached unprecedented heights. At a
time when the American export of popular culture is second only to its export of aerospace technology and when 70 percent of the $20-billion-dollar-
a-year American music business revenue is made outside of the United States
(Huey 1990, 50), Madonna's visibility and numbers overseas (her sales
abroad are more than double her domestic sales) are hard to overlook.

But the real value that Madonna has to offer a multinational conglomerate cannot be calculated in sales figures alone. In addition to her direct
profit-making potential, Madonna's highly recognizable visage can be con-
veniently employed—on the cover of corporate reports, for instance—as a
flexible, readily identifiable icon for the industry. Next to Bugs Bunny, Madonna is probably the most effective corporate symbol currently in the possession of Time-Warner, and thus, she can project some much-needed personality onto a global but faceless media-entertainment giant (Goodman
1992, 51). Notice how, then, Madonna—as star—becomes one way for a
corporation to express its relation to the totality. But, even more telling, notice how this is the same sort of emblematic deployment, found in the world
of multinationals, that Meaghan Morris argues takes place with some regularity in cultural theory: here, Madonna as cultural analyst's mask; there,
Madonna as corporate identity.[9]

Intriguingly, these various appropriations don't seem to have especially
altered or invalidated Madonna's public persona. Regardless of whoever
adopts her star for whatever purpose, Madonna appears to remain the resil-
ient end result of her own creative self-fashioning.[10] Maybe this is because,
as Andrew Goodwin (1990, 272) maintains, despite the different "attempts
to expose the marketing of the star aura in pop, [they have] failed precisely
because the discourses of authorship remain dominant, and because large
sections of the pop audience refuse to consume self-consciously." Although
the ascendance of Madonna can be read as the triumph of a certain kind of
knowing inauthenticity (what Larry Grossberg [1989, 265] calls "authentic
inauthenticity"), it can also be seen as an example of pop audiences' continuing belief in "fairly traditional notions of creativity and authorship"
(Goodwin 1990, 271). As long as Madonna acts "as the guarantor of the
truth of the discourse of her stardom" (Dyer 1991, 139), she remains an au-

thentic artist in the eyes of the fans. Meanwhile, those who see Madonna as inauthentic—as "boring," a "fake," "a slut who screwed her way to the top," possessing "no talent" (comments from an informal poll conducted by Williams and Martinez [1991, 21])—perceive the legitimacy of her stardom as constructed elsewhere. Given that popular arguments around the concept of authenticity aren't likely to be discarded anytime soon (Madonna's biggest fans and detractors will continue to debate whether she *is* or *is not*), it might be more worthwhile to consider how the elsewhere of the discourse of authenticity isn't where it used to be.

That is to say, one of the most significant changes in the social production of stardom over the last two or three decades is where the rhetoric used to authenticate stars is now enacted. In the past, this rhetoric worked—more or less—behind the back of the star. Any affirmative answers given to questions about authenticity usually required that one look below the surface for what seemed like an essential moment of truth: a certain gesture, a flash of spontaneity, a glimpse of what was supposedly hidden. Richard Dyer (1991, 138–139) has distinguished three "markers" of authenticity: "lack of control, lack of premeditation, and privacy." These markers work together, he argues, to construct a rhetoric of authenticity that is powerful "so long as it is not perceived as a rhetoric" (Dyer 1991, 137). And herein lies the change.[11] The star can no longer simply remain oblivious to his or her own authenticizing rhetoric but must be seen to consciously engage this rhetoric (bring it to the surface) and, subsequently, attempt to control its effects.

This change in how the discourse of authenticity is constructed offers one possible explanation of why, with Elvis Presley, there was such an unfailing sense of an original who only later came to be corrupted (from elsewhere) by the machinery of simulation and the cult of celebrity. "This is why Elvis is the King: King of the passage into the better world of recording. Sun King of the total abstraction of the body, of its sounds and images, of its waste in the face of recording" (Wark 1989, 28). Because Elvis's authenticizing discourse—not unlike Lester Bangs's claim about solipsism—lay outside his domain, it could and eventually did lead to his undoing (so to speak). If it seems that, especially when Elvis is limited, there is usually a certain almost religious reverence for the *real* Elvis, perhaps it is because the real Elvis was always there—most profoundly—when he seemed at his most unreal. This might explain one of the reasons why Presley impersonators appear to prefer the King at his most flamboyantly kitschy and spectacular.[12]

Although Elvis himself was finally unable to escape his own "promotional simulacra" (Kroker, Kroker, and Cook 1989, 96),[13] his impersonators—in an attempt to give back to Elvis a more perfect version of his myth—reverse the route by which he was lost, working back toward a recovery of the real body through a performed abstraction of its recorded work. Elvis serves, then, as an image, a voice, a body to be appropriated or inhabited, but, more than anything else, he offers a way to travel back and forth between those previously commonsensical notions of the real or the authentic and those things that appear as mere reproduction.[14] It is hard, then, to imagine the real Elvis within today's culture because, as Greil Marcus (1990, 122) claims, "the impossibility of Elvis Presley as a conscious cultural actor . . . buries him beneath his culture, the culture he inherited, the culture he made, and the culture that then to such a great degree remade itself according to his promises, complexities, contradictions, and defeats."

It is these lessons—think of them, perhaps, as a variation on what it means to learn from Las Vegas—that Madonna, for one, has followed so well.

> There can no longer be much doubt that Madonna now regards celebrity itself as her art, or that she plies it with such gut instinct and manipulative savvy that all past and present practitioners—all those Swedish nightingales and sultans of swat and little tramps and cleopatras and blond bombshells and rebels without a cause and king pelvises . . . seem like stumbling naifs by comparison (Christgau 1991, 31).

In this regard, the video for Madonna's song "Material Girl" can be seen—retrospectively—as a key, defining moment in her career and a wake-up call for many of her commentators as well. With its knowing homage of sorts to Marilyn Monroe's song-and-dance number "Diamonds Are a Girl's Best Friend," its self-conscious disjunction of the singer and the song as ironic commentary on the then-predominant image of Madonna as Boy Toy, and the infinite regress of its interplay within and between Madonna's complex assemblage of personae and characters, *Material Girl* showed—more clearly than any of her other videos until that point—that Madonna was trying to intervene in and influence the shape that her own emerging mythology would take. As Judith Williamson (1985, 46–47) noted at the time, "Madonna is not just a star; she is about *being* a star. Her whole image is a constant reference to the process of stardom." After that, Madonna was pulling her own strings and ours, too.

Madonna's stardom, from *Material Girl* onward, has continued by this same means of elaborate self-referral, both to herself as star and to the processes of stardom. It could be one of the best performance strategies to take in a social world where "the entire space of signification has begun to be reconstituted as one vast, implosive and multiply interconnected promotional culture [where] self-promotional careerism—Hobbes plus Narcissus—has been installed as the normalized form of adaptive behaviour and identity" (Wernick 1988, 193–194). Blame it on systematic changes in the music industry, on the inescapable networks of our promotional culture, on the "me" decade, or on Andy Warhol,[15] but the solipsism that Lester Bangs perceived as *outside* threatening to engulf the domain of Elvis (and culture in general) has moved *inside,* way inside; solipsism has become one of the constitutive features of stardom itself.

It is the closed circuit of Madonna's stardom ("the pure pleasure [of] turning the audience into a giant bedroom mirror" [Hoberman 1991, 51]) that's on display, front and center, in her film documentary *Truth or Dare:* a film that is split almost equally between Madonna being the star and Madona (psycho)analyzing her own motivations for being a star. In one of the more intentionally revealing moments of this movie, Warren Beatty, having reached a new level of frustration, bemusement, and horror, exclaims; "She doesn't want to *live* off-camera, much less talk." And so it is that Madonna works, self-consciously, at the gap—real or not—between private and public, premeditated and planned, vulnerable and invulnerable, subject and object.

It is a closed circuit, yes, but that doesn't mean that the audience—or especially the critic—is excluded from its workings.

> In postmodernist space, the activity of the audience is self-inscription. One is invited to create meaning in the text by writing oneself there. There is an extent to which this has always been true in all expressive media [but] the shift of emphasis signals a shift of activity. Texts which intend polysemy, which do not police meaning but instead invite it, do not encourage identification, a psychological response, but displacement, a spatial activity. For within the text, we displace the star (Michaels 1987, 91).

But before this change of emphasis, star texts used to work differently. Elvis was, to some degree, displaced by the discourse that came to be deployed by the new forms of stardom: a discourse of power and control. Ultimately, as Greil Marcus (1990, 122) notes, "A new Elvis Presley could not build an empire elsewhere because there is no elsewhere; all territory is occupied by power." The only Elvis who can find an elsewhere in contemporary society (and who has done so quite successfully) is an Elvis free of his own corporeality, an ephemeral Elvis.[16] In the second of the three temporally contiguous stories that compose the movie *Mystery Train* (a film largely about displacement), Elvis Presley materializes before a frightened female motel guest who is sitting, wide-eyed, with the bedsheets tucked up under her chin. Elvis seems embarrassed to be there, to be elsewhere, to be everywhere, to be anywhere. He apologizes profusely. "I must have got the wrong address or something, " he says. "I, I better be going. I gotta go." And he dissolves back into the ether.

Not given to disintegrating, Madonna's stardom depends on her drawing directly from the discourse of power: "It's a great feeling to be powerful. I've been striving for it all my life. I think that's just the quest of every human being: *power*" (Sessums 1990, 148). And it seems virtually impossible, in fact, to encounter a write-up (popular or academic) about Madonna that doesn't come around to address this theme (see the chapters by Tetzlaff, Pribram, Bordo, and Mandziuk in this volume alone!). Because it has long held its own particular perspective on the terrain of power, critical theory displaces and is displaced by Madonna. It is, at times, an awkward dance. Turn this way and you stare into the camera (as Michaels [1987, 91] concludes, "I have bought another five minutes of fame"). Turn the other direction and you might see Baudrillard, Frith, Jameson, Morris, Deleuze, or Barthes. These are the complicated pleasures of being interpreted and interpreter, of being analyzed and analyst, of being a star and starstruck. Just be careful of who leads in this dance.

THE IMMACULATE CONNECTION: YOU CAN DANCE FOR INSPIRATION

> Well, I'd like to cite Arendt's banality of evil (you thought I'd have something off-the-wall up my sleeve), in fact it's more appropriate than ever, dissociate while administering pain hi-ho, in front of the console, phoning your broker, stroking your hairless leg, "evil" itself can stand redefining, which perhaps I'll get to, though in a roundabout way, since it is harder than ever to be plain, that is, you are plain but is it plain that's received?, heck no, the language all unstuck, thus Madonna and her whirling navel will describe a broad sphere of effluence, so to speak, inflicting all species of pleasure, so to speak, and if this seems elusive, take heart, there are these constants: dollars and power, though their acquisition and implementation signify a more various collusion, collusion in what?, in keeping the good poor good and poor, in keeping the electrified wire (now wireless) hooked to your genitals, yes yours.
> —Harold Jaffe, "Madonna"

Nothing more is up *this* sleeve (though maybe a dance card is in my hand). But, in conclusion, I'd like to note just two remaining items: The first concerns a methodological decision, and the second addresses the cognitive map.

About Reality

Rather than getting too concerned with making distinctions about *real seeming* and *being,* this chapter has often purposefully ignored what might be seen as their differences. For example, instead of saying something like "Madonna seems to exert control over her career," it was easier to erase *seems* from the equation. I've tried not to let the resulting assertions ("Madonna exerts control") stand unsupported but, instead, attempted to account for some of the reasons why such a statement might offer an effective description. Increasingly frustrated—in earlier drafts—with continually drawing a line that separated appearance from reality, I decided that it was simpler to make a line that might connect them (and, in the process, cancel each of them out).

Years ago, Georg Lukács (1971, 204) wrote: "It is true that reality is the criterion for the correctness of thought. But reality is not, it becomes—and to become the participation of thought is needed." It is a similar notion of *becoming* that is found, as well, in the work of Deleuze and Guattari (1987, 239): "Becoming is a verb with a consistency all its own; it does not reduce to, or lead back to, 'appearing,' 'being,' 'equaling,' or 'producing.' " Madonna is, in this sense, in a perpetual state of becoming. Becoming what? At the very least, because she embodies the process of stardom itself, she is always a becoming-star. But beyond fancy conceptual nomenclature, where exactly does this get us?

At one very basic level, it offers a kind of constant reminder that cultural criticism and theory can always do better than devote an inordinate amount of time to disclosing the *real* nature of things. This often simply replays the old "cultural dupe" thesis (i.e., the critic or analyst is charged with the responsibility of revealing to the masses how they are living only in a state of real seeming, or—at best—possessing an enlightened false consciousness). But, even more, this notion of *becoming* allows for a rethinking of what constitutes the boundaries of analysis. To paraphrase a discussion between Dick Hebdige and Iain Chambers (Chambers 1988, 612–615), discovering the limits of your particular conceptual frame means to hear the sound of "logic escaping." But it's necessary to try to bring this excessive logic back into the analysis, to reinscribe it "for what it signals are precisely those transformatory powers that threaten to make our present analysis redundant by producing something new: a new reality" (Chambers 1988, 615). This, then, is not to deny "the real" but to bring it back in—to recognize the real effects of analysis, of texts, of language on the world where they're practiced.[17]

This chapter has more than its fair share of logic escaping (and, admittedly, not all of it beyond my control). I can't pretend to have brought us any closer to the "real" Madonna (tossing out the differences between seeming and being in favor of becoming doesn't mean adopting an asymptotical theory model of reality). Indeed, there are always those excesses that will remain excessive, unexplained, a mystery, and therefore, pleasurable.

"Ontologically slippery" was how J. Hoberman (1991, 51) described *Truth or Dare*: "Watching this film is like watching a photograph come up in a developing tray, the image coalesces before your eyes." In *Truth or Dare*, Madonna challenges her audience to take her word for it, to separate the carefully constructed from the absolutely authentic. (Does it work? Is it effective?) In her own self-produced representation, are we seeing the *real* Madonna? She responds:

> People will say, "She knows the camera is on, she's just acting." But even if I *am* acting, there's a truth in my acting. It's like when you go into a psychiatrist's office and you don't really tell what you did. You lie, but even the lie you've chosen to tell is revealing. I wanted people to see that my life isn't so easy, and one step further than that is, the movie's not completely me. You could watch it and say, I still don't know Madonna, and *good*. Because you will never know the real me. Ever. (Hirschberg 1991, 168).

Likewise, Lester Bangs (1987, 336)—in an incredible moment of inspired ventriloquism—becomes Elvis Presley, back with a vengeance:

> You rock critics and "deep thinkers," you were using me, projecting some fantasy of rebellion on me. I certainly wasn't rebelling against anything, ever. . . . Don't come 'round with your *National Enquirer* or your Peter Guralnicks and Greil Marcuses, not to mention your Geraldo Riveras. Just don't come 'round at all. . . . I still do take some slight comfort in the fact there's something about me, some weird quality, that you haven't been able to figure out yet, none of you. I never could either. I guess I was something.

Even after the best-intentioned textual analyses, complex mapping of effectivities, and sympathetic assemblage of voices, sometimes the farthest reaches of the territory can only be adequately acknowledged in, ironically, the most mundane manner: "Madonna, you know, she's really something."

About the Cognitive Map

Finally, I must concede that I'm not exactly sure how one might successfully complete a cognitive map.[18] Nevertheless, it is important to find the means to re/connect ideological maps (of things like the movement of multinational capital, as well as the critical-political consciousness) with the experiential maps of everyday life (see, e.g., Grossberg 1992). Yes, it's projecting far too much on Madonna to think that she offers some way to close the distance between me and you. But if we listen and watch closely enough, I swear sometimes there's a glimpse of how it might be done. On MTV's tenth anniversary special, "MTV 10," Madonna delivered a stream-of-consciousness monologue directly into the camera. She was supposedly addressing MTV (but we know better). She began:

> I'm here because I wanted to talk to you about "us" and all that we've been through. I wanted to talk about me and you. I remember when we first met . . .

Acknowledgments

The third section of this chapter was written with assistance from Harris Breslow. Extra special thanks go to Stan Denski, Jackie Seigworth, Gilbert Rodman, Kirsten Lentz, and, most especially, Cathy Schwichtenberg, who has more patience than an editor should be allowed.

NOTES

1. Speaking of kings and queens: For those who put stock in such coincidences, Elvis Presley died on August 16, 1977, and Madonna was born on August 16, 1958. I'm also reminded of an album by Robyn Hitchcock entitled *Queen Elvis* from which he released the single, "Madonna of the Wasps." For an argument about the intrinsically solipsistic nature of video (and Madonna), see Cubitt (1991, 60–64). With the continued ubiquity of Elvis, asking the question, "What comes after Elvis?" might be considered more than a little presumptuous. For the reasons why it so often feels inappropriate to write about Elvis in the past tense, see these discussions on Elvis after Elvis: Marcus (1985, 1990), Spigel (1990), Wark (1989), and Tharpe (1979).

2. Fredric Jameson (1991) might actually anticipate such a willful "misreading" of his cognitive map. In the final pages of his *Postmodernism, or, The Cultural Logic of Late Capitalism,* Jameson describes an earlier critical analysis he had done of the film *Dog Day Afternoon* as a preliminary attempt at mapping the ways in which "the possibility of class figuration in the [film's] content . . . is projected out onto the world system on the one hand, and on the other articulated by the form of the star system proper" (1991, 416).

3. When Barry King (1987, 159) asserts that stars must "carry the burden, given the powerful mimetic thrust of popular cuture, of representing a seemingly more comprehensive view of everyday (and not so everyday) life than is available to those of us who remain within the confines of work and locales," he arguably erects an overly simplistic model of culture with the superstructure serving as mere reflection of the base.

4. See Frith's (1991a) "Brit Beat" column from the *Village Voice.* It details a Madonna profile that was broadcast on the British TV program *Arena.* A variety of critics were assembled to comment on the Material Girl, but, in the end, "when Madonna herself made it clear that she knew *exactly* what she was about, the British critics switched off. " (Also of note is the fact that the Unit for Criticism and Interpretive Theory at the University of Illinois proclaimed Madonna the "organic intellectual" of the month in August 1991.)

5. To be fair to Fiske, he does make the effort elsewhere to account for Madonna's singularity, as well as her potentialities for cultural resistance. It is his assertion that Madonna is *only* intertextual that is most troublesome here.

6. Translator Brian Massumi (1987, xv) asks the reader to consider these same questions in his foreword to Deleuze and Guattari's *A Thousand Plateaus.*

7. A *Vanity Fair* cover story offers a tidy allusion to some of these themes. In the midst of a careful description of the interior of Madonna's home in Hollywood Hills, the reader learns this seemingly minor detail: "On the kitchen counter, audiotapes of

Joseph Campbell's *The Power of Myth* lie stacked beside rap tapes of Public Enemy"
(Sessums 1990, 142). With all of these cues present, one is left only to imagine that
otherworldly scratch-mix where Joseph Campbell joins militant rapper Chuck D in
his proud and vengeful boast that Elvis was "simple and plain," so that, finally,
"you've got to fight the power, fight the power [of myth]!"

8. As this book went to press, Madonna did indeed sign a contract with Time-
Warner, rumored at nearly $60 million. The terms of the contract confirm much of the
speculation in this section of the chapter. The *New York Times* (Holden 1992, B1)
reported that "Madonna in partnership with Time-Warner will form her own multimedia entertainment company, Maverick. . . . Mr. Levin [Gerald M. Levin, the president and co-chief operating officer of Time-Warner] cited the Madonna agreement as
a critical step in helping to bring the division of Time-Warner closer together through
Madonna-generated work that had multiple lives in music, film, video and book formats."

9. To some degree, this is yet another consequence of what has been called the international boom in cultural studies (see the introduction to *Cultural Studies* [1992,
Grossberg, Nelson, and Treichler, eds.]). But see also Dick Hebdige (*New Statesman,*
December 1989, 40–41) on what cultural theory and politics might be able to learn
from the construction of corporate identities.

10. In fact, the closest that Madonna has ever come to allowing herself to be out-
right appropriated or subsumed by the mythology of some other pop cultural artifact
(i.e., Pepsi-Cola and the infamous "Like a Prayer" ad debacle) lasted only the twenty-
four hours (or so) that passed before she released her controversial video for the same
song. Pepsi officials pulled their spot and their Madonna tour sponsorship almost immediately.

11. Dyer's remarks on authenticity take place in a discussion about film stars, and it
should be acknowledged here that, though Madonna and Elvis both starred in movies,
their stardom is obviously more closely affiliated with popular music. But though the
"markers" that Dyer identifies have, then, always worked a bit differently in the case of
popular music—inhabited at once more intensely and more loosely—I would maintain that the place from which these markers signify has changed dramatically in the
last twenty years. The change is essentially, as I see it, that where once the "truth" of a
performance was to be inferred from what was beneath or below the surface, today it
is, more often than not, found on the surface.

12. It is "spectacular" mostly in the sense that Guy Debord (1983) attaches to *spectacle,* that is, the "spectacle is not a collection of images, but a social relation among
people, mediated by images" (paragraph 4). Also see Spigel (1990) for details on the
social relationships maintained between Elvis impersonators (especially at conventions) and for information on the professional and ethical code that they feel honor
bound to follow.

13. This feeling of total entrapment is described by Lester Bangs (1987, 335) (who
is writing as if he *were* Presley): "The point is that something I started doing to make
people know I existed started rubbing out my existence, a little at a time, day by day, I
could feel it going, seeping away, steady and calm . . . and nothin' comin' in to replace
it. And I knew nothin' ever would."

14. In some sense, Elvis impersonators might be understood as enacting some version of what Jameson (1991) has referred to as (modernist) parody, which requires a certain amount of respect for the idiosyncracies of some inimitable style; whereas Madonna and her wanna-bes might be recognized as operating more generally within the postmodern realm of pastiche. For an insightful reading of how the discourse of parody and pastiche can be deployed around discussions of Madonna, see Curry (1990).

15. Christgau (1990, 72) has remarked that, above all, Madonna has shown a "profound understanding of Andy Warhol." David Harvey (1989, 171), in his *The Condition of Postmodernity,* writes that "rampant individualism fits into place as a necessary, though not a sufficient, condition for the transition from Fordism to flexible accumulation." It's a change that Harvey believes began around 1972.

16. See Wark's (1989) "Elvis: Listen to the Loss" and Marcus's (1985) "The Dead and the Quick." Baudrillard (1988) offers a hypothesis about death and power in his book *America.* It is the dead, Baudrillard (1988, 115) writes, who can outperform the living because they can move more quickly and make more efficient use of power.

17. See Grossberg (1992), in particular Chapter 1 and the section on "Materialism and Effectivity: The Real."

18. But I'm in good company because Fredric Jameson (1988) begins his preliminary essay on this subject, "Cognitive Mapping" (from *Marxism and Intepretation of Culture,* pp. 347–360) by stating: "I am addressing a subject about which I know nothing whatsoever, except for the fact that it does not exist." This is hardly an auspicious beginning for anyone who hopes to follow his model.

REFERENCES

Anderson, S. (1989). "Forgive Me, Father. " *Village Voice,* April 4, pp. 67–68.

Ansen, D. (1990). "Magnificent Maverick." *Cosmopolitan,* May, pp. 308–311.

Arrington, C. (1991). "Madonna in Bloom: Circe at Her Loom." *Time,* May 20, pp. 56–58.

Bangs, L. (1987). *Psychotic Reactions and Carburetor Dung.* New York: Alfred A. Knopf.

Barthes, R. (1972). *Mythologies.* (A. Lavers, trans.). New York: Hill and Wang.

Baudrillard, J. (1988). *America.* (C. Turner, trans.). New York: Verso.

Bennett, T. (1990). *Outside Literature.* New York: Routledge.

Best, S. (1989). "Jameson, Totality, and the Poststructuralist Critique." In D. Kellner (ed.), *Postmodernism/Jameson/Critique.* Washington, D.C.: Maisonneuve Press, pp. 333–368.

Bordo, S. (1990). " 'Material Girl': The Effacements of Postmodern Culture." *Michigan Quarterly Review* 29, no. 4 (Fall): 653–677.

Bradby, B. (1990). "Freedom, Feeling, and Dancing." *OneTwoThreeFour* 9 (Autumn): 35–52.

Chambers, I. (1988). "Contamination, Coincidence, and Collusion: Pop Music, Urban Culture, and the Avant-Garde." In C. Nelson and L. Grossberg (eds.),

Marxism and the Interpretation of Culture. Urbana: University of Illinois Press, pp. 607–615.

Christgau, R. (1990). "Decade: Rockism Faces the World." *Village Voice,* January 2, pp. 65–73, 88.

———. (1991). "Madonnathinking Madonnabout Madonnamusic." *Village Voice,* May 28, pp. 31–33.

Cubitt, S. (1991). *Timeshift: On Video Culture.* London: Comedia Press.

Curry, R. (1990). "Madonna from Marilyn to Marlene—Pastiche and/or Parody." *Journal of Film and Video* 42, no. 2 (Summer): 15–30.

Debord, G. (1983). *Society of the Spectacle.* Detroit, Mich.: Black and Red Press.

Deleuze, G., and Guattari, F. (1987). *A Thousand Plateaus.* (B. Massumi, trans.). Minneapolis: University of Minnesota Press.

Dyer, R. (1982). *Stars.* London: BFI Publishing.

———. (1991). "A *Star Is Born* and the Construction of Authenticity." In C. Gledhill (ed.), *Stardom: Industry of Desire.* New York: Routledge, pp. 132–140.

Fiske, J. (1989). *Understanding Popular Culture.* Winchester, Mass.: Unwin Hyman.

Frith, S. (1988a). "Art Ideology and Pop Practice." In C. Nelson and L. Grossberg (eds.), *Marxism and the Interpretation of Culture.* Urbana: University of Illinois Press, pp. 461–475.

———. (1988b). "Video Pop: Picking Up the Pieces." In S. Frith, (ed.), *Facing the Music.* New York: Pantheon, pp. 88–130.

———. (1988c). *Music for Pleasure.* New York: Routledge.

———. (1991a). "TV Guides." *Village Voice,* January 15, p. 72.

———. (1991b). "Art of Poise." *Village Voice,* April 9, p. 74.

Goodman, F. (1992). "Big Deals." *Musician,* January, pp. 39–51, 97.

Goodwin, A. (1990). "Sample and Hold: Pop Music in the Digital Age of Reproduction." In S. Frith and A. Goodwin (eds.) , *On Record: Rock, Pop and the Written Word.* New York: Pantheon, pp. 258–273.

Grossberg, L. (1986). "History, Politics, and Postmodernism: Stuart Hall and Cultural Studies." *Journal of Communication Inquiry* 10, no. 2 (Summer): 61–77.

———. (1988). "Wandering Audiences, Nomadic Critics." *Cultural Studies* 2, no. 3 (October): 377–390.

———. (1989). "MTV: Swinging on the (Postmodern) Star." In I. Angus and S. Jhally (eds.), *Cultural Politics in Contemporary America.* New York: Routledge, pp. 254–268.

———. (1992). *We Gotta Get Outta This Place: Popular Conservatism and Postmodern Culture.* New York: Routledge.

Grossberg, L., Nelson, C. and Treichler, P. (1992). *Cultural Studies.* New York: Routledge, pp. 1–22.

Harvey, D. (1989). *The Condition of Postmodernity.* Oxford and Cambridge, Mass.: Basil Blackwell.

Hebdige, D. (1989). "The Image Religion." *New Statesmen and Society,* December 1, pp. 40–41.

Hirschberg, L. (1991). "The Misfit." *Vanity Fair,* April, pp. 160–168, 196–202.

Hoberman, J. (1991). "Blond on Blond." *Village Voice,* May 14, pp. 51, 56.

Holden, S. (1992). "A $60 Million Deal for the Material Girl." *New York Times,* April 20, pp. B1, B4.

Huey, J. (1990). "America's Hottest Export: Pop Culture." *Forbes,* December 31, pp. 50–60.

Jaffe, H. (1989). "Madonna." *Polygraph* 2/3: 37–40.

Jameson, F. (1988). "Cognitive Mapping." In C. Nelson and L. Grossberg (eds.), *Marxism and the Interpretation of Culture.* Urbana: University of Illinois Press, pp. 347–360.

––––––– . (1991). *Postmodernism, or, The Cultural Logic of Late Capitalism.* Durham, N.C.: Duke University Press.

Kellner, D. (1989). "Jameson, Marxism, and Postmodernism." In D. Kellner (ed.), *Postmodernism/Jameson/Critique.* Washington, D.C.: Maisonneuve Press, pp. 1–42.

King, B. (1987). "The Star and the Commodity: Notes Towards a Performance Theory of Stardom." *Cultural Studies* 1, no. 2 (May): 145–159.

Kroker, A., Kroker, M., and Cook, D. (1989). *Panic Encyclopedia.* New York: St. Martin's Press.

Lukács, G. (1971). *History and Class Consciousness: Studies in Marxist Dialectics.* (R. Livingstone, trans.). Cambridge, Mass.: MIT Press.

Marcus, G. (1982). *Mystery Train.* New York: E. P. Dutton.

––––––– . (1985). "The Dead and the Quick." *Artforum* 23, no. 6 (February): 66–71.

––––––– . (1990). "Still Dead: Elvis Presley Without Music." *Art Forum* 29, no. 1 (September): 117–123.

Massumi, B. (1987). "Translator's Foreword: Pleasures of Philosophy." In G. Deleuze and F. Guattari, *A Thousand Plateaus.* Minneapolis: University of Minnesota Press, pp. IX–XV.

McClary, S. (1991). *Feminine Endings: Music, Gender, and Sexuality.* Minneapolis: University of Minnesota Press.

McRobbie, A. (1992). "Post-Marxism and Cultural Studies: A Postscript." In L. Grossberg, C. Nelson, and P. Treichler (eds.), *Cultural Studies.* New York: Routledge, pp. 719–730.

Michaels, E. (1987). "My Essay on Postmodernity. " *Art and Text* 25 (June–August): 86–91.

Morris, M. (1988). "At Henry Parkes Motel." *Cultural Studies* 2, no. 1 (January): 1–17, 28–47.

––––––– . (1990). "Banality in Cultural Studies." In P. Mellencamp (ed.), *Logics of Television.* Bloomington: Indiana University Press, pp. 14–43.

––––––– . (Forthcoming). "The Man in the Mirror: David Harvey's 'Condition' of Postmodernity." *Theory, Culture, and Society.*

Pond, S. (1990). "The Industry in the Eighties. " *Rolling Stone,* November 15, pp. 113–117.

Probyn, E. (1989). "Take My Word for It: Ethnography and Autobiography." *Journal of Communication Inquiry* 13, no. 2 (Summer): 18–22.

Schwichtenberg, C. (1990). "Postmodern Feminism and Madonna: Toward an Erotic Politics of the Female Body." Paper presented at the National Conference on Rewriting the (Post)Modern, University of Utah, March 30–31.

Sessums, K. (1990). "White Heat." *Vanity Fair,* April, pp. 142–148, 208–214.

Spigel, L. (1990). "Communicating with the Dead: Elvis as Medium." *Camera Obscura* 23 (May): 176–205.

Tharpe, J. (1979). *Elvis: Images and Fancies.* Jackson: University Press of Mississippi.

Wark, M. (1989). "Elvis: Listen to the Loss." *Art and Text* 31 (December–February): 24–28.

Wernick, A. (1988). "Promotional Culture." *Canadian Journal of Political and Social Theory* 12, no. 1–2: 180–201.

Williams, S., and Martinez, J. (1991). "1990 Madonna Symposium Survey Results." *Frighten the Horses* 4 (Winter).

Williamson, J. (1985). "The Making of a Material Girl." *New Socialist* 31 (October): 46–47.

_____ . (1986). *Consuming Passions.* New York: Marion Boyars.

Young, R. (1991). *White Mythologies: Writing History and the West.* New York: Routledge.

Zuidervaart, L. (1989). "Realism, Modernism, and the Empty Chair." In D. Kellner (ed.), *Postmodernism/Jameson/Critique.* Washington, D.C.: Maisonneuve Press, pp. 203–227.

About the Book and Editor

Various cultural theories (foremost among them, postmodernism) have figured in the debate over the politics of representation. These theories have tended to look at representation in the context of either audience enablement or commercial constraint; that is, do the images empower the public or inhibit it? One key area consistently overlooked has the been the study of subcultural or subordinate groups who appropriate what is traditionally considered "mainstream."

The Madonna Connection is the first book to address the complexities of race, gender, and sexuality in popular culture by using the influence of a cultural heroine to advance cultural theory. Madonna's use of various media—music, concert tour, film, and video—serves as a paradigm by which the authors study how images and symbols associated with subcultural groups (multiracial, gay and lesbian, feminist) are smuggled into the mainstream. Using a range of critical and interpretive approaches to this evolving and lively cultural phenomenon, the authors demonstrate the importance of personalities like Madonna to issues of enablement and constraint.

Are "others" given voice by political interventions in mass popular culture? Or is their voice co-opted to provide mere titillation and maximum profit? What might the interplay of these views suggest? These are some of the questions the authors attempt to answer. Some celebrate Madonna's affirmation of cultural diversity. Others criticize her flagrant self-marketing strategies. And still others regard her as only a provisional challenge to the mainstream.

Cathy Schwichtenberg is assistant professor of speech communication at the University of Georgia.

About the Contributors

ANNE BARTON WHITE is a doctoral student in mass communication research in the School of Journalism and Mass Communication at the University of North Carolina at Chapel Hill. She is interested in politics and gender, representations of women in the media, and women's interpretations of media messages. She is currently investigating the construction and interpretation of images of high-profile women, such as Madonna, and women in politics.

SUSAN BORDO is associate professor of philosophy and holds the Joseph C. Georg Chair at Le Moyne College. She is the author of *The Flight to Objectivity: Essays on Cartesianism and Culture* (1987) and coeditor of *Gender/Body/Knowledge: Feminist Reconstructions of Being and Knowing* (1989). Her current book, *Unbearable Weight: Feminism, Western Culture, and the Body,* is forthcoming.

JANE D. BROWN is professor and direct or Graduate Studies in the School of Journalism and Mass Communication at the University of North Carolina at Chapel Hill. She has coedited *Media, Social Science, and Social Policy for Children* (1985) and has published a number of articles on adolescents' use and interpretation of media, especially music videos. Currently, she is investigating how adolescents use the mass media as they construct personal identities.

LISA HENDERSON is assistant professor of communication at the Pennsylvania State University. She is also a lesbian activist and writes about sexual politics, cultural theory, and the production and consumption of popular media.

E. ANN KAPLAN is professor of English and comparative literature and director of the Humanities Institute at the State University of New York at Stony Brook. She has published widely in the areas of feminist film theory and media studies. Her books on feminist and psychoanalytic theory and popular culture include *Women and Film: Both Sides of the Camera* (1983) and *Rocking Around the Clock: Music Television, Postmodernism, and Consumer Culture* (1987). She is currently working on *Motherhood and Representation: 1830–1960.*

ROSEANN M. MANDZIUK is assistant professor of speech communication at Southwest Texas State University, where she teaches rhetorical criticism and theory, media studies, and cultural approaches to communication. She is journal editor of *Women's Studies in Communication* and the author of several essays that apply feminist critical perspectives to analyses of documentary, historical, and media discourses.

MELANIE MORTON has a B.A. in liberal arts from the New School for Social Research and is currently a doctoral candidate in the University of Minnesota's Department of Comparative Studies in Discourse and Society.

THOMAS K. NAKAYAMA is an assistant professor of rhetorical studies in the Department of Communication at Arizona State University. He has published on such topics as race and gender in cultural studies, postmodernism, and alternative forms of public discourse.

CINDY PATTON is a critic and writer. She is the author of *Sex and Germs: The Politics of AIDS* (1985) and *Inventing AIDS* (1990) and has contributed to numerous volumes on gay studies and on AIDS. She is assistant professor of rhetoric and communication at Temple University. She is completing a book on sexual representation.

LISA N. PEÑALOŽA, assistant professor of marketing at the University of Colorado, has published a number of articles on immigrant consumer acculturation. Her research brings a critical perspective to the analysis of subcultural and gender issues in marketing and consumer research. She is currently completing an ethnographic study of Mexican immigrants in Southern California.

E. DEIDRE PRIBRAM is an independent film- and videomaker and an assistant professor of film/video at the Pennsylvania State University. She is the writer and director of *The Family Business,* an independent feature film, and the editor of *Female Spectators: Looking at Film and Television* (1988).

LAURIE SCHULZE teaches film and television studies in the Mass Communications Department at the University of Denver. She has published articles on female bodybuilders, made-for-TV movies, made-for-TV movies about female bodybuilders, and Madonna fans. She is currently finishing her dissertation on Madonna and cultural studies.

CATHY SCHWICHTENBERG, assistant professor of speech communication at the University of Georgia, has published numerous articles on postmodernism, gender, and popular culture. Her current research focuses on the construction of masculinity through body-enhancing technologies, and she is the author of *Approaches to Popular Culture* (forthcoming).

RONALD B. SCOTT is assistant professor and assistant chair for the Department of Mass Communication at Miami University of Ohio. He has written on the representation of African Americans in the mass media and teaches courses in production, media writing, criticism, and minorities in the media.

GREG SEIGWORTH is pursuing his Ph.D. in cultural studies in the Department of Speech Communication at the University of Illinois at Urbana-Champaign. He has been a lecturer at the College Conservatory of Music in Cincinnati, Ohio, and in the Department of Communication and Theatre at Indiana University at Indianapolis. He has been a popular music critic and a professional recording engineer.

DAVID TETZLAFF teaches film and television production in the Department of Mass Communication at Miami University in Oxford, Ohio. He also makes documentary films and writes essays on the politics of popular culture.

Index

323

T #0262   081024 - C0 - 234/156/17 - PB - 9780367309114 - Gloss Lamination